"Lord, I believe; help thou mine unbelief."

Mark 9:24

ROD W. JEPPSEN

Pathway Publishing

Lord I Believe; Help Thou Mine Unbelief

The author assumes full responsibility for the content
and organization of this material.

Quotations and lyrics appearing on pages
iii, v, x, xi, xii, 5, 10, 14, 28, 29, 40, 47, 49, 54, 55, 60, 61, 62, 63, 64, 65, 67, 68, 80, 82, 88, 89,
90, 95, 96, 100, 103, 104, 109, 112, 113, 114, 115, 121, 124, 125, 136, 144, 148, 149, 152, 153,
155, 156, 157, 161, 163, 164, 168, 169, 170, 173, 176, 177, 183, 189, 193, 197, 198, 199, 204,
205, 207, 209, 212, 215, 216, 217, 219, 221, 229, 233, 236, 239, 242, 244, 252, 261, 265, 267,
268, 270, 273, 280, 290, 308, 310, 311, 317, 318, 322, 326, 327, 328, 333, 334, 338, 339, 341,
342, 343, 345, 346, 347, 352, 354, 355, 357, 359, 364, 366, 372, 374, 375, 376, 377, 378, 383,
384, 385, 386, 387, 388, 389, 390, 397, 401, 403, 407, 408, 409, 412, 413, 416, 419, 425, 427,
429, 434, 435, 439, 441, 442, 443, 444, 445, 446, 447, 449, 453
The Church of Jesus Christ of Latter-day Saints
Used by permission.

Cover design: Phil Hunter, Market Design Media
Book layout and design: Jeremy Ames
Photo back cover: Busath Photography, Laura Bruschke

Pathway Publishing
P.O. Box 95122
South Jordan, UT 84095-0122
801-253-3138

Library of Congress Control Number
2005904122
ISBN 0-9661898-2-5

10 9 8 7 6 5 4 3 2 1

Praise for "Lord, I believe; help thou mine unbelief":

When I first suspected my husband had a pornography problem I felt a myriad of overwhelming emotions: fear, hurt, anger, desperation, and unbelief. For years I carried these unspoken emotions by myself. . . . This book became the help I had hungered for. . . .

It was as though I had found a friend to identify with me as I read other people's feelings that matched my own. It helped me to understand that my feelings were not abnormal or "bad." As funny as it is, I couldn't put this book down. . . . the lessons I learned helped me to move forward.

—Z. Z.

Counselor/therapist Rod Jeppsen (a specialist in treating sexual addictions) has created an excellent workbook for spouses and other family members who associate or live with those afflicted with this disorder. The core of it is the Articles of Faith found in the LDS religion and scriptures.

I like the way Jeppsen has structured his workbook format that goes beyond just a good read. The author actively engages the reader requiring both spiritual and intellectual effort. This is an active therapy which can be used by individuals alone or in group settings. There is a great deal of wisdom and practical advice dispensed by someone who has been in the trenches many years, giving a helping hand to many who have endured much and repeatedly had their hope challenged.

—Victor B. Cline, Ph.D.

This book helps us understand that "Earth has no sorrow that Heaven cannot heal." For me, it has become a companion book to my scriptures. I have marked and highlighted my copy of it and have read and re-read it. I have gained immeasurable strength and knowledge through it. My understanding of the Atonement and my testimony of the Savior and His healing power have increased immensely. Brother Jeppsen taught me lessons about the Savior that I never knew.

—A. F. B.

This book fills an empty space for the spouse, and other "loved ones," of those hooked on pornography and all its attendant evils.

For every individual caught in the trap of sexual addiction, there will be more who suffer in a wake that follows in ever-expanding, debilitating circles. Jeppsen's book will accomplish its intended purpose in stemming the tide while providing protection and comfort to the many loved ones of the addict. By closely following the concepts and assignments herein, the sufferer will be able to free him/herself from being endlessly spiritually engulfed. It will help whole families by giving them concrete ways to squarely face the enemy, and with spiritual power, come off conqueror.

The relevant and inspired words of living and ancient prophets, brought to light in this work, are in themselves strengthening and life-giving. Wisely, the author has woven truths of the gospel and the power of the Atonement with the many threads of self-doubt, discouragement, and hurt in such a way that healing takes place and freedom is achieved.

The timing of the book is inspired. As twenty-first-century technology makes its inroad into the private lives of countless individuals in ways never known before, this workbook gives the reader spiritual insights to withstand the flood-tide of evil that is attempting to seep into the heart of every home. It is interesting and most heartening to realize that the antidote for it all is within the simple, yet powerful, words of ancient and modern servants of our Eternal Father in Heaven. Thanks to Jeppsen's sensitivity to the needs of the suffering spouse, this workbook makes those words available to all.

—Friend and Mentor
   Jonathan M. Chamberlain, Ph. D.

Lord, I Believe; Help Thou Mine Unbelief is a long awaited tool for women whose spouses are struggling with pornography. Wives can find solace in the spiritual principles and support in the psychological guidance. It presents a step by step approach for the journey a wife can make in order to maintain her emotional health and be a support for her husband in a positive way.

We can only change ourselves but we can be a catalyst for change in others through healthy boundaries, a firm spiritual foundation, and charity. Satan is waging war upon our brothers, so I am very grateful to have this resource for the many women in this difficult situation.

—Abbie Vianes, MA in Professional Counseling

Brother Jeppsen lovingly reaches out to aid the victims of compulsive sexual behaviors and to minister to their needs, sustain them, and help them carry on and even to forgive. But in reality his book is far-reaching and will help each and every one of us! We all have habits and undesirable behaviors we want to change—some more terrible than others. . . . We all suffer the consequences of not only our own sins, but those of others—sometimes our most-loved ones! We all will have burdens that seem unbearable. Brother Jeppsen uses counsel, encouragement, stories, quotes, and special messages of hope from our modern-day prophets and church authorities as he helps us understand how to heal "the Lord's way."

—H. L. B.

With all he's done to help individuals struggling with compulsive sexual behaviors, I'm delighted that Rod Jeppsen has now written a book to help their loved ones. Lord I Believe; Help Thou Mine Unbelief is a comprehensive resource that provides much of the hope and help they need.

I've heard people say, "Why don't the scriptures and the brethren say more about addiction?" Rod's thorough research and big-picture grasp of the problem showed me just how much revelation we have received regarding how to best address these difficult issues. This book will bless many lives, and I will be using it with my clients for years to come.

—Mark Chamberlain, Ph.D.
   author of *Wanting More* and coauthor of *Willpower Is Not Enough*

In the world of sexual addictions and pornography use, the spouses of those involved in these dark behaviors are many times ignored and neglected. Their need for understanding and support is profound as they struggle with feelings of betrayal, loss, and distrust. In this book, Rod W. Jeppsen has provided practical and spiritual guidance for spouses dealing with these difficult issues. The principles presented are sound and, if applied, will provide healing and strength.

—Dan Gray, LCSW

Acknowledgements

I'm thankful to my wife and family for their love and support. In addition, I am very grateful for so many who have helped to complete this book. Even though I had a great desire to write a book for loved ones who are helping family members or friends to conquer compulsive sexual behaviors, it could not have been possible without the expertise and input from others.

Darla Isackson was the content editor for this book. Her grasp of gospel principles as well as her editing skills provided more flow to the text and improved the clarity and readability. I appreciate Annette Wheeler for nurturing and massaging the text to make it more poignant and real.

I am also thankful for the following who reviewed parts or all of the manuscript and made so many suggestions, B.R., T.P., C.P., A.W., D.R., C.B.B., M.C., G.G., K.J., K.S., P.J., S.D., and D.D. The editing and personal insights from each of these individuals made the book more real and practical, to get at the heart of the matter.

Without the expertise of Dr. Allan Roe, who has spent years counseling couples, this book would not be as helpful and on target as it needed to be. I'm grateful to him for reviewing the entire manuscript, making editorial and other suggestions, as well as consenting to include several of his practical charts and summaries.

Finally, I am grateful to Dr. Jonathan M. Chamberlain who helped me fine-tune the Twelve Principles for Emotional and Spiritual Healing, and made other suggestions to the manuscript. He has been a friend and mentor for many years.

This book is dedicated to you—the family member—who is trying so hard to help your loved one overcome compulsive sexual behaviors. May you receive peace through your faith, work, and the healing power of the Savior's Atonement.

Table of Contents

Preface

The initial discovery that a loved one is struggling with one or more facets of compulsive sexual behaviors generates a variety of responses, including shock, confusion, fear, self-blame, bitterness, betrayal, inferiority, anger, hopelessness, humiliation, and more. One spouse related feeling as though "time was suddenly suspended as a crushing avalanche of frightening thoughts converged at once, sending me spiraling into an engulfing void of hopelessness."

Another stated simply: "This can't be true. It's just a bad dream and I will soon wake up!" There are few things as personally traumatizing as when a spouse violates covenants and chooses to engage in pornography or other compulsive sexual behaviors. If a spouse is using drugs or alcohol, it is so much easier to view the usage as the spouse's problem. But compulsive sexual behaviors violate trust and emotional and sexual intimacy and may feel like a personal attack. Another wife commented, "I feel so crushed and hurt. I also fear if others find out about my husband's problem, they will judge me."

The parents of a young man shared their dilemma upon learning of their son's entrenchment in a homosexual lifestyle as follows: "We can't believe that this is our son. Why would he choose such a lifestyle?"

The jolting, unexpected, and unfamiliar nature of this kind of disclosure or discovery initially creates a sense of embarrassment, shame, and fear of what others might think or feel about our situation if they were to ever find out. Living in fear may cause us to make choices that are counterproductive and even harmful to us and our loved ones. Unchecked fear becomes the catalyst for further isolation.

Additionally, the fact that society condones and even encourages discussions regarding drug and alcohol addiction, while avoiding the topic of sexual addiction, lends further evidence that we are alone in our circumstances. This sense of alienation, if unchecked, may even lead us to pull away from the Savior and our Heavenly Father.

The desire to withdraw and remain in a state of emotional and even physical isolation because of the fear of someone else finding out about our loved ones' compulsive sexual behaviors may even lead to silence and inaction on our part. Such response may inadvertently send the message that we condone the behaviors and possibly serve as an aid to keep our loved ones stuck in the addiction. If we are not careful, this tendency toward isolation or silence may even prevent us from feeling God's awareness of our situation and His love for us and our loved ones. On the flip side, moments of isolation and solitude can be healing. One wife expressed:

> *My isolation was the reason I turned to God. He was the only one I could talk to who understood and had the power and ability to help. In my grief and isolation, He comforted, instructed, and taught me. If I had others to talk to, I may have missed this wonderful spiritual help.*

Though our loved ones may have made choices that alienated them from feeling the love of the Savior and His light, we can choose to walk toward His light—the light of Christ. The Savior has promised to guide and comfort all those who mourn, regardless of their circumstances. The Savior said:

> *Come unto me, all ye that labour and are heavy laden, and I will give you rest.*
>
> *Take my yoke upon you, and learn of me; for I am meek and lowly in heart: and ye shall find rest unto your souls.*
>
> *For my yoke is easy, and my burden is light (Matt. 11:28-30).*

During the nights when we feel alone, we can focus our faith, hope, and prayers upon feeling His love, peace, and presence as found in the familiar consoling hymn: "O Savior, stay this night with me; Behold, 'tis eventide" ("Abide with Me; 'Tis Eventide," *Hymns,* 165).

AVOID THE GUILT TRIP

One of our first reactions to the news regarding our loved ones' compulsive addictions might have been, "Where did I go wrong?" Many reactions may have followed such as, "If I had been a better spouse (or parent), this would not have happened." "If I had only been more sexually responsive, this could have been avoided." Often we carry feelings of guilt and anger for not recognizing the warning signs of our loved ones' behaviors sooner. God has provided a way for us to eliminate any guilt for He has "taken away the guilt from our hearts, through the merits of his Son" (Alma 24:10).

We should not consider the compulsive behaviors of our loved ones to be the result of some mistake that we have committed. Elder Richard G. Scott explained this principle:

> *If you are free of serious sin yourself, don't suffer needlessly the consequences of another's sins. As a wife, husband, parent, or loved one, you can feel compassion for one who is in the gall of bitterness from sin. Yet you should not take upon yourself a feeling of responsibility for those acts. When you have done what is reasonable to help one you love, lay the burden at the feet of the Savior. He has invited you to do that so that you can be free from pointless worry and depression. As you so act, not only will you find peace but will demonstrate your faith in the power of the Savior to lift the burden of sin from a loved one through his repentance and obedience* (*Ensign,* Nov. 2002, 88).

President Gordon B. Hinckley, speaking to parents of wayward children, gave this advice, which applies to all relationships, "They may do, in the years that come, some things you would not want them to do, but be patient, be patient. You have not failed as long as you have tried. Never forget that" (Salt Lake University Third Stake Conference, 3 Nov. 1996, in *Ensign,* July 1997, 72). All we can do in life is try—try to do the best we can.

We are blessed for trying. Trying means we have not given up. We should avoid looking at the struggles of our loved ones as failure on our part. A healthy approach is, "I have tried and will continue to try!" Just because our loved ones may choose not to change, it does not mean we have not tried. Remember, if we have tried we have not failed.

THE GERMAN PIE

Shortly before the Civil War, a group of German-speaking European immigrants who belonged to a religious group known as the Community of True Inspiration settled in Amana, Iowa. They established the Amana Colonies, divided into seven different villages, encompassing over 20,000 acres of land. Originally a communal system, today the Amana Colonies are mostly a tourist attraction. When I am in the area on business, I drive there to enjoy their wonderful German pie, which is similar to pecan pie with raisins and coconut added. It is even more delicious when topped with a scoop of rich vanilla ice cream. I have told my wife on several occasions how fresh, flavorful, and delicious the pie tasted after a perfect German meal.

On one business trip, as I was eating German pie for dessert, I decided to take some home so my wife could experience the flavorful taste and no longer have to rely on my word. I purchased two boxed pies and decided the safest place for them would be in the trunk of the rental car. I knew they would stay nice and cool since it was February. I then drove to Omaha and stayed overnight in a hotel. Early the next morning I drove to the airport, took the pies out of the trunk, and carefully carried them into the airport and onto the plane. I stowed them in the overhead compartment during my flight to Salt Lake City.

Before I got into my own car, I opened the pie boxes to check the condition of each pie. They both looked fine. When I arrived home, I shared the exciting news with my wife that I had purchased not only one German pie, but two. I showed her the pies and she responded, "This will make a great dessert for us after supper." Supper came and went, and it was soon time for the good stuff—dessert. I cut part of the pie into pieces and placed large scoops of vanilla ice cream on each piece.

I took my first bite and tasted quite a different flavor than I had expected! A second bite confirmed that the pie tasted like some kind of chemical. I was puzzled at first and took a third bite. Then I recognized the taste. The pie tasted like the scent of a new car. Suddenly it all made perfect sense—the pies had been in the trunk of the rental car for about twelve hours before I flew to Salt Lake City, and the "new car" smell had slowly seeped into the crust of the freshly baked pies.

The pies looked fine in the boxes and on our plates, but the taste was terrible—even nasty. What appeared good was *not* good! I had worked hard to get the pies safely home, and I was so disappointed.

The Drug of Lust

Although we are addressing something far more serious than the flavor of pies, there are some pertinent parallels to the compulsive sexual behaviors our loved ones are entrenched in. Over a period of time (a lot longer than twelve hours), the drug of lust slowly and cleverly worked its way into our loved ones' lives, just like the "new-car" scent slowly seeped into the pie crusts. Just as the "new car" scent destroyed the pies, lust can and does destroy relationships and lives.

What is lust? Elder Richard G. Scott explained: "Satan promotes counterfeit love, which is lust. It is driven by a hunger to appease personal appetite. One who practices this deception cares little for the pain and destruction caused another. While often camouflaged by flattering words, its motivation is self-gratification" (*Ensign*, May 1991, 35).

Our loved ones did not realize the extent of the damage they were sustaining by taking the drug of lust—nor did we recognize the side effects that would impact our lives. Of course it is true that they were aware of the choices they were making and also aware that they were wrong choices, but they were not aware of the insidious side effects of those choices. Lust is a spiritually devastating drug—it has no mercy, it has no love, and it possesses the capacity to filter into a person's life in far more devastating ways than the "new car" smell invaded the pie crust. The drug of lust goes into the body and brain like a slow IV dripping into the bloodstream. Over the years it can penetrate every cell, yet the damage being caused is seldom recognized until the devastating invasion is revealed.

Suddenly we realize that what we thought we had we do not have. Our relationship with our loved ones, like the pie, may have appeared to be okay on the outside. Perhaps others have commented about how our family seems to have it all together. However, lust is deceitful, and we suddenly discovered that we did not have the relationship we thought we had with our loved ones nor the family unit we thought we had. In many cases we begin to wonder who this loved one really is. Often we stand back and say, "I don't even know him" or "I thought I knew her." This is all very shattering to our emotional and spiritual well-being.

Our greatest spiritual and emotional challenges come when our lives take a serious detour from what we expected, when the choices of a loved one jeopardize the well-being of our family or marriage or both. One woman explained, "All of a sudden I felt as if my life's work—my family—was all for nothing. It seemed as though all of us, including the children, had been caught in a net from which there was no escape. We were doomed because of the overwhelming extent of my husband's sexual addiction."

Because of the impact our loved ones' addictions have on our families, it is easy to view our loved ones as the enemy. In reality, our enemy is Satan and the drug of lust. We need to make every effort to stay focused on the real problem and not turn against our loved ones. Satan wants us to view our loved ones as the problem so that we do not have the time and emotional energy left to work on the real issues. It is essential for our loved ones to discover their own individual emotional "triggers" that cause them to reach for the drug of lust. This is their responsibility. If they are serious about changing, they will make every effort to seek help, to learn, to be honest, and to implement a new lifestyle. They do not need to work through the change process alone. If they seek the Spirit, they will be guided and directed. Our loved ones need healing, we need healing, and our relationship needs healing. If we listen and act on the promptings from the Holy Ghost, we will come to know the underlying issues that need to be resolved before healing can take place.

Some loved ones will take the proper steps to bring the real issues into focus. Others, however, will choose to remain stuck in the compulsive sexual behaviors, addicted to the drug of lust. In such cases Satan would have us believe that all is lost and that our ability to find true joy and happiness is forever limited by the choices of another. That is one of Satan's most clever lies. Regardless of the choices of others, joy, happiness, peace, and comfort are available to each of us.

> *Grace be to you and peace from God our Father, and from the Lord Jesus Christ.*
>
> *Blessed be God, even the Father of our Lord Jesus Christ, the Father of mercies, and the God of all comfort;*
>
> *Who comforteth us in all our tribulation, that we may be able to comfort them which are in any trouble, by the comfort wherewith we ourselves are comforted of God* (2 Cor. 1:2-4).

THE HEALING POWER OF THE ATONEMENT

Beyond the healing that the Savior's Atonement can provide for a loved one entrenched in compulsive sexual behaviors, it also offers us, as spouse and family members, strength, peace, and healing beyond our own as we face some of life's most daunting challenges. The Savior props us up when we emotionally struggle. When we are mentally and physically drained and drop off, He brings us back. He is always there! The burdens that seem unbearable at the moment can be lifted. The hopelessness we feel can be replaced with hope.

We can know and feel that our Savior is with us and will not leave us alone. The Savior said, "And I will also ease the burdens which are put upon your shoulders, that even you cannot feel them upon your backs, . . . and this will I do, . . . that ye may know of a surety that I, the Lord God, do visit my people in their afflictions" (Mosiah 24:14). The Savior is always there. If we seek Him, He will ever be with us!

Introduction

It is common at first disclosure or discovery of our loved ones' compulsive sexual behaviors for that finding (pornography, masturbation, fornication, adultery, homosexual and lesbian behaviors, child sexual abuse, etc.) to consume all our waking hours. Self-blaming, confused, bitter, betrayed, resentful, or angry thoughts often come in random, alternating waves: "How can this really be happening to me?" or "How stupid could I have been not to see this coming?" or "How did I miss the signs?" or "How could my spouse do this to me?" or "Why do I have to pay a price for someone else's mistakes?" We ask these questions hoping for answers. Some answers come soon, others come later, and some never come. We do not need answers to every question to feel whole and to keep moving toward healing. "And the people, when they knew it, followed him: and he received them, . . . and healed them that had need of healing" (Luke 9:11).

CONTENTS

Set in the framework of the *Twelve Principles for Spiritual and Emotional Healing* (which follow herein) is a compilation of scriptural references, quotations by apostles, and statements by those who have been personally involved in helping loved ones overcome compulsive sexual behaviors. Statements from actual people have been included: (1) To make the book more personal; (2) To enhance the ability of the reader to relate; and (3) To help you realize that you are not alone on this journey because others have been down this difficult road before—a road that they did not choose; (4) To give guidance and direction on the healing path; and (5) To give peace and hope in the Savior. For purposes of confidentiality, the names of these individuals have not been included. These statements were shared with me through e-mails, letters, telephone conversations, or personal interviews.

We will discuss the choices our loved ones have made and the resultant emotional, mental, spiritual, physical, and even financial pain those choices brought. There is hope that our loved ones will use the same agency they exercised to get into the behaviors to choose to walk another path. There is hope for wholeness, peace, and happiness for those of us who love them, even if they never choose to take the necessary steps to be free from the addiction to the drug of lust.

WORKBOOK FORMAT

The workbook format of this book offers the reader an opportunity to gain personal understanding, clarity, and direction regarding the issues surrounding a loved one's compulsive behaviors.

Facing tough realities and finding peace, hope, and the necessary direction is not easy, but it can be done. Trying to do it alone would be much more painful and difficult for us than it needs to be. Accepting the help of others, especially the power of the Atonement, will heal our pain and lift our burdens and generate a wholeness we initially judged impossible.

This workbook was designed to help us identify what we can control and what we cannot. This distinction is very important since so much unhappiness in life comes from trying to control things we have no power over. Throughout the workbook the male pronouns including he, his, him, and himself are frequently used. This does not mean that men are the only gender involved with compulsive sexual behaviors, because some females are too. However, to make the text flow, I chose the male pronouns.

EXERCISES

The assignments throughout this workbook have proven helpful to others dealing with a loved one's compulsive sexual behaviors. These writing exercises will help you uncover your own truths regarding your own healing as well as insights regarding your loved one's road out of compulsive sexual behaviors. It's not necessary to go in order of the chapters. For example, if you are working with a professional counselor and he or she recommends that you do some work on setting and keeping boundaries, then you can jump ahead to Principle 7 (Personal Honesty with Ourselves and Others is Essential to Learn How to Set and Keep Boundaries) and proceed through that chapter first. Keep a note pad or journal handy as you do the exercises because you may wish to write more than will fit in the space provided in the book. In addition, you may not wish to respond to every question. If a response does not come to mind, move on.

Unwanted Feelings

At times you may feel a strong desire to set the book aside, but I encourage you to complete it. You no doubt will discover that working through the exercises brings to the surface high levels of unwanted feelings such as anger, resentment, bitterness, jealousy, abandonment, guilt, anxiety, and more. If you avoid facing feelings that you need to face, healing will be delayed. On the other hand, if you complete all of the exercises—even though they may be temporarily difficult and painful—you will acquire in the process the skills necessary to deal with these emotions.

The best approach is to take time to complete the exercises over a period of many weeks or months. Give yourself time to ponder, think, and reflect. If you need to stop and take a day or two away from the book and the exercises, do so and then continue. There is no "drive-through," quick-fix, behavioral change program—healing takes time. The real key to healing is applying what you learn in the exercises to your everyday life. It is not enough just to fill in the blanks. By practicing and applying the principles for healing daily, we change our view-point, get renewed hope, gain insightful perspective, and find wholeness and peace. Our strength to continue comes from the Savior. "They that wait upon the Lord shall renew their strength; they shall mount up with wings as eagles; they shall run, and not be weary; and they shall walk, and not faint" (Isa. 40:31). We can continue the journey with renewed strength from Him.

Blessing of Hope

There is no question that at times we will be overwhelmed with discouragement and hopelessness. Healing, balance, and wholeness come as we listen to and follow the Spirit. Learning how to apply the healing power of the Atonement in our lives is paramount. Just as our own healing is a result of our connection with the Savior, we cannot do the healing for our loved ones. That healing is between our loved ones and Christ. We can choose to focus on our own issues and our own healing. It is an individual endeavor. If we and our loved ones both seek healing and wholeness, our relationship will find much higher ground. If our loved ones choose to remain stuck in the sexual addiction, we must remember that we can still become whole and find peace and balance in our lives. As we are strengthened by the Spirit and in our own progression, we can learn to ask, "How can I grow from this experience?" "What would the Lord have me learn from this painful event in my life?"

The Savior promised peace and hope for our future. He said: "Peace I leave with you, my peace I give unto you: not as the world giveth, give I unto you. Let not your heart be troubled, neither let it be afraid" (John 14:27). While peace is obtained through the Savior's love and Atonement, it will take a great deal of endurance to continue on this healing journey. "He healeth the broken in heart, and bindeth up their wounds" (Ps. 47:3).

We can experience a degree of success relatively soon. Reflecting on what you have endured and accomplished in the past may give you hope for the future: "We believe all things, we hope all things, we have endured many things, and hope to be able to endure all things" (A of F 13).

Our hope and faith in the Atonement of Christ allows us to continue: "What is it that ye shall hope for? Behold I say unto you that ye shall have hope through the atonement of Christ and the power of his resurrection, to be raised unto life eternal, and this because of your faith in him according to the promise" (Moro. 7:41).

Because of Christ and His Atonement, all is not lost. Elder Boyd K. Packer said, "I know of no sins connected with the moral standard for which we cannot be forgiven. I do not exempt abortion. The formula is stated . . . 'Behold, he who has repented of his sins, the same is forgiven, and I, the Lord, remember them no more' (D&C 58:42)" (*Ensign,* May 1992, 68). We can be saved and so can our loved ones. It is a matter of choice. We need to make choices that allow healing and the Atonement to work in our lives, and so do our loved ones.

CHANGE IS A PROCESS

Changing behaviors involves time, effort, faith, commitment, repentance, and maintaining a high degree of hope. In the process of changing, our loved ones may stay stuck for a while before they are able to move on. Again, we cannot force another person to change. We can only work on our own issues and lean on the Savior's sure promise of hope, healing, and wholeness. Each step of progress draws us closer to our final goal—becoming one with Christ.

We can know that God is watching over us in our hour of need. Elder Jeffrey R. Holland gave this encouragement: "Even if you cannot always see that silver lining on your clouds, God can, for He is the very source of the light you seek. He does love you, and He knows your fears. He hears your prayers. He is your Heavenly Father, and surely He matches with His own the tears His children shed (*Ensign,* Nov. 1999, 36).

THANK YOU

I am grateful that you are willing to go through this workbook. I wrote this book hoping that others can benefit from the insights, stories, comments, and healing of those who have been down a similar path. This healing path will not be easy. It will be difficult, very difficult, but with the Savior's help we can succeed! President James E. Faust stated: "Everybody in this life has their challenges and difficulties. That is part of our mortal test. The reason for some of these trials cannot be readily understood except on the basis of faith and hope because there is often a larger purpose which we do not always understand" (*Ensign,* Nov. 1999, 59).

There are many things about our current situation that we do not understand; however, faith and hope in the Savior will get us through. The Savior reassures us of His presence during our journey: "I will go before your face. I will be on your right hand and on your left, and my Spirit shall be in your hearts, and mine angels round about you, to bear you up" (D&C 84:88). We can be comforted knowing that the Savior's love, protection, and guidance are with us. Who is better qualified to walk with us every step of the way?

Our Heavenly Father is also as close to us as we will allow, "When life's perils thick confound you, Put His arms unfailing round you. God be with you" ("God Be with You Till We Meet Again," *Hymns,* 152). God and Christ can comfort us each day if we allow Them into our lives.

TWELVE PRINCIPLES FOR SPIRITUAL AND EMOTIONAL HEALING

The Twelve Principles for Spiritual and Emotional Healing are based on the Articles of Faith. President Thomas S. Monson, speaking about the Articles of Faith, asked, "Can you think of a more firm foundation, a more basic philosophy to guide any of us than the Articles of Faith?" (*Ensign,* Feb. 2002, 2).

※ Principle 1: Agency—We Choose Our Behavior.

The 11th Article of Faith states that we have the right to choose how to worship Almighty God, and we know that right of choice extends to every area of our lives: "We claim the privilege of worshiping Almighty God according to the dictates of our own conscience, and allow all men the same privilege, let them worship how, where, or what they may" (A of F 11).

※ Principle 2: We Are Responsible for Our Behavior.

"We believe that men will be punished for their own sins, and not for Adam's transgression" (A of F 2).

※ Principle 3: The Godhead Has Perfect Love for Us.

"We believe in God, the Eternal Father, and in His Son, Jesus Christ, and in the Holy Ghost" (A of F 1).

"We believe that the first principles and ordinances of the Gospel are: . . . fourth, Laying on of hands for the gift of the Holy Ghost" (A of F 4).

※ Principle 4: With Faith, We Can Surrender Our Trials to the Lord Jesus Christ—He Invites Us to.

"We believe that the first principles and ordinances of the Gospel are: first, Faith in the Lord Jesus Christ" (A of F 4).

"We believe . . . that Christ will reign personally upon the earth" (A of F 10).

✳ Principle 5: Our Only Hope Is Christ's Atonement and Its Power to Heal—Spiritually, Emotionally, Mentally, Socially, and Physically.

"We believe that through the Atonement of Christ, all mankind may be saved, by obedience to the laws and ordinances of the Gospel" (A of F 3).

"We believe in the gift of . . . healing" (A of F 7).

✳ Principle 6: Your Bishop Is Called of God; Work Hard to Build a Strong Support System with Him and Other Trusted Individuals.

"We believe in the same organization that existed in the Primitive Church, namely, . . . pastors, teachers, evangelists, and so forth" (A of F 6).

"We believe that a man must be called of God, by prophecy, and by the laying on of hands by those who are in authority, to preach the Gospel and administer in the ordinances thereof" (A of F 5).

"We believe all that God has revealed, all that He does now reveal, and we believe that He will yet reveal many great and important things" (A of F 9).

✳ Principle 7: Personal Honesty with Ourselves and Others Is Essential to Learn How to Set and Keep Boundaries.

"We believe in being honest, true, chaste" (A of F 13).

"We believe in being subject to kings, presidents, rulers, and magistrates, in obeying, honoring, and sustaining the law" (A of F 12).

✳ Principle 8: God's Words Have Healing Power; Search and Ponder His Words Daily.

"We believe the Bible to be the word of God as far as it is translated correctly; we also believe the Book of Mormon to be the word of God" (A of F 8).

✳ Principle 9: Personal Revelation Is Available through Prayer and Fasting; We Can Embrace Revelations from Our Prophets.

"We believe that the first principles and ordinances of the Gospel are: . . . fourth, Laying on of hands for the gift of the Holy Ghost" (A of F 4).

"We believe in the same organization that existed in the Primitive Church, namely, apostles, prophets" (A of F 6).

"We believe in the gift of tongues, prophecy, revelation, visions" (A of F 7).

"We believe all that God has revealed, all that He does now reveal, and we believe that He will yet reveal many great and important things" (A of F 9).

Lord, I Believe, Help Thou Mine Unbelief

�֍ **Principle 10: Being Kind and Forgiving to Self and Others Is Healing— So Is Giving Service without Reward.**

"We believe in being . . . benevolent, . . . and in doing good to all men" (A of F 13).

✖ **Principle 11: We Are Protected when We Obey the Laws of the Land and Seek that which Is Good.**

"We believe in being subject to kings, presidents, rulers, and magistrates, in obeying, honoring, and sustaining the law" (A of F 12).

"If there is anything virtuous, lovely, or of good report or praiseworthy, we seek after these things" (A of F 13).

✖ **Principle 12: Learning from the Past Will Help Us to Live Well in the Present, and Give Us Hope for the Future.**

"We believe all things, we hope all things, we have endured many things, and hope to be able to endure all things" (A of F 13).

PRINCIPLE 1

Agency—We Choose Our Behavior

CHAPTER OVERVIEW

We experience so many emotions once we learn that our loved ones have engaged in compulsive sexual behaviors. Our emotions go all over the board like a bottle of black ink thrown against a white wall. The ink splatters into hundreds of blotches, strange spots, and little dots. Each ink spot represents some emotion—big or small. We may have big globs of emotions in one area and little dots in other areas, even though we may have tried to clean up our emotional state. One wife shared:

> *I was so angry, hurt, and disgusted with my husband when I learned about his pornography problem. I asked myself a hundred times why he would do this to us. My emotions were so volatile, and I had no time to process them. I didn't know what to feel or how to feel because my emotions fluctuated so much. What made matters worse is that I had no one to share my feelings with. In the past I had turned to my husband for emotional support, but I just couldn't do that this time—I was too angry. I became emotionally numb and felt all alone.*

No two people respond the same way when learning about the compulsive sexual behaviors of loved ones. The discovery may come when we receive a confession, catch our loved ones, or when someone informs us about it. It is even more painful if our loved ones deny it, lie about it, or are defensive or evasive. It is so painful and difficult to hear. Our emotions usually wander all over the place; it is not easy for them to find a home. Some emotions we want to keep, others we want to manage, diffuse, or throw away—surrender. We choose which emotions we keep and which ones we discard. Like the saying goes, "It is easier said, than done." We want to do some emotional house cleaning, but usually we do not know how or where to begin.

A common response is, "This cannot be happening to me. It must be some kind of nightmare." It can hurt even more, however, when we realize that it is happening to us, that we didn't dream it up; it is reality. We often ask ourselves, "How can we get our lives back?" "Will our lives ever be normal again?" "Will I ever be able to forgive and trust again?"

We have to begin healing from where we are today. Part of healing is accepting our current state and being willing to move forward from where we are.

It can be helpful to hear what others have learned along their journey. By learning from others, we can facilitate our own healing. The Holy Ghost can and will give us direction as we seek it: "By the power of the Holy Ghost ye may know the truth of all things" (Moro. 10:5).

 ## CHAPTER OBJECTIVES

At the conclusion of this chapter you should—

1. Understand that your response to your loved one's behavior is uniquely yours.
2. Realize the importance of accepting your feelings; recognize your humanness, and your right to feel the way you do.
3. Realize the importance of prayerfully evaluating and determining who needs to know about your loved one's behavior.
4. Understand agency and how it applies to you and your loved one.
5. Identify in writing your feelings—pain, anger, etc.
6. Understand that sexual addiction is a symptom of the problem or problems rather than the problem itself.
7. Know how you can benefit by being more assertive with your loved one and begin practicing assertiveness.
8. Understand the "stages of loss" and learn to recognize your current emotional stage.
9. Learn how to surrender to God the negative effects of the "Why me?" syndrome.
10. Recognize when you feel the emotion of anger, experience it, and decide at what level you want it to escalate; then use it to enhance your healing.

11. Recognize that it will take time to work through all of the issues surrounding your loved one's choices.
12. Understand how to avoid staying stuck in the victim role.
13. Realize that you are not captive and that you have many choices available.
14. Learn and apply the spiritual principles that others have discovered through prayer and scripture study that will help you deal with your emotional pain.
15. Believe and accept the truth that the ultimate source of peace is the Savior.

EVERYONE RESPONDS IN DIFFERENT WAYS

There is no easy way for our loved ones to tell us that they have been engaging in compulsive sexual behaviors or to be confronted by us because we have found out. It is one of the most frightening ordeals they have to face during the repentance and healing process. They worry, "What is going to happen once I tell my spouse everything that has been going on?" "Will my spouse leave me?" "What will the bishop think of me?" A teenager or young adult often wonders, "What will my parents, bishop, and/or priests quorum advisor think?"

Similarly, there is no easy way to hear the news that our loved ones have been engaging in harmful compulsive sexual behaviors—that they have been living a deceitful life. Notice the variety of responses of parents and spouses as they learned that their spouse, son, or daughter, was living a double life:

"I felt so unloved, rejected, and unaccepted when I learned that my husband was viewing pornography. To think that he got excited looking at those pictures was abhorrent to me."

"I can't image my son being involved in a gay lifestyle. I don't know why or how come. My emotions are so 'numbed out.'"

"As soon as my husband told me the truth about his affair, I was sick to my stomach. My first reaction was, 'I don't even want him to touch me ever again. I don't want him to see me naked. I don't want him to be near me.'"

"Suddenly I understood the source of the oppressive, noticeable darkness I'd felt in our home for so many years. I worried about the effect that it may have had on our children."

These responses from others are exactly that—their responses: resentment, hurt, pain, and anger expressed in different ways. Even though there may be some similarities, no two individuals will respond in exactly the same way to such devastating news or discovery. Based on our individual background and experiences, we see life from different perspectives.

▶ Think about your own feelings when you found out your loved one was involved in compulsive sexual behaviors. Briefly write about the emotions you felt at that pivotal moment.

_____

_____

_____

_____

_____

_____

Even though there are differences in our perspectives, we all have at least two things in common: (1) We did not choose to be in this situation, and (2) We are filled with varying, sometimes conflicting, emotions. You may even feel as Nephi did in light of his brothers' unrighteous decisions: "O, then, why is it, that ye can be so hard in your hearts? Behold, my soul is rent with anguish because of you, and my heart is pained; I fear lest ye shall be cast off forever" (1 Ne. 17:46-47).

Similarly, Jacob, when declaring the results of acts of unrighteous husbands, stated: "Ye have broken the hearts of your tender wives [husbands, parents, or children], and lost the confidence of your children [spouse or parents], because of your bad examples before them; and the sobbings of their hearts ascend up to God against you. And because of the strictness of the word of God, which cometh down against you, many hearts died, pierced with deep wounds" (Jacob 2:35).

Your heart may feel as though it has been pierced and wounded. The pain does not go away no matter how much you want it to. It really hurts!! But God has promised the blessing of healing when He offered, "A new heart also will I give you, and a new spirit will I put within you: and I will take away the stony heart out of your flesh, and I will give you an heart of flesh" (Ezek. 36:26). These are hope-filled, comforting words which can turn the tide in favor of much needed peace and healing.

What does this scripture mean to you: "A new heart also will I give you, and a new spirit will I put within you?"

_____

_____

_____

_____

_____

WHO SHOULD KNOW?

When we are in emotional pain, we may want to run, hide, close ourselves off from the world, and pretend that our loved ones' problem was just a bad dream; Other days we may look for opportunities to vent our frustrations and anger to anyone who will listen. A more helpful approach involves a prayerful, pondering posture regarding whom to tell and how much detail to divulge. Learning to trust our spiritual insights and prayerful decisions is critical during this time.

We need to let the Spirit be our guide and we especially need to avoid saying things to other family members in a spirit of revenge. The Spirit can guide us for good. Elder Richard G. Scott stated, "A powerful testimony is grounded in the personal assurance that the Holy Ghost can guide and inspire our daily acts for good" (*Ensign,* Nov. 2001, 87). While there is no universal right or wrong regarding this decision, a good "rule of thumb" may be to tell only those who absolutely need to know and who have the ability to help. There are some important considerations to help us evaluate whom to trust with such sensitive information:

- Will this person be able to offer gospel-centered guidance? Initially, the bishop, branch president, or stake president is the best resource for guidance, help, and understanding.

- Is there a safety issue regarding children or other family members?

- When we share information regarding our loved ones' addictions, we open ourselves up to receiving unsolicited conflicting advice that can play with our minds and impact self-trust.

- If family members know about our loved ones' sexual behaviors, they may find it difficult to continue to accept them as part of the family circle.

We should always keep shared information about our loved ones confidential unless we are prompted otherwise. If it becomes necessary to share the information, we should only do so after we think it through wisely, get inspiration, and are confident that it is necessary. There may be times when we talk with the bishop, family members, or other trusted individuals where we need to disclose necessary information. We should tell our loved ones what we are going to disclose to others. This is particularly important when a divorce has occurred and the children want to know why. Confidentiality should be maintained as much as possible. Confidentiality fosters trust. Effective communication needs trust. We place ourselves and our relationships at risk when we jeopardize trust. However, when abuse of children, the disabled, or the elderly has occurred, we must always take appropriate steps to protect the victims. We also have a legal responsibility to immediately report such abuse to law enforcement agencies.

AGENCY—THE GREAT TEACHER

An experience my wife and I had on a plane illustrates clearly how the choices of one person can affect many others. On February 8, 2002, the date of the opening ceremonies for the Salt Lake Winter Olympics, my wife and I were returning to Salt Lake City after a business trip to Texas. After the airplane door closed, the flight attendant explained the special rules that were in place because of this momentous event. One of these rules was that no passenger could stand, attempt to get something from the overhead compartment, or move about the cabin during the last thirty minutes of the flight. As we left the Dallas/Fort Worth Airport, the flight attendant explained this rule a second time over the intercom.

Our flight was rather uneventful. About fifteen minutes before the no-standing period would begin, the captain came on the intercom and explained the rule a third time. He added one additional warning: "If anyone stands or moves about the cabin the last thirty minutes of the flight, the plane will immediately be diverted to Colorado Springs. In such event, we will be grounded approximately five hours in Colorado until the opening ceremonies are over. Only then will we continue on to Salt Lake City."

We assumed that all of the passengers were hoping as strongly as we were that no one would stand up. The captain continued, "If you need to use the restroom or change a diaper, now is a good time to do it, since the thirty-minute rule will begin in about fifteen minutes."

The next time the captain's voice was heard, he said, "We are now starting the thirty-minute rule—no one can stand, attempt to get something from the overhead bin, or move about the cabin. Thank you for your cooperation."

About ten minutes later a man in his early twenties seated next to a window stood up, spread one leg over the passenger next to him, and stood up in the aisle. Every passenger that could see him standing was shocked. We all looked at him with, "What do you think you are doing?" written all over our faces.

The young man walked to the rear of the plane. My wife and I were seated on the third to the last row, and I stared at him as he walked down the aisle. I must admit I was thinking, "You idiot!" He glared back at me as though to say, "What are you looking at me like that for?"

As the young man walked toward the rear of the plane, the flight attendant told him to return to his seat. He did not respond, and so she directed him back to his seat using strong hand motions. He seemed a little stunned but followed her command.

The flight attendants were on their phones communicating with the captain. Our hearts sank and we thought, "Oh well, it's been awhile since we've been in Colorado."

A flight attendant attempted to speak with the young man, but he knew only enough English to tell her that he could not speak English.

As she returned to her position at the rear of the plane, I asked her why the man stood up. She said, "He does not speak English."

Another passenger who heard her response called out, "Well, he shouldn't even be on this plane if he can't speak English."

Others joined in with similar remarks and statements of disgust. We were all sure we were going to Colorado just because one guy broke a rule he couldn't even understand.

However, the captain granted mercy because the passenger who stood did not speak the language and did not hear or understand the rule. The captain decided that redirecting the plane to Colorado would not serve justice and granted mercy. The plane continued to Salt Lake City and landed on schedule.

There is really no behavior or sin that is solo. One person's choice can affect so many people. Our loved ones' choices affect us and many others. This young man made a choice that could have impacted the lives of many passengers even though he did not know the consequences of that choice. The passengers could have been affected spiritually, emotionally, mentally, socially, physically, and financially. Similarly, our loved ones may make choices without comprehending how they may impact us spiritually, emotionally, mentally, socially, physically, and financially.

How have your loved one's choices affected you?

_____

_____

_____

_____

_____

_____

There is no question that our loved ones' choices have impacted us. At times we may cry out that our loved ones receive justice and at other times we may plead mercy. "And now, the plan of mercy could not be brought about except an atonement should be made; therefore God himself atoneth for the sins of the world, to bring about the plan of mercy, to appease the demands of justice, that God might be a perfect, just God, and a merciful God also" (Alma 42:15).

What is the relationship between the captain on the plane who granted mercy and our Lord and Savior, Jesus Christ?

_____

_____

_____

_____

_____

_____

DO WE SPEAK THE LANGUAGE?

We and our loved ones understand to some degree the communication of God. We have felt His promptings and have received direction from the Holy Ghost. We can know the truth about our situation through the Spirit because "the Comforter . . . was sent forth to teach the truth" (D&C 50:14).

But with all of this direction and guidance, how many times have we disobeyed a commandment? Has it been because we chose not to follow? Perhaps we did not hear the warning signs through the Spirit, or perhaps we failed to understand the language of the Spirit.

How many strangers have judged us at such times? How many of our loved ones have judged us? Their remarks might have been, "You should know better than that." "Those behaviors are not normal." "What in the world are you thinking?" "You idiot." Such comments are much more hurtful than the expressions of disgust heard on the plane because they come from those who are closest to us rather than strangers. We seldom remember what strangers say to us, but often we carry for a long time what loved ones say to us.

Initially we may want to lash out like the passengers on the plane, but we should work diligently to choose a different approach. What we want to say is probably what we should not say. We can begin by asking our loved ones a question, "How can I best help you get through this difficult time?" "What are ways that I can support you?" "When I need to share my feelings of frustration and concern, can I share them with you?" These are questions that give us a place to begin.

INNOCENT VICTIMS OF COMPULSIVE SEXUAL BEHAVIORS

When our loved ones make wrong choices, we may think or make comments such as, "What were you thinking?" "Don't you care about us?" "I want to get inside your head and try to figure out why you did such a thing." "I just want to scream at you over and over again." "I feel so angry I could hit you."

As innocent victims, we had no choice in regard to the behaviors chosen by our loved ones, but simply because in mortality we travel in the same "plane" as our loved ones, we also suffer the consequences of their choices. When children are involved, they too become victims. A wife observed:

> It is easy to be the victim when I had actually been victimized since such enormous hurt had been inflicted upon me because of my husband's behaviors. Even though I was finally able to let it go, I realized years later that I had continued to play the victim role on behalf of my children. After all they had lost so much and endured so much through no fault of their own. If I didn't carry the victim torch of injustice for them, who would? (Ouch . . . letting go of that one was tough!)

As victims, we experience many emotions. Along with the anger, we too may develop feelings of guilt, low self-esteem, or other negative feelings that get in the way of our own healing.

In what ways have you been a victim of your loved one's behaviors?

_____

_____

_____

_____

Regardless of what circumstances we find ourselves in, we can, through the Atonement of Christ, be empowered to free ourselves from staying stuck in the victim role.

One person wrote:

> *I am a survivor of childhood physical, emotional, and sexual abuse. I no longer view myself as a victim. The change has come from inside me—my attitude. I do not need to destroy myself with anger and hate. I don't need to entertain thoughts of revenge.*
>
> *My Savior knows what happened. He knows the truth. He can make the judgments and the punishments. He will be just. I will leave it in His hands. I will not be judged for what happened to me, but I will be judged by how I let it affect my life. I am responsible for my actions and what I do with my knowledge.*
>
> *I am not to blame for what happened to me as a child. I cannot change the past, but I can change the future. I have chosen to heal myself and pass on to my children what I have learned.*
>
> *The ripples in my pond will spread through future generations* (*Ensign*, Sept. 1997, 19).

We certainly have been hurt. We certainly have emotional and spiritual pain, but as this person wrote, "I no longer view myself as a victim. The change has come from inside me—my attitude." There is no question that our loved ones have been involved with serious compulsive behaviors and this does impact us emotionally and in many other ways too. It will take time to walk through the emotional quagmire that has been created. As we sort through all of the hurt, accept the feelings we are experiencing, and realize that we are human and have the right to our feelings, we can then begin to choose ways to soften or diffuse some of the negative emotions that usually make us feel trapped. Running away from the uncomfortable feelings or telling ourselves we should not feel angry is not healthy for us because it usually makes us feel guilty and inappropriate guilt compounds our emotional stress and self-value. As we make small steps of progress and choose healthy ways to deal with the negative emotions, we will avoid feeling hopeless even though we may experience strong feelings of disappointment and sadness along the healing path.

Over time, we work to change our viewpoint, perspective, or belief about our loved ones' behaviors. Here is one perspective from a wife:

> *I married a returned missionary in the temple. We both come from very active families. I had done all the things I had been taught while growing up in the Church. I knew that I would be blessed for marrying in the temple and having a forever family.*
>
> *My husband began looking at pornography when he was quite young—ten or eleven. He cleaned up his behavior to go on a mission, but continued it once he returned home. I did not know he had a pornography problem until after we were married. He didn't know he was addicted even though he knew it was wrong. About three years after our marriage, my husband committed adultery. My world came crashing down. Everything I had worked for was gone—temple covenants, relationships, the righteous family, and much more. I felt so vulnerable and unacceptable. I hurt all over inside emotionally. The pain occupied almost every waking hour.*
>
> *Once I realized and accepted that the Atonement could cover adultery, I had a very comforting feeling. I realized that temporally things would not be the same, but they did not have to stay that way if my husband continued the repentance process. I knew it would not be easy, but we would and did get through it.*
>
> *It's been almost nine years since those dark days, but we have stayed together, grown closer to each other, and learned much about the Atonement.*

As this woman's perception changed by understanding the power of the Atonement, so did her feelings. She no longer felt like a victim or that all was lost. She understood that there would be painful days ahead, but there was a way to get through it and she would find it. And she did. In addition, her husband made the effort to change. There are few things that would help us more with our healing than to see improvements and the discontinuation of our loved ones' compulsive behaviors. The husband's repentance and changes were a blessing for him, his wife, and their family. Some of our loved ones will choose not to change (at least for now). However, we still need to move forward with our own healing, whether our loved ones do or do not change. We usually begin this process by changing our perception about our situation.

🌿 In what ways can you change your perspective or beliefs about your present situation and your loved one's compulsive behaviors so that you will be empowered to move forward with your healing?

TRYING TOO HARD (OVERFUNCTIONING)

One of the first obstacles we confront is the overwhelming desire to fix everything and make it all better right now. Our attitude may be, "I just want this problem done and over with. I don't want to keep dealing with this." So we work extra hard to solve our loved ones' problems when they should take responsibility and solve their own problems. We can support our loved ones by listening, sharing thoughts and feelings, discussing and setting a plan of action, and working together, but eventually our loved ones have to be the ones to solve their own problems. Here is an example of a wife trying too hard to help her husband overcome his pornography problem:

- She initiates and has sex more often with her husband.

- She asks him frequently throughout the day how he is doing and if he has had any temptations.

- She monitors all of his email and deletes any junk mail that might be inappropriate.

- She discontinues any magazine subscriptions that she subscribed to that may show women in swimsuits or advertise lingerie.

- She researches and purchases an Internet filtering system to block out pornography.

It's not that any one of these choices is necessarily inappropriate, but it may be destructive for the wife to be working so hard to fix her husband's problems. Why? The list of solutions created by the wife does not include the two most important items: (1) Does her husband want to change? (2) How much effort is he willingly or unwillingly putting forth to make the changes happen? Attempting to rescue her husband, though understandable, is not realistic—in fact, it is counterproductive. Why? Because it takes away the husband's responsibility to change and to prove to himself that he has the power to do so. It's also counterproductive because the wife can't continue the life of a policewoman or detective forever. Furthermore, she can't spend all of her energy on her husband's problem because she will have nothing left for herself or other family members. Eventually, she will get burned out, discouraged, and want to stop trying. She has other responsibilities such as taking care of herself, her desires and needs, children, church calling, civic duties, perhaps work, and much more. She can talk with her husband and determine together what areas of improvement need to be made, but the husband is still responsible for his behavior and needs to decide to do something about it. Even though it is a natural inclination to try to solve our loved ones' problems, we need to know where our responsibility ends.

What are ways that you can be supportive to your loved one, but still realize and allow him to be responsible to stop his inappropriate sexual behaviors?

_____

_____

_____

_____

_____

NOT DOING ENOUGH (UNDERFUNCTIONING)

On the flip side of trying too hard to rescue our loved ones is the risk of not doing enough or not doing anything. One wife responded to her husband's pornography usage with, "Oh well, my husband gets really moody if I say anything about stopping it so when he is looking at pornographic magazines, I just close the bedroom door and leave him in the bedroom by himself." This wife's response is not wise since she is indirectly condoning her husband's behavior. There are choices we can make to set boundaries (Boundaries are discussed in Principle 7) and ways we can deal with our emotions in healthier ways. (How to deal with our emotions is discussed in Principles 4 and 5)

🌿 **Are there choices you can make now to help yourself and to let your loved one know that his behavior is unacceptable?**

We want to learn how to balance our efforts and be consistent in our approach. There are two extremes—trying too hard and not doing enough. Understanding the real underlying issues will help us to achieve a balanced approach.

REAL UNDERLYING ISSUES

In most cases, the underlying issues, the root causes of our loved ones' addicting behaviors, started many years ago and have been growing ever since. It is easy to think that the acting out of the compulsive behaviors is the problem, but in reality, the acting out is merely a symptom of the underlying problem(s). For healing, wholeness, and hope to emerge, the root issues must be identified, confronted, diffused, and eliminated.

Those underlying issues are best brought to light through spiritual nudgings, insights, and promptings that come to us and our loved ones. To the degree that we are willing to face even the difficult truths illuminated through the quiet whisperings of the Holy Ghost, healing, hope, peace, and comfort will replace fear, confusion, doubt, and anger. Elder Richard G. Scott expressed the process this way:

> *I have found that because of our Father's desire for us to grow, He may give us gentle, almost imperceptible promptings that, if we are willing to accept without complaint, He will enlarge to become a very clear indication of His will. This enlightenment comes because of our faith and our willingness to do what He asks even though we would desire something else* (*Ensign*, Nov. 1995, 17).

Essential to the healing process is understanding that our loved ones resorted to inappropriate sexual behaviors (for the most part) to escape the reality of unpleasant and unwanted emotions. Most individuals caught up in such behaviors will not want to accept that truth, for doing so means facing those very issues and emotions they attempt to avoid through the drug of lust. Loneliness, low self-esteem, rejection, resentment, boredom, and anger are common issues at the very heart of compulsive sexual behaviors.

One important key to help us successfully navigate through the healing process is to learn to deal with the issues head-on instead of trying to ignore them or go around them. This process usually involves facing things we really don't want to face. Learning to be assertive is so important for our emotional well-being.

MEETING DESIRES WITH ASSERTIVE BEHAVIOR

What is assertive behavior? It is identifying our inner desires and being willing to share them with our loved ones in a sensitive, sensible way. The purpose of assertive behavior is to make our desires known and to be on equal footing with our loved ones. We have the right to be heard and so does our loved one. We should keep a written record of what style of assertiveness works for us and what does not. We may have varying degrees of success depending on the person we are interacting with and the actual situation. We should recognize that we have the right and the choice to be assertive. However, our choice is whether we want to be assertive, not whether our loved ones will respond to our assertiveness. We generally have better feelings about ourselves when we are assertive, especially in the long run. It's usually better to state our preferences and not to have them met, than not to say anything at all. Here are the four S's to keep in mind when using assertive behavior:

Selective—We need to determine with whom and under what circumstances we will be more assertive or less assertive. Every situation does not require assertive behavior. We may choose to let some situations slip by almost unnoticed. The point is *we choose*. We make the selection of what is important enough to us to be assertive about.

Sensitive—We should be sensitive to our loved ones, but still recognize that we have desires or wishes too and would like to have them met. In order for our desires to be met, we need to let our loved ones know what they are. We can do this in a firm, but kind way. We also recognize that our loved ones have desires and wishes too and may say "no" to our wishes.

Sensible—Be sensible. After we choose to be assertive or non-assertive in a particular situation, we still need to be sensible on how we proceed. Use common sense.

Begin Slowly—We should begin slowly and work to become assertive. We may not be successful at our first attempt. As we begin to be more assertive, we should choose a situation that is most likely to have a positive outcome. This will provide us with a good foundation to become more assertive. Early failures can be very discouraging. However, one failure or several failures is not reason enough to stop trying assertive behavior. Here are three different situations with *passive, aggressive,* and *assertive* responses for each.

Situation: I am in the mood for a fresh bowl of soup and salad, . . .

Passive Behavior
. . . but when my husband asks me where I want to eat I just say, "It doesn't matter to me." My husband chooses his favorite—a place that serves hamburgers and fries. (I go along and don't say anything even though I really wanted a nice salad and bowl of soup. I get resentful that I continually sacrifice my preferences for what my husband wants.)

Aggressive Behavior
. . . and tell my husband, while I'm pointing my finger at him, that I will not go to any place unless I can choose it. (I raise my voice and give my husband an ultimatum to get what I want—a restaurant that serves soups and salads.)

Assertive Behavior
. . . and suggest a place that I would prefer to go. I know that my husband does not especially like this place because it does not sell hamburgers. I recognize that my wishes are important and suggest to him that next time we can go to a place of his choosing or to a place that serves both. I am open to a discussion and want to respect his desires too. (I state my preferences and make them known. I recognize my husband's desires and am willing to discuss or brainstorm ways that both of our desires may be met.)

Situation: I want to get a filtering or block-out program for the Internet since my husband has had problems looking at pornography, but each time I suggest it my husband says, "There are too many good sites that inadvertently get blocked out with filtering software."

Passive Behavior
. . . I don't know if what he is saying is true or not, but he usually says he knows what is the best thing to do, so I just won't say anything any more.

Aggressive Behavior
. . . I yell at my husband and tell him that he is wrong and I will prove it to him by purchasing the filtering software and getting the neighbor to install it on the computer if he doesn't want to. (I have used anger and attacked my husband's knowledge about filtering software and involved a third party to get what I want.)

Assertive Behavior
. . . I tell my husband that I am not sure exactly how the software works but that it is really important for me to have some assurance that pornography cannot easily be accessed in our home. I suggest that we learn more about filtering software together by saying, "I would really like to learn more about filtering software. Can we gather information together and perhaps find a solution?" (I have been very assertive on what I prefer, but still recognize that my husband may not agree. I recognize that he can still choose to get or not to get more information, but have firmly stated my preferences.)

Situation: I'm not in the mood for sexual intimacy . . .

Passive Behavior
. . . but I will tell him it's okay and just go along. (Quite often I feel pressured or forced to have sexual intimacy and that makes me angry, but I don't say anything.)

Aggressive Behavior
. . . and won't be until you start helping around the house. You never help with anything!" (I raise my voice and shake my finger at him. I have used sexual intimacy as a weapon to get what I want.)

Assertive Behavior
. . . but I will try and see where it goes. If nothing happens, then I would like to try it again on another night." (Tonight I have chosen to have sexual intimacy, but have also set some boundaries, if it doesn't work out. I could also choose not to try tonight and suggest we try again tomorrow night. It's my choice.)

We can think about being more assertive and how these positive steps will help us to deal with our pain and eventual healing. However, for this to happen we actually need to *take* the assertive steps in order to get the results we desire.

Why is passive behavior so detrimental to your healing?

_____

_____

_____

_____

_____

What is the difference between aggressive behavior and assertive behavior?

_____

_____

_____

_____

_____

Think about your relationship with your loved one. In what areas of your relationship do you need to be more assertive?

_____

_____

_____

_____

_____

_____

�] Evaluate your relationship with your loved one and determine in which areas of your relationship you need to be more assertive. Decide to begin with one most likely to succeed.

_____

_____

_____

_____

_____

🌿 Perhaps role-playing situations can be helpful. Which friend could assist you to role-play your assertiveness and give you feedback? How will you benefit by role-playing your assertive behavior with a friend? Would tape recording or video recording the role-play be helpful for you?

_____

_____

_____

_____

_____

🌿 When will you actually initiate this new behavior with your loved one?

_____

_____

_____

_____

_____

Assertiveness is a skill, and we need to be aware of the difference between assertiveness and aggressiveness. By knowing the difference we can monitor ourselves and work to stay in the assertive position. In some situations we may choose not to be assertive at all because we may feel physically threatened. Also, just because we are assertive does not mean our loved one will respond in the way we desire. Another caution is not to become overly zealous with the new assertiveness skills. Overuse of assertive behavior may become very annoying to our loved ones and make it difficult for them to be around us. We should keep in mind the four S's: Be **Selective**, Be **Sensitive**, Be **Sensible,** and Begin **Slowly**.

What can we expect in the coming days, weeks, and months? During this intense period of healing, we can expect our emotions to ebb and flow, often accompanied by a sense of loss due to our expectations of what our life *should* be. The sudden loss of stability, relationships, order, love, virtue, trust, respect, honor, blessings, covenants, sealings, and priesthood undermine our vision, hope, and sense of well-being. The stages we go through when we suffer such serious losses mirrors the process one encounters when facing the death of a loved one. In a very real way we do in fact experience death—the death of our perceived, former relationship with our loved ones.

THE STAGES OF LOSS

We have experienced losses: the loss of a relationship, the loss of innocence, the loss of dreams and hopes, and the loss of what life could have been.

In her book *Questions and Answers on Death and Dying,* Dr. Elizabeth Kubler-Ross focused her professional career on understanding and helping those who lose loved ones to death by identifying five stages of loss. These stages include denial, anger, bargaining, depression, and finally acceptance.

While our loved ones who engage in destructive sexual behaviors remain alive, we too, often experience these same five stages—though often not in any particular order. For instance, we may begin at the denial stage and jump to the depression stage, or we may go from the bargaining stage back to the denial stage. It may be helpful to consider our experience in light of each of these stages and identify our own reactions to our loved ones' compulsive sexual behaviors.

Denial: The first stage of loss is *Denial.* We refuse to believe that the experience is actually happening. We want it to magically go away. We think we will wake up one day and discover that we had a bad dream and that everything will be okay. We feel certain that our spouse or son or daughter would not do this to us, and so it cannot be true. This is only something we read about in a book or see on TV. It is not something that happens to our family. We think this might happen to people who don't go to church, but surely not to people who attend church regularly, try to live the gospel, serve in callings, and hold family home evenings. After all, we have been taught that we will be blessed for living the gospel—and this is not a blessing!

The denial stage may also find us using thought patterns such as:

He's a wonderful father and husband. He's always held leadership positions in the Church and has blessed so many lives. He just has this pornography problem. Our children don't know about it, so it isn't affecting them at all. I know he tries hard to overcome his problem, and it does not bother me that much because he treats me kindly and never has pornography in our home.

The wife who shared this statement is still in denial about the seriousness of the problem.

🌿 **What thoughts do you have about the denial stage? Did you experience the denial stage? Are you in the denial stage now?**

_____

_____

_____

_____

_____

Anger: The next stage of loss is *Anger*. During this stage we become very angry, primarily at our loved ones, but sometimes at the situation. We are human. We are supposed to have emotions and are entitled to feel them. We may say things like, "What's wrong with my spouse? Can't he use self-control?" Or, "How did my son or daughter get involved in this sexual relationship before marriage?" We become angry because of the choices made by our loved ones, and this very fact makes us angry. We are usually angry at ourselves too. We may say things like, "Why didn't I see this coming?" "How could I have been so stupid?" "I should never have trusted him." "Why do I have to be the one to suffer when I didn't do anything wrong?"

One wife shared:

I felt all alone. I could not talk to anyone. I did not want to talk to my husband because I was just too angry. I saw our wedding picture on the nightstand and wondered, "How could he do this to me?" I did not want to see him. I was afraid to see him for fear that I would yell and scream at him in front of the children.

The anger stage usually comes and goes. It becomes very frustrating because one minute we feel our anger is manageable and the next minute we feel out of control. It's important to recognize that our degree of anger is tied to the amount of pain that we feel. It's also common to feel guilty for being so angry at our loved ones, but we can diffuse the guilt by accepting our humanness and recognizing it will take time to work through the anger. In addition, we can ask ourselves, "Why should I feel guilty for having human emotions like anger unless I act on it in unrighteous ways?" Our emotions are divine attributes that separate us from other creations.

How would you compare your past or present thoughts, emotions, and behaviors to the anger stage?

When we are asked to state how we feel about our loved ones' behavior, the emotion that is most commonly identified is anger. There is nothing wrong with feeling the emotion of anger unless it motivates us to say or do things that are harmful and not helpful. We are usually angry at our loved ones and their behaviors. President Brigham Young gave this poignant advice: "Do not get so angry that you cannot pray; do not allow yourselves to become so angry that you cannot feed an enemy—even your worst enemy, if an opportunity should present itself. There is a wicked anger, and there is a righteous anger" (*Discourses of Brigham Young,* 269). Once we feel the emotions of anger and recognize them, what choices do we want to make? How can we use the emotion of anger righteously and to our advantage?

You Are Using Your Anger

Right— To make things *better,* if it helps you to:	Wrong— To make things *worse,* if it causes you to:
Identify threats	Be more miserable
Motivate yourself to solve problems	Break something important
Be more assertive	Make situations worse
Eliminate frustrations	Be more dysfunctional
Express your thoughts and feelings	Lose a needed job
Maintain or restore your rights	Violate your own ethics
Get desired results, be more productive	Break a rule of your home, school, work, or commandments
Set limits to protect needed boundaries	Break a law of your city, state, or country
Prevent others from taking advantage of you	Use your anger as an offensive weapon
Resist unreasonable demands	Lose things
Make better choices	Make your emotions worse
Replace unwise choices	Make others' emotions worse
Achieve more, be more successful	Get a bad reputation
Protect yourself from abuse	Injure yourself or someone else
Protect yourself from physical harm	Cause yourself headaches, sleeplessness, or ulcers
Solve disagreements	Cause yourself anxiety, fear, depression, or guilt
Become more effective	Have people get even with you
Be happier	Be lonely because people avoid you
Be proud of yourself	Lose self-respect
Be yourself	Lose important people

Used by permission. © 1999 Allan Roe, Ph.D.

Anger is a real emotion. We do feel anger. At what level do we want our anger to escalate? We do not want to run from the emotion of anger, but rather be able to use it in a positive way that produces the results we desire. The question we might ask ourselves is, "Once I feel anger, what choices do I want to make?"

After reviewing the chart (page 23), how can you manage your anger to get productive results? (Ways to deal with our emotions in healthy ways are discussed in Chapter 4 and 5.)

Bargaining: Another stage of loss is *Bargaining*. At this stage we may try to work a deal with God. We may tell God that if He will take this trial away or quickly make it all better, we will stop doing things that are wrong and serve Him more. We may tell Him that we will work harder at improving our life if He will just lift this load from our shoulders. During our prayers, we may tell God all kinds of things we would be willing to do in return for what we want—a quick fix.

Learning of his wife's involvement with another man, one husband said:

> *Lord, if thou wilt just help me get through this, I'll serve thee. I'll do my Church callings and be faithful for the rest of my days. I have not always done what I could have or should have, but I'm willing to turn over a new leaf and make changes. I want to get the help that I need right now. I want to have this pain go away.*

We make all sorts of deals with God and try to talk Him into our solution and hope that He will come through. Have you experienced the bargaining stage or something that may be similar?

Depression: Another stage of loss is *Depression*. Depression comes with the hard realization that this situation is for real and that it is actually happening to us. A feeling of hopelessness and despair usually sets in because we are finally willing or have been forced to face the reality of our situation and realize there is no quick fix. A feeling of being boxed in with no escape routes is a common emotion. Feeling that we are overwhelmed and all alone with no one to help us increases our feelings of hopelessness. Sometimes we feel numb—feeling no emotion, shutting down, feeling dead inside—like life is just a big blur. Sometimes we can drown in too much feeling, obsessing, or experiencing anxiety, and panic.

We may have daily thoughts of not knowing what the future will bring and not caring about the future or we may be terrified to even think of the future.

We may not want to go places where someone might see us, regardless of whether or not they know what we are experiencing. We must be careful to avoid thinking that "everyone knows" and everyone is out there talking about us.

We typically experience a lack of concentration and may find difficulty in doing our daily tasks. We may not hear what others are saying or see what they are doing even when we are in the same room.

We may be tuned out to the world around us because we are so consumed by the intensity of our present problem and pain, which is usually the first thing we think about when we wake up in the morning and the last thing on our mind when we retire at night. If we have nightmares or wake up in the middle of the night, it haunts us then too.

A thought that may often cross our mind is, "Will things ever get better?" We find that there are few if any individuals we can share our feelings with, and this makes our situation more difficult.

Isolation and depression are often found together. A wife commented:

> *I never ever thought this would be me. My whole world has collapsed around me. I've tried to do what's right—and now this! I don't deserve it. I had nothing to do with what my husband did. I feel hurt and cheated.*
>
> *I have days when I just don't want to get out of bed and face the world. I just don't have the energy any more. I feel so helpless. I don't know how much longer I can continue.*

How would you describe yourself emotionally in regard to the depression stage?

_____

_____

_____

_____

_____

It's very important to recognize when we need medical attention. Our diet, exercise, and many other factors can impact our emotional well-being and our level of depression. If there is a prolonged period of depression (this could be several days or a few weeks) where daily tasks are difficult to accomplish, please seek medical advice. It's important for a medical professional to properly diagnosis each person and provide the necessary care.

Acceptance: The final stage of loss is *Acceptance*. Depending on what stage we may be in now, the idea of ever accepting the situation may seem elusive and impossible.

Acceptance does not in any way mean that we approve of our loved ones' choices, but it means that we accept the truth about our situation, that we accept the reality of the pain and hurt, and that we recognize the need to make the best choices possible to deal with the situation in a healthy way.

- We should focus on what we feel prompted to do now, today, regardless of the fact that we can't see very far down the road.

- We should accept that our loved ones need help and that we need help.

- We should seek help that is Christ-centered.

- We should accept the fact that love requires work—hard work.

- We should accept the fact that our loved ones may not choose to accept our love, see the truth, or make the necessary changes, but that we will be okay nonetheless.

If our loved ones do not immediately choose the path to wholeness and freedom from their addictive behaviors, we must accept the fact that it is a process that will take time—a journey, not a one-day hike.

We must accept the truth that through the Savior's love and Atonement we will make it through this painful time, regardless of what our loved ones choose to do.

We should move forward with faith, trusting that the Savior is "the Only Begotten of the Father, full of grace, equity, and truth, full of patience, mercy, and long-suffering, quick to hear the cries of his people and to answer their prayers" (Alma 9:26).

As we move through the loss stages, our emotions will be very volatile. We should realize that to some degree we are a victim of our loved ones' choices and that we are also suffering the consequences of his or her choices.

We should accept the reality of the situation we are in without feeling hopeless about it.

🌿 **Have you experienced moments of acceptance when you felt that you *could* get through this ordeal? What are they?**

_____

_____

_____

_____

_____

WHY ME?

"Why me?" is a common question asked. We so desperately seek an answer. Since we usually do not find an immediate answer to the question, we have little closure.

A husband, after learning about his wife's compulsive sexual behaviors, complained, "What did I do to deserve this?" His statement implies that he was somehow guilty of some sin too! President Thomas S. Monson described how life's situations bring much pain:

> *It may safely be assumed that no person has ever lived entirely free of suffering and tribulation, nor has there ever been a period in human history that did not have its full share of turmoil, ruin, and misery.*
>
> *When the pathway of life takes a cruel turn, there is the temptation to ask the question "Why me?" Self-incrimination is a common practice, even when we may have had no control over our difficulty. At times there appears*

to be no light at the tunnel's end, no dawn to break the night's darkness. We feel surrounded by the pain of broken hearts, the disappointment of shattered dreams, and the despair of vanished hopes. We join in uttering the biblical plea "Is there no balm in Gilead?" We feel abandoned, heartbroken, alone" (Ensign, May 1998, 52).

It is common and natural at this time in the healing process to ask "Why me?" It is usually difficult to accept that the pain we experience comes from the choices of our loved ones. We never thought that our hurt would come from someone within our family! This is one of the reasons it is so painful. This was not caused by someone outside the family unit—it was not an external event. Naturally, we want an answer to "Why me?"

Elder Neal A. Maxwell suggested that the answer lies in asking "what" rather than "why":

As we confront our own . . . trials and tribulations, we too can plead with the Father, just as Jesus did, that we "might not . . . shrink"—meaning to retreat or to recoil (D&C 19:18). Not shrinking is much more important than surviving! Moreover, partaking of a bitter cup without becoming bitter is likewise part of the emulation of Jesus.

Continuing, we too may experience moments of mortal aloneness. These moments are nothing compared to what Jesus experienced. Nevertheless, since our prayers may occasionally contain some "whys," we too may experience God's initial silence (see Matt. 27:46).

Certain mortal "whys" are not really questions at all but are expressions of resentment. Other "whys" imply that the trial might be all right later on but not now, as if faith in the Lord excluded faith in His timing. Some "why me" questions, asked amid stress, would be much better as "what" questions, such as, "What is required of me now?" or, to paraphrase Moroni's words, "If I am sufficiently humble, which personal weakness could now become a strength?" (see Ether 12:27) (Ensign, Nov. 1997, 22-23).

The question "What is required of me now?" opens a whole new world for spiritual exploration and refinement. A spouse reflected, "I stopped asking myself 'what if,' and starting dealing with 'what is.'" By looking at "what is," we have a reality check to monitor where we are now and what we need to do. Questions like "What is it that I need to do today?" "What is in my heart?" "What is the best choice I can make right now?" can help us stay grounded and deal with today's issues. Elder Dallin H. Oaks expressed how experiences in "the furnace of affliction" can help us to become what God wants us to become:

Most of us experience some measure of what the scriptures call "the furnace of affliction" (Isa. 48:10; 1 Ne. 20:10). Some are submerged in service to a disadvantaged family member. Others suffer the death of a loved one or the loss or postponement of a righteous goal like marriage or childbearing. Still others struggle with personal impairments or with feelings of rejection, inadequacy, or depression. Through the justice and mercy of a loving Father in Heaven, the refinement and sanctification possible through such experiences can help us achieve what God desires us to become (Ensign, Nov. 2000, 33–34).

What are some of our mortal experiences that Elder Oaks said place us in "the furnace of affliction?"

_____

_____

_____

_____

_____

_____

_____

What have you discovered about the mortal experiences that you are currently experiencing?

_____

_____

_____

_____

_____

_____

_____

The key to our healing is to focus on how God would have us walk through a particular challenge rather than wondering why this happened to us. President

George Q. Cannon taught that we can get through every trial if we "connect" with God, have faith in Him, and keep His commandments:

> *No matter how serious the trial, how deep the distress, how great the affliction, He will never desert us. He never has, and He never will. He cannot do it. It is not His character. He is an unchangeable being; the same yesterday, the same today, and He will be the same throughout the eternal ages to come. We have found that God. We have made Him our friend, by obeying His Gospel; and He will stand by us. We may pass through the fiery furnace; we may pass through deep waters; but we shall not be consumed nor overwhelmed. We shall emerge from all these trials and difficulties the better and purer for them, if we only trust in our God and keep His commandments.* (Collected Discourses, 2:185).

It's important to note that President Cannon promised that "we shall emerge from all these trials and difficulties the better and purer for them, if we only trust in God and keep His commandments." Furthermore, President Cannon did not say the trials or difficulties would be taken away or be easy. The words from Hymn 85, "How Firm a Foundation," remind us that God will be with us through our trials:

Verse 3
Fear not, I am with thee, O, be not dismayed,
For I am thy God, and will still give thee aid;
I'll strengthen thee, help thee, and cause thee to stand,
Upheld by my righteous, omnipotent hand.

Verse 4
When through the deep waters I call thee to go,
The rivers of sorrow shall not thee o'er-flow,
For I will be with thee, thy troubles to bless,
And sanctify to thee thy deepest distress.

Verse 5
When through fiery trials thy pathway shall lie,
My grace, all sufficient, shall be thy supply.
The flame shall not hurt thee, I only design
Thy dross to consume and thy gold to refine.

In our trials and difficulties, we experience growth and progression—to become what God wants us to become. We do not know what our loved ones may choose to do, and we cannot control them anyway, but we can choose to trust in God and keep His commandments so that we can emerge from these trials and difficulties.

One wife confirmed this truth:

> *I never felt so close to my Heavenly Father as I did during the ordeal of dealing with my husband and his pornography problem. I caught a glimpse of what it is like when one of God's children goes astray. I thought about all of God's children who are lost in some way and how the pain and sorrow must affect God. I only had one loved one that was lost, but God has had so many.*
>
> *I felt God's presence and wanted so much to do all I could do to stay close to Him in my prayers and by the way I lived. I did not want to add to God's sorrow.*

A mother whose son was struggling with pornography reflected, "I have never prayed so hard in my life. I have fasted more than ever before and I have frequently attended the temple and included my son's name on the prayer rolls."

🔖 **Pray about and ponder about your current trial. How can you apply what President Cannon taught?**

_____

_____

_____

_____

_____

_____

WHY ARE WE CALLED VICTIMS?

We are victims because we never chose to be where we are right now. Someone close to us, a loved one, made choices to engage in compulsive sexual behaviors, and now, to one degree or another, we are experiencing the destructive consequences of his or her choices.

Suffering consequences from the choices that others make is not an easy burden to bear; however, Christ can and will help us carry the load until we are ready to surrender it all to Him.

Recognizing that we did not make the choices that led to the consequences is important because we cannot afford to waste emotional and spiritual energy packing around unnecessary guilt. We are not responsible for what our loved ones choose to do. Agency is an eternal principle.

Even when others' exercise of agency emotionally rips apart our hearts, God still allows our loved ones to choose to engage in compulsive sexual behaviors. We need to recognize that our loved ones—not us—made the choices to engage in the behaviors, and healing for our loved ones cannot really take place until they accept full accountability and responsibility for past choices and are willing to repent of those choices.

AVOID STAYING STUCK IN THE VICTIM'S ROLE

As loved ones, we want to be careful that we do not get or stay stuck in the victim's role. There is a big difference between recognizing that we are innocent victims and then moving on with our lives and choosing to stay stuck in the victim's role and embracing self-pity, low self-esteem, resentment, and anger.

By being aware that we *could* easily get stuck in this role, we can choose not to. We can still feel the hurt and pain, but realize that we are not powerless in regard to our choices for dealing with them.

To some extent we are all affected by the negative choices of those around us. An empowering truth emerges when we realize that we can choose to no longer remain stuck in the negative emotions and behaviors brought on by the choices of others.

WHAT IF MY LOVED ONE CHOOSES NOT TO CHANGE?

Some of our loved ones may choose not to change. We have agency to make our own choices. The Holy Ghost will lead us to what is best for us and our healing. One wife expressed:

> *After years of beating myself up for my husband's acting out episodes, I finally realized that it was not my job to heal him or to make him better. That was between him and God. My role was to be a good person, the best I could be, and my husband's response to me, whether it be good or bad, was not about me, but about him.*

Our loved ones may not make the necessary changes. They may choose to stay "stuck" in their behaviors. What then? I suppose our feelings, tears, and sorrow are similar to what God feels on a daily basis watching His children stay "stuck" in unhealthy patterns and behaviors that separate them from Him.

Only God knows where our loved ones will end up if they persist in their unwillingness to change and what circumstances they need to bring them a change of heart. The Savior reminds us, "Nevertheless, ye shall not cast him out of your synagogues, or your places of worship, for unto such shall ye continue to minister; for ye know not but what they will return and repent, and come unto me with full purpose of heart, and I shall heal them; and ye shall be the means of bringing salvation unto them" (3 Ne. 18:32). The phrase, "For ye know not but what they will return and repent," is a powerful reminder that we do not know all the experiences that might help our loved ones to change nor do we know who will choose to repent. As our loved ones have experiences that help them to "return and repent," Christ has promised, "I shall heal them." Regardless of what our loved ones decide to do, we can know that we are loved by God and that He sees way beyond our mortal view. He will direct us. A wife shared:

> After meeting with our counselor for several months, I finally said, "What if my husband does not choose to change?" The counselor's response made me very angry at the time. He said, "You can't change your husband, but you will be okay." He repeated, "You will be okay."
>
> I left his office unsure about how I was going to handle having full responsibility for a home, children, food, and more. I cried all the way home, but I also felt the truth of his words.
>
> Now, twelve years later, I have come to know for myself that what he said was true. I have been okay. It has been very hard at times, but I know that God is near and He will guide and direct me. I know that the Holy Ghost has given me guidance and direction at the very moment I needed it the most. I have awakened in the middle of the night and received the guidance I needed for the next day. I have not been alone. I have been okay.

This woman felt impressed to stay in the relationship. She has been okay. The Savior will help us so that we will be okay, too. We can know what is best for us and our loved ones regarding our relationship.

Whatever our decision, we will still have moments when we are discouraged and depressed: "Now when our hearts were depressed, and we were about to turn back, behold, the Lord comforted us, and said . . . bear with patience thine afflictions, and I will give unto you success" (Alma 26:27). We have His assurance that He will help us get through this difficult time as we stay connected with Him.

🌿 **How has the Lord comforted you?**

_____

_____

_____

_____

_____

_____

_____

Our loved ones may choose to face their situation with honesty and courage, or they may choose to remain stuck in the behaviors. Regardless of the choices our loved ones make, we can accept our emotions, learn to manage them, and soften and diffuse them, so that over time we experience a personal healing process.

The scriptures teach, "But behold, he did deliver them because they did humble themselves before him; and because they cried mightily unto him he did deliver them out of bondage; and thus doth the Lord work with his power in all cases among the children of men, extending the arm of mercy toward them that put their trust in him" (Mosiah 29:20). We too can be delivered from whatever bondage we may feel that we are in because of our loved ones' choices.

Our loved ones can be delivered too! The Deliverer is the same for each of us—the Savior of the world! Our walk towards healing and peace requires faith and trust in the Savior that He can and will deliver us from feelings of hopelessness and discouragement. He will direct our walk throughout the process if we allow Him to.

After the truth is out about our loved ones' behaviors, it is easy to let our minds wonder about the future. What impact will this knowledge have on our relationship with our loved ones, children, extended family, friends, neighbors, and others? What will this do to our eternal family unit? Questions such as these are common, but cannot be answered now or in the near future. It will take a great amount of faith to get from where we are now to the next turn on the healing path. The difficult part for us is the unknown. We cannot see around the next corner, no matter how much we would like to. We want to know how everything is going to turn out and we want to know right now. We want to know what the future holds and don't want to wait to find out. Impatience postpones our healing. When this impatience creates unnecessary emotional stress, it's important that we still make healthy choices. We can choose what to do when our loved ones violate covenants.

Violation of Covenants

(Masturbation, pornography, fornication, adultery, homosexual and lesbian behaviors, child sexual abuse, or any other compulsive sexual behaviors violate covenants.)

What Makes the Situation Worse	What Makes the Situation Better
Purposely say hurtful things to your loved one.	Talk about your own feelings and needs.
Try to get even with your loved one by inflicting emotional pain upon him or her.	Stay close to the Spirit so you can respond appropriately.
Demand that your loved one change first before you make any effort to change.	Discuss your situation with the bishop. Get help by reading books or meeting with a professional counselor.
Demand that your spouse make important decisions right now, such as, "You need to decide right now to work on the marriage or leave."	Work together to set realistic goals to improve your marriage. Find out why the marriage is broken and learn what needs to be done to fix it. Be willing to implement what you learn. If your spouse is unwilling to work on the marriage, eventually you will need to decide what is best for you.
Take all the blame yourself for your spouse's compulsive sexual behavior.	Recognize that if your loved one is not happy in the marriage, he or she has a responsibility to tell you. Also, be willing to go to counseling, get help, and work to make changes on the real issues.
Beat yourself up for your loved one's behavior and punish yourself.	Recognize that your loved one is responsible for his or her behavior.
Make impulsive decisions when emotionally out of control.	Calm down and postpone any major decisions until you are emotionally stable.
Require spouse to do more than is humanly possible. "You need to tell me every time you are being tempted."	Be realistic and look for progress over a period of time. Work together to set achievable goals.
Pretend that there are no problems that need to be addressed and just try to avoid and put the whole ordeal behind you.	There are issues in every relationship that can be improved. Find out what they are and work together to improve them.

What Makes the Situation Worse	What Makes the Situation Better
Try to control your spouse so he will not do it again.	Recognize that there is nothing you can do to assure against relapses. Agency is at play here and the choice whether to relapse or become whole is totally in the court of the offender. Ask your spouse to write down what he is willing to do to change. This should be a detailed statement of exactly what he will or will not commit to do. Take time to consider that written statement of willingness and then prayerfully decide whether or not it is appropriate to stay in the relationship. Base your decision on your spouse's willingness or unwillingness to take full responsibility for and follow through to make the necessary changes.
Tell friends and family members (when it's not a necessity) about your loved one's problem just to try and win them over to your side.	Keep the matter confidential except with a few people who can help in the matter. However, there may be reasons for more than a few people to know especially if child abuse has occurred. The offender had agency and chose to act on impulses. Now the loved one must make choices regarding the family including the children, extended family, etc. Allow the agency of others to also come into play, whether they will be charitable or otherwise. When handled correctly, an extended family can be a tremendous support structure and should not be circumvented for the comfort of the offender. If he is serious about changing, he will welcome all support and not be offended if others have to know.
Yelling, screaming, arguing, and fighting with your spouse.	Talk. Listen and listen and listen. Respect each other and the right to have differing opinions.
When talking to your loved one use the words you, your, always, and never. For example, "You never do anything right."	When talking to your loved one try to use the words us, we, our, or I and me. For example, "I feel really hurt because of your viewing pornography. What can we do to work through this issue?"

What Makes the Situation Worse	What Makes the Situation Better
Skirting around the issues to avoid confrontation.	Tell your loved one what is on your mind and what you see as the problem. Focus on the solutions to problems. Be willing to explore the underlying issues that perpetuate the problems. Seek professional help to learn healthier ways of dealing with those issues.
Keep obsessing about your loved one's compulsive behavior which encourages the anxiety and anger to continue to mount.	Work on your own issues and set appropriate boundaries that allow you to facilitate your own healing.
Escape the pain by running away from your feelings or by feeling guilty for having negative emotions.	Accept your feelings. Know that you are human and have the right to your own feelings.

© Used by permission [chart modified]. © 1995 Allan Roe, Ph.D.

WE HAVE MANY CHOICES / TAKE ACTION

If we are waiting for external events to change before we act or make choices, we may be waiting a long time. Remember, we always have choices. We can be proactive and begin making them. We can take action. We can still keep our own personalities and be assertive. We can say to ourselves, "You can still be you!" Taking action will usually reduce our anxiety and fear because we realize that we have choices and that there are many things we can choose to do. Think about riding a bicycle; it is difficult to maintain balance or to turn the front wheel unless the bike is moving. Staying in motion, even though it may be slow at times, still gives us some momentum. Doing nothing and waiting for our loved ones to change is not wise; in fact, it is emotionally unhealthy for us to feel that our loved ones hold us captive. Making healthy choices and taking positive action frees us! Here are some choices and actions we can take:

- I can choose to get a book and read more about how to deal with sexual addictions.

- I can choose to set boundaries so I know where my responsibilities begin and end.

- I can choose to meet with my bishop and initiate appointments.

- I can choose to establish a support system.

- I can choose to join an LDS-based support group. (Refer to page 454.)

- I can choose to get individual personal counseling.

- I can choose to learn from others who have been in a similar situation and how they dealt with loved ones who chose compulsive sexual behaviors.

- I can choose to attend the temple.

- I can choose to work on my own issues and become a better person.

- I can choose to read and ponder the scriptures.

- I can choose to pray.

- I can choose to use therapeutic writing to record my thoughts and feelings.

- I can choose to work to get in touch with my feelings and realize I am human and am entitled to my feelings.

- I can choose to explore ways to deal with my feelings that produce a healthier outcome.

- I can choose to learn about ways to let go of inappropriate feelings of guilt I might experience because of my loved one's behaviors.

- I can choose how I want to respond to my loved one's behavior.

- I can choose music that will improve my mood and strengthen my spirit.

- I can choose to meditate.

- I can choose to rediscover a hobby or begin a new one.

- I can choose to reduce tension with aerobic exercises.

- I can choose to eat nutritional foods that will help me feel better.

- I can choose to learn to be more assertive and role-play assertiveness with a trusted friend.

- I can choose to stay in the relationship and try to work through the issues.

- I can choose to separate from my spouse. (This is one of the last choices after much thought, personal prayer, fasting, pondering, counseling with the bishop, etc. However, where any form of abuse is taking place, separation is certainly an appropriate option. The different forms of abuse are discussed in Principle 11.)

- I can choose to divorce my spouse. We certainly do not advocate divorce. However, it is an option when a spouse refuses to admit he has a problem, will not change, will not meet with the bishop, or will not go to counseling and his behavior is placing his wife and children at risk. This is a very important decision and requires much thought, personal prayer, fasting, pondering, counseling with the bishop, etc. over a period of time. It is wise to wait until your emotions and thought processes are stable enough to make such an important decision.

What are some additional choices you can make?

I can choose to _____

I can choose to _____

I can choose to _____

I can choose to _____

Satan wants us to feel we have no choices because of our loved ones' behavior and that we are stuck and have no way out. This is not true! We have so many choices now and in the future. The Spirit will lead and guide us so we can see all of our choices. As we respond to the Spirit and make choices with the guidance of the Holy Ghost, we will be led and directed each step of the way through the healing journey. Healing is a process—one step at a time.

ONE STEP AT A TIME

For now, we need to take the next step with faith. After traveling that distance, we look for the next step. We keep this as our motto, "One step at a time. One day at a time. One week at a time. One year at a time." That is really all we can do, and some days even that will be very difficult.

It is important that we stay focused on the short distances and not spend emotional energy on the long journey. If we have the faith to cover the short distances, the long journey will take care of itself. President Gordon B. Hinckley shared this experience:

> *Long ago I worked for one of our railroads whose tracks threaded the passes through these western mountains. I frequently rode the trains. It was in the days when there were steam locomotives. Those great monsters of the rails were huge and fast and dangerous. I often wondered how the engineer*

dared the long journey through the night. Then I came to realize that it was not one long journey, but rather a constant continuation of a short journey. The engine had a powerful headlight that made bright the way for a distance of 400 or 500 yards. The engineer saw only that distance, and that was enough, because it was constantly before him all through the night into the dawn of the new day (Ensign, May 2002, 72).

Our painful journey through the winding roads and difficult terrain will be lit in short distances. Christ and the Holy Ghost will light our way if we allow Them. Their light will never burn out. We can choose whether or not to block Their light by responding in negative ways to our loved ones' behaviors. We may not have any idea what choices we will make next week, but we do know what steps we are inspired to make this hour and we can make them and follow through.

We usually experience moments when we can't see beyond today. It's all we can do emotionally to think about today—even the next hour may be foggy and difficult to see. We get through painful experiences by focusing on what we can do today. We may get overwhelmed to think about much more. Over time the days add up to weeks and the weeks add up to months, until one or two years have passed. President Gordon B. Hinckley reminded us of this eternal principle:

The Lord has spoken of this process. He said: "That which doth not edify is not of God, and is darkness. That which is of God is light; and he that receiveth light, and continueth in God, receiveth more light; and that light groweth brighter and brighter until the perfect day" (D&C 50:23–24).

And so it is with our eternal journey. We take one step at a time. In doing so we reach toward the unknown, but faith lights the way. If we will cultivate that faith, we shall never walk in darkness (Ensign, May 2002, 72-73).

What suggestions did President Hinckley have for moving forward with faith?

How will moving forward with faith free you from the victim's role?

_____

_____

_____

_____

_____

_____

We do not have all the answers right now, and we cannot guess what the future will bring. That's why our journey requires faith, work, and reliance on the Spirit. One woman expressed:

> *I just about drove myself crazy trying to find answers for all of the "what ifs." I would catch myself trying to think too far into the future. When I realized what I was doing, I corrected my thoughts and tried to stay focused on the things I needed to get done today. Writing down the things I needed to do on paper helped me to stay on track.*

If we try to do all of the work ourselves rather than relying on the Lord and the promptings from the Holy Ghost, we will fail. The scriptures teach, "Cursed is he that putteth his trust in man, or maketh flesh his arm, or shall hearken unto the precepts of men, save their precepts shall be given by the power of the Holy Ghost" (2 Ne. 28:31).

What can you do to trust in the Lord and focus on the here and now?

_____

_____

_____

_____

_____

_____

_____

_____

REVIEW OF PRINCIPLES

How would you describe agency to a child?

_____

_____

_____

_____

How does agency apply to you and your loved one?

_____

_____

_____

_____

_____

How can understanding and accepting your loved one's agency help you in your healing?

_____

_____

_____

_____

_____

In what areas of your relationship with your loved one do you need to be more assertive?

_____

_____

_____

_____

_____

How will you practice assertive behavior?

_____

_____

_____

_____

_____

What are the stages of loss? How has each stage of loss impacted you (denial, anger, bargaining, depression, and acceptance)?

_____

_____

_____

_____

_____

What stage of loss are you currently experiencing?

_____

_____

_____

_____

_____

_____

Why is it important for you to accept your feelings and emotions and recognize your humanness and right to feel the way you do?

_____

_____

_____

_____

_____

How can you avoid the "Why me?" syndrome?

How can you avoid being trapped in the victim's role?

What have you learned about your own ability to heal, even though your loved one may choose to stay stuck in compulsive behaviors?

What choices can you make now that will help you stay on the healing path?

Record any other insights or thoughts that have come as you have read this
chapter.

_____
_____
_____
_____
_____
_____
_____
_____
_____

What is the single most important principle or concept you have learned from
this chapter?

_____
_____
_____
_____
_____
_____
_____
_____

With whom can you share this important principle or concept in the next
week?

_____
_____
_____
_____
_____

CALMNESS BREAK

Once a day take a few minutes to relax and unwind. Go to the same place each day. This may be a quiet room in the house or elsewhere. Get in a comfortable chair or lie on your bed.

As you unwind, compare the difference between having tense muscles and relaxed muscles. Start with your right arm. Put your hand in a fist and tighten up all the muscles in your hand and arm. Tighten your muscles to the point that they are firm, but not enough to cause a muscle spasm. Now relax your fist. Slowly open your hand and feel the muscles relax. Get every muscle to relax. Enjoy the relaxation. Now tighten up your muscles on your right hand and arm again. Now relax them. Try to relax the muscles even more. You can now use this same process for relaxation with all your body parts from your face muscles all the way down to your toes.

What have you discovered?

MESSAGES OF HOPE

Elder Joseph B. Wirthlin: "Even when the winds of adversity blow, our Father keeps us anchored to our hope. The Lord has promised, 'I will not leave you comfortless,' and He will 'consecrate [our] afflictions for [our] gain.' Even when our trials seem overwhelming, we can draw strength and hope from the sure promise of the Lord: 'Be not afraid nor dismayed . . . for the battle [is] not yours, but God's'" (*Ensign,* Nov. 1998, 27).

Elder Jeffrey R. Holland: "I think of those who suffer from sin—their own or someone else's—who need to know there is a way back and that happiness can be restored. I think of the disconsolate and downtrodden who feel life has passed them by, or now wish that it would pass them by. To all of these and so many more, I say: Cling to your faith. Hold on to your hope. 'Pray always, and be believing.' Indeed, as Paul wrote of Abraham, he 'against [all] hope believed in hope' and 'staggered not . . . through unbelief.' He was 'strong in faith' and was 'fully persuaded that, what [God] had promised, he was able . . . to perform'" (*Ensign,* Nov. 1999, 36).

PRINCIPLE 2

We Are Responsible for Our Behavior

CHAPTER OVERVIEW

We do not know why our loved ones chose to engage in compulsive sexual behaviors. Most of the time even they don't know or understand all the reasons either. However, by learning about the compulsive sexual behaviors cycle and how it works, we can free ourselves from carrying unwarranted guilt about our loved ones' choices. This knowledge and understanding will allow us to stay focused on our own personal issues rather than being preoccupied with our loved ones' behaviors.

In our search for answers, we no doubt have asked ourselves time and time again, "How did our loved ones get so deeply involved in these behaviors?" There is not a quick or easy answer to this question. Our loved ones have the responsibility to seek answers and can through repentance, self-evaluation, and counseling discover some conclusions, but probably will never have a complete answer. However, lack of complete answers to this question need not delay our loved ones' healing or our healing unless we allow it. One thing we know for sure is that no person on earth is exempt from temptation, and anyone who entertains inappropriate thoughts too long, can fall into unacceptable behaviors.

President James E. Faust, speaking in a priesthood session of general conference, declared, "One of the great myths in life is when men think they are invincible. Too many think that they are men of steel, strong enough to withstand any temptation. They delude themselves into thinking, 'It cannot happen to me.' . . . Brethren, it can happen to any of us at any time. So much of our course in life is influenced by forces we only partly perceive" (*Ensign,* May 2002, 46).

Temptation extends no mercy but is cunning and deceptive and often packaged in such a way as to be very enticing. Anyone who is not aware of the danger of the temptation and who does not choose to flee may easily fall prey to it. When a person chooses to give way to a particular package of temptation, the natural consequences are automatically included—though they may not be spelled out, even in fine print. These consequences may not be evident initially, but they eventually do appear. There are no exceptions.

Anyone who succumbs to a particular temptation can fall into a cycle of compulsive behaviors linked to that temptation. The unhealthy pattern repeats itself again and again, and over a period of time the pattern becomes ingrained.

 ## CHAPTER OBJECTIVES

At the conclusion of this chapter you should—

1. Know that you can heal even though all of your questions about your loved one and his behavior may not be answered.
2. Know the stages in the compulsive sexual behaviors cycle.
3. Know the differences between lust and love.
4. Understand that there are underlying issues (usually emotional) that cause the behaviors and cause your loved one to stay "stuck" in the behaviors.
5. Understand that it will take time for your loved one to resolve the underlying emotional issues that trigger the compulsive sexual behaviors cycle.
6. Know the difference between a loved one's "lapse" and "relapse" and how you can prepare yourself and respond in a self-enhancing way.
7. Know the difference between open-ended questions and closed-ended questions and why open-ended questions are more effective.
8. Learn how to recognize if your loved one is serious about making changes to overcome his inappropriate behavior.
9. Know that the Spirit will offer peace, comfort, and insight to soften and smooth some of the "rough road" during this time of transition.
10. Understand the value of "journaling" your thoughts and feelings.
11. Try to keep a journal and practice emotional cleansing through writing.

Unanswered Questions

Right now you probably have more questions than answers. Two of the most common questions are: "Why did this happen?" and "How did my loved one get involved in compulsive sexual behaviors?"

Although I do not pretend to have complete answers to these questions, I do have some insights that may help. I will try to explain what goes on inside the mind of a person who engages in compulsive sexual behaviors.

As we discuss this sensitive subject, it is imperative that we remember to always *focus on the problem, not on your loved one who has the problem.* The loved one who chooses to engage in the compulsive behaviors often has one personality that is wonderful, thoughtful, and courteous, but the other side is often irritable, edgy, and angry. Being caught in the middle between the two sides presents a whole "bag" of challenges for those who want to help.

The truth about our loved ones is often difficult to perceive as a result of their ambivalent behaviors. Here is an experience shared by a husband that can help us understand compulsive behaviors.

Parable of the Chocolate Chip Cookies

My wife and I were going on a business trip to Texas. On the day of the departure, she spent the morning alone at home. She was busy and stressed out and wanted to get some relief before the trip.

I returned home from my office in the early afternoon and found my wife busy in the kitchen.

I asked, "What are you making?"

She responded, "I'm making chocolate chip cookies to take to our friends in Texas."

I was surprised since my wife was on a diet and chocolate chip cookies were not on it. I also thought it was strange for her to be making cookies for the friends that we would be visiting on our trip, since she had never done so before.

I said nothing more and continued to pack my luggage. The smell of fresh chocolate chip cookies permeated the house. How could one resist just one cookie? Neither of us was able to resist; however, we still had three dozen choc-olate chip cookies neatly layered between tin foil in a box to take on the trip.

On the airplane my wife asked, "Would you get me just one cookie from the box in the overhead compartment?"

I responded to her request, and it wasn't too long before my wife said, "Just one more cookie."

We ate supper at the hotel that evening. Afterwards, chocolate chip cookies became a great bedtime snack—just one more cookie each.

The next day I was in a seminar from 8:00 A.M. to 5:00 P.M. My wife was alone in the hotel room. She brought books to read and craft items to keep her busy.

When I returned from my all-day seminar, the first layer of cookies was gone from the box.

The second day my seminar concluded, and we were on our way to visit our friends. We were just about ready to leave the hotel room when I remembered the cookies my wife had made, and I asked, "What about the cookies?"

My wife's quick response was, "There's not enough left to give to anyone."

Addressing the underlying emotional issues behind this story, we can focus on the feelings, thoughts, and choices that led this woman to bake and eat three dozen cookies when she was on a diet. Focusing on the triggers which drive a given compulsive cycle is the first step toward resuming a positive direction, sanity, and wholeness. Like the woman in the parable, are there certain times of the day when a person is more susceptible to eating cookies than other times? Are there moments or situations when she craved cookies? Did she use chocolate chip cookies to make her feel good and provide a short-term burst of energy—only to fall down to lower energy levels afterward? Is she likely to eat more cookies when she is bored or tired? Does she crave cookies when she is under stress? Does she cover up her stress while eating chocolate chip cookies? What are the underlying emotional issues regarding the behaviors that she chose that took her in the opposite direction from the goals that she had set for herself?

To truly address the problem, we need to realize that there are underlying feelings, thoughts, and choices that lead our loved ones to compulsive behaviors. The behaviors are usually a symptom of underlying emotional issues that our loved ones need to resolve in a healthy way. "Satan sometimes tempts us through our emotions. He knows when we are lonely, confused, or depressed. He chooses this time of weakness to tempt us to break the law of chastity" (*Gospel Principles,* 240-241). President Spencer W. Kimball said: "We live in a sterile age, or so it seems—an age when young people [also older people] turn to sex to escape loneliness, frustration, insecurity, and lack of interest" (*The Teachings of Spencer W. Kimball,* 271). Recognizing the underlying issues provides the comfort of knowing that our loved ones' compulsive behaviors are not about us. Of course, we have a part in the relational aspect with our loved ones, but it is our loved ones' responsibility to identify the underlying emotional issues that trigger the compulsive behaviors and learn to deal with them in better ways so they can escape the behavior.

A wife shared this insight:

> *Once I learned about the compulsive sexual behaviors cycle, it was a great relief for me. I no longer felt the guilt or blamed myself for what my husband had chosen to do. At first I thought that if I had been more sexually responsive this would not have happened. Now I recognize that my husband's inability to deal with his own unwanted emotions is the driving force behind the compulsive behaviors. I do recognize that I have a part in our relationship and I can work to improve our relationship, but I am not responsible for my husband's feelings and emotions that lead to his unhealthy choices.*

Once we see that our loved ones' behaviors are tied directly to their inability to deal with their own unwanted emotions, we free ourselves from unwarranted guilt and stop blaming ourselves for their choices.

⚑ How does knowing that your loved one's behaviors are usually tied to his underlying emotional issues free you from unwarranted guilt?

_____

_____

_____

_____

_____

_____

Now let's go back to the chocolate chip cookies. Did the wife have an opportunity to cease her behavior several times along the way? Why couldn't she just say no? After all, she had already made a commitment not to eat cookies while she was on her diet. If we make commitments, we should keep them. Right? What is the likelihood of her limiting herself to one cookie? Did the one cookie satisfy her craving or just increase it? This man's experience with his wife involved cookies, but it could be any *mood-altering* choice that affects the "feel-good" part of the brain. How does a woman on a diet end up eating almost three dozen cookies?

Here is the compulsive behaviors cycle as it relates to this woman:

1. Feeling: She felt stressed getting ready for the trip and wanted some relief. We don't feel the same level of stress while we are eating cookies. We cover up the stress with a mood-altering choice. For the moment the stress is gone and temporarily there is a good feeling. That's how we get stuck in compulsive behaviors. Remember, compulsive mood-altering choices only work in the short-term and ultimately have negative consequences.

2. Thought: She got the thought in her mind, "I want some chocolate chip cookies. They would lift me up and give me an energy boost." Then she rationalized or tricked herself into thinking it was a good idea by saying, "I will bake them for a friend."

3. Behavior: She watched all of the ingredients go into the mixing bowl. After the dough was made, she tasted a little bit that "accidentally" got on her finger. She tells herself (rationalizes), "It's okay to eat a little bit of the dough because that's not a cookie. Right? My diet restricts me from eating cookies, but there is nothing that says I can't have cookie dough." She smelled the fresh cookie aroma from the oven. She surrounded herself with the temptation and then caved in and ate "just one." She could live with herself by saying, "The temptation was just so overpowering that I simply could not stop."

4. Addiction: She told herself, "After all, one little cookie will not affect my diet." Then she ate one more and one more until the cookies were almost gone. How did she first get introduced to chocolate chip cookies as a "feel-good" treat? She probably did from a family member, friend, neighbor, or cookbook, or else she may have discovered them on her own.

In similar ways our loved ones learned compulsive behaviors. All too often this four-step process to compulsive behaviors (feeling, thought, behavior, addiction) gets us in the behaviors and keeps us there. Consequently the addiction causes even more negative feelings, completing the addictive cycle.

President Joseph F. Smith outlined the compulsive behaviors cycle very clearly:

1. Feeling: "In the mad rush of life for worldly honors and for the possession of the perishable things of this earth men do not stop before they get weary, and they do not rest before they become faint."

2. **Thought:** "They appear to think that what is necessary for them when they become weary and faint is to take stimulants to refresh themselves, that they may be able to run a little farther for a few moments."

3. **Behavior:** "In this way the man of business braces himself up by taking strong drinks. The housewife and the mother who has become faint, feels that she must, in order to keep up her strength, take a cup of tea, and thus brace up her nerves and strengthen herself for a little while that she may be able to finish her day's work."

4. **Addiction:** "Resorting to the aid of stimulants and drugs that go far to injure our systems and make us slaves to an acquired appetite" (*Collected Discourses,* 4 [Apr. 7, 1895]).

This statement might well have been taken from a recent general conference address, but look again at the reference and note that the statement was made in 1895. However, President Smith's inspired words are very applicable to our day and time. The last two words in this quotation *acquired appetite* are extremely important to ponder.

No one is born with compulsive appetites. A person must choose them and feed them somewhere along the way. Early choices in life can lead a person to be a slave to addictions. President Gordon B. Hinckley admonished:

> *I plead with you boys tonight to keep yourselves free from the stains of the world.*
>
> *You must not indulge in sleazy talk at school. You must not tell sultry jokes. You must not fool around with the Internet to find pornographic material. You must not dial a long distance telephone number to listen to filth. You must not rent videos with pornography of any kind. This salacious stuff simply is not for you. Stay away from pornography as you would avoid a serious disease. It is as destructive. It can become habitual, and those who indulge in it get so they cannot leave it alone. It is addictive* (*Ensign,* May 1998, 49).

The good news is that anyone can be healed and freed from pornography or other compulsive sexual behaviors through repentance and the Atonement. When a person recognizes they have made poor choices, it's easy for them to feel guilt, self-pity, and shame. These are emotions that can cause them to reach again for their drug of choice because they create internal conflict and tension. Elder Russell M. Nelson explained this cycle:

> *Danger lurks when we divide ourselves with expressions such as "my*

*private life," "my professional life," or even "my best behavior." Living life in
separate compartments can lead to internal conflict and exhausting tension.
To escape that tension, many people unwisely resort to addicting substances,
pleasure seeking, or self-indulgence, which in turn produce more tension,
thus creating a vicious cycle (*Ensign, Nov. 2000, 17).

This end of the cycle causes it to repeat itself again and again if our loved ones
do not deal with the guilt, shame, and other consequences in a Christ-centered
way. We all need to be careful to deal with our emotions in healthy ways instead
of looking for something to cover up the emotional pain of the original bad
choice or its detrimental consequences. Once we have committed to a goal, how
do we move forward when we experience a lapse? What should this woman do
after eating almost three dozen cookies? Ponder the following questions:

- Since this woman had a lapse on her diet, should she just stop dieting?

- Should she say, "I can't do this anymore" and return to her old eating habits?

- Should she beat herself up and tell herself how terrible she is for eating the
  cookies?

- What does she gain by looking at the lapse as a complete failure?

- What does she gain by replaying the incident in her mind and then thinking
  what a rotten, terrible person she is for lapsing?

- What does she gain by replaying all the other times where she attempted a
  diet and was not successful?

- What does she gain by telling herself that she has blown it again and is no
  good to her family or others if she can't make a commitment and keep it?

- What does she gain by comparing herself to all the women she knows who
  have chosen to diet and have been successful?

**✍ If this woman were your best friend and told you about her diet and
the experience of eating the cookies, what advice would you give her?**

_____

_____

_____

_____

✒ If your loved one lapsed as he or she is working to overcome compulsive sexual behaviors, what advice would you give him or her?

_____

_____

_____

_____

_____

Let's look back at the woman and her cookies. She will gain nothing by thinking about the negative. By doing so she will most likely become more discouraged and depressed, which in turn will tempt her to return to her addiction. With feelings of discouragement and depression, she does not have the emotional and spiritual power necessary to get out of the inappropriate behaviors and to move forward. By accepting the lapse as part of dieting, admitting it happened, and saying "I can learn from this" and "I will know what to do next time," she empowers herself with emotional and spiritual strength to continue.

We too are empowered to stay on the healing path and to draw on the Savior's love and power when we consider a lapse to be a learning experience rather than a failure. Is a failure disappointing? Terribly so! Does the lapse bring back the emotional baggage once again? Yes, it does! The feelings of resentment, bitterness, and anger quickly bubble back to the surface. One wife expressed her frustration this way:

> *About one month after I started dating my husband, he told me about his pornography problem. I was shocked because he didn't seem to be the type of guy to be doing this. He was so kind to others and to me that it just seemed so out of character. At the same time, I didn't want to get more involved with him and fall more in love unless I had some spiritual confirmation to continue the relationship. I felt good about continuing the relationship and we were married about six months later. We have been married for seven months now and my husband has looked at pornography twice. While we were courting, he slipped up a couple of times. With each incident, I seemed to get angrier. The first time I seemed to have a lot of patience and understanding, but now the anger just seems to take over and it takes me longer to work through it. Instead of working through it in a few hours, it now seems to take me a day or so.*

This newlywed's feelings are so real and so common. She is certainly entitled to her feelings. She is vulnerable. She has been hurt and a natural emotional reaction is anger.

Nephi had two unsuccessful attempts at obtaining the plates of brass before he succeeded. With each attempt he learned what would not work. His efforts were learning experiences, not failures. Before Nephi and his brothers made their first attempt to obtain the plates, he started on a very positive note: "I will go and do the things which the Lord hath commanded, for I know that the Lord giveth no commandments unto the children of men, save he shall prepare a way for them that they may accomplish the thing which he commandeth them" (1 Ne. 3:7).

How did Nephi respond to their first unsuccessful attempt to obtain the plates? He declared, "As the Lord liveth, and as we live, we will not go down unto our father in the wilderness until we have accomplished the thing which the Lord hath commanded us" (1 Ne. 3:15).

How did Nephi respond to their second unsuccessful attempt to obtain the plates? He stated:

> *Let us go up again unto Jerusalem, and let us be faithful in keeping the commandments of the Lord; for behold he is mightier than all the earth, then why not mightier than Laban and his fifty, yea, or even than his tens of thousands?*
>
> *Therefore let us go up; let us be strong like unto Moses; for he truly spake unto the waters of the Red Sea and they divided hither and thither, and our fathers came through, out of captivity, on dry ground, and the armies of Pharaoh did follow and were drowned in the waters of the Red Sea* (1 Ne. 4:1-2).

Whether we are talking about obtaining the plates of brass, dieting, or working to change compulsive behaviors, we usually discover that it is not easy. We often realize that change does not occur simply because we want to change or even when we first attempt to change. It may take more than one attempt, as it did for Nephi, to obtain the plates. In fact, it will probably take many more attempts.

We should avoid thinking that since we are now attempting to change there will be no eating of the cookie dough or cookies. This absolute, 100 percent, all-or-nothing change model is not healthy since change usually requires learning with some lapses. Both learning and lapses are necessary parts of the healing process, and we should take them in stride and move forward in the direction the Lord wants us to go.

If the wife, who is on the diet, learns from this experience so that she will avoid making the same mistake in the future, has she grown and progressed? Isn't she still on the diet? Isn't she still going to lose the weight if she continues on the diet? Yes! The answer is to continue. Continue the course. Don't give up. Our loved ones are responsible to get out of compulsive sexual behaviors. No one can do it for them. We can be supportive and provide encouragement, but they have to decide to change and then make a real effort to do so. Now that this woman has had a lapse with her diet, what can her husband or other loved ones do to help her? Ponder the following questions:

- Should her husband criticize her and tell her that he knew she would not be able to change?

- Should her husband make fun of her and tease her?

- Should her husband constantly nag her about the diet and how she does not stick with it?

- Should her husband recount all the times she has tried to go on a diet and has been unsuccessful?

- Should her husband bring up other areas she has tried to change like being more organized and remind her that she can't do that either?

- Should her husband run through a list of his wife's relatives and give examples of how none of them has been able to reach their goals?

- What is gained by her husband telling other family members what she did?

- What is gained if her husband withdraws himself and does not talk to her?

- What is gained if her husband becomes angry at her and yells and screams?

- What is gained if the husband uses the wife's lapse as a weapon and states that he will not help her clean the house as punishment?

Why are these behaviors or actions so detrimental to a loved one who has lapsed?

🔖 If your spouse had broken his or her diet, how could you be supportive and help him or her get back on the diet and meet the goal?

_____

_____

_____

_____

_____

The Prophet Joseph Smith taught: "Nothing is so much calculated to lead people to forsake sin as to take them by the hand, and watch over them with tenderness. When persons manifest the least kindness and love to me, O what power it has over my mind, while the opposite course has a tendency to harrow up all the harsh feelings and depress the human mind" (*Teachings of the Prophet Joseph Smith*, 240).

🔖 How can you apply this principle to your loved one?

_____

_____

_____

_____

_____

How do you think the wife would have felt if her husband had used this approach with her? What can we do to help our loved ones? "Take them by the hand, and watch over them with tenderness." Show kindness and love. This helps our loved ones to know that they can love themselves because others love them. It helps them have power over the negative thought patterns that keep them mired in the compulsive behaviors. As a result, our loved ones are more likely to give up the negative thinking that "I am a loser and will never change."

How powerful is this approach? The Prophet taught, "*Nothing* is so much calculated to lead people to forsake sin as . . . tenderness . . . kindness and love."

The idea that we show tenderness, kindness, and love to our loved ones does not mean in any way that we condone their behaviors. Elder Russell M. Nelson reminds us, "Real love for the sinner may compel courageous confrontation— not acquiescence! Real love does not support self-destructing behavior" (*Ensign,* May 1994, 71). One wife decided,

> *I could go to work and provide income for my family, but feel impressed not to do so for now. I worked through the early years of our marriage and could return to the workplace, but since my husband lost his job because he was looking at pornography at work, I think it's best to let him figure out what to do. I will help him rewrite his resume, do some job networking, give him encouragement, but not go to work. I could probably get a job in my field sooner than he could in his profession, but this would not be helpful to him or allow him to experience the consequences of his behaviors.*

This wife felt good about her decision and that it would help her husband to experience the consequences of his behaviors. She decided that getting a job and going to work would be supporting him in his compulsive sexual behaviors. This wife was able to support him positively by helping him with his resume, doing job networking, and giving words of encouragement.

How can you apply Elder Nelson's statement to you and your loved one?

Our loved ones are caught between light and darkness. When they have some success in overcoming the behaviors, they walk closer to the light. When they fall or slip, they can easily drift toward darkness. By encouraging our loved ones to keep trying even when they slip, we will give them an opportunity to leave the darkness and seek the light.

The scriptures provide light. Even when we slip and fall, we can get back on course and receive light by reading and pondering the scriptures. Elder Henry B. Eyring counseled:

There has been a war between light and darkness, between good and evil, since before the world was created. The battle still rages, and the casualties seem to be increasing. All of us have family members we love who are being buffeted by the forces of the destroyer, who would make all God's children miserable. For many of us, there have been sleepless nights. We have tried to add every force for good we can to the powers swirling around the people who are at risk. We have loved them. We have set the best example we could. We have pled in prayer for them. A wise prophet long ago gave us counsel about another force which we may, at times, underestimate and thus use too little. . . . And now, as the preaching of the word had a great tendency to lead the people to do that which was just—yea, it had . . . more powerful effect upon the minds of the people than the sword, or anything else, which had happened unto them—therefore Alma thought it was expedient that they should try the virtue of the word of God (Alma 31:5) (Ensign, May 1999, 73).

We can use the word of God to strengthen us and to keep us in the light, so that we are part of that force for good. We seek to become this force for good so we have the spiritual power to deal with the situation even though our loved ones may have little desire to change. By being on solid spiritual footing ourselves, we are more likely to be an influence for good to those around us. Perhaps by our examples, our loved ones may seek the word of God

THE COMPULSIVE SEXUAL BEHAVIORS CYCLE

In order to understand the compulsive sexual behaviors cycle, we first need to define the term. Let's consult the dictionary. The word *compulsive* means "driven by an irresistible inner force to do something" (*Encarta World English Dictionary* [North American Edition], 2001, Microsoft.)

This is the bottom line. Our loved ones have an irresistible inner force to engage in compulsive sexual behaviors even though it places their life, their family, their Church membership, their career, their reputation, their health, and their finances at risk. Why is this inner force irresistible? Because our loved ones have bought Satan's lies and have taken the drug of lust. By so doing they begin to believe exactly what Satan wants them to believe—that the behaviors are irresistible, that there is not much they can do to resist them. The Satanic logic is, "If the behaviors can't be changed, why even try?" President Thomas S. Monson warned, "Avoid any semblance of pornography. It is dangerous and addictive. If you continue to view pornography, your spirit will become desensitized and your conscience will erode" (*Ensign*, Nov. 1990, 97).

Our loved ones, through repentance and Christ's Atonement, can be freed from the behaviors and Satan's grip if they so choose. President James E. Faust gave this hope:

> *We challenge the powers of darkness when we speak of the perfect life of the Savior and of his sublime work for all mankind through the Atonement. This supernal gift permits us, through repentance, to break away from Satan's grasping tentacles (Ensign, Sept. 1995, 6).*

🌿 **In order for your loved one to be freed from the behaviors, what did President Faust say was required?**

_____

_____

_____

_____

_____

One of the risks in writing this book is implying that all people with compulsive behaviors get involved in the same way and stay in the behaviors for the same reasons. This is definitely not the case. However, there are certain patterns that are very common. By learning about these patterns, we can see that the behaviors that our loved ones choose are not about us, but about them and their emotional and spiritual deficiency.

Compulsive sexual behaviors are usually emotional and spiritual problems, not sexual. President Spencer W. Kimball reminds us that there are unmet needs when someone engages in compulsive behaviors:

> *Jesus saw sin as wrong but also was able to see sin as springing from deep and unmet needs on the part of the sinner. This permitted him to condemn the sin without condemning the individual. We can show forth our love for others even when we are called upon to correct them. We need to be able to look deeply enough into the lives of others to see the basic causes for their failures and shortcomings (Ensign, Aug. 1979, 5).*

By looking beyond the compulsive sexual behaviors, we can begin to see that unmet needs of our loved ones are the driving force behind the behaviors.

Knowing some of the basic causes for our loved ones' behaviors can help us separate our loved ones from those behaviors.

How does the compulsive sexual behaviors cycle usually begin? Quite often our loved ones were introduced to the behaviors by a family member, friend, relative, neighbor, or they discovered it on their own through experimentation, a book, magazine, or the Internet. Regardless of how the behaviors started, it is so important to understand that they are learned behaviors.

Our loved ones were not born with compulsive sexual behaviors. President Spencer W. Kimball declared:

> *Satan tells his victims that it is a natural way of life; that it is normal; that [these] kind of people [are] born "that way" and that they cannot change. This is a base lie. All normal people have sex urges and if they control such urges, they grow strong and masterful. If they yield to their carnal desires and urges, they get weaker until their sins get beyond control (The Teachings of Spencer W. Kimball, 276).*

If they so desire, our loved ones can unlearn the behaviors. They can get out of them and stay out. Once they were introduced to the behaviors, they continued with very small, nearly imperceptible steps, oblivious to the truth about what was really happening. This is the way Satan operates. With each progressive step, our loved ones' thought processes became clouded. Because they let the darkness in, they were carefully led into Satan's trap. Elder Henry B. Eyring said:

> *The enemy of righteousness also works in little steps, so small that they are hard to notice if you are thinking only about yourself and how great you are. Just as truth is given to us line upon line and the light brightens slowly as we obey, even so, as we disobey, our testimony of truth lessens almost imperceptibly, little by little, and darkness descends so slowly that the proud may easily deny that anything is changing. . . . One of the effects of disobeying God seems to be the creation of just enough spiritual anesthetic to block any sensation as the ties to God are being cut (Ensign, July 2001, 9).*

The scriptures teach the same principle and if we are not careful, we can be led astray:

> *And others will he pacify, and lull them away into carnal security, that they will say: All is well in Zion; yea, Zion prospereth, all is well—and thus the devil cheateth their souls, and leadeth them away carefully down to hell (2 Ne. 28:21).*

Our loved ones became a victim of Satan's evil plan to cheat their souls and lead them carefully down to hell. Notice how the word *carefully* is used here—very slowly with a well-laid-out plan. One man shared:

> *It took eleven years into my marriage before I committed adultery. I never thought I would ever commit adultery. I had been on a mission and married in the temple. It started with pornography when I was very young. I first saw a magazine when I was around six years old. As a teenager, I had a few magazines that I kept hidden away from my parents. After I was married, I worked for a disaster clean-up company and it just so happened that a fire burned down an adult book store and our company was hired to clean it up. During the clean-up, I had access to videos, magazines, and books that were not destroyed in the fire. This got me into pornography deeper and deeper. I started flirting and doing things with a lady at work until I did something that I never thought I would do—commit adultery.*

Lust kills love and slowly controls our loved ones' behaviors. Most people who take drugs never thought they would get "hooked." Neither did our loved ones. One of the challenges with lust is that these individuals may not have realized at the time that they were "buying into" Satan's lies because the movies, song lyrics, books, magazines, CDs, DVDs, and Internet sites depict lust as love. The drug of lust is taken in slowly over a period of years, and so it becomes very difficult for our loved ones to distinguish between love and lust. Why couldn't we see all the signs of lust? Because it is very easy for our loved ones to cover their tracks. It is not like alcohol or drugs where we can readily detect by smelling, by looking into eyes, or by observing odd behavior. The adversary is very cunning in promoting the drug of lust.

THE DRUG OF LUST

Satan tries to convince the world that lust and love are the same. What is lust? Elder Richard G. Scott explained,

> *Satan promotes counterfeit love, which is lust. It is driven by a hunger to appease personal appetite. One who practices this deception cares little for the pain and destruction caused another. While often camouflaged by flattering words, its motivation is self-gratification* (Ensign, May 1991, 35).

The Lord says that marriage between a husband and wife permits a couple to share sexual intimacy as *one* of the ways to express love. There are also *many* other ways to express love. Satan rarely shows any other way. That's part of his trap. Satan uses authors, writers, and producers who listen to his voice to depict lust and call it love. Satan says that sex equals love—if you have sex, you are in love. The distinction between lust and love is clearly taught by President Gordon B. Hinckley: "Let me say that any young man who asks for sexual favors from a young woman whom he may be dating on the basis that he loves her is saying in the strongest terms that he does not love her. Such an expression is one of lust and not of love" (*Ensign,* June 1996, 5).

The drug of lust, not love, is the driving force in all compulsive sexual behaviors. Wherever compulsive sexual behaviors are found, so will there be lust. *All compulsive sexual behaviors are burned in lust, including gay or lesbian homosexual relationships.*

> *For this cause God gave them up unto vile affections: for even their women did change the natural use into that which is against nature:*
>
> *And likewise also the men, leaving the natural use of the woman, burned in their lust one toward another; men with men working that which is unseemly, and receiving in themselves that recompense of their error which was meet* (Rom. 1:26-27).

We must always remember that there is one common enemy—Satan. Our loved ones have been trapped by Satan and the drug of lust. Yes, they made the choices that led into the trap, but the real problem is the drug of lust. When they made their choices, they did not consider all the consequences regarding their marital relationship, their family, or God. Elder Russell M. Nelson teaches:

> *The abuse of the power to love can result in no love at all. Only its cheap facsimiles of lewdness and lust remain in the wake of pleasure without conscience. Instead of feasting at the banquet table of bounteous love with his own posterity, one is left with scraps from the table—only the refuse from what might have been* (*Ensign,* Nov. 1984, 31).

These are painful consequences to suffer, and it is only when our loved ones are able to set aside the drug of lust through repentance and the power of the Atonement that they see the whole range of painful, hurtful consequences of their thoughtless choices. They can learn to "bridle all [their] passions, that [they] may be filled with love" (Alma 38:12). Our loved ones *can* learn how to surrender the drug of lust and embrace love.

As the scriptures teach, "Love and the will of God will abide in us forever. Walk in the Spirit, and ye shall not fulfil the lust of the flesh. For the flesh lusteth against the Spirit, and the Spirit against the flesh: and these are contrary the one to the other: so that ye cannot do the things that ye would" (Gal. 5:16-17).

Let's paraphrase this scripture: "Ye cannot do the things that ye would while ye take the drug of lust." Our loved ones who choose the drug of lust cannot be the husband, wife, son, or daughter they could be if they had not been taking the drug. This is one of the reasons we often think, "I don't know this person anymore."

Over time our loved ones' consciences may have become dulled. It is important that we attack the drug of lust—not each other. In order to receive the blessings of a pure and loving life, they must surrender the drug of lust. However, they may not choose to do so. They may choose to forfeit the blessings, and that does not mean we will lose the blessings from our righteous choices.

The biblical prophets have taught about the drug of lust and its end result:

> *But every man is tempted, when he is drawn away of his own lust, and enticed.*
> *Then when lust hath conceived, it bringeth forth sin* (James 1:14-15).

> *For all that [is] in the world, the lust of the flesh, and the lust of the eyes, and the pride of life, is not of the Father, but is of the world.*
> *And the world passeth away, and the lust thereof: but he that doeth the will of God abideth for ever* (1 Jn. 2:16-17).

What choices can you make to further your healing even if your loved one chooses not to give up the drug of lust?

_____

_____

_____

_____

_____

LUST IS ADDICTIVE

Similar to alcohol, tobacco, and drugs, lust is very addictive. It will attack any victim regardless of age. Self-mastery and a firm relationship with our Savior are the ultimate defenses.

President Gordon B. Hinckley explained the addictive nature of lust: "There is so much of filth and lust and pornography in this world. . . . You can't afford to indulge in it. You just cannot afford to indulge in it. You have to keep it out of your heart. Like tobacco it's addictive, and it will destroy those who tamper with it" (*Ensign*, Aug. 1997, 6–7).

President Hinckley said that lust and pornography were addictive. What does *addictive* mean? It refers to any behavior individuals continue in spite of the fact that it is making their lives worse. In addition, when one tries to give up the drug, negative, even painful, withdrawal symptoms are experienced.

DRUG TOLERANCE

Once a person has reached a tolerance level for a drug (which can happen very quickly), the same dosage does not produce the same stimulation to the "feel-good" part of the brain. Those who use alcohol, drugs, or tobacco, talk about how their need continually escalated so that eventually they required more frequent or stronger dosages. The original amount soon has minimal effect—the user feels no high.

In regards to pornography, a person may originally become stimulated and excited from soft pornography but later will resort to hard-core pornography to produce the same high or rush. One person said, "I didn't think I had a problem until I realized how explicit the pornography is that I am viewing now compared to the pornography I viewed six or eight months ago." After one reaches the tolerance level with hard-core pornography, they may maintain at a plateau. However, lust has no boundaries. Elder David B. Haight taught:

> *Pornography is not a victimless crime. Who are its victims? First, those who either intentionally, or sometimes involuntarily, are exposed to it. Pornography is addictive. (See Ensign, March 1984, 32–39.) What may begin as a curious exploration can become a controlling habit. Studies show that those who allow themselves to become drawn to pornography soon begin to crave even coarser content. Continued exposure desensitizes the spirit and can erode the conscience of unwary people. A victim becomes a slave to carnal thoughts and actions. As the thought is father to the deed, exposure can lead to acting out what is nurtured in the mind (Ensign, Nov. 1984, 70).*

There can be no love for self, others, or God when lust is present. Elder Neal A. Maxwell explained: "When we breach the seventh commandment, we thus hurt ourselves and others, too. When we are unhappy with ourselves, other people suffer. In this sense, there is no sin which is private! Furthermore, lust prevents the development of true love and thereby blocks us from keeping the first and second great commandments" (*Ensign,* Feb. 1986, 20).

Drug Withdrawal

The withdrawal part of the addiction occurs when our loved ones try to stop taking the drug of lust and experience mental, emotional, and physiological withdrawal symptoms. We hear about withdrawals that users of tobacco, drugs, or alcohol experience when they try to quit. The pattern is similar for those attempting to quit the drug of lust. One man described his withdrawal symptoms: "I have used pornography for so many years, I don't know if I can live without it. When I try to stop, I'm irritable and get a knot in my stomach that doesn't seem to go away."

Elder Marvin J. Ashton shares the level of commitment it takes to change:

> One may ask, "What must I do to break the chains that bind me and lead me away from the path our Savior would have us follow?" These chains cannot be broken by those who live in lust and self-deceit. They can only be broken by people who are willing to change. We must face up to the hard reality of life that damaging chains are broken only by people of courage and commitment who are willing to struggle and weather the pain (*Ensign,* Nov. 1986, 15).

To give up the drug of lust takes a tremendous amount of effort, faith, prayer, and surrendering. Even though we can be supportive in many ways, our loved ones have to make the choice to give up the drug, and they must have the fortitude to weather the storm during withdrawal. It may be the most difficult thing they will ever do. President Ezra Taft Benson taught:

> We should not invite the devil to give us a stage presentation. Usually, with our hardly realizing it, he slips into our thoughts. Our accountability begins with how we handle the evil thought immediately after it is presented. Like Jesus, we should positively and promptly terminate the temptation. We should not allow the devil to elaborate with all his insidious reasoning (*Ensign,* Mar. 1989, 4).

Think about the cookies again. The longer the person thinks about it, rationalizes it, smells the aroma from the oven, and looks at the fresh baked cookies, the more difficult it becomes to resist "just one."

At first some of these principles may be difficult to understand because we usually do not share the problem with our loved ones. We do not know what life and temptations are like for them, and they really do not know what life and temptations are like for us. One wife commented, "If my husband really loved me, he would not be looking at pornography." This may seem to be a very rational way to think, but when we look at the husband's behavior as an addiction, it is not a rational statement. Why? The very reason it is called an addiction is that in spite of the fact the husband might love his wife and know each time he engages in the compulsive sexual behavior that it hurts her, he still continues the destructive behavior. This is such a painful addiction for the wife to see in her husband because in many ways she feels it is a personal attack on her. Here are some questions that might help in understanding the complexities of our loved ones' addiction:

- At what age did your husband (wife or child) begin his compulsive sexual behaviors?

- What types of compulsive sexual behaviors did your loved one begin with? (It usually begins with masturbation and pornography.)

- During your loved one's adolescent years, how many times or how often was he exposed to pornography or other sexually stimulating experiences?

- How many years has your spouse been involved with compulsive sexual behaviors before you were married?

- Prior to your marriage did your spouse ever think that he had a real addiction?

- Did he ever receive professional counseling specifically to treat the addiction or confess it to the bishop?

- What type of attitude and openness regarding sex did your spouse's family share while he or she was growing up? Did they talk about sexual intimacy in healthy ways and teach their children about sex education in a timely and sensitive manner? Or was sex a secret that no one ever talked about?

- What type of personality did your spouse have during his teenage years? Was he quiet? Did he have very many friends? Was he popular?

- Did he have healthy normal relationships with the opposite sex or was he sexually inappropriate?

- How easy is it for your spouse to identify what he is really feeling and share it with you?

- How assertive is your husband when he has an emotional need to ask you for your help?

- As you look at your spouse's siblings or other extended family, are there other family members who also have a pornography and/or other addictions?

- What type of family dynamics were/are present in your spouse's family? Do they openly discuss problems and deal with them, or are they passively secret about solving problems and hope they will just go away? Is one or the other parent very controlling? Does one or both parents struggle with perfection-ism—expecting themselves and each child to be perfect? How much trust existed among family members?

These questions are not to cast blame on any one person or family member, but to recognize that addiction is very complex and has many facets. There are so many aspects of an addiction. There are many experiences that feed the addiction. Often we cannot pinpoint how and why the behavior began, but we can pose questions that help us to see the complexity of the addiction. Part of our loved ones' healing is learning about themselves by reflecting on their past and trying to put the pieces together to make some sense as to how this negative behavior began. Seeking professional counseling can help them. After looking at the broad spectrum of addictions with all their complexities, it becomes more rational to see why it is very possible for a husband to say he loves his wife and still not be able to stop his compulsions. In most cases, the husband had the addiction for many years before he met his wife.

As you review the list of questions about addiction, which questions, from your perspective, are applicable to your loved one's compulsive sexual behaviors?

_____

_____

_____

_____

_____

_____

🖋 How does learning more about the complexities of addiction help you in your healing?

_____

_____

_____

_____

_____

PLAN *FOR* BUT DO NOT PLAN *TO* HAVE A LAPSE

It is so very painful when our loved ones lapse. Such lapses bring back all of the emotional baggage once again—the mistrust, resentment, hurt, fear, self-blame, bitterness, betrayal, inferiority, anger, hopelessness, and more. One wife said, "Here we go again, I'm being dragged through this mess one more time. I just can't do it anymore." Although it is very hard to get refocused after our loved ones lapse, we should let our emotions settle down before we make any major decisions.

Let's think back during our elementary school days when we participated in fire drills. Our school principal and teachers were planning *for* a fire but not planning *to* have a fire. What is the difference? If we plan *for* a fire, we are more likely to stay calm and keep our heads if there is a fire. How do we plan *for* a fire? We outline an evacuation plan. We practice the execution of the plan. We sound the fire alarm and begin. We tell the children to stay calm and to walk single file from the classroom. The teacher leads the way. The teacher's calmness and poise sets the example for each student to follow. We teach the children the buddy system—to watch out for one another. After each class is safely outside, we take roll and make sure that everyone is accounted for.

This is how we plan *for* a fire. Just because we plan *for* a fire it would not give license for an arsonist to set a fire. Similarly, just because we plan *for* a lapse in inappropriate behaviors it would not give our loved ones license to act out. If we plan *for* a fire, we will likely be more calm, think more rationally, and get through it with fewer injuries if a fire occurs. We experience the same benefits by planning for a lapse. We are more likely to stay calm, think rationally, and experience less emotional injury if one occurs.

Our natural tendency is to say, "I don't even want to *think* about a lapse. That would be terrible!" But what if we used that same logic regarding fire drills?

"I don't even want to *think* about a fire. That would be terrible!" A fire could happen—and it might. Therefore, the wisest thing we can do is to be prepared in case a fire occurs. Similarly, the wisest thing we can do is to prepare for the possibility that a lapse might happen.

How do we prepare *for* a lapse? We talk openly to our loved ones about preparing for a lapse in sexual acting out or dishonesty. If a lapse occurs, what would we do? Our loved ones have the responsibility to tell us about the lapse. Healing requires complete honesty with self and others. How soon will our loved ones tell us about the lapse? How much information do we want to know about the lapse? What will the consequences be? What can our loved ones learn from the lapse to significantly reduce the possibility of future lapses? How can we be supportive to each other after a lapse? What could the husband say to the wife? What could the wife say to the husband? How can we involve the bishop or branch president? What would we do to stay on the healing path? What additional things will the loved ones do to prevent a future lapse?

They could meet regularly with the bishop, get professional counseling, attend support groups that are gospel-centered, and be open and honest.

Here are some questions you can ask yourself if your loved one lapses:

- What is the best way I can help myself?

- What are the ways I can receive inner strength and support?

- Is there someone I trust with whom I can share my feelings and thoughts?

- How can my immediate and extended family help me?

- How can my home teachers and visiting teachers help me?

- How can the bishop help me?

- How can I accept God's perfect love for me?

- How can I rely upon the Atonement of Christ to get through the pain?

- What has helped me in the past during other lapses?

- How can I continue to work on my own issues?

- How can I set firm boundaries and expectations?

- How can I take this painful experience and draw closer to Christ?

- What has Christ promised He would do for me?

At these critical times Satan would like us to "throw in the towel" and just quit trying. He will do everything he can to sidetrack us and make us believe that it is impossible to deal with this situation or that it is impossible for our loved ones to make the necessary changes. Change for us and our loved ones usually occurs in very small steps. Satan will focus on the negative when our loved ones have a "slip-up" during the healing process. He will whisper in our minds that the lapse is certain evidence our loved ones cannot change. If we are not careful, the "slip-up" can be blown out of proportion and disrupt the course of healing. This does not mean in any way that we should not discuss or address the lapse, but we should find helpful ways to deal with it that work for us and increase the probability that it won't recur. Both the issues we face as couples and the counterproductive ways we may have communicated in the past can easily recur. Although we will need to learn new ways that work for us, old patterns are not easy to break.

One thing we can discuss with our loved ones is how much information we want to know when there is a lapse. We should make it perfectly clear that we prefer that they tell us about a lapse immediately after it happens. For instance, we need to let them know that we want them to come to us and say plainly, "I slipped up last night. I got on the computer and looked at pornography." Requiring our loved ones to be responsible to tell us the truth is a better approach than policing their behaviors or interrogating them. Part of their healing is taking responsibility for their own behaviors. If we police them, we may hinder them from taking responsibility.

How can you help your loved one to take full responsibility for his or her behaviors?

_____

_____

_____

_____

_____

_____

On the other hand, some of our loved ones choose to stay in the behaviors, lie, tell half-truths, and deceive us to "cover their tracks." In these situations, we should "do our homework" and gather information in advance so that we know the seriousness of their behaviors and have the information to confront them at an appropriate time. To trust loved ones to be honest and open when they have a "track record" of repeating their acts and keeping them a secret is foolish.

Here are some areas to discuss with your loved one when you are attempting to learn how to trust again:

HONESTY ABOUT A LAPSE

- Do you want your loved one to tell you each time there is a lapse?

- How would you like to be told this information—face-to-face, by phone, email, a short note?

- Do you want to know immediately—within twenty-four hours—or later?

- Do you want to know detailed or general information?

- Do you want a set time and place to discuss this information, such as a Sunday afternoon, following supper, etc.?

OPEN-ENDED QUESTIONS

The more we can use open-ended questions the better. Open-ended questions allow our loved ones to share feelings and information that they need and want to share at that time. If we don't ask open-ended questions, we may end up doing work our loved ones should be doing. It may take awhile before our loved ones are ready to share. We should let them know that we expect them to tell us about their acting out; however, some information we do not need to know and should not ask for. We should also realize that we will never get answers to all of our questions—nor do we need answers to all of them in order for our individual healing to take place. Here are some questions that others have used to approach their loved ones:

- "Is now a good time for me to ask a few questions?"

- "It must be difficult to talk about all the surrounding issues, but it helps me and my emotions as we talk about them. Can we continue, or would you rather choose a different time?"

- "How can I best help you during your time of need?"

- "How will we know if progress is being made?"

- "How will we track the progress?"

- "If you had a wish list of things that would help you during this time, what would you include on that list?"

- "What boundaries need to be set?"

- "How can we set limits on what we talk about so that we don't violate each other's "space" as we work through these difficult issues?"

- "Will you let me know when you want to take a break from talking about this issue?"

- "Can I tell you what would work for me?"

- "How can we know what each other expects?"

- "How can we meet each other's expectations?"

We must make every effort not to use the information our loved ones share against them. Any information used against them will discourage them from sharing more. In fact, if we use shared information as a weapon to attack or punish, they will often withdraw and close off. Withdrawal from others is very unhealthy and can lead our loved ones to resort to acting out. Staying connected with others keeps them on the healing path. We should make a personal commitment not to bring up information disclosed during a healthy discussion when we later find ourselves in a moment of anger.

We should make every effort to focus on the small positive steps taken by our loved ones. We should give our loved ones credit for every step of progress. At times we may have to look hard to see little successes and be willing to compliment loved ones for them. Our encouragement can go a long way during the initial healing process.

The healing process needs time to work. Many times those in the behaviors have said, "My family accepts me for who I am, not for what I have done, and that has made such a difference for me and how I feel about myself." Even though we can accept the person and not accept his behaviors, we should not blindly put ourselves or others at risk. We must first recognize that our loved ones are sons or daughters of God and then set firm boundaries and make decisions that are in our own best interest and according to the Spirit.

Avoid Endless Questioning

We naturally want answers to the "whys?" We want to know why and how this all happened. If we are patient as we seek for answers and understanding, we will let our loved ones share information when they are ready. Knowing every little detail does not change the act and often only adds insult to injury. Furthermore, knowing every detail may make us obsess about them and make it more difficult to forgive because we paint a picture in our heads that is very difficult to discard. Even though we may desperately want to know every detail, it is best that we do not ask for them or allow our loved ones to volunteer them. When we continually ask questions, we may condition our loved ones to withhold information, which is counterproductive to healing. Here are some questions to ask ourselves:

- What am I feeling right now? What feelings are deep down inside my soul?

- How will I benefit from knowing more details about my loved one's behaviors?

- Will knowing more details about my loved one's behavior make it harder or easier to deal with my pain?

- Once details are lodged in my brain, how will I remove them later if I decide that they are bothersome?

- What details do I need to know right now?

What have you discovered about your feelings and what is important for you to know right now to continue your healing?

_____

_____

_____

_____

_____

_____

_____

Our loved ones still have the responsibility to be open and honest, but perhaps we could agree on how and in what setting this could best be accomplished. Bringing appropriate information to the light and discussing it in the right setting *facilitates* healing. We want to show support for our loved ones' efforts to overcome their problems, but at the same time we need to be open and honest with our feelings and emotions.

It takes a lot of hard work, faith, and courage to stay on our healing journey. Even when our loved ones have started on the healing path, we still have some questions and doubts. Perhaps we could define this state as "cautious hope." One wife shared:

> *I hope and pray that my husband and I can beat this without any other incidents. I know in my heart that if anything happens again with my husband that I will not start over again. It is a hard thing to battle addiction, and at times exhausting. I keep walking myself through the things we have talked about, and it seems to help me a lot to be able to keep a positive perspective.*
>
> *My husband and I are doing well. The strange thing about all of this is that I feel like I understand what has happened, and we are really trying to put new habits in the place of old habits that were destructive. We really don't argue about any of this, but the hardest, most exhausting part is that the road is long and you can come to many crossroads where it can go either way. It's realizing that this is a lifelong struggle, and there is no certain cure. It's the uncertainties that make me hesitate when it comes to other parts of my life, such as the decision to have more children. Will these uncertainties subside at some point for me?*
>
> *I am learning so much about what I can and can't control, and there is a lot of fear that goes along with that. I think that I am doing well, and yet it tires me so much sometimes.*

This woman has experienced some healing and so has her husband. Just because we are on the healing path, however, it does not mean that doubt and fear are gone. Choosing to deal with the doubts and fears in healthy ways keeps us on the healing path. This woman has identified her own issues and the husband has identified some of his issues. Together they have discovered unhealthy patterns that were adding fuel to the compulsive fire, and they are working to replace the unhealthy patterns with healthy patterns. As she continues her healing and places faith in Christ and believes that she will be led through each crossroad in life, she will be blessed and will have less fear as she continues on with hope: "Behold, verily, verily, I say unto you that mine eyes are upon you. I am in your midst and ye cannot see me" (D&C 38:7).

ABSTINENCE EXPERIENCE

Many times loved ones speaking about family members say, "I just don't get it. What thrill does he get by looking at pornography? I can't imagine anyone getting addicted to something like that." Since pornography is not something we choose, it is often very difficult to understand why our loved ones choose it. Often we do not understand what it is like for our loved ones unless we have an experience that is somewhat similar, although not identical. Following is an experiment that might give you some insights. Give some serious thought to this experiment which points out one of the many things we can do to gain more empathy and compassion for our loved ones—to try to see life through their eyes, but still not in any way condone their behavior. We might also discover something that we may want to change in ourselves. Select one thing you eat or drink every day or almost every day that is not good for you. What are some things that for the most part are not healthy, but enjoyable? Here are some suggestions of items you could choose from:

Caffeine drinks

Cakes and cookies

Pastries

Candy

Chocolate

Potato chips

French fries

Ice cream

Add your own special favorites to the list:

_____

_____

_____

_____

_____

Make a selection before you continue reading. Now make a commitment to abstain from this item for sixty days. Sixty days is not that long, is it? Get a note pad or journal and write your commitment down. Then record your plan. How are you going to go for sixty days without eating or drinking this particular thing? Every day for the next sixty days record your experiences. Write your thoughts, feelings, and emotions. Notice the temptations that you face. Watch how you rationalize. See how others influence you. Watch how the media impacts you. If you lapse and eat or drink the item you selected, record how that makes you feel. Keep the journal for the entire sixty days, whether or not you have a lapse. The most important part of this experiment is the journal. At the end of the sixty days summarize your experience.

What did you learn from this experiment? How has this experiment benefited you?

_____

_____

_____

_____

_____

_____

The real purpose of this experiment has little or nothing to do with the item you selected. By doing this experiment, what most people discover is that to some degree they have developed a mental, emotional, and physiological dependence on the item. This is discovered in the journal writing. We see how we have "bought into" the idea that we need this food or drink to make it through the day to perk us up and to make us feel better.

Similarly, our loved ones choose compulsive sexual behaviors for some of the same reasons. This is why we say that compulsive sexual behaviors are not usually a sexual problem, but rather an emotional and spiritual problem. If you have read over this experiment and not committed to do it, please reconsider. My experience is that most people will significantly benefit from this experience. Please try it. I do not want to imply in any way that this list of food and drinks are sinful and equal in seriousness to our loved ones' compulsive sexual behaviors. They are not. However, there is usually a parallel between our emotional patterns and the choices we make and our loved ones emotional patterns and their choices, although, our loved ones' choices are very destructive. President Spencer W. Kimball said, "Self-mastery . . . is the key, and every person should study his own life, his own desires and wants and cravings, and bring them under control" (*Ensign*, Oct. 1985, 6).

🌿 If you have decided to read on and not try this experiment, what are some of your reasons?

_____

_____

_____

_____

_____

_____

TIME LINE FOR CHANGE

One of the most common questions we ask is, "How long will it take for my loved one to change his behavior?"

Once, while working with a couple, the wife asked me this question and I answered, "How about if I let you answer that question with an experiment?"

She responded, "What do you mean?"

I explained the abstinence experiment, and asked her to choose a food or drink she particularly enjoyed on a regular basis. It had to be something she knew wasn't good for her and that she would like to give up. She selected a soft drink that she drank two or three times a day. She agreed to begin abstaining immediately.

What was the result? She made it three days without the soft drink and then drank one. She never stopped again; she went right back to her previous pattern of two or three a day.

Consequently, the next session she admitted that she had discovered part of the answer to her own question.

What was the answer? "It's hard to change."

I agreed, "Yes, it is!"

"But there is a big difference between my behavior and his," she quickly exclaimed. "What I am doing is not a sin, but what my husband is doing is a sin."

"I wholeheartedly agree!" I replied. "But we are not talking about whether or not something is a sin. Rather, we are talking about our compulsions and how our thoughts, feelings, and behaviors drive them." I continued, "What you chose to give up for sixty days and what your husband is working on to give up for the rest of his life are very different. However, both of these behaviors are driven by the same basic motivation. The reason you found it so difficult to change is that you usually engage in your compulsion to drink a soft drink because you want to change your mood and produce an immediate 'rush' or 'feeling-good' sensation—so does he. In addition, both of the behaviors (pornography and certain soft drinks) are also addictive in nature, and so doubly hard to quit."

With less intensity than before, she replied, "I'm starting to see what you mean. I never thought of it that way. No wonder it is so hard for him to change."

Answering this wife's question in this manner worked for her, but it may not work for all of us. Consider this example: Fold your arms. Look and see how you folded them. Is your right arm over your left arm or is your left arm over your right arm? Now, refold your arms with the opposite arm on top. How does that feel? Does it seem uncomfortable? Unless you consciously think about it, if I asked you to fold your arms again, you would do it the same way that you have always done it. To refold your arms a different way, you would have to consciously think about it every time.

Loved ones who have engaged in compulsive sexual behaviors have to "refold" their *minds*. It takes time for this to happen. Quite often the pattern seems to be: Some progress and then no progress; some progress and then no progress. Eventually more steady progress will be made by loved ones who really want to make the change and work at it. President Ezra Taft Benson taught:

> *The scriptures record remarkable accounts of men whose lives changed dramatically, in an instant, as it were: Alma the Younger, Paul on the road to Damascus, Enos praying far into the night, King Lamoni. Such astonishing examples of the power to change even those steeped in sin give confidence that the Atonement can reach even those deepest in despair.*
>
> *But we must be cautious as we discuss these remarkable examples. Though they are real and powerful, they are the exception more than the rule. For every Paul, for every Enos, and for every King Lamoni, there are hundreds and thousands of people who find the process of repentance much more subtle, much more imperceptible. Day by day they move closer to the Lord, little realizing they are building a godlike life. They live quiet lives of goodness, service, and commitment. They are like the Lamanites, who the*

Lord said "were baptized with fire and with the Holy Ghost, and they knew it not" (3 Ne. 9:20) (*Ensign,* Oct. 1989, 5).

What are we supposed to do with our time while our loved ones are going through the change process? We should be following the same process—trying to change and improve our own behaviors.

President Thomas S. Monson, speaking about the Savior, shares an important key: "By learning of Him, by believing in Him, by following Him, there is the capacity to become like Him. The countenance can change, the heart can be softened, the step can be quickened, the outlook enhanced. Life becomes what it should become. Change is at times imperceptible, but it does take place" (*Ensign,* May 1996, 51).

If change is imperceptible, that means it will be difficult to see. It also means that it will be easier to see what has not changed instead of what *has* changed. We want to watch carefully so we can see the small steps of progress made by our loved ones. It is so much easier to dwell on what our loved ones are not doing, rather than on what they are doing. We all benefit when we cut them a little slack and provide a listening ear and an open heart.

Often they fear our response to this question, "If I told you everything that I have done, would you still love me?" Even though our loved ones have made choices that caused us pain and sorrow, they want to be loved and accepted as much as we do.

How long should it take our loved ones to heal? There are so many opinions in regard to this question. Generally speaking, people are firmly on the healing path when they can go for one year without any acting out of the behaviors. This also means that our loved ones are not blaming others for their choices. They take full responsibility for where they have been and the choices they have made. This time period should not discourage us or make us too optimistic. One year is a good benchmark, but to stay the healing course continued effort must be made.

It is something to work toward. It is not the same for all people. Some heal in shorter time periods and others may require longer time periods to accomplish the same healing process. Each person is an individual and the healing will be determined by the amount of effort our loved ones make, their desire to repent, and their reliance on the Atonement of Christ. Christ says that He will heal all of us if we come unto Him, but He does not give us a timetable. That's because we choose our own timetable.

He [She] Is Probably *Serious* About Changing If He:	He [She] Is Probably *Not Serious* About Changing If He:
Has made up his own rules for staying out of compulsive sexual behaviors and is following them.	Was caught or reported by someone else rather than him admitting to it or confessing.
Takes responsibility for his making changes.	Lies, is evasive, is sneaky, tells half truths, only tells if asked or has a secret life.
Decides to see a counselor on his own rather than being forced or told to by someone else.	Runs away, hides or won't talk about his behaviors, feelings, thoughts, and fantasies.
Goes to professional counseling sessions.	Is less religious or church-going than usual.
Is working in counseling sessions.	
Does all homework given by his therapist.	Is defensive, using denial, minimizing, rationalization, blame, guilt trips, etc. to avoid dealing with his problems.
Meets regularly with the bishop.	
Does all homework given by his bishop.	Pretends or tries to convince others that there are no problems, that they are already taken care of, or that they are no big deal.
Is open and willing to talk about what he does, thinks, and feels.	
Is honest.	
Is working on his issues daily.	Acts as if he is the victim and seeks sympathy.
Is working more on what he needs to change than on what he thinks his spouse needs to change.	Tries too hard to make a quick-fix deal. He will say he is sorry and will promise not to do it anymore—if everyone will just forgive, trust, not talk about it, and forget about it.
Gives wife the space and closeness she needs.	
Shows he understands the hurt he has caused loved ones.	Puts himself in tempting situations and won't talk about it.
Works on repairing the hurt he has caused her.	Wants his wife to okay or go along with his addictions.
Is trying to find out what caused his addictions to prevent it from happening again.	Continues to do his addictions.
Takes care of personal and family needs.	Feels cheated that he can't continue his addictions.
Talks and acts with respect.	Has more criticisms or blame for others than for himself.
Works to earn trust and forgiveness.	

He [She] Is Probably *Serious* About Changing If He:	He [She] Is Probably *Not Serious* About Changing If He:
Is dependable in taking care of family, occupation, and religious responsibilities.	Is angry, moody, resentful, critical, or out of control.
Sets specific, measurable goals and achieves them.	Wants to go back to the way things were before getting caught, rather than improving and growing.
Solves problems that were caused by his addictions.	Makes impulsive decisions; has impulsive behaviors.
Lives the standards of the Church.	Keeps punishing himself.
Has made significant changes, is different.	Makes promises rather than changes.
	Only thinks about his own needs and wants.
	Is manipulative, using inappropriate techniques such as demands, fear, guilt, or threats to get what he wants.
	Tries to get people to take his side.
	Uses other addictions like alcohol or drugs to avoid dealing with his real problems.
	Does not live the standards of the Church.
	Is not willing to put in the time or effort to fix things.

HEALING TAKES TIME

Some of our loved ones may not choose to change, but others will. Hopefully most will! Here is one story of a man who has stayed on the healing path. His wife shared:

> *It will soon be a whole year since my husband has viewed any pornography. I have seen an incredible difference in him. He is so content and wonderful. He really and truly is. It has been so exciting for me to finally have my companion in my life—clean and worthy.*
>
> *So this is my question: As I have read through your books, I have learned*

that it actually is always a temptation (which is hard for me to know and understand). I don't mean the weakness. Since it's been almost one year and he has changed incredibly, do you think through your experience with working with others that it is over now for my husband? Do you think he will ever look at pornography again?

He says he is so happy, that it is in the past now, and he is grateful for the changes he has made in his life. He's the happiest he has ever been.

Please tell me in all honesty, do you think he will ever view it again?

This was my response.

It is so good to hear from you! You were led by the Spirit as you reached out to help your husband. It is good to hear that your husband has worked hard on his issues and you have worked on yours and the marriage is healing.

Regarding your question about your husband, the key for any person to stay on the healing path is to continue to do those things that got them on the path. As we continue to deal with our emotional problems in a healthy way, we can continue to stay on the healing path. Compulsive sexual behaviors are not about sex or pornography but about underlying emotional problems and spiritual issues that need work. Compulsive sexual behaviors just cover up the pain.

Healing is so much like daily exercises. If we want to stay physically fit, we need to exercise regularly and watch our diet. How long do we exercise and watch our diet? For the rest of our lives. The same is true of the healing path. We have to do our emotional and spiritual exercises daily to stay on the healing path.

If we choose not to exercise and eat properly, it does not take too long to get out of shape. Similarly, we take the same risk with our emotional and spiritual lives if we do not take care of them.

PRACTICE EMOTIONAL CLEANSING THROUGH WRITING

Writing can increase our hope and help us hear the voice of the Spirit. It can help us see the truth—truth is light and hope. The two major types of writing that we will discuss are therapeutic journal writing and therapeutic letter writing. Both forms of writing will help us deal with our trials in a healthy way and increase our level of hope.

Therapeutic Journal Writing

We can keep a daily "feelings" journal apart from our formal record of life's important events—one that allows us to put our thoughts, feelings, and emotions on paper. Writing has proven very helpful in the process of cleansing us of bottled-up troubled emotions. Writing gives us permission to express our feelings. We may feel safer writing our thoughts and feelings on paper rather than discussing them with someone. When we write down our experiences or feelings, they seem more real and usually more manageable. We should not concern ourselves with grammar, spelling, or punctuation. We just start writing and let the thoughts, feelings, and ideas flow. We can cross out words, write between lines, underline, or mark the journal in any way we choose. Unresolved feelings of anger, resentment, bitterness, rejection, abuse, etc., are emotional infections. Writing in journals, where we are honest and open on paper, is like draining the infection out of our body.

Infections in the body usually begin in a small area and spread over time. Emotional infections are no different. If not attended, physical infections in the body can spread and eventually cause severe illness or loss of limb or life. Likewise, if we do not cleanse our emotional infections, they can cause long-term illness, emotional devastation, and even spiritual death. The right kind of medical treatment can cure infections early on. One way we can begin to remove emotional infections early is by writing out thoughts and feelings every day. It is a cleansing, healing process.

If we have really bad feelings, we may not want to take the chance that anyone else will read our "venting." Even rereading it ourselves can be counterproductive, because it is reprogramming the very thoughts we are trying to rid ourselves of. To avoid this, we can simply tear up and throw the paper away when we are finished. The idea is to get the negative feelings, the emotional infection, out of our system. Honest "writing therapy" does this very effectively.

Analytical writing, on the other hand, can help us see thinking errors and distortions and let the light of the Lord return. Many of our emotional infections begin with unrealistic expectations, rationalizations, distorted thinking patterns, or emotional imbalance. If we do not inject a high dosage of reality or correct thinking, we inadvertently allow the infection to spread.

By consistently self-monitoring our thoughts, feelings, and emotions, we can cleanse our emotional "pus pockets" and be more emotionally healthy. We can track where we are with our emotional well-being and hold ourselves accountable.

Journal writing can help us see on paper where we are emotionally and can help us with emotional cleansing and healing. We can reflect on previous months of journal writing and observe the small steps of progress in our emotional well-being.

Each day we should identify the good choices or small things we have done for healing. In our journals we can give ourselves credit for even the tiniest accomplishment or step of progress. We can also write about forgiving ourselves for inappropriate choices or behaviors that we have made. We can write weekly goals at the beginning of each week and report the progress each day in our journals.

Keeping a journal where we record our innermost thoughts and feelings encourages honesty with self, provides clarification of our emotions, and enhances self-understanding. Journal writing also gives us the chance to self-monitor our emotions. There is great value in being honest with ourselves in regard to where we are emotionally.

🌿 **What date will you begin your journal writing?**

Therapeutic Letter Writing

Being honest on paper when writing a letter may be easier for us than talking to the person. When it is not appropriate or when the timing is not right for us to talk to someone who has offended or hurt us in some way, writing them a letter (which may only be for our own emotional processing) can provide much-needed emotional cleansing and clarification of our feelings. Careful consideration should be given before we confront someone about an issue regarding a hurtful experience. Praying, discussing the difficult situation with family members when appropriate, counseling with the bishop, and talking with others whom we trust are powerful resources at our disposal.

Often the process of writing a letter is very healing. We write our feelings and thoughts in a letter form, *but rarely, if ever, mail the letter.* Here is what one man experienced from his counseling and letter writing:

> *About two months into the [counseling] process, my therapist suggested one way to get my anger out and reconcile my feelings toward Dad. He proposed that I write a letter to my father—a letter that would probably never be sent—containing everything I had always wanted to say but had never said.*
>
> *It wasn't the first time I'd thought about writing a letter, but the suggestion was the motivation I needed to begin the project. And it was a project! I*

thought of my years of unhappiness as a child and knew that a few pages of unfocused anger just wouldn't suffice. If I was going to do this, I was going to do it right.

I decided to convey every memory I could think of— bring each one into the light, study it, and determine what each had done to me. When finished, I hoped to better understand myself and, hopefully, my father (Ensign, Aug. 1994, 22).

What did this man hope to gain by writing the letter?

_____

_____

_____

_____

_____

What would you hope to gain by writing a letter to someone?

_____

_____

_____

_____

Let's continue with this man's experience:

The journey [letter writing] took more than three months and almost 24,000 words. I prayed for the Spirit of the Lord to bless me so that this experience would turn to my good. The writing became part of my personal history, illustrating the subtle things parents do that can adversely affect their children's self-esteem, even reaching into their adult lives. I saw that words can hurt just as much as the back of a hand or a leather belt. It was the words my father shouted at me that affected me the most and became the hated habit I was passing on to my own children (Ensign, Aug. 1994, 24).

As you read these next paragraphs, consider the honesty regarding this man's feelings.

Today is April 22. I will most likely never send this letter to you [Dad]. It deals with my childhood, growing up in our home. Most of the time it wasn't really home but a kind of hell. I have many regrets from those years, and one of them is having few memories of really happy, secure times in our family. The memories I recall are mostly ones of fright, anxiety, and sometimes even terror.

I want to let go of the past that has haunted me all my life. Years ago I thought I had forgiven you. But the baggage remains. I haven't really felt the full expression of forgiveness. I hope this letter will help me reach that destination. . . .

The letter began with me pointing finger after accusing finger; my writing sometimes barely kept up with my emotions as I recalled nightmarish incidents of physical and mental abuse. I still felt guilt as I recalled the slaps, shouts, and cries heard outside my closed bedroom door. Inside my room, I listened, wanting to do something but too terrified to move, conditioned not to get involved. I wrote of my father's choosing not to be involved in my life, doing nothing to build trust and respect. I wrote of my wish that a favorite uncle could have been my father instead of the man who sat at the kitchen table with his ever-present wine bottle and glass, oblivious to the needs of his family. I wrote of the most bitter pill I had to swallow—that my father never apologized to me or admitted when he was wrong. I summed up a particularly difficult entry noting that all the little boy inside me wanted was a regular dad, a dad who loved him (Ensign, Aug. 1994, 22, 24).

Being honest with our feelings and emotions is very healing.

📖 **How do you think this man benefited from being so honest regarding his feelings and emotions?**

_____

_____

_____

_____

_____

By writing the letter, this man learned about himself, his father, and many other important things:

Each week through my prayers and in my discussions with the therapist, the letter helped supply insights and direction. Through the Spirit, I began to see a different side of my father. I realized that Dad's illness—alcoholism—prevented him from being the kind of father I needed. I accepted the probability that Dad, without realizing it, had passed on to me what he had learned from his father. And finally I understood that Dad had probably done the best he could with what he had.

The Spirit brought me insight after insight. . . .

And what of the letter? It sits at home, telling the story of my journey from despair to peace and what I learned along the way. The letter concludes with this August entry: "It is my dream that all my children will grow up knowing beyond any doubt of my love for them, that their childhood memories will be filled with happy times, and that they will carry forward a legacy of love to their children—my grandchildren. The road to this dream will not be smooth, but I am determined to see it fulfilled."

Between God and my inbred stubbornness, it will be done (Ensign, Aug. 1994, 24–25).

This man never mailed the letter. There was no need. Healing had taken place, and the goal of inner peace and serenity had been reached.

Most letters we write for emotional cleansing are never sent. We cannot change the past and we cannot change another person, but we can change the way we perceive the whole situation to get ourselves unstuck from the past. As we write, the Holy Ghost often reveals to us truths we had not suspected, softens our hearts toward those who hurt us, and helps us see the hurt they were carrying. When we are able to finally diffuse the hurt and anger, we allow ourselves to move on and progress.

Writing is an amazing tool in the process of forgiving others and learning to love and forgive ourselves.

Who are some individuals to whom you need to write an emotional cleansing letter? (You may choose to use codes or abbreviations.)

When will you begin your first letter?

REVIEW OF PRINCIPLES

How do your behaviors relate to the Parable of the Chocolate Chip Cookies?

_____

_____

_____

_____

_____

_____

What is the correlation between the chocolate chip cookies and your loved one's compulsive behaviors?

_____

_____

_____

_____

_____

_____

What are some of the common underlying emotional feelings that drive compulsive behaviors?

_____

_____

_____

_____

_____

_____

_____

What have you learned about the drug of lust? Why is it important for your loved one to give up the drug?

_____

_____

_____

_____

_____

Did you choose something you really enjoy eating or drinking several times a week and agree to abstain from it for sixty days? If so, what have you learned so far?

_____

_____

_____

_____

_____

If not, what are some of the reasons you chose not to do the exercise?

_____

_____

_____

_____

_____

Is it possible that some of your reasons are the same justifications that your loved one uses to stay stuck in his or her compulsive behaviors?

_____

_____

_____

_____

What have you learned about the difficulty of changing human behavior?

_____

_____

_____

_____

_____

Why is it important that you do not try to change or heal by yourself, but that you apply the Savior's perfect love and Atonement?

_____

_____

_____

_____

_____

How can therapeutic journal writing help you during your healing? When will you begin?

_____

_____

_____

_____

_____

Record any other insights or thoughts that have come as you have read this chapter.

_____

_____

_____

_____

_____

What is the single most important principle or concept you have learned from this chapter?

_____

_____

_____

_____

_____

_____

With whom can you share this important principle or concept in the next week?

_____

_____

CALMNESS BREAK

Seriously think about providing some simple act of service today. Could you call a few good friends and tell them that you really appreciate friendship? Could you compliment a member of your family on something he has done well? Could you write a short note? What is something you could do to surprise your family that would cost under $5? What simple act of service could you do today?

_____

_____

_____

_____

MESSAGES OF HOPE

Elder Joseph B. Wirthlin: "As I read and ponder the scriptures, I see that developing faith, hope, and charity within ourselves is a step-by-step process. Faith begets hope, and together they foster charity. We read in Moroni, 'Wherefore, there must be faith; and if there must be faith there must also be hope; and if there must be hope there must also be charity.' These three virtues may be sequential initially, but once obtained, they become interdependent. Each one is incomplete without the others. They support and reinforce each other. Moroni explained, 'And except ye have charity ye can in nowise be saved in the kingdom of God; neither can ye be saved in the kingdom of God if ye have not faith; neither can ye if ye have no hope'" (*Ensign*, Nov. 1998, 26).

Elder James E. Faust: "Free agency, given us through the plan of our Father, is the great alternative to Satan's plan of force. With this sublime gift, we can grow, improve, progress, and seek perfection. Without agency, none of us could grow and develop by learning from our mistakes and errors and those of others" (*Ensign*, Nov. 1987, 35).

The Godhead Has Perfect Love for Us

CHAPTER OVERVIEW

The emotional pain and uncertainty of our situation can overwhelm us to the point where we may wonder "Where is God?" When we have so few people we can talk to about our situation, feelings of loneliness and isolation may overpower us.

One wife lamented, "I just want some peace. My husband's problem is on my mind constantly. I can't seem to escape it. I feel so overpowered at times. I can't deal with the constant inner turmoil. It's eating me alive." We can diffuse these unwanted feelings by making an effort, perhaps more than we have ever done before, to stay connected with God through our thoughts and prayers.

Elder Richard G. Scott assures us, "In this uncertain world, there are some things that never change: the perfect love of our Heavenly Father for each of us; the assurance that He is there and will always hear us" (*Ensign,* Nov. 2001, 87). These reassuring words that God is present and always listening can provide comfort.

Even though there are many uncertainties, many questions, and few answers, Elder Neal A. Maxwell gave this encouragement, "We can know, right now, that God knows us and loves us individually!" (*Ensign,* Nov. 2002, 18).

Furthermore, we can be taught by the Holy Ghost what we should do in our circumstances. "The Comforter, [which is] the Holy Ghost, whom the Father will send in my name, he shall teach you all things" (John 14:26). The Holy Ghost will teach us whatever we need to know to deal with our circumstances. Feelings of comfort will prevail over loneliness and isolation if we allow them into our souls. The Lord said, "You shall receive my Spirit, the Holy Ghost, even the Comforter, which shall teach you the peaceable things of the kingdom" (D&C 36:2). Isn't peace what we seek? Our relationship with the Savior can bring us lasting peace, for He is "Wonderful, [The] Counsellor, The mighty God, The everlasting Father, The Prince of Peace" (Isa. 9:6).

 ## CHAPTER OBJECTIVES

At the conclusion of this chapter you should—

1. Realize that you may not trust your loved one because of his past and/or present behavior. This is normal and okay.
2. Understand that in order to begin trusting your loved one you will need evidence that he is changing.
3. Know how to deal with a loved one who chooses to lie.
4. Continue to trust in God even though you may not be able to trust your loved one.
5. Know that God and Christ love you perfectly and know your needs.
6. Understand why a good relationship with God and Christ is important to the healing process.
7. Recognize what you cannot control and be willing to let it go—surrender to God.
8. Understand how the "surrender prayer" can release you from the things you cannot control.
9. Avoid letting the problem—your loved one's behaviors—separate you from God's love and direction.
10. Recognize how fear can distance you from God's love and the Savior's Atonement.
11. Know that the Holy Ghost can and will direct you as you seek His inspiration.
12. Know how to feel and respond to the promptings of the Holy Ghost and begin to know the truth of all things.

IN WHAT AND IN WHOM CAN WE TRUST?

Usually trusting our loved ones who have betrayed our trust is very difficult. We have been wounded. We have been hurt in so many ways. We usually feel very vulnerable. It will be hard to trust our loved ones until they start changing their behavior and begin to warrant our trust. However, we want to avoid carrying any mistrust toward our loved ones into our relationship with God and His Son. That is the real risk of not trusting our loved ones. However, if we begin to trust our loved ones and they act out again, where does that leave us? One wife expressed:

My husband often says to me, "When are you going to start trusting me again?" In a way I thought that he was just directing the blame on me. When am I going to start trusting him? I wanted to ask him, "When are you going to change and stick with it? When are you going to be completely honest with me?" The painful part about my husband's comments is that I do feel guilty for not trusting him. I feel like I should trust him, but I don't. There have been so many false starts. I have been dragged through this mess for almost fifteen years.

This wife's response is common. We should make it clear to our loved ones that there are two parts to being able to trust again: (1) Permanently changing their behaviors, and (2) Truthfulness about their thoughts, feelings, and behaviors. Think of the child who took several cookies from the jar and was approached by his mother about the missing cookies. If the child says, "Yes, I took the cookies," then the mother has to deal mostly with the child's cookie-taking behavior. Let's suppose that the child said he did not take the cookies and the mother later found crumbs and a half-eaten cookie in his room. Now the mother asks again, "Did you take the cookies?" This time the child admits and tells the truth. Now the mother has to deal with the child's cookie-taking behavior and his lying behavior.

The child really needs to improve in two areas: (1) Learn not to take cookies or other items without getting permission, and (2) Learn not to tell lies. If the child continues to take cookies, but is truthful every time he is asked, the mother still will not be able to trust him with cookies because his behavioral track record shows that he will probably continue to take cookies. Perhaps the mother could hide the cookies or not bake cookies, but that is not the point. The point is how can the son learn both self-control and honesty? Perhaps, the mother can sit down and discuss consequences with her son. What should we do if this happens again? What the mother can do is make clear that neither behavior is acceptable.

Furthermore, she can talk about how painful it is to deal with his stealing, but that it is much more difficult to handle his stealing *and* lying.

Our loved ones have at least two areas that need improvement in order to earn our trust: (1) Learn how to surrender the compulsive sexual behaviors, and (2) Learn to be open and honest about their behaviors or lapses.

We want our loved ones to continue to surrender their negative behaviors—work hard to give them up—but we also want them to be open and truthful about their behaviors and lapses. We want and expect the truth! Lies, half-truths, defensiveness, evasiveness, and living a secret life are not acceptable. We need the truth so that we can make decisions with the Spirit that are best for us. It is very important that we communicate this to our loved ones. We want them to know that it usually hurts us much more if they lie than if they just tell the truth. It is difficult enough to deal with our loved ones' acting out, but lies make the situation much more painful and emotionally difficult to handle.

One wife shared: "It really hurts me when you explain why you were late coming home, and then I learn later that the reason you gave for being late was not true. Lying about why you were late hurts me so much more than the real reason you were late. I want and expect the truth!"

Consider these questions:

- What is your definition of trust and what is your loved one's definition?

- What emotions do you feel when you are not able to trust?

- Can you share these uncomfortable emotions with your loved one?

- What is your definition of honesty and what is your loved one's definition when it comes to being truthful regarding compulsive sexual behaviors?

- Why are openness and honesty in the relationship so important for you to be able to trust again?

- Is it your loved one's behaviors that are not allowing you to trust or is it his dishonesty about behaviors, or both?

- Why is it important to have trust restored in the relationship?

- Have you told your spouse what it would take in order to trust again?

- What effort is your spouse making so you can trust again?

- What effort are you making to trust your spouse again?

🔰 In order for trust to be restored in your relationship with your loved one, what changes would need to take place in the relationship and with your loved one's behaviors?

_____

_____

_____

_____

_____

One wife shared what she had learned about forgiveness and trust:

> *I had previously assumed that forgiving would be extremely difficult if someone had greatly offended me. But as the hurt, anger, and bitterness began to fade, I realized that I still loved Jim. Forgiveness then seemed to come naturally. What was most difficult, though, was rebuilding my trust in him.*
>
> *Many couples find it impossible to rebuild that trust. I feel that I was fortunate. Jim's sincere repentance and his desire to prove trustworthy helped tremendously. But I also know that Satan frequently introduced thoughts of distrust into my mind to keep our marriage from becoming strong and sacred (*Ensign*, Aug. 1988, 24).*

If our loved ones are sincerely repenting, being honest, and truthful, it is certainly easier to begin building trust in the relationship. But what if our loved ones are not willing to repent or to be honest and truthful?

WHO IS THE REAL PERSON?

Frequently our loved ones play the role of the "nice guy" in the public eye and only display the characteristics of the addict when they are at home. One wife explained her experience with a husband entrenched in sexual addiction in this way:

> *His personality in public is in direct contrast to the side the children and I see at home. This has been very confusing over the years as I've tried to figure out who he really is. It has been even more confusing for our children, who have experienced this dichotomy in a very destructive way.*
>
> *My efforts to reach out to my husband, to offer help, or to address the*

issues as I see them seem futile. It is as though he lives encased in a formidable, protective barrier that is impenetrable even to love.

Before we were married, I saw only his "public" face. Now I see the
whole devastating truth. I've also come to realize that his addiction and
abusive behaviors are generational. Because of his "nice guy" image in public, friends, neighbors, and even ecclesiastical leaders discount much of what
I experience and feel as his wife. It just doesn't match their view of him.

My only peace comes on my knees when I plead for guidance and insight.
Heavenly Father has given me the ability and strength to keep going.

When those we normally rely on for support cannot or will not see the truth
regarding our loved one, we are left to suffer the pain alone. In some cases, others
who do not understand the whole situation may believe we are the only ones who
need help or they may believe our actions or inactions somehow caused the behavior. The dilemma regarding how much about our loved ones' behaviors to reveal
and how much to keep to ourselves proves challenging. This uncertainty can create emotional agony that rips us apart. One wife explained her torn feelings:

Each time I break down and cry in front of my mother about my plight
she says, "But your husband is so good in many areas. He provides for the
family. He is well-liked in the neighborhood. He goes to church every Sunday.
He does a lot with the kids. You go on family vacations. I think you just need
to hang in there and keep doing more to support him."

My mother's comments, though well-intended, are so hurtful. I felt that
I was the guilty one for not supporting him enough. At the same time I was
torn because I did not want her to know how many affairs he had had while
we have been married. I couldn't disclose everything I wanted to because
part of me wanted to protect my husband and protect my extended family
from knowing everything.

The sad part was I started distancing myself from my mom because of
her inferences that my problems would be solved if I would just work harder
to keep the marriage intact. Consequently, my husband's behavior not only
impacted our relationship, but also distanced my relationship with other
family members.

Staying on the healing path requires great faith. Our loved ones respond in
many different ways when they confess or are caught in their compulsive sexual
behaviors. Their attitudes fluctuate all the way from recognizing the addiction
and voluntarily seeking help to confessing only because they got caught and
continue to show a high degree of denial and unwillingness to change.

Common responses from loved ones suffering from sexual addiction, though varied, carry the same message of blame as illustrated below:

Response #1: A husband says to his wife:

> *"I would not be looking at pornography if you had sex with me more often."*

When our loved ones are caught in the act of compulsive sexual behaviors, they quickly turn the whole situation around and try to make us feel that we are the ones to blame. They may even succeed in getting us to carry unwarranted guilt for their behavior.

We have to be very careful that we do not get caught in the same trap that our loved ones are in. If we are not careful, Satan can sell us the same "bill of goods" that lust is really part of love! This can happen when a wife attempts to appease her husband by dressing sexy and buying into the idea that maybe if she were as provocative and alluring as the porn stars, she could keep her husband from looking at pornography.

There is a big difference between being sexually responsive and buying into Satan's lies that pervert true love into lust. If our loved ones were addicted to drugs and alcohol, we would not consider buying those drugs and giving some to them when they so desired. We should really consider at what level we want our intimate relationship.

Response #2: When a wife questioned her husband's relationship with a woman at work, he responded:

> *"I am not involved with her in any intimate way. We only discuss business when we attend conventions away from home."*

We know from the facts that our loved ones are sexually acting out, but they vehemently deny it. They tell lies to cover up their compulsive sexual behaviors.

Response #3: A son reluctantly said:

> *"If you want me to, I will go to counseling."*

When our loved ones are caught in the act of compulsive sexual behaviors, they quickly admit, ask for forgiveness, and attend counseling—but only to please us. However, they are not ready (often because they are not willing) to change from the inside and really work on their underlying issues. Consequently, their healing is postponed and they stay stuck in the behavior.

Response #4: A husband angrily stated:

"I accept you as you are with all your weaknesses, so you should accept the way I am."

Our loved ones shun responsibility for their decisions. The underlying message is that we have weaknesses too, and so theirs are justified.

Response #5: Our loved one says:

"I recognize that I have a problem. I need help to solve it. I will find a counselor and commit to attend counseling. I know the Lord can help me. I need to rely on Him more."

Our loved ones voluntarily admit that they have a problem and they are actively working on healing, including meeting with the bishop, attending counseling, and making some changes.

The best scenario is loved ones who immediately confess their compulsive sexual problems, desire to get help, and do so. Many of them, however, will not take the first step—admit that they have a problem and take full responsibility for it. They may even try to pretend that their behavior does not bother them, but President Harold B. Lee made it clear: "If I were to ask you what is the heaviest burden one may have to bear in this life, what would you answer? The heaviest burden that one has to bear in this life is the burden of sin" (*Ensign,* July 1973, 122).

When loved ones engage in compulsive sexual behaviors, such a course brings darkness into their lives, and sometimes we have moments when we can see, feel, or experience that darkness too. One wife commented, "I could sense when my husband had acted out again. Darkness just seemed to be present." As we stay close to the Savior, the darkness will leave. The scriptures record the light we can receive from the Savior: "He is the light and the life of the world; yea, a light that is endless, that can never be darkened." (Mosiah 16:9). His light helps us to overcome the "natural man."

WHEN LOVED ONES LIE

Our loved ones fall into two broad categories; those who tell the truth and really work hard to change and those who lie to us and make little or no effort to change. Many of our loved ones try to "cover their tracks" by telling us lies.

Discovering that our loved ones have lied to us is like having the wind knocked out of us and being knocked to the floor. We might even feel physically sick. We have committed ourselves to this loved one; how could he or she lie to our face? We can find ourselves torn between love and hate. We love the person we married and hate the same person for lying to us. We usually say, "If he would just tell me the truth, I could accept it. But it's the constant lying that makes it so hard." Or "If he is lying about this, what other secrets does he have?"

The scriptures teach, "Wherefore putting away lying, speak every man truth" (Eph. 4:25). Most of us could deal with the truth, but it is the untruths that play with our minds. One woman said, "I thought I was going crazy. Lie after lie just kept coming. I was so confused and mixed-up and often said, 'Is there any truth at all?' I tried to think about other things, but I just couldn't. I really and truly thought I was going crazy."

We sometimes fall for the lies because our loved ones sound so convincing. Their body language, voice inflection, and level of intensity all seem to say they are telling the truth. Also, our loved ones can quickly turn things around and attempt to make us feel like we are the guilty party for not believing them. They may say, "I have always trusted you, and so why aren't you trusting me when I'm telling you the truth?" Or "If you really loved me, you would believe me." Or "That's the real problem—you never believe me."

For several reasons we are inclined to believe our loved ones even when they lie. With a marital relationship, we have entered into a trusting relationship. We have opened our hearts, minds, and bodies to someone whom we chose to marry and therefore chose to trust. Initially, we do not believe our loved ones are lying because we choose to and want to believe they are telling the truth. Once we realize we have been "blind sided" and discover that our loved ones have deceived us, it takes time to digest. It is extremely hurtful to realize that our loved ones have lied and deceived us for so long. Furthermore, we may not want to face the reality that they would lie to us. In our hearts we cling to the belief that anyone involved in an intimate relationship with us would surely tell the truth. Even when we discover the truth behind the lies, it's easy for us to deny it. One wife shared:

> *I don't know if words can describe my feelings when I learned that my husband had been involved in an affair for two years. It was more than I could comprehend. At first I denied it. But the awful realization began to crush me. I cried whenever I was by myself, but in public I pretended that things were fine. I stopped eating and dropped to ninety-five pounds. The world around me seemed to be unfocused, and sometimes I felt that I couldn't even move (Ensign, Aug. 1988, 22).*

Learning the truth impacts each of us differently, but a common thought is, "I can't believe that he would do this to me!" The scriptures warn, "Take heed to yourselves, that your heart be not deceived, and ye turn aside, and serve other gods, and worship them" (Deut. 11:16). This scripture cautions us to not allow our hearts to be deceived. If we brush aside our loved ones' lying or tell ourselves that they would not lie when evidence shows that they have, we are putting ourselves in danger.

Our loved ones become snared in Satan's trap of lies. If we don't want to believe they are lies when evidence shows otherwise, we are in denial. If we continue to believe the lies, we can be stuck in phony feelings of false security. Eventually the false security will crumble. When we've been believing their lies and then finally face the terrible truth, we may get caught up in another one of Satan's traps of hate, bitterness, and revenge. Even though it may seem natural to experience these emotions, getting stuck with them for long periods of time will keep us from following the commandment to "Love the Lord thy God with all thy heart, with all thy might, mind, and strength; and in the name of Jesus Christ thou shalt serve him" (D&C 59:5).

We are also putting ourselves in danger if we choose to believe our loved ones' lies, and in a very real way start lying to ourselves. If we are in these circumstances, we need to get out of denial and accept the reality that our loved ones often lie to us to "cover their tracks," to get what they want, to try to look good, or to live a double life. Some want to continue to take the drug of lust and still keep their families intact because their thinking is distorted and they believe Satan's lie that they can have both. Furthermore, they often want us to accept them with their compulsive sexual behaviors and often say, "That's just the way I am." They may even state that if we truly loved them we would accept them as they are and go along with their unacceptable behaviors. We will need to continually remind ourselves that we can still feel and show love toward our loved ones without condoning their behaviors. We must not buy into Satan's lies and think that the behaviors are natural and that there is nothing that our loved ones can do to change. We do not have to accept our loved ones' compulsive sexual behaviors in any way.

HOW TO ASSERTIVELY RESPOND TO OUR LOVED ONES WHO LIE

Satan lied from the beginning. He is deceptive and deceitful. When our loved ones choose to walk away from light and truth into Satan's traps, they often use his tactics to cover their tracks. They may lie, stretch the truth, make misrepresentations, make up stories, tell half-truths, or withhold information. They may say or do anything they think will appease us. This distortion of truth may be the result of some or all of the following:

First, they may still be in denial. Denial means they will not admit they have a problem. They think, "I don't have a problem with pornography because I can stop at any time."

Second, our loved ones may lie to us because they are rationalizing their behavior. Rationalization occurs when our loved ones realize that they have a problem but try to convince themselves that there is a good reason for what they do. They rationalize by saying things like, "If my wife were willing to have sex more often, I would not need to look at pornography."

Third, our loved ones may use minimization to downplay the effects of their addiction. Minimizing is another form of denial. "I only view pornography once in a while so it's not a real problem for me."

Fourth, they may believe they can avoid the consequences of getting caught. Often this tactic works for a time. One wife shared:

My husband had been involved with a woman in a hotel room where smoking was allowed. When he came home I could smell smoke all over his clothes. When I confronted him about the smoke smell, he quickly gave a response that sounded so logical at the time. He said, "I stopped by a family in the ward to see how they were doing and we talked for quite a while." (The family was less active and both the husband and wife smoked.)

One of the reasons I thought he was telling the truth was he did not hesitate with his answer. When I asked the question, he gave an immediate response. I thought at the time that his reply made perfect sense.

Months later while washing his clothes, I found a motel room receipt from a motel in our city. I immediately had a sick feeling. Why would he have a receipt in his pocket from a motel in our town? It was then that I started wondering about his responses to my questions over the past year or so.

At first I did not want to believe it might be true. I did not want to think that he would do this to me.

There is a real danger that we may also slip into a trance of self-deception. We are in denial if we say, "I'm sure there is a good reason that my husband has this receipt to a local motel. I would not want to confront him and stir up the pot."

Denial is lying to ourselves by saying there is not a problem with our loved ones' behavior. Denial from our loved ones and denial from ourselves means that we get lies from two sources.

We cannot control whether our loved one stays in denial, but we can choose to get out of denial ourselves by being aware of lies we tell ourselves in an attempt to avoid dealing with painful realities. We can quickly cut off this source of lies by facing up to the fact that our loved ones have chosen compulsive sexual behaviors that create discomfort and suffering for us. When we are caught in a web, it is impossible to free ourselves until we come out of denial, admit we are in the web, and become willing to face it and deal with it.

Our loved ones can rationalize their behaviors, and if we are not careful, we can rationalize their behavior too. A woman rationalized, "I know my husband is on the Internet late at night and views pornography. But he is a good provider for our family. This is his only weakness." Rationalizing and excusing behavior that is clearly wrong can keep us stuck in unhealthy emotional behaviors too. We can become an enabler by not setting firm boundaries and by not letting our loved ones know that viewing pornography or any other compulsive sexual behavior is clearly wrong and that we do not approve of it in any way. We cannot be passive. Silence usually condones behaviors. By not sharing our thoughts and feelings, we might feed the fires of their rationalizations.

CONFRONTING OUR LOVED ONES ABOUT THEIR LYING

Addictive sexual behaviors are not something we can smooth over and pretend are minor problems. Violating covenants is a serious matter. Many times our loved ones' "reasons" don't make sense and evidence tells us otherwise.

It is therefore very important that we confront our loved ones about their lying. Usually this is not an easy thing to do—particularly if our loved ones are still in denial. While they try to make it appear that nothing will faze them, underneath all of their lying and denial are their unmet needs driving the addictions and pleasure seeking. They have never learned the difference between pleasure and joy. They no longer have the self-mastery and eternal perspective to find joy. They are hiding from all the emotions they don't want to feel and don't know how to deal with. Unfortunately, our loved ones have used us and others in unhealthy ways as they have tried to get what they want. They don't realize their needs can be met only from within by facing their problems and by developing a relationship with the Savior.

Our loved ones' compulsive sexual behaviors (and the deceptions that went

with them) violated our trust, but their continued lying compounds our mistrust. We tell ourselves that they would not lie to us when in fact some have,
are now, and will usually continue to lie, until they are confronted. Even a well-
thought-out confrontation may not stop them from lying, but confrontation is
still essential.

Our loved ones are responsible for stopping their lies and all other inappropriate behaviors. While we need to consider the impact of the way they were
raised, their friends, their perceptions about consequences, etc., there are still
no excuses for lying. Even if they claim that they lied to us because they did not
want to hurt us by telling the truth (they somehow think ignorance protects us
from the consequences of their bad choices), there are no excuses for lying. The
fact is that some still choose to lie to us, and lying is not acceptable behavior
in a trusting relationship. Without trust and without the truth, we don't have a
healthy relationship. So in order to continue in the relationship, we must confront them about their lying.

BE WELL-PREPARED

A word of caution: Be sure you have prepared a well-laid-out plan before you confront your loved one. Know what you are going to say. It is best to write it down
and read what you have written. Also consider your loved one's "track record"
when you have confronted him on other issues. Has he ever hit you, pushed you
down, held you in a room, or stood in a doorway so you could not leave? If so,
this is physical and emotional abuse. If there is a history of past abuse, make sure
you are in a safe place when you confront him. Perhaps a third party could be
close by in another room. A public setting like a restaurant may be a good choice.
If you are working with your bishop, perhaps it could be done in his office. If you
are not working with your bishop, you might consider discussing your situation
with him before you proceed. If you are meeting with a professional counselor, a
full disclosure of your situation and concerns is very appropriate and important.
Counseling together with a counselor can provide self-confidence, good judgment, and a positive, well-defined spiritual path to follow.

PARTIAL DISCLOSURE

When confronted, our loved ones may choose to tell us only part of the truth.
This is much like a salesman who does not make full disclosure on a product.
When we ask, "Can we use this vacuum to clean draperies?" His response may

be, "Yes, it does a real nice job on draperies." We think the salesman answered the question; however, after purchasing the vacuum we learn that we must buy a $75 attachment in order to clean draperies with our new vacuum. The drapery attachment was included in other vacuums we were pricing, and the salesman was well aware that we were price shopping and were very price conscious. He therefore chose not to disclose all the information so we would choose his vacuum. He was likely more concerned about his commission than our well-being.

Similarly, our loved ones may be more concerned about having their own wants met and keeping their "cover." At the moment they may have little or no sensitivity for us nor concern about our needs. They often lack empathy. They often lack real feelings. To some extent they have lost their conscience.

President Thomas S. Monson warned, "Avoid any semblance of pornography. It is dangerous and addictive. If you continue to view pornography, your spirit will become desensitized and your conscience will erode" (*Ensign,* Nov. 1990, 97). Yes, our loved ones have become desensitized and very selfish. Usually they have a shorter, impulsive view of life and what they want. Many times our loved ones make partial disclosure of information just like the vacuum salesman did. They withhold information that had we known about we never would have "bought into" the deal in the first place. When we ask them why they didn't tell us the whole story, they often respond, "Well, you never asked me." Once again they try to push the blame onto us.

Our situation with them is much more serious than with the vacuum salesman. We are dealing with human lives in a relationship that requires trust. We need all the pertinent information. Our loved ones' lies or partial disclosure can prevent us from making the best decisions for ourselves and those closest to us, perhaps children and extended families. We are making decisions about our future and considering whether we should attempt to rebuild the relationship or dissolve it. We need and should expect the truth! Nothing less is acceptable.

Absolute full disclosure is required to begin the process of restoring trust. This does not mean we need to know every explicit detail. Such details could be damaging to our healing. A flat statement such as, "I had an affair and committed adultery" or "I was involved in a gay relationship for six months" would be adequate for the moment. When we ask for full disclosure from our loved ones, we should expect them to tell us that they committed adultery if such is the case rather than "We were involved—we were just touching each other." Our loved ones cannot fully heal without telling us the truth and the full extent of their involvement, and we often cannot heal if we get too many of the explicit details. We need to achieve a healthy balance. We need accurate information regarding our loved ones' compulsive sexual behaviors so that we can determine what is best for us, our children, and our family. We need this information so we can determine whether we are going to stay and try to rebuild the relationship or leave the marriage. One reason our loved ones might withhold information is out of fear that we will do just that—leave the marriage.

FACING THE TRUTH

Lying compounds our mistrust. We may wonder what else they have lied about to us. Trust is lost immediately but cannot be restored immediately. Such restoration takes a great deal of time and work and usually requires a 180-degree turnaround by our loved ones. We often find ourselves wanting to double check everything they tell us. Consequently, our loved ones often say, "Don't you trust me?" or "When are you going to start trusting me again?" The question is not "When am I going to start trusting again?" but "When are you going to have a consistent record of being trustworthy?" We need evidence. The direct answer to their questions is: "At the present time there is no trust between us, and it will take some time and work on your part to restore that trust."

The point we want to stress is the "present time." Whether trust can be restored in the future depends largely on our loved ones' consistent actions and behaviors, not ours. Often loved ones want to blame us for not trusting them. However, for trust to be restored we need positive action by our loved ones to back up their words. One wife shared, "Until my husband started doing what he said he was going to do, I could not trust him again." We should avoid feeling guilty because we do not, for now, trust our loved ones who have lied to us. To give trust too soon before it is earned would be foolish. Trust is not a "freebie;" it is something one earns.

Before you begin trusting your loved one again, what changes would need to take place with his or her behavior?

_____

_____

_____

_____

_____

🖉 Have you felt guilty for not trusting? In which ways can you let go of your feelings of guilt? Why is letting go of your feelings of guilt so important for your healing?

_____

_____

_____

_____

_____

_____

Tolerance

Someone close to us may ask why we put up with our loved ones' behaviors. One reason we do so is that we have built up a tolerance for their behaviors. We put up with more and more lies and compulsive sexual behaviors because they come on so gradually. At first their lying and other forms of manipulation were alarming to us, but over time they may seem somewhat normal.

It is important that we request and listen to feedback from others we trust and determine if what they tell us regarding our loved ones' behaviors has merit. Sometimes an outsider can give us feedback that we do not want to hear but need to hear in order to recognize how much we have tolerated over the years. Hopefully this can snap some sense of reality back into us so that we can get out of denial and seek the help we so desperately need.

🖉 As you reflect on your loved ones behaviors over the past several years, has his destructive behavior escalated over time? What are some possible examples?

_____

_____

_____

_____

_____

_____

God Knows Us and Has Perfect Love for Us

Athough we may have lost trust in our loved ones, we do not need to lose trust in the Lord or in His power to guide, sustain, and deliver us. We believe in God and His perfect love for us, His children, yet we may still have the following questions in our minds: Does God really know me personally? Does He know my situation and needs? Does He understand my pain? Will He really come to my rescue? Will He be there when I call upon Him? How can I know?

Elder Richard G. Scott, speaking of the Father and the Son, reminds us, "They continue to love us perfectly, each one of us, individually. Yes, they are all-powerful and all-knowing; their works extend eternally, yet their love for each of us is personal, knowing, uncompromising, endless, perfect" (*Ensign,* May 1988, 61).

Trust in the Savior

President James E. Faust stated: "In an increasingly unjust world, to survive and even to find happiness and joy, no matter what comes, we must make our stand unequivocally with the Lord. We need to try to be faithful every hour of every day so that our foundation of trust in the Lord will never be shaken" (*Ensign,* Nov 2004, 18).

The yearning of our hearts may be similar to the prayer of the psalmist:

> *Hear me speedily, O LORD: my spirit faileth: . . .*
> *Cause me to hear thy loving kindness in the morning; for in thee do I trust: cause me to know the way wherein I should walk; for I lift up my soul unto thee.*
> *Deliver me, O LORD, . . .*
> *Teach me to do thy will; for thou [art] my God: thy spirit [is] good; lead me into the land of uprightness.*
> *Quicken me, O LORD, for thy name's sake: for thy righteousness' sake bring my soul out of trouble* (Ps. 143:7-11).

The prayer of the psalmist can truly give us comfort. The power of prayer to lift us above our present state can give us the reassurance we truly need. The Lord can deliver us from our pain and from whatever bondage we might find ourselves. Here is the mission statement for our deliverance: "But if ye will turn to the Lord with full purpose of heart, and put your trust in him, and serve him with all diligence of mind, if ye do this, he will, according to his own will and pleasure, deliver you out of bondage" (Mosiah 7:33).

How can you apply the principles from this scripture to your own deliverance?

_____

_____

_____

_____

_____

SURRENDER TO GOD

One way we can show our trust in God is to surrender our concerns to Him through prayer. Sometimes our self-reliance or pride gets in the way of our being able to rely on God and receive His direction. One wife, whose husband committed adultery, confided:

> [I] learned to trust in the Lord. I had previously believed that I was a capable, independent, self-sufficient person, able to handle difficult situations and crisis calmly and well. But when I found myself totally incapable of coping on my own, I discovered the difference between leaning on the arm of flesh and relying on the Savior. In learning to walk by faith, I learned how the Lord can comfort and relieve anguish; how He can teach us wisdom, justice, and mercy; how He can lead us. Elder Neal A. Maxwell tells us that "we can . . . actually do as Peter urged and cast our cares upon the Lord (see 1 Pet. 5:7); He is familiar with them, including even the feeling of being forsaken (see Mark 14:50; Mark 15:34). Nothing is beyond His redeeming reach or His encircling empathy" (Ensign, Aug. 1988, 24).

SURRENDER PRAYER / LET GO OF THE UNHEALTHY EMOTIONS AND LET GOD TAKE THEM

In order for us to heal from the pain and hurt, we need to decide what portion of the situation we can control and what portion we need to let go of and surrender to God. A surrender prayer can be helpful in letting go of things we cannot control.

When we are struggling with feelings of resentment and anger toward our loved one, we can say a surrender prayer: "Heavenly Father, I need Thy help. I have feelings of resentment and anger in my heart toward my loved one. I am willing to let them go, but I need Thy help. I want to give them up to Thee because I cannot have them in my life and still worship Thee with a true and honest heart. Help me, Father, that I might have the strength to surrender these feelings to Thee. I love Thee, Father, and am grateful to be Thy daughter."

A simple surrender prayer can go a long way. It does several things for us:

- It helps us recognize what we can control and what we cannot control.

- It reminds us that our healing is based on what we are willing to surrender to the Lord. President Ezra Taft Benson taught: "You do change human nature, your own human nature, if you surrender it to Christ. Human nature has been changed in the past. . . . And only Christ can change it" (*Ensign*, July 1989, 4). When we surrender our anger, we leave the door wide open for love to flow in to fill the void. We choose one or the other throughout the day by how we choose to think about humankind.

- We remember to thank God and express our love for what He has given us. Gratitude and love go together. We can choose love or anger. A personal surrender prayer may help us in choosing love when faced with challenges.

Should we use the surrender prayer only when we have unwanted feelings and emotions? Certainly not! We should use the prayer consistently to entrust our loved ones' situations and behaviors to the Lord's divine power. If we have the Spirit, if we are guided by and have faith in Christ, we can also see who might need a prayer as we move about our day's work. What a blessing to surrender our unwanted feelings and emotions and to turn over our loved ones' behaviors and problems to the only true source of help and healing.

The surrender prayer can help eliminate selfishness and allow us to let go of self-pity or other feelings that prevent us from healing. Remember that the attitude, "I deserve to be angry and upset as long as I want," is a form of selfishness and pride and is not healthy. These attitudes can keep us stuck in compulsive behaviors too! President Ezra Taft Benson reminded us: "Selfishness is one of the more common faces of pride. 'How everything affects me' is the center of all that matters—self-conceit, self-pity, worldly self-fulfillment, self-gratification, and self-seeking" (*Ensign*, May 1989, 6).

Lamoni's father understood this principle of surrender: "O God, Aaron hath told me that there is a God; and if there is a God, and if thou art God, wilt thou make thyself known unto me, and I will give away all my sins to know thee" (Alma 22:18).

How do we give away all our sins? We surrender. Surrendering and healing go together. Holding on to the hurt and pain impedes healing. Elder Neal A. Maxwell expressed this surrender process: "If faithful, we end up acknowledging that we are in the Lord's hands and should surrender to the Lord on His terms—not ours. It is total surrender, no negotiating; it is yielding with no pre-conditions" (*Ensign*, May 1985, 72).

We begin the surrender process by giving up our unhealthy emotions. We begin by giving up harsh feelings that we may harbor toward our loved ones. We begin by giving up our selfish and fearful desires to hold onto the hurt, pain, and anger—we hand them over to God. We begin by developing more faith in Christ, the Rock, the Sure Foundation, the Physician of our souls. This surrendering process is challenging. It will take time—perhaps even a lifetime!

Elder Joseph B. Wirthlin reminds us: "Though you may feel weary, though you sometimes may not be able to see the way, know that your Father in Heaven will never forsake His righteous followers. He will not leave you comfortless. He will be at your side, yes, guiding you every step of the way" (*Ensign*, Nov. 2001, 27).

After prayerful consideration, write your own surrender prayer.

_____

_____

_____

_____

_____

As we turn to Heavenly Father and Jesus Christ, healing can begin. The Spirit will begin to take control of the natural man. The natural man [woman] is often full of resentment, bitterness, shame, and anger. We don't have to stay stuck or trapped in these unhealthy emotions. We can be freed!

> *For the natural man is an enemy to God, and has been from the fall of Adam, and will be, forever and ever, unless he yields to the enticing of the Holy Spirit, and putteth off the natural man and becometh a saint through the atonement of Christ the Lord, and becometh as a child, submissive, meek, humble, patient, full of love, willing to submit to all things which the Lord seeth fit to inflict upon him, even as a child doth submit to his father"* (Mosiah 3:19).

LISTEN TO THE VOICE OF GOD

As we choose to continue moving forward, we do not know what the future will bring. But we do not need to feel alone, and we do not need to live in fear. Even though we still have many unanswered questions, God and Christ are always there to be our anchor in the stormy seas—our lighthouse to safely guide us to shore. Sometimes they calm the storm, and sometimes they calm the storm *within us.* They offer the peace that only divine help can give. We need Their help consistently. We need Their voices to encourage us along. Because God is our Father and Christ is our brother, we can recognize Their voices if we are willing to listen and not be deceived.

One day early in December my backyard neighbor, Phil, asked if I would come to his house and watch their three children if the delivery of their fourth child turned out to be an emergency. Phil and his family were new to the area and did not know very many people. I told Phil I'd be happy to help and never thought more about it. Several days later the phone rang around 2:30 a.m.

It was Phil; the moment had arrived. "Can you come over quickly? We need to leave right now. My wife is in labor!" His wife's previous deliveries were fast, and so every minute counted. I put on my sweat pants and top, slid on my high-top tennis shoes without taking time to lace them, grabbed my ski parka, and walked out my back door without even combing my hair. I was at their back door within two to three minutes. I must have been quite a sight; however, they had more important things to worry about than my appearance.

Phil said, "Thanks for coming so quickly. You can sleep on the couch here in the family room. The kids are upstairs sleeping in their beds." With a final, "Thanks again for coming," they left for the hospital. The house was quiet, and I curled up on the couch and went to sleep.

About 6:00 a.m. I heard a voice calling, "Dad!"

As I woke up, I realized one of Phil's children was calling him, and I started up the stairs. When I was part way up, the child yelled with more intensity, "Dad!!"

The upstairs was dark except for the small night light shining in the hallway. I was not sure which bedroom to enter; I had never been in their upstairs before. In the first bedroom I could not see a child.

As I started for the next bedroom, the child yelled a third time. His voice was an urgent plea for help, "Dad!!!"

I entered the second bedroom, and with the light from the hall, I could see five-year-old Jordan sitting up in bed.

I said, "Jordan, I'm not your dad." Just as the words came out of my mouth, I realized by the look on his face that I should not have said that.

Since I was standing in the door, I blocked most of the light so Jordan could not see my face. I quickly said, "Jordan, I'm Rod. Your next-door neighbor."

Still there was no response. I tried to help him relax by saying, "I live behind your house. You play with my daughters, Mindy, Lisa, and Kristen."

Still no response from Jordan. At that moment I heard Phil's voice calling me from downstairs.

"Phil, I'm up here in Jordan's bedroom," I called. Phil came up the stairs; he did not turn on the light, but quietly entered the room.

I gave Phil a quick update, "Jordan woke up just a few minutes ago and I came up to console him, but he is still scared."

Phil said, "Jordan are you okay?"

For the first time Jordan responded, "Yes, Dad, I'm okay."

Jordan could not see his father's face either, but he knew his father's voice. Jordan did not respond to me, the imposter, but he recognized his father's voice. With his father present, he was no longer frightened, but calm.

Jordan was calm, and said, "Yes, Dad, I'm okay."

Like Jordan, we may feel we are in the middle of a nightmare. We feel scared and confused; we are crying out for help! Our Father will hear our prayers and come to our rescue, just as Phil did for Jordan. If we have trained our spiritual ears to listen to our Father's voice, we will know that He is present. We can be at peace when we hear and respond to our Father's voice, just as Jordan was quickly at peace.

Our Lord will not forsake us. "Wherefore, I am in your midst, and I am the good shepherd, . . . He that buildeth upon this rock shall never fall. And the day cometh that you shall hear my voice . . . and know that I am" (D&C 50:44-45).

FEAR AND WHAT IT DOES TO US

We have a lot of reason to fear the unknown. Often the more we think about the future the more we fear it. Here are some things that others have worried about or feared:

- If I stay with my spouse, won't people who know of his problem think I am insecure?

- If I leave him, will they blame me?

- Whom can I really talk to?

- Can I trust anyone?

- Will I ever be able to trust again?

- How will I act in social settings?

- What if someone in the ward finds out about my spouse's problem? Then everyone will know. I would be so embarrassed.

- Since my spouse attended a disciplinary council, I'm so embarrassed that all of those men know of my spouse's problem. I wonder what those men think of me.

- Who will baptize our son when he turns eight?

- What will I tell my son when he asks why his dad cannot ordain him to the priesthood?

- When my daughter asks why her dad is not partaking of the sacrament, what should I say to her?

- At times I feel that I have to compete with the women my husband has seen in the pornographic magazines.

- Sometimes I feel pressure to engage in demoralizing behaviors to satisfy his sexual wants.

- At times I feel I need to lose weight, start working out more, or dress differently.

- I don't feel that I will ever be able to trust my spouse again.

The unknown future, with so many unanswered questions, can create fear. How can we deal with fear in a healthy way? We can start by establishing firm boundaries with our loved ones. Some of the above questions should be answered by our loved ones. Why should we feel responsible to answer questions that our loved ones have the responsibility to answer? For example, a mother says, "What will I tell my son when he asks why his dad cannot ordain him to the priesthood?" Let dad accept responsibility for his behaviors and answer the question. The mother should say, "Son, please ask your dad that question."

We should determine which questions are important for us to answer and which ones should be directed to our loved ones. We can minimize fear and undo stress by telling others to talk directly with our loved ones. Our future depends on the choices we make now and the boundaries we set for ourselves and our relationships.

🔖 What are some of your fears? How can you diffuse them?

_____

_____

_____

_____

_____

_____

DIFFUSING FEAR

Fear can separate us from God. Why? Because we spend so much of our time worrying about what might happen that we have little time left to focus on our own issues and our relationship with Him.

> *And we have known and believed the love that God hath to us. God is love; and he that dwelleth in love dwelleth in God, and God in him* (1 Jn. 4:16).
>
> *There is no fear in love; but perfect love casteth out fear: because fear hath torment. He that feareth is not made perfect in love* (1 Jn. 4:18).

Knowing and accepting God's perfect love for us dispels fear. When we focus on God's love, we avoid spending an inordinate amount of time worrying about our loved ones. Are we concerned? Yes, but we should avoid worrying because worry creates a wedge between us and God. It puts us in a bad frame of mind: "Fear hath torment." Even though our loved ones have committed serious sins, we should avoid feelings of hate. We can hate our loved ones' behaviors, but not our loved ones. "If a man say, I love God, and hateth his brother, he is a liar: for he that loveth not his brother whom he hath seen, how can he love God whom he hath not seen?" (1 Jn. 4:20).

One woman expressed that her fear was diffused by regularly reading this passage of scripture:

> *Verily, verily, I say unto you, ye are little children, and ye have not as yet understood how great blessings the Father hath in his own hands and prepared for you;*
>
> *And ye cannot bear all things now; nevertheless, be of good cheer, for I will lead you along. The kingdom is yours and the blessings thereof are yours, and the riches of eternity are yours.*

And he who receiveth all things with thankfulness shall be made glorious; and the things of this earth shall be added unto him, even an hundred fold, yea, more.

Wherefore, do the things which I have commanded you, saith your Redeemer, even the Son Ahman, who prepareth all things before he taketh you;

For ye are the church of the Firstborn, and he will take you up in a cloud, and appoint every man his portion.

And he that is a faithful and wise steward shall inherit all things (D&C 78:17-22).

WRITING A LETTER TO OUR LOVED ONES

How can we deal with moments of fear? One way we can diffuse fear is by writing a letter to our loved ones, stating the new set of rules we will play by and focusing on the four areas explained below. This will allow us to see our present situation more clearly. Once we have it down on paper, we can edit, revise, and make needed changes as we receive more inspiration. Taking time to write our solutions to a problem on paper is therapeutic, and the problem often seems more manageable. It may also be good to read the letter to someone you trust before you read it to your loved one, remembering confidentiality. The play director holds a dress rehearsal before the performance, the seamstress makes a muslin before cutting expensive fabric, and the pressman does a mockup of a book before it is printed. We should do our own "dress rehearsal."

When we are satisfied that the letter says all we wish to communicate, before reading it to our loved ones, we need to share the ground rules for the open letter experience and ask that they accept and agree to follow them:

1. We will select a time and place that is appropriate to read the letter. (We will clearly state that the reason for having it in writing is to make sure all our thoughts and feelings are expressed and shared accurately.)

2. We will ask that we be allowed to read the letter out loud in its entirety before we entertain any comments or discussion.

3. We will ask for their respect during the letter reading and assure them that we will give them the same respect listening to their comments when the reading is completed.

4. We will assure our loved ones that we have scheduled enough time for them to share their thoughts and feelings following the letter.

In order to diffuse fear, we need to address the issues "head-on." We really cannot effectively try to go around them. Having a written plan in the form of a letter to our loved ones can diffuse fear as we articulate and communicate our desires and share details that they may not realize we know.

Each of the four letters in the word **"FEAR"** is one focus area to include in the letter. "**F**" is for **Facts**, "**E**" is for **Expectations**, "**A**" is for **Anchor**, and "**R**" is for **Reply**. Let's discuss them one at a time.

F is for **Facts**: In the letter we want to focus on the facts. What do we know about our loved ones' behaviors? What do we know to be the facts? What is the evidence? Are there credit card receipts, phone bills, Internet sites, web site addresses, e-mails, phone calls from third parties who shared information, canceled checks, or confessions?

It is very important that we stick with these facts. We should avoid becoming a detective, but sometimes it is necessary to make an informed decision. Furthermore, some evidence just falls into our hands. For example, one wife got her husband's wallet off the chest of drawers to pay for Girl Scout cookies and found a condom in it. He had just returned from a one-week business trip. These are the types of facts to include in the letter. It is not necessary for the wife to accuse the husband of committing adultery, but it is important to include in the letter that she found a condom in his wallet following his recent business trip.

Keep in mind that we are not judging our loved ones, just stating the facts. In the letter we should say: "Here are the facts. I'm not judging you, I'm just stating what I know." Even though a loved one has tried to hide the facts or cover up his behaviors, the truth will be made known. Elder Richard G. Scott explains Satan's tactics, "Satan strives to convince one that sins can be hidden from others, yet it is he that causes them to be revealed in the most compromising circumstances" (*Ensign*, Nov. 2002, 87).

E is for **Expectations**: We want to include in the letter what we expect from our loved ones in the coming days, weeks, and months. Our expectations need to be very clear. We must tell our loved ones that we will not tolerate any more lies. We expect the truth! We also expect our loved ones to disclose the extent of their behaviors so that we do not have to keep asking and wondering. We have the right to know how involved they have been in compulsive sexual behaviors.

We expect our loved ones to meet with the bishop or stake president and begin the repentance process. We expect that our loved ones will get counseling, apply what they learn in counseling, and continue to stay engaged in the counseling process. We expect them to follow through on assignments given by the bishop or counselor. We should be willing to commit to attend counseling with our loved ones. Both of us may benefit from counseling.

It is important to remember that we prefer that our expectations be met, but realistically they may not be. We should realize that we can deal with this even though we do not like it. It will be difficult if our loved ones do not meet our expectations, but we can continue on and find peace, comfort, and joy. At some point in time we will decide whether we should stay in the marriage or not.

A is for **Anchor**: We should explain in the letter to our loved ones that we did not choose the rough waters we are in—they did. But because we were on the same raft, we got taken downstream as well. We must let our loved ones know that we are going to the shore and setting anchor. This means we will no longer allow them to control us and pull us underwater because they choose to get pulled under. We need to be very firm and let them know that this is where we get off. This is where we will set anchor. We can get plenty of help from those on the shore, and we will do just that—get the help we need.

We also set anchor so that we can think and make decisions undisturbed for a while. It is here that we begin the demanding and burdensome task of sorting through our unpredictable volatile feelings and emotions, maybe without our loved ones around. We need time, perhaps a day or two or several days, depending on our circumstances, to find a way to make some sense of the situation and to decide what we will do from here. We may feel trapped and incapable of knowing what is best for us.

These feelings will change if we allow them to. We may know through the Spirit what we should do, although obtaining that direction will take faith and patience. *"And it came to pass that so great was their faith and their patience that the voice of the Lord came unto them again, saying: Be of good comfort, for on the morrow I will deliver you out of bondage"* (Mosiah 24:16). We do not need to stay stuck in this mental and emotional bondage.

🖉 **Where is the best place for you to sort through your thoughts and feelings? Would you like to be alone or have someone with you? How could you arrange for the time to work through your thoughts, feelings and emotions?**

_____

_____

_____

_____

_____

_____

Through the Spirit, we can see that we have many options. We can choose to set firm boundaries and not let our loved ones walk over us. We can choose our responses to our loved ones' behaviors. We can choose to stay in the marriage and rebuild, or we can choose to divorce. The choices our loved ones make will help us make decisions and choose problem-solving behaviors. With the Lord's help we can see that we have choices; we can free ourselves from the feeling that we are in bondage. We can be delivered as we exercise patience and faith in the Savior and follow the promptings of the Spirit.

Taking the space and time we need will help us get anchored with the Spirit and clearly see our choices. Also, we can avoid the risk of telling other family members too much about our situation right now. We need time to feel the hurt and to work through it. If we tell family members prematurely, we may regret it. We may get unsolicited advice that conflicts with our own inclinations and spiritual promptings. Such advice can cause us more emotional conflict and unrest.

Our firm anchor response in the letter may surprise our loved ones because in the past we may have allowed them to emotionally "push us around." We may have given in too often to their requests and demands in an attempt to smooth things over. We may have denied, avoided, or ignored behaviors that we will no longer tolerate.

We should remind ourselves daily that we must stay anchored in Christ. We stay focused on Him as we deal with the unpleasant reality that our loved ones may be, at least for now, "led about by Satan, even as chaff is driven before the wind, or as a vessel is tossed about upon the waves, without sail or anchor" (Morm. 5:19). We anchor our own boat and set our own boundaries. We have chosen a different path. We know that "whoso believeth in God might with surety hope for a better world, yea, even a place at the right hand of God, which hope cometh of faith, maketh an anchor to the souls of men, which would make them sure and steadfast, always abounding in good works, being led to glorify God" (Ether 12:4).

By using God and Christ as our anchors, we can be sure and steadfast. This is what we need for healing and this is what our loved ones need us to do in order for them to begin to see the consequences of their behaviors and the pain they have caused. Even if they choose not to see the pain ("Who being past feeling have given themselves over unto lasciviousness, to work all uncleanness with greediness" [Eph. 4:19]), we can stay anchored and have the peace of Christ in our lives. Then we can set a course that the Lord would have us travel.

R is for **Reply**: When our loved ones want a reply regarding what we intend to do about staying married, divorcing, or any other matters, we should let them know that we will respond when we are ready. They want a quick fix. They often want to know if we are going to try to work things out or just divorce. They need to be told that they were the one that put the relationship in danger; therefore, it is their responsibility to repair any damage that was done. They are usually afraid that we will choose to leave them, and they are often afraid of being alone.

Sometimes they may cry, shower us with gifts, plead for our forgiveness, or make promises to sway the scales in their behalf. We should not fall for these behaviors. We need to see long-term permanent changes. They need to see the consequences of their choices. They have used us and their addictions to get what they wanted rather than getting their needs met from within and by having a relationship with the Savior. In many cases they need to see what they are about to lose because of their choices before they decide to change those choices.

They must see that their behaviors are not something we will smooth over and pretend that they are a minor problem. Violating covenants is a serious matter. Yes, our loved ones can be forgiven, but there is a lot of work to do on their part before they can expect us, the Church, or the Lord to forgive them. The Lord still has perfect love for them, but forgiveness takes time and a great deal of effort on their part—sometimes more than they expect or are willing to give.

Elder Robert D. Hales provided some important counsel to parents of teenagers. His insights are also applicable to those of us who are dealing with the negative consequences of family members who have been caught in the snare of compulsive sexual behaviors. Elder Hales said:

> *Every family can be strengthened in one way or another if the Spirit of the Lord is brought into our homes and we teach by His example.*
>
> *Act with faith; don't react with fear. When our teenagers begin testing family values, parents need to go to the Lord for guidance on the specific needs of each family member. This is the time for added love and support and to reinforce your teachings on how to make choices. It is frightening to allow our children to learn from the mistakes they may make, but their willingness to choose the Lord's way and family values is greater when the choice comes from within than when we attempt to force those values upon them. The Lord's way of love and acceptance is better than Satan's way of force and coercion, especially in rearing teenagers (Ensign, May 1999, 34).*

As you ponder Elder Hales' comments, how can you apply his teachings with the relationship you have with your loved one?

_____

_____

_____

_____

_____

_____

_____

_____

_____

_____

_____

Even during uncertain periods we can know that the Savior is near and will assist us. President Gordon B. Hinckley assured:

> *We know not what lies ahead of us. We know not what the coming days will bring. We live in a world of uncertainty. For some, there will be great accomplishment. For others, disappointment. For some, much of rejoicing and gladness, good health, and gracious living. For others, perhaps sickness and a measure of sorrow. We do not know. But one thing we do know. Like the polar star in the heavens, regardless of what the future holds, there stands the Redeemer of the world, the Son of God, certain and sure as the anchor of our immortal lives. He is the rock of our salvation, our strength, our comfort, the very focus of our faith.*
>
> *In sunshine and in shadow we look to Him, and He is there to assure and smile upon us* (*Ensign*, May 2002, 90).

If we stay anchored to the Savior and trust that He will help us in our very hour of need, we can experience joy and receive strength during our pain. When Christ is in our lives, so is joy, regardless of our present condition. He knows our pain and will come to our rescue if we truly seek Him and do all we can on our own to reduce the pain.

What are some ways you can achieve inner peace and solace?

How will God, Christ, and the Holy Ghost be part of your inner peace? Can you achieve it without Them?

How can you act with faith?

How can you show love for your loved one even though you do not accept his or her behaviors?

▓ Read 1 Corinthians, Chapter 13 with an open mind and heart. Record the impressions that come to your mind as you ponder these verses.

_____

_____

_____

_____

_____

_____

_____

▓ Read the chapter again and record any additional spiritual insights you discover.

_____

_____

_____

_____

_____

_____

TRUST IN GOD HELPS US REDUCE ANXIETY

Our relationship and trust in God will help us to think clearly and stay calm during potentially explosive times. This will help to reduce anxiety. Anxiety includes worry, distress, and uneasiness about our situation. An extreme level of anxiety is usually present as we work through our issues and try to be supportive to our loved ones trying to change.

We can benefit by breaking anxiety into bite-sized pieces. If we focus on what's going to happen in the next month, year, or five years, we can become so overwhelmed and discouraged that it will be hard to get on the healing path or stay there. A positive approach is to focus on those things that we need to do between now and lunch. At lunch we focus on those things that we need to accomplish between now and dinnertime. During dinner we focus on the rest of the evening.

How will you break your day into smaller time periods so you can focus on shorter blocks of time and avoid being overwhelmed?

We handle our anxiety by breaking it into pieces that we can handle. Some days even smaller chunks of time will be all that we can handle. On other days we can focus on the entire day without feeling overwhelmed. The situation will affect many thoughts, emotions, relationships, and decisions. We also need to sort these out and try to deal with them one at a time. It is important to remember that we only need to do what we can do. President Brigham Young taught this encouraging principle:

> *We all occupy diversified stations in the world, and in the kingdom of God. Those who do right, and seek the glory of the Father in heaven, whether their knowledge be little or much, or whether they can do little or much, if they do the very best they know how, they are perfect. . . .*
>
> *If the first passage I have quoted is not worded to our understanding, we can alter the phraseology of the sentence, and say, "Be ye as perfect as ye can," for that is all we can do, though it is written, be ye perfect as your Father who is in heaven is perfect. To be as perfect as we possibly can, according to our knowledge, is to be just as perfect as our Father in heaven is. He cannot be any more perfect than He knows how, any more than we. When we are doing as well as we know how in the sphere and station which we occupy here, we are justified in the justice, righteousness, mercy, and judgment that go before the Lord of heaven and earth (Journal of Discourses,* Vol. 2, 129–130, Brigham Young, Dec. 18, 1853).

🔯 What are your impressions as you read President Young's statement?

_____

_____

_____

_____

🔯 In what ways has President Young's statement given you comfort?

_____

_____

_____

_____

_____

AVOID THE PANIC MODE

Because of all the stress we are under, it usually doesn't take much to get a volatile, emotional response from us or from our loved ones—even panic. What is panic? Webster's Dictionary defines panic as "a sudden overwhelming fear, with or without cause, that produces hysterical or irrational behavior." When panic strikes, we may experience "shortness of breath, chest pains, and other discomforts, choking or smothering sensations, and fear of 'going crazy' or losing control" (*Diagnostic and Statistical Manual,* 4th edition, 2000).

It is so easy to get into a panic mode. When we are hysterical, our emotions are out of control. We often experience intense apprehension and fearfulness about the future. Under these conditions, it is very difficult to be rational. When we are irrational, our behaviors are illogical; they do not make sense to those around us.

Being in a panic mode is counterproductive to the healing process. Why? Because it is likely to motivate impulsive choices that create pain, which only adds to the pain caused by our loved ones' behaviors. Panic responses to our loved ones' behaviors may include, but are not be limited to:

- I asked my husband to leave immediately. He stayed in a motel for about two weeks.

- Once I discovered my wife was emotionally involved with another man over the Internet, I yelled, screamed, and pushed her.

- I punished my spouse by not talking to him for about ten days.

- I kept questioning my spouse until he told me every sexual detail.

- I asked my husband how my intimate relationship with him compared to the other woman.

- I told my spouse that he could not sleep in the same bed.

- I told my spouse that I would not have sex with him.

- I continually checked up on my spouse so I would know where he was every minute.

- I called a neighbor and had him install a computer tracking program, without my husband's knowledge, so I would know which websites he visits.

- I demanded that my spouse never see or talk to the other woman again.

- I called the woman who was involved with my husband and told her what a rotten person she was for having an affair with my husband.

- I made my son call his gay friends, while I stood by him, and tell them that he was not going to talk with them ever again.

- I secretly researched all the information I could about the woman my husband had the affair with so that I could compare myself to her.

- I joined a health club and immediately started a weight-loss program to show my husband what he would be missing if he left me.

- I bought an entire new wardrobe so I could feel good about myself.

- I purchased new furniture for the house, which we couldn't afford.

- I went on an eating binge and ate everything in sight.

It's very important to note that a few of the behaviors listed above *may* be appropriate in order to establish boundaries and to protect us and our innocent children. However, they should be done calmly, logically, and guided by inspiration, not in a panic. If child abuse has occurred, our first efforts must be devoted to the children and their protection. This means the person who committed the abuse should not be in the home. Immediate reporting to law enforcement agencies is required. Contacting the bishop and seeking professional counseling by someone trained to work with victims of abuse are important and urgent actions. It is also important that the one who committed the abuse get counseling.

However, it is important to avoid the panic mode and not overreact. It is also important that we not let our panic cause us to freeze and do nothing. Meeting with the bishop may give us time to cool down and think more clearly so we can avoid making irrational choices. When our minds have cleared, we are better equipped to make good decisions. We should try to think of all the ramifications and then act. We should not enable our loved ones by dismissing their behaviors or waiting too long to act.

✒ **What are other appropriate or inappropriate things you may have done as your first reaction when you were told about or discovered your loved one's compulsive behaviors?**

_____

_____

_____

_____

_____

Here are some ways to deal with panic thoughts, feelings, and behaviors:

- Write down your fears and concerns so you can see them on paper. This allows you to see your situation as another person might see it. Once you get it all on paper, you can decide how to best move forward. Writing it down allows you to look at your circumstances more objectively.

- Decide that you will work through your problems even though it may be difficult.

- Be aware of your feelings—accept them, express them, and keep them in control.

- Use breathing control exercises to reduce the symptoms. Take deep breaths and exhale slowly.

- Begin an exercise program—walking, jogging, swimming, aerobics, etc.

- Engage in activities that are emotionally relaxing.

- Use your sense of humor and don't forget to laugh at yourself.

- Recognize your strengths, talents, and abilities and use them to deal with the problems.

- Become more assertive—express your thoughts and feelings assertively.

- Learn what thinking errors you might have and work to change them.

- Develop a self-talk message that is positive and relaxing.

- Seek a professional evaluation and follow the suggested treatment plan.

- If medications are prescribed by a mental health professional, take them as prescribed.

- Read your favorite scriptures and hymns with your own voice into a recorder at a time when you are calm and relaxed. (Try to record at least thirty minutes.) This exercise will serve as a reminder that you can be calm.

Consider the following scriptures:

> *And I was led by the Spirit, not knowing beforehand the things which I should do* (1 Ne. 4:6).

> *And it came to pass that there was no contention in the land, because of the love of God which did dwell in the hearts of the people* (4 Ne. 1:15).

> *Pray always, that you may come off conqueror; yea, that you may conquer Satan, and that you may escape the hands of the servants of Satan that do uphold his work* (D&C 10:5).

> *Angels speak by the power of the Holy Ghost; wherefore, they speak the words of Christ. Wherefore, I said unto you, feast upon the words of Christ; for behold, the words of Christ will tell you all things what ye should do* (2 Ne. 32:3).

> *Thou hast suffered afflictions and much sorrow, because of the rudeness of thy brethren [husband, wife, child, sibling, friend]. Nevertheless, Jacob, . . . thou knowest the greatness of God; and he shall consecrate thine afflictions for thy gain* (2 Ne. 2:1-2).

My name is Jehovah, and I know the end from the beginning; therefore my hand shall be over thee (Abr. 2:8).

And ye cannot bear all things now; nevertheless, be of good cheer, for I will lead you along (D&C 78:18).

Behold, I will go before you and be your rearward; and I will be in your midst (D&C 49:27).

Consider the following verses of "I Need Thee Every Hour," (*Hymns*, 98):

I need thee every hour,
Most gracious Lord.
No tender voice like thine
Can peace afford.

I need thee every hour,
In joy or pain.
Come quickly and abide,
Or life is vain.

Throughout the day and night you can play the recording and listen to the words of inspiration and comfort in your own voice. Notice the calmness of your voice and make the choice to stay calm. The scriptures and words from the hymns provide inspiration, hope, and direction to help us deal with the trials of life.

Use "I will" Thoughts and Statements

We can also remind ourselves that the situation we are in is very difficult, uncomfortable, and demanding, but we can get through it—and we will. Our thoughts might include:

"This is so difficult, but **I will** get through it."

"I do not like what I'm going through, but **I will** solve it."

"This is so hard, but **I will** deal with it."

"This is very painful, but **I will** continue each day—one day at a time."

Using "I will" statements empowers us to continue to deal with this situation in a spiritually healthy way even though it is very hard and emotionally draining. "I will" statements have more commitment than "I might," "I'll try," "I should," or "If I can." "I will" is empowering because we exercise our agency and choose to do it. We have greater inner strength and are more likely to rely on divine help when we make the choice. We can learn from those who said, "I will," in the scriptures, and we can move forward with greater resolve and do what needs to be done.

> Now Lamoni said unto Ammon: I know, in the strength of the Lord thou canst do all things. . . ***I will*** go with thee (Alma 20:4).

> And Simon answering said unto him, Master, we have toiled all the night, and have taken nothing: nevertheless at thy word ***I will*** let down the net (Luke 5:5).

> ***I will*** arise and go to my father, and ***will*** say unto him, Father, I have sinned against heaven, and before thee (Luke 15:18).

> Behold, God is my salvation; ***I will*** trust, and not be afraid (2 Ne. 22:2).

> O Lord, I have trusted in thee, and ***I will*** trust in thee forever (2 Ne. 4:34).

> Yea, my God will give me, if I ask not amiss; therefore ***I will*** lift up my voice unto thee. (2 Ne. 4:35).

> I, Nephi, said unto my father: ***I will*** go and do the things which the Lord hath commanded, for I know that the Lord giveth no commandments unto the children of men, save he shall prepare a way for them that they may accomplish the thing which he commandeth them (1 Ne. 3:7).

These "I will" statements can also remind us of those things we **will not** do. Elder George Q. Cannon taught:

> Our only preservation is in living near to God, day by day, and serving him in faithfulness, and having the light of revelation and truth in our hearts continually, so that, when Satan approaches, we will see him and understand the snare that he has laid for us, and we will have the power to say, "O no; God being my helper, ***I will not*** yield to it; ***I will not*** do that which is wrong; ***I will not*** grieve the Spirit of God; ***I will not*** deviate from the path that my Father has marked out for me; but ***I will*** walk in it (*Journal of Discourses*, 11:173-74, Oct. 8, 1865).

As we improve our relationship with God—one day at a time—we can have the light of revelation and truth in our hearts.

WHOM CAN WE TRUST?

Sometimes we spend too much time worrying about our loved ones, their behaviors, and our inability to trust them. Consequently, we deplete our emotional energy. What can we accomplish when we have no emotional energy left? When we are worn out and feel downtrodden, we put ourselves at risk for more upheaval. If we don't take care of our own emotional reservoir, who will? We want to be careful that we do not freely give from our own emotional reservoir to the point that there is nothing left for us. We want to preserve, maintain, and replenish our own emotional reservoir to cover this unexpected drought.

Being prepared for the future means having enough spiritual water to take care of ourselves. One way to replenish our spiritual reservoir is to focus our emotional energy on those whom we can trust and continue to strengthen those relationships. We should spend our emotional, spiritual, and mental energy developing the following areas of trust:

- Trust in God and Christ.

- Trust in Their promises.

- Trust in Their will.

- Trust in Their wisdom.

- Trust in Their timing.

- Trust in Christ's Atonement. Know and accept that He can heal all wounds—even your wounds.

- Trust the words of the prophets and apostles.

- Trust inspired Church leaders (branch presidents, bishops, stake presidents).

- Trust in prayer.

- Trust in fasting.

- Trust in the scriptures.

- Trust yourself, your thoughts, impressions, promptings from the Holy Ghost, and answers to prayers.

- Trust that you can and will make wise decisions and be able to solve problems.

- Trust your talents, abilities, and righteous desires.

- Trust yourself and your ability to move forward even though it is very difficult.

- Trust your relationships with family or other close friends who give support and strength.

By focusing our emotional energy on those whom we can trust, we will be empowered to develop more trust in ourselves, in God, and in His Son. Our goal is to become what God desires us to become in the process of working through our own issues. Elder Richard G. Scott explained: "Your agency, the right to make choices, is not given so that you can get what you want. This divine gift is provided so that you will choose what your Father in Heaven wants for you. That way He can lead you to become all that He intends you to be. That path leads to glorious joy and happiness" (*Ensign,* May 1996, 25). The healing power of the Atonement will lift us up.

President Gordon B. Hinckley reminds us:

> *Pray for wisdom and understanding as you walk the difficult paths of your lives. If you are determined to do foolish and imprudent things, I think the Lord will not prevent you. But if you seek His wisdom and follow the counsel of the impressions that come to you, I am confident that you will be blessed* (*Ensign,* May 2003, 100).

TRUST IN GOD

Over the years I have heard statements by others expressing how devastated they felt regarding their loved ones' behaviors and how their poor choices have impacted their lives. The unrelenting pain and horror seemed at times unbearable. How can we find the strength to go on when we don't know what the future may bring? Here are statements of concern from others, followed by answers from the scriptures that encourage us to trust in God:

Statement:
"This is the worst thing that I have ever gone through. I can't sleep. I can't eat. I have so much emotional stress. What did I do to deserve this?"

Trust in God:
> *Whosoever shall put their trust in God shall be supported in their trials, and their troubles, and their afflictions, and shall be lifted up at the last day* (Alma 36:3).

Statement:

"I have no one to talk with about this situation. I don't feel close to my husband anymore. I don't feel that I can share my thoughts and feelings with him. I am just too angry most of the time."

Trust in God:

Trust in him at all times; [ye] people, pour out your heart before him: God [is] a refuge for us (Ps. 62:8).

Statement:

"I am so concerned about the future. I don't know what is going to happen. I don't know how things will end up with our marriage and family. I'm so afraid of what could happen."

Trust in God:

Behold, God is my salvation; I will trust, and not be afraid; for the Lord JEHOVAH is my strength and my song; he also has become my salvation (2 Ne. 22:2).

Statement:

"When will all of this pain go away? When will I stop hurting so much? I have carried this burden for so long! I don't know if I can keep going."

Trust in God:

And I will also ease the burdens which are put upon your shoulders, that even you cannot feel them upon your backs, even while you are in bondage; and this will I do that ye may stand as witnesses for me hereafter, and that ye may know of a surety that I, the Lord God, do visit my people in their afflictions (Mosiah 24:14).

I would that ye should remember, that as much as ye shall put your trust in God even so much ye shall be delivered out of your trials, and your troubles, and your afflictions, and ye shall be lifted up at the last day (Alma 38:5).

Statement:

"I am so confused; I don't know what I should do. One day I make a decision about something and think I feel good about it, but the next day I am totally confused again and can't move ahead."

Trust in God:

In thee, O LORD, do I put my trust: let me never be put to confusion (Ps. 71:1).

Trust in the LORD with all thine heart; and lean not unto thine own understanding.

In all thy ways acknowledge him, and he shall direct thy paths (Prov. 3:5-6).

Statement:

"At times I want to get even with my spouse. I want my spouse to hurt as much as I do. I just want my spouse to have to go through what I have been through. This would teach him a lesson."

Trust in God:

But behold, he did deliver them because they did humble themselves before him; and because they cried mightily unto him he did deliver them out of bondage; and thus doth the Lord work with his power in all cases among the children of men, extending the arm of mercy towards them that put their trust in him (Mosiah 29:20).

Statement:

"My family thinks I should divorce my spouse. Even some of my friends say I should not put up with his behavior any more. I'm torn between what my family wants me to do and what I feel the Lord wants me to do."

Trust in God:

O Lord, I have trusted in thee, and I will trust in thee forever. I will not put my trust in the arm of flesh; for I know that cursed is he that putteth his trust in the arm of flesh. Yea, cursed is he that putteth his trust in man or maketh flesh his arm.

> *Yea, I know that God will give liberally to him that asketh. Yea, my God will give me, if I ask not amiss; therefore I will lift up my voice unto thee; yea, I will cry unto thee, my God, the rock of my righteousness. Behold, my voice shall forever ascend up unto thee, my rock and mine everlasting God* (2 Ne. 4:34-35).

FAITH AND COURAGE

It will take a great deal of faith and courage to focus on our own issues. The Lord's counsel to Joseph Smith is applicable to our situation, "Be patient in afflictions, for thou shalt have many; but endure them, for, lo, I am with thee, even unto the end of thy days" (D&C 24:8).

We can sing "When Faith Endures" (*Hymns*, 128):

> *I will not doubt, I will not fear; God's love and strength are always near.*
> *His promised gift helps me to find an inner strength and peace of mind.*
> *I give the father willingly my trust, my prayers, humility.*
> *His Spirit guides; his love assures that fear departs when faith endures.*

The Savior has promised that He will help us and lift us up: "And now it came to pass that the burdens which were laid upon Alma and his brethren were made light; yea, the Lord did strengthen them that they could bear up their burdens with ease, and they did submit cheerfully and with patience to all the will of the Lord" (Mosiah 24:15). We too carry real burdens because of our loved ones' choices. We too can be lifted up. Read the scripture again and insert your name in the blank line.

> *And now it came to pass that the burdens which were laid upon _____were made light; yea, the Lord did strengthen [him or her] that [he or she] could bear up [the] burdens with ease, and [he or she] did submit cheerfully and with patience to all the will of the Lord"* (Mosiah 24:15).

The Lord will lift our burdens when we turn to Him, move forward with patience, and strive to do His will. This will take a great amount of faith. We hold on to hope for our loved ones with faith, not control. If we attempt to control others, then we are not using faith. Faith can get us through so that we can be comforted and know that "this too shall pass." How do we know this? Because of our faith!

REVIEW OF PRINCIPLES

How can you teach the perfect love of God and Christ to someone who has sinned?

_____

_____

_____

_____

_____

_____

How can you use the surrender prayer in your healing?

_____

_____

_____

_____

_____

_____

_____

What are ways you can diffuse fear?

_____

_____

_____

_____

_____

_____

_____

How can you know if it is wise to begin to trust? Whom will you trust?

What can you do to deal with being overwhelmed and panic in a healthy way?

How can the Holy Ghost comfort you at this time?

What have you done to accept the peace and comfort the Holy Ghost offers?

How can you work toward and accept the peace the Savior has promised?

Record any other insights or thoughts that have come as you have read this chapter.

What is the single most important principle or concept you have learned from this chapter?

With whom can you share this important principle or concept in the next week?

_____

_____

_____

CALMNESS BREAK

Some loved ones have found that writing poetry is a healthy way to deal with their feelings and emotions. Here is what one woman discovered about love:

> *Love is a process of giving pieces of ourselves away,*
> *And by doing so discovering what we are capable of becoming.*
> *Love is a canvas we paint and repaint over and over again*
>   *as our lives change and grow—*
> *Adding color when needed, sunshine after life's storms, and rainbows*
> *Following despair and sadness to remind us of how beautiful*
>   *things can be and are;*
> *Giving us hope for a brighter and better tomorrow.*
> *Loving is the most natural—best part of ourselves—of our existence.*
> *Allowing past heartaches and sorrow to take from us*
> *Our willingness or ability to love and be loved;*
> *Goes against the very nature of our souls and reason for being.*
> *While there are some who desperately reach for love, yet too afraid*
>   *to fully embrace it,*
> *For whom love is always just beyond their reach.*
> *There are others who make love happen;*
> *Forging past fear, vulnerability, and insecurity **to find the priceless***
>   ***truth about love.***
> *When given freely, it expands the soul and increases one's capacity to be;*
> *To be kind, charitable, happy, to be free.*

We cannot control who does and does not love us.
What we can do, however, is gift Love and Respect.
Gifting love and respect regardless of circumstances
Says everything about our ability to love
And nothing about the receiver of our gift.
Love invites laughter, increases joy, enlightens understanding,
Magnifies compassion, and sustains life.
Love is a catalyst for change and a playground for growth.
Love heals wounds, mends hearts, endures hardship, and lifts spirits.
Love is the power and force which governs the universe.
When we become a part of that force we are changed forever.
Becoming a piece of the picture that makes us whole.

Written by: Donna Root

MESSAGES OF HOPE

Elder Joseph B. Wirthlin: "The Savior's love extends to everyone—the weak and the strong, the courageous and the fearful, the sinner and the righteous. Because Jesus loved his followers and because they knew he loved them, he was able to speak openly and honestly with them. He reproved Peter at times because he loved him, and he wanted to help him become all that he was capable of becoming. And because Peter knew that the Lord loved him, he was able to accept the reproof and grow from it" (*Ensign*, Sept. 1995, 37).

Thomas S. Monson: "Some point the accusing finger at the sinner or the unfortunate and in derision say, 'He has brought his condition upon himself.' Others exclaim, 'Oh, he will never change. He has always been a bad one.' A few see beyond the outward appearance and recognize the true worth of a human soul. When they do, miracles occur. The downtrodden, the discouraged, the helpless become 'no more strangers and foreigners, but fellowcitizens with the saints, and of the household of God' (Eph. 2:19). True love can alter human lives and change human nature" (*Ensign*, Dec. 1971, 132).

PRINCIPLE 4

With Faith, We Can Surrender Our Trials

to the Lord Jesus Christ—He Invites Us to

CHAPTER OVERVIEW

Most of us experience the need to turn the issue of our loved ones' compulsive sexual behaviors over to the Lord. In the short-term we may have done well with the burden, thinking naively that this ordeal would quickly end and that our lives would be normal again. We soon learn, however, that there is no quick and easy solution and that we simply do not have the mental, emotional, physical, or spiritual strength to continue carrying the load by ourselves.

When we turn our trials over to the Lord, we surrender them to Him. Surrender means that we are willing to admit that we cannot solve our problems without Him, that we accept His help and His perfect love, and that we are willing to become what He desires us to become because of this experience. Surrendering our wills to Christ brings victory over the trials, peace during and after the trials, and the miracle of healing.

These blessings require faith in the compassion and Atonement of the Savior. The miracle of healing comes by our yielding our will and choosing to drop at His feet the burden that we are carrying because of our loved ones' choices. We must believe that through our faith we can surrender to the Lord our feelings of discomfort, bitterness, fear, resentment, and anger about our loved ones' behaviors.

In many ways we are like children who are discovering how painful life can be and how much our lives are affected by the choices of others. We did not choose to be in this situation. Our loved ones' choices generated the situation along with the emotional burdens and obstacles. That burden may at times feel almost unbearable. In response to such circumstances, the Savior invited, "Come unto me, all ye that labor and are heavy laden, and I will give you rest" (Matthew 11:28). The Savior can and will give us rest as we choose to "come and fear not, and lay aside every [burden]" (Alma 7:15). We must take our burdens to Him.

We can receive no greater blessing in our lives than to become a new person, born again with His image in our countenances, allowing us to walk in the way of truth, peace, and joy, even in the midst of challenges! With faith in Christ, this goal is achievable. "We believe that the first principles and ordinances of the Gospel are: first, Faith in the Lord Jesus Christ" (A of F 4). "We believe in the gift of . . . healing" (A of F 7).

 ## CHAPTER OBJECTIVES

At the conclusion of this chapter you should—

1. Understand that increased faith in the Lord Jesus Christ will help heal your soul.
2. Be aware of ways you can increase your faith in God and Christ.
3. Accept and allow Christ to help you during your time of healing.
4. Have a better understanding of how trials can help you become more converted to the gospel of Jesus Christ.
5. Realize that no one is exempt from trials.
6. Understand the need to be very assertive when dealing with your loved one's deceit.
7. Be able to identify irrational thought patterns that postpone healing and work to replace them with rational thought patterns that enhance healing.
8. Work to increase your patience and accept the Lord's timetable for healing.
9. Understand that through Christ and His Atonement, a broken heart can be healed.

OVERCOMING THE NATURAL MAN THROUGH CHRIST

The gospel of Jesus Christ is like a huge hospital. We have agreed to be admitted. We have all checked in. We are waiting to be seen by the Physician. The time arrives, and He comes into the room and makes His diagnosis, "I have checked you over and you have the 'natural man disease,'" He reports.

Puzzled, we ask, "The what?"

He responds, "The natural man disease."

We ask, "How severe is this disease?"

"The natural man disease is a very serious ailment because 'the natural man receiveth not the things of the Spirit of God: for they are foolishness unto him: neither can he know them because they are spiritually discerned'" (1 Cor. 2:14).

We ask, "How long has this disease been around?"

He responds, "The natural man is an enemy to God, and has been from the fall of Adam" (Mosiah 3:19). He politely tells us there are other patients He needs to see. He writes a prescription and thanks us for coming.

We quickly ask, "How long do I need to take this medicine?"

He responds, "For the rest of your life."

We arrive at the pharmacy, get the prescription filled, and read the label: "Yield to the enticings of the Holy Spirit, and [put] off the natural man and [become] a saint through the Atonement of Christ the Lord, and [become] as a child, submissive, meek, humble, patient, full of love, willing to submit to all things which the Lord seeth fit to inflict upon [you], even as a child doth submit to his father" (Mosiah 3:19). We so eagerly want to be cured from such a terrible disease that we resolve to faithfully take the medicine every day.

The first few weeks we experience a noticeable difference in how we view God, others, our trials, and ourselves because we are really trying to follow the directions on the prescription. But before too long we get busy and forget to take the medicine. We skip a day here and there and think that it won't matter. As we slack off, we quit seeing any significant changes and say to ourselves, "I don't think this medicine is doing any good. I feel just the way I did before. There is no reason to keep taking it if it's not going to work."

In a moment of discouragement we stop taking the medicine altogether. We lose hope and soon feel awful, and so we schedule another appointment to see the Physician. One of His first questions is, "Are you still taking the prescription?"

We quickly respond, "No, because it wasn't doing any good."

"How do you know it wasn't doing any good?" He asks.

"Because I didn't feel better!" We answer.

He gently reminds us, "I will give unto the children of men line upon line, precept upon precept, here a little and there a little; and blessed are those who hearken unto my precepts, and lend an ear unto my counsel, for they shall learn wisdom; for unto him that recieveth I will give more; and from them that shall say, We have enough, from them shall be taken away even that which they have" (2 Ne. 28:30).

We feel a little embarrassed by what He just said. Sensing our feelings, He reassures us: "Learn of me, and listen to my words; walk in the meekness of my Spirit, and you shall have peace in me" (D&C 19:23).

We quietly leave and make a commitment to try once again. Sometimes we get worn out trying, but, little by little, we learn and grow.

> What are the virtues that one needs to acquire in order to overcome the natural man or woman?

_____

_____

_____

_____

_____

_____

> How will this trial help you to acquire these virtues?

_____

_____

_____

_____

_____

_____

FAITH IN THE LORD JESUS CHRIST

Faith in the Lord Jesus Christ allows us to cast our burdens upon Him and trust that He will help us and guide us even though the paths are unknown. One woman expressed, "If I just knew for sure how this was going to end, then I could go on. But it's the uncertainty that I cannot deal with."

Knowing how something is going to turn out is not faith. Elder Dallin H. Oaks said, "I also know that strength is forged in adversity and that faith is developed in a setting where we cannot see ahead" (*Ensign,* May 2003, 97). Ponder Elder Oaks' statement.

 Record the impressions or thoughts that come to you as you consider his words:

_____

_____

_____

_____

_____

_____

BUILDING FAITH IN GOD AND THE LORD JESUS CHRIST

A great deal of faith in God will be required to get through our current trials—more than we have exercised before. How can we use faith to effectively get through this trial? How can we increase our faith?

Elder Richard G. Scott shared these principles:

> *"You will gather the fruits of faith as you follow the principles God has established for its use.*
>
> *Some of those principles are:*
>
> - *Trust in God and in His willingness to provide help when needed, no matter how challenging the circumstance.*
> - *Obey His commandments and live to demonstrate that He can trust you.*
> - *Be sensitive to the quiet prompting of the Spirit.*
> - *Act courageously on that prompting.*
> - *Be patient and understanding when God lets you struggle to grow and answers come a piece at a time over an extended period.*
> - *Motivating faith is centered in trust in the Lord and in His willingness to answer your needs. For 'the Lord . . . doth bless and prosper those who put their trust in Him.' The consistent, willing exercise of faith increases your confidence and ability to employ the power of faith"* (*Ensign*, May 2003, 76).

These are truly powerful principles that can help us increase our faith in God and His Son. Some seem so simple that they are easy to overlook. Let's review each principle one at a time.

🌿 "Trust in God and in His willingness to provide help when needed no matter how challenging the circumstance." How can you apply this principle in your present situation?

_____

_____

_____

_____

_____

_____

🌿 "Obey His commandments and live to demonstrate that He can trust you." How can you most effectively accomplish this principle?

_____

_____

_____

_____

_____

_____

🌿 "Be sensitive to the quiet prompting of the Spirit." How can you put yourself in a position to be sensitive to the Spirit? How will the Spirit speak to you?

_____

_____

_____

_____

_____

_____

🌿 "Act courageously on that prompting." How can you act courageously on the promptings of the Spirit?

_____

_____

_____

_____

🌿 "Be patient and understanding when God lets you struggle to grow and answers come a piece at a time over an extended period." How can you submit to God's timetable? How do answers often come and over what period of time?

_____

_____

_____

_____

_____

If we cast our burden upon the Lord, He will help us get through this difficult time. Hymn 110, "Cast Thy Burden upon the Lord," provides comfort.

Cast thy burden upon the Lord,
And he shall sustain thee.
He never will suffer the righteous to fall.
He is at thy right hand.
Thy mercy, Lord, is great
And far above the heav'ns.
Let none be made ashamed
That wait upon thee.

Elder Robert D. Hales gave this encouragement: "As we put our faith in the Lord and keep our focus on the eternities, we will be blessed to be able to accept whatever trial we are given, for life on earth, as we know it, is only temporary, and, if we endure it well, the Lord has promised us: 'And, if you keep my commandments and endure to the end you shall have eternal life, which gift is the greatest of all the gifts of God (D&C 14:7)'" (*Ensign,* May 1998, 77).

This is a wonderful promise! But even with promised blessings, accepting this trial is not easy because of the natural man and woman instincts that we all possess. Our natural tendency is to question the Lord. Why did this happen to me? What did I do wrong? When will this be over? When will You take away my pain? When will You take away my trial?

No One Is Exempt from Trials

We all face trials regardless of our age, bank account, skills, gender, or even our testimony. We may wonder if anyone really cares and understands what we are going through. Elder Robert D. Hales expressed:

> *Some experiencing pain may feel that the Brethren do not have an understanding of their trials and tribulations. We do care from the depths of our hearts.*
>
> *Over the past twenty years, I have also learned a great deal about how the Lord cares for each of us. What I have begun to understand is that every one of us has challenges, pain, and opposition. None of us is exempt from the realities of mortality. "For it must needs be, that there is an opposition in all things (2 Ne. 2:11)" (Ensign, Mar. 1996, 15).*

Conversion to the Gospel of Jesus Christ

It seems to be a human tendency to want to grow and progress without pain or difficulties. However, no matter how much we listen and learn in priesthood meetings, Relief Society, Sunday School, or sacrament meetings, we have to apply what we learn in real life—outside the church building. Only real-life trials allow us to apply the teachings of the gospel in our lives, and this is when the real growth takes place.

We grow when we are stretched to our limits and then muster enough courage and faith to go on. Sometimes we are amazed at what we have endured and learned from in the past, and those memories can help us do what we need to do now to get through this difficult time.

It is often hard to believe that the experience we are going through with our loved ones can help us to become more converted to the gospel of Jesus Christ but it can. Elder Russell M. Nelson emphasized, "Yes, every test, every trial, every challenge and hardship you endure is an opportunity to further develop your faith (see D&C 63:11; D&C 101:4)" (*Ensign,* Nov. 1990, 75).

Our initial feelings of shock, confusion, fear, self-blame, bitterness, betrayal, inferiority, hopelessness, humiliation, and anger may drive us away from God rather than toward Him. If we are aware of these feelings and make a determined effort to change our course and move toward God, we can quickly get back on the healing path.

The difficulty of our journey is compounded when the very family member who was generally there for us is the one who has created this trial for us to endure. Sometimes we think that it would be much easier for us to bear if only it had been an accident or if someone outside the family had created this trial for us.

We must remember, though, that in most cases our loved ones did not go out with the intention to purposely create a trial for us. Only through pleasure seeking and taking the "drug of lust" did they make choices that resulted in such difficult consequences for them and for us. Because they were caught up in the short-term pleasures of their compulsions, they did not see the long-term consequences and trials they were creating for us.

Very seldom do our sexually addicted loved ones recognize the seriousness of their choices and the all-encompassing impact and consequences they have on us. Furthermore, our loved ones cannot see the painful consequences of their behavior until they humble themselves, repent of their sins, and strive to live the commandments. One reason the whole situation is so frustrating for us is that they often cannot see the consequences of what they have done and what they continue to do by engaging in destructive behavior.

Regardless of whether our loved ones decide to change, how can these trials help us draw closer to the Savior? The entry entitled *"Conversion"* in the Bible Dictionary states, "Complete conversion comes after many trials and much testing" (*Bible Dictionary,* 650). If we look at our present situation as a trial, burden, or affliction and recognize that it has the potential to give us some spiritual benefit and eventually a "complete conversion," then with that eternal perspective and Christ's power we can muster up the spiritual strength to continue our healing even though it will not be easy.

We should recognize that our trial will not last forever. It will come to an end. As we reflect on past trials that we have endured, we can see that this is true. It may seem endless now, but the day will come when the suffering is over. Sometimes our trial ends because our perspective changes from seeing our plight as a trial to seeing it as a process that is helping us to become more converted to the gospel of Jesus Christ.

📖 According to the *Bible Dictionary,* when does complete conversion take place?

_____

_____

_____

_____

_____

TRIALS—ARE THEY A CURSE OR A BLESSING?

Elder Orson F. Whitney taught:

> *No pain that we suffer, no trial that we experience is wasted. It ministers to our education, to the development of such qualities as patience, faith, fortitude and humility. All that we suffer and all that we endure, especially when we endure it patiently, builds up our characters, purifies our hearts, expands our souls, and makes us more tender and charitable, more worthy to be called the children of God, and it is through sorrow and suffering, toil and tribulation, that we gain the education that we come here to acquire* (quoted in *Improvement Era,* Mar. 1966, 211).

Each trial will eventually prove to be a great blessing to us if we allow it to become such. Elder Wilford Woodruff taught:

> *In the dispensations and providences of God to man it seems that we are born to suffer pain, affliction, sorrows and trials; this is what God has decreed that the human family shall pass through; and if we make a right use of this probation, the experience it brings will eventually prove a great blessing to us, and when we receive immortality and eternal life, exaltation, kingdoms, thrones, principalities and powers with all the blessings of the fulness of the Gospel of Christ, we shall understand and comprehend why we are called to pass through a continual warfare during the few years we spent in the flesh* (*Journal of Discourses,* Vol.18, 33).

President Brigham Young explained, "God never bestows upon His people, or upon an individual, superior blessings without a severe trial" (*Journal of Discourses,* 3:205–206).

No Witness Until After the Trial of Faith

Moroni taught, "I . . . would speak somewhat concerning these things; I would show unto the world that faith is things which are hoped for and not seen; wherefore, dispute not because ye see not, for ye receive no witness until after the trial of your faith" (Ether 12:6).

To gain a witness or conversion, we must experience trials. The trials precede the witness. In the middle of our trial we may think that our trial is so much more difficult than trials that other people experience here in mortality—but this is not true. Every trial is difficult. When we think it would be nice to trade our trial for a different one, we need to remember that our trials provide the precise learning experiences we need in order to develop the virtues we most desire. For example, we usually want to develop more faith in the Lord Jesus Christ, but we struggle when we are faced with trials that would do exactly what we desire—develop more faith in Christ! Elder Robert D. Hales counseled, "Often we do not know what we can endure until after a trial of our faith. We are also taught by the Lord that we will never be tested beyond that which we can endure (see 1 Cor. 10:13)" (*Ensign,* May 1998, 76).

We believe that this life is a test and that we came here to gain experiences that would help us to become more godlike. Elder M. Russell Ballard explained:

> *We mortals have a limited view of life from the eternal perspective. But if we know and understand Heavenly Father's plan, we realize that dealing with adversity is one of the chief ways we are tested. Our faith in our Heavenly Father and his beloved Son, Jesus Christ, is the source of inner strength. Through faith we can find peace, comfort, and the courage to endure. As we trust in God and his plan for our happiness with all our hearts and lean not unto our own understanding (see Prov. 3:5), hope is born. Hope grows out of faith and gives meaning and purpose to all we do. It can give us comfort in the face of adversity, strength in times of trial, and peace when we have reason for doubt or anguish (Ensign, May 1995, 23–24).*

Patience in Our Trials—
Accepting the Lord's Timetable

Turning our problems over to the Lord means that we are willing to go along with His timetable. Sometimes we want and expect a quick solution to our problems. Our impatience can create considerable stress and anxiety. These emotions are usually unhealthy because with such pressures we cannot think clearly and may make choices that distract from our healing.

President Thomas S. Monson reminds us: "Life is full of difficulties, some minor and others of a more serious nature. There seems to be an unending supply of challenges for one and all. Our problem is that we often expect instantaneous solutions to such challenges, forgetting that frequently the heavenly virtue of patience is required" (*Ensign,* Sept. 2002, 2).

How can you be more patient with yourself as you work through your healing?

What are some ways you can be more patient as you reach out and try to help your loved one?

It will take some time for a broken heart to heal. Increased patience is one way we can set aside our will and embrace God's will.

WHAT WE BECOME IS MORE IMPORTANT THAN THE TYPE OF TRIAL WE ENDURE

We can become closer to the Savior as we allow Him to walk with us and help us during our times of need. Wealth and poverty can both be trials. Elder Dallin H. Oaks shared: "The blessings of adversity extend to others. I know it was a blessing to be raised by a widowed mother whose children had to learn how to work, early and hard. I know that relative poverty and hard work are not greater adversities than affluence and abundant free time" (*Ensign*, May 2003, 97).

Alma asked a series of questions in Alma, Chapter 5. In fact, he asked over 40 questions in the entire chapter, including the following:

> *And now behold, I ask of you, my brethren [sisters] of the church, have ye spiritually been born of God?*
>
> *Have ye received his image in your countenances?*
>
> *Have ye experienced this mighty change in your hearts?*
>
> *Do ye exercise faith in the redemption of him who created you?* (Alma 5:14-15).

Clearly the important question is "What have we become in the process of going through trials?" Alma did not ask what trials we endured to receive His image in our countenances. Nor did he ask what experiences we had that brought a mighty change in our hearts. Does it make any difference what trial we have if the end results are accomplished? If we become what God wants us to become, does it matter which trial got us to that point?

FAITH AND WORKS

Faith in the Lord Jesus Christ will help us get through the pain and sorrow we now feel. The Lord will do His part to help, and He expects us to do what we can to help ourselves. Elder Russell M. Nelson reminds us, "Remember that faith and prayer alone are seldom sufficient. Personal effort is usually necessary to accomplish your heart's desire. 'Faith, *if it hath not works,* is dead, being alone.'"(James 2:17; see also James 2:18, 20, 26; Alma 26:22)(*Ensign*, Nov. 1990, 75).

What are some things you can *do* now to "receive His image in your countenance" and improve the way you feel about your present situation?

_____

_____

_____

_____

_____

Avoid Constant Replaying of the Hurt

We have been hurt—terribly hurt. But we invariably add more hurt when we choose to consistently replay in our minds our loved ones' past behaviors. When we think about our loved ones' behaviors and the emotional pain they have caused us, it is natural to respond with feelings of bitterness, fear, resentment, hatred, and anger. Choosing to cling to these emotions over long periods of time, however, saps our emotional strength and can make us feel helpless. What plays across our minds determines the flow of our emotions for "as he thinketh in his heart, so [is] he" (Prov. 23:7).

To avoid being consumed with bitterness, resentment, fear, or hateful and angry feelings toward our loved ones, we must avoid constantly thinking about their choices and past behaviors. We certainly don't want to deny that it happened and sweep it under the rug, nor do we want to soften the natural consequences that our loved ones have to pay or cover up for them in any way.

Instead we must concentrate on identifying irrational thought patterns and actively replacing them with the new rational thought patterns we are developing. To continue our healing, each irrational thought pattern needs to be replaced by a rational thought pattern.

Thought Patterns

Irrational Thought Pattern: "Committing adultery is the worst thing that he could have ever done to me. My life is ruined. Our family is ruined. I can never, ever be happy again."

Rational Thought Pattern: "It is very sad and disheartening that he chose to commit adultery. It has ripped me apart. It is very discouraging, and some days it is so hard to go on. I have every right to feel discouraged and even depressed at times. But do I want these emotions to escalate? What choices can I make now that I feel these emotions? I can choose to respond to my husband's behavior in a self-enhancing way that empowers me to move forward even when it is difficult. I can begin by looking ahead at the next three to four hours. What can I do during this time to help myself? What needs do I have? How can I get my needs met during this painful time? Whom can I include in my support system? What part can the bishop play? How can I draw nearer to God and feel His love for me?"

Irrational Thought Pattern: "I have done a terrible job as a parent. If I had been more attentive to my son's needs during his adolescent years, he would never have become involved in the gay lifestyle. I can never forgive myself for not being there for him."

Rational Thought Pattern: "I am a parent with my own weaknesses. I may not have been there all the time, but that is not a requirement for being a good parent. My son needed opportunities to make his own choices and learn from his experiences. He is fully accountable to God for his behavior. I will choose to respond to my son's gay lifestyle by supporting him as a son of God, but not condoning his behavior. I can choose to be kind and loving to my son and not beat myself up for my son's behavior."

Irrational Thought Pattern: "I have not been a good wife. I have not met my husband's sexual needs. I can never be sexy like the women in the pornography magazines. I don't have the shape or anything else it takes. I feel so ugly and unacceptable most of the time."

Rational Thought Pattern: "I am human. I have feelings and emotions. My husband is responsible for his behavior. I certainly have some things I can improve upon, just like all human beings, but that does not make me a bad wife. I am not in competition with the women in the pornography magazines. I will choose not to let my husband's behaviors put me into a mindset where I think I am competing with them. I will not compete with lust. I will choose love over lust. My husband needs to make the same choice."

Write your own irrational thought patterns and then write a rational thought pattern replacement.

Irrational Thought Pattern

_____

_____

_____

_____

Rational Thought Pattern

_____

_____

_____

_____

_____

Irrational Thought Pattern

_____

_____

_____

_____

_____

Rational Thought Pattern

_____

_____

_____

_____

_____

Irrational Thought Pattern

_____

_____

_____

_____

_____

Rational Thought Pattern

_____

_____

_____

_____

_____

We only have so much emotional energy each day, and we do not want to weigh ourselves down by dwelling on irrational thoughts that use up our strength. By using rational thought patterns to replace irrational ones, we can begin to look forward with hope. We replace lies with truth, darkness with light. We do not forget the past, but we also do not want to remain captive to it.

Rational thought patterns allow us to move through past challenges toward a joyful, peaceful tomorrow. Irrational thought patterns are like small leaks in our boat. Eventually there is too much water in the boat and we start to sink. Rational thought patterns repair the holes in the "boat of life," preserving the energy we need to paddle against the currents of life.

Will there still be turbulent waters ahead? Yes! Will there still be winds and waves fighting against us? Yes! Yet we can safely reach our destination because the Savior will lead us and not forsake us. Our lifeline and boatmate is the Lord. President Spencer W. Kimball encouraged:

> *The Savior urged us to put our hand to the plow without looking back. In that spirit we are being asked to have humility and a deep and abiding faith in the Lord and to move forward—trusting in him, refusing to be diverted from our course, either by the ways of the world or the praise of the world . . . There is so much yet to be done! Let us, then, move forward; let us continue the journey with lengthened stride. The Lord will lead us along, and he will be in our midst and not forsake us* (*Ensign,* May 1980, 81).

This experience has taken us to the very edge—the edge of extreme emotional pain. We feel that pain often. As we move forward with our rational thought patterns, we can begin to show our trust in the Savior. We slowly give up the past hurt and reach out for a relationship with our Savior. The scriptures counsel:

> *I count not myself to have apprehended: but [this] one thing [I do], forgetting those things which are behind, and reaching forth unto those things which are before,*
> *I press toward the mark for the prize of the high calling of God in Christ Jesus* (Philip. 3:13-14).

Moving forward with a relationship with God and Christ is the key to our healing. We can stay connected to God as we take time to find quiet moments to pray, meditate, read scriptures, sort out our feelings, and get connected with the Spirit and ourselves. A solid relationship with God will help us to diffuse our natural inclination to be angry at our loved ones.

AVOID DOUBLE AND TRIPLE ANGER

The feelings of anger we experience toward our loved ones are very real, intense, and overwhelming. We are human and have feelings of anger. We want ways to deal with our anger so it does not separate us from God and the Spirit. Furthermore, since we have been taught not to harbor bitter feelings or be angry toward others, we may turn our anger toward ourselves. In truth, we are usually angry at our loved ones *and* ourselves—double anger. Our anger was first directed at our loved ones, and then we added anger at ourselves for the way we reacted—self-blame. We are then dealing with anger from two directions and may not realize it.

When a child strays and engages in compulsive behaviors, we may experience three-way anger: (1) Anger at the child; (2) Anger at ourselves for our failings—including being angry at the child; and (3) Anger at our spouse. We may feel that our spouse did not assist the child in a helpful way during critical periods of life. We might think, "If my spouse had been a better father, my son would not have embraced the gay lifestyle." Or "If my wife would have stayed closer to our teenage daughter, she could have talked through her problems and would not have gotten pregnant." When we have double or triple anger brewing within us, our feelings can become intense. However, we can choose to recognize the anger, admit it, learn from it, surrender it, and keep striving to do better. One woman shared:

> *My husband came home from work and said he had resigned. Resigned? For what reason? "As you know, I signed an agreement with my boss that if I used the company's computers to view pornography again, I would be terminated. I was the only one in the office late Thursday and started to look up some information on the Internet for work and then just got this urge to go to one porn site. After the first site I went to another one, then another. About two hours later, I realized what I had done, and wrote my letter of resignation because I knew they had the tracking software and I would be fired once they looked at the reports."*
>
> *I was so upset at my husband for looking at pornography again. He knew the consequences. What about our house payment and food? Was he just thinking about himself again? I just lost it when he told me what he had done. I wanted my husband to see how angry I was, and so I started slamming doors, yelling, and screaming. I just kept slamming every door in my path. I made our oldest daughter (who is six) start crying. She had never seen me this way before. She was scared.*

*About two hours later I had calmed down enough to talk to my husband.
He apologized for what he had done and could see the pain it had caused.
We both decided to talk to the children about my angry outburst. Without
telling them the details, we told them I got real upset and responded in anger.
This seemed to be very healthy for the kids to discuss it and let them talk
about how they felt.*

This woman was angry and had every right to feel the anger and she did. The
emotion of anger is a human emotion, but it's how we choose to handle it after
we feel it that either takes us toward our intended goal or away. The next section
discusses how we can soften or diffuse anger.

USING YOUR *FEET* TO WALK THROUGH THE ANGER

We usually do not like anger and the captive feelings that it brings, but we
do not know how to relinquish it. Heaven knows most of us have tried and
tried. Here's a formula that works: We Feel it. We Experience it. We Express it.
Finally, to let go of anger we can use our *FEET* and walk Through it. Let's look
at each step.

Feel it. We usually recognize when we are getting angry. We should
know ourselves well enough to feel the anger coming on. If we are aware,
we can stop it before the anger gets supercharged and becomes explosive. We've heard the advice before to count to ten, but many times we
do not implement it. Elder Neal A. Maxwell admonished: "In significant
moments of self-expression, we can first count to ten. Such thoughtful
filtering can multiply our offering by ten as a mesh of reflective meekness
filters out destructive and effusive ego" (*Ensign,* May 1999, 23).

Experience it. We should recognize that anger is an emotion. We are
human. Humans become angry at times. We should not necessarily run
from anger, nor should we embrace it. We should experience it and then
deal with it appropriately by expressing it honestly to our loved ones or
to God, then letting it go.

Express it. Directing our anger at the person's behaviors rather than
at the person will usually relieve the intensity. In the example above,
when the husband announced to the wife that he had resigned from his
job because he had used the company's computer and Internet to view
pornography, the wife could have said, "I am very upset that you viewed

pornography again. I can't tell you how angry I am. I am not angry at you, but I am very angry at your behaviors." It is not easy to separate the two, and we often have only seconds to make the attempt; consequently, many times we forget. This does not mean we have failed, nor does it mean that the goal is impossible to achieve. We may not have remembered this time, but we can try to do better next time. We can use the surrender prayer. We can express and surrender our anger to God: "Heavenly Father, I feel so angry right now. I cannot believe the way I feel. I want to surrender these hateful, angry feelings to Thee. I want to give them up, but I need Thy help. Help me surrender. Help me let go. Help me keep trying."

Walk **Through** it. In our previous example, the wife and husband talked through the anger with their children after the incident. To discuss and express their feelings in a calmer setting was very helpful because it relieved the anxiety and fear the children had experienced. It allowed the wife to accept herself as a daughter of God and still dislike the way she had responded. The husband could see that his decision affected more people than himself. He could see the pain that his behaviors created for his innocent wife and children.

We should avoid judging ourselves or our loved ones for isolated moments of anger. Just because we have moments of anger we should not conclude that we are a terrible spouse, parent, sibling, or friend. It may be true that our behaviors at the time we were angry were not good, but we are still sons and daughters of God. We are good at heart. We have divine potential, even though we may display bad behaviors. If we keep replaying our moments of anger, it's likely that we will develop more self-anger with each replay. Striving to do better is a wiser course of action. Elder Joseph B. Wirthlin reminds us:

> *In most cases, growth comes slowly—one step at a time. We understand this when it comes to mastering a musical instrument, becoming an accomplished athlete, or flying a jet aircraft. Yet, we often can scarcely forgive ourselves when we don't make the progress we expect in all areas of our own lives.*
>
> *Great sculptors and artists spend countless hours perfecting their talents. They don't pick up a chisel or a brush and palette, expecting immediate perfection. They understand that they will make many errors as they learn, but they start with the basics, the key fundamentals first.*
>
> *So it is with us. (Ensign, Nov. 2003, 80).*

❧ As you strive to improve, how do you feel about yourself and your progress after reading this quote?

_____

_____

_____

_____

_____

❧ In what ways can you deal with your anger in healthy ways?

_____

_____

_____

_____

❧ How can you separate moments of anger (your behaviors) from your identity as a son or daughter of God?

_____

_____

_____

_____

_____

❧ How would you benefit by visualizing a moment when you could be very angry at your loved one and see yourself walking through the experience in a healthy way?

_____

_____

_____

_____

_____

AVOID THE NEGATIVE THOUGHTS
THAT FUEL ANGER'S FIRES

Anger, like most emotions, needs fuel to keep burning. What is the fuel we often give it? It is the continual replaying in our minds of the negative thoughts we have about our loved ones. Each time we replay the negative thoughts, our anger burns brighter. The anger is always there—morning, midday, and night. We get tired of it and are fearful because we don't know for sure what power the fires of anger may have over us.

From the experiences of Lehi and his family when leaving Jerusalem, we learn about faith, humility, endurance, patience, repentance, blessings, hope, and trying again. There is one more principle we often overlook—how to deal with anger. Can Laman and Lemuel's bad example motivate us to give up our anger? Do we learn from them the fate of those who choose to hold onto their anger? We know that Laman and Lemuel had feelings of anger toward Nephi. Let's suppose that I had Laman in for counseling. Suppose he really wanted to eliminate anger toward his brother and have a working relationship. Where would I begin? Perhaps I would invite him to tell his story about his brother and father and why their family left Jerusalem. I'm quite sure he would go into detail about how hard it was to leave their comfortable home, belongings, and riches. Recounting the story about how they obtained the plates of brass, losing their "gold and silver, and all manner of riches," would probably take most of the first session.

When I welcome him back to the second session, I would ask, "How do you feel, Laman, about your level of anger toward your brother this week. Have you noticed an increase or decrease?"

He more than likely would respond: "Oh, nothing has changed! It's still there. I'm very angry!"

I would ask, "What is it that you tell yourself in order to stay angry at Nephi?"

"What do you mean?" he would ask.

I respond, "In order to stay angry at someone, you have to say some very negative things to yourself about that person."

He quickly replies, "I don't tell myself anything—the thoughts just happen because they're true."

I don't want to confront Laman at this point, and so we continue to talk and discuss other possibilities that could be the source of his anger. Laman always points at Nephi.

"Nephi is the cause of my anger. If he would stop doing what he is doing, I would be just fine."

As the session continues, Laman is more willing to recognize some of the things he replays in his mind to stay angry at Nephi, such as:

> *[Nephi] hast declared unto us hard things, more than we are able to bear* (1 Ne. 16:1).

> *We have wandered much in the wilderness, and we have suffered much affliction, hunger, thirst, and fatigue; and after all these sufferings we must perish in the wilderness with hunger.*
> *They did murmur. . . against [Nephi]* (1 Ne. 16:35-36).

> *Let us slay . . . our brother Nephi, who has taken it upon him to be our ruler and our teacher, who are his elder brethren* (1 Ne. 16:37).

> *He says that the Lord has talked with him, and also that angels have ministered unto him. But behold, we know that he lies unto us; and he tells us these things, and he worketh many things by his cunning arts, that he may deceive our eyes, thinking, perhaps, that he may lead us away into some strange wilderness; and after he has led us away, he has thought to make himself a king and a ruler over us, that he may do with us according to his will and pleasure* (1 Ne. 16:38).

> *Our brother is a fool, for he thinketh that he can build a ship; yea, and he also thinketh that he can cross these great waters* (1 Ne. 17:17).

More sessions may be needed for Laman to uncover all the terrible things he says to himself in order to stay angry at Nephi.

Finally, I feel it is time to say, "Here is my suggestion, Laman. Write this list of negative thoughts down so you will be aware of what you have used in the past to stay angry at Nephi. Then whenever you catch yourself saying one of these statements to yourself, you can choose to change it so you do not become angry."

"What do you mean?" is Laman's reply.

"Let me give you an example. As we review your list, the last negative thought you use to stay angry at Nephi is, 'Our brother is a fool, for he thinketh that he can build a ship; yea, and he also thinketh that he can cross these great waters' (1 Ne. 17:17). When you catch yourself saying this to yourself, change it to, 'My brother may do foolish things at times, but that does not make him a fool. I don't really like my brother's choice to go across these great waters, but he has his agency and can do as he pleases.'"

Laman interrupts, "It sounds like you are playing mind games with me!"

I agree, "It may appear that way, but it's hard to feel an emotion without first thinking something that triggers it."

During our next session, I would prepare a worksheet for Laman and have him write positive replacements for his negative thought patterns:

What I Have Told Myself to Stay Angry at Nephi

"We have wandered much in the wilderness, and we have suffered much affliction, hunger, thirst, and fatigue; and after all these sufferings we must perish in the wilderness with hunger."

They did murmur . . . against [Nephi] (1 Ne. 16:35-36).

What I Will Choose to Tell Myself to Surrender Anger

"It has been so hard in the wilderness. I did not like it at all, but I got through it and learned a lot even though it was very difficult. Looking at the past, we have been able to get through the difficult times even though at the time it did not look like we would. I will continue to look for solutions even though it is hard."

You may be saying to yourself, "Now, come on, Laman was the wicked one and didn't have a testimony that Nephi was being led by God. That was his problem. It wasn't about anger!" But doesn't anger get in the way of our worship of God? Can we stay angry for long periods of time and still have the Spirit? Elder Robert D. Hales reminds us: "The Holy Ghost will withdraw. He cannot be with us if we are angry in our hearts" (*Ensign,* Nov. 2003, 31). If we are without the Holy Ghost, where does that leave us?

What chance does Laman have to let go of anger if he continues to replay in his mind these negative thoughts about Nephi? What is the end result of thinking this way about someone? The scripture is clear: "And after this manner did my brother Laman stir up their hearts to anger" (1 Ne.16:38).

Is it possible that we, in a similar way as Laman, say negative thoughts to ourselves to stay angry at our loved ones? The fact that we see ourselves as the "good guys" and our loved ones as the "bad guys" does not change the validity of the principle.

Choose to Tell Ourselves a Positive Thought Replacement

What are some positive substitutions we can choose to deal with unwanted feelings and emotions? Here is a positive substitution using the previous example.

What I Have Told Myself to Stay Angry at My Loved One

"My husband is a fool for looking at pornography. He talks about all of these great changes he is going to make, but he can't do it. He is never going to do it. The possibility of his changing is about as likely as getting in a row boat in New York and paddling to Europe."

What I Will Choose to Tell Myself to Surrender Anger

"My husband has made some foolish mistakes. Looking at pornography is one of them. I do not like it when he does foolish things, but he is not a fool. He has divine potential within him to change if he will choose to. I can be supportive without enabling him, but he has his agency. I will continue to draw on the Lord's power and Spirit in order to get through the hurt I have."

LETTING GO OF THE ANGER

We begin the process of letting go of the negative feelings by changing what we tell ourselves about our loved ones. Elder Joseph B. Wirthlin counseled:

We must let go of the negative emotions that bind our hearts and instead fill our souls with love, faith, and thanksgiving.

Anger, resentment, and bitterness stunt our spiritual growth. Would you bathe in impure water? Then why do we bathe our spirits with negative and bitter thoughts and feelings?

He further explained:

You can cleanse your heart. You don't have to harbor thoughts and feelings that drag you down and destroy your spirit. . . . Every day drain from your heart the feelings of resentment, rage, and defeat that do nothing but discourage and destroy. Fill your heart with those things that ennoble, encourage, and inspire (Ensign, Sept. 2001, 11).

When you are angry at your loved one, what are you usually telling yourself?

_____

_____

_____

_____

🔖 When you have some peace and contentment, what are you telling yourself about your loved one?

_____

_____

_____

_____

_____

Letting go of the hurt will not be easy. Trusting that God will help us takes faith, but over time it can be done. A wife whose husband committed adultery shared:

> *Finally I learned that we must let go of the past. The Apostle Paul said, "But this one thing I do, forgetting those things which are behind, and reaching forth unto those things which are before, I press toward the mark" (Philip. 3:13–14).*
>
> *I was counseled that I could not begin a new life unless I could turn my back on the old one. Rehashing the events that had transpired, recrimination, and retribution could serve no worthy purpose. In time I was able to do this, and I have never regretted that I did (Ensign, Aug. 1988, 24).*

We need to choose to let anger go. It does not seem to disappear on its own, and so we must use our agency and decide to let anger go. It is not easy, but it can be done. Elder Dallin H. Oaks explained, "The first principle of the gospel is faith in the Lord Jesus Christ, who gives us the light and the strength to overcome the obstacles of mortality and to use our God-given agency to choose the behavior that will lead us to our divine destiny" (*Ensign,* Oct. 1995, 14).

Try to identify your own unhealthy thought patterns and write healthy replacements.

🔖 What I told myself to stay angry at my loved one:

_____

_____

_____

_____

🌿 What I will choose to tell myself to surrender anger:

_____

_____

_____

_____

_____

🌿 What I told myself to stay angry at my loved one:

_____

_____

_____

_____

_____

🌿 What I will choose to tell myself to surrender anger:

_____

_____

_____

_____

_____

🌿 What I told myself to stay angry at my loved one:

_____

_____

_____

_____

_____

_____

What I will choose to tell myself to surrender anger:

_____

_____

_____

_____

_____

How can we surrender anger? How can we let it go? Hasn't the Lord spoken to us?

> *And it came to pass that the Lord was with us, yea, even the voice of the Lord came and did speak many words unto them [Laman and Lemuel], and did chasten them exceedingly; and after they were chastened by the voice of the Lord they did turn away their anger, and did repent of their sins, insomuch that the Lord did bless us again with food, that we did not perish* (1 Ne. 16:39).

Most of us who try to give up anger make some progress and then hit a brick wall. We try to climb over and cannot. We try to go around it and cannot. We try to dig a tunnel under it and we run out of energy. Eventually we discover that with Christ at our side we can walk right through that wall. One wife shared her joy:

> *I had worked and worked, prayed and prayed, fasted and fasted to get rid of my anger. It all seemed to no avail. Every place I went it followed me like a dog on a leash. At the store, at my children's school, on vacation, at church, in the temple, everywhere. Then one day while watching a TV program that showed victims' families sharing their thoughts toward a mass murderer, I was touched by the Spirit like never before. One woman said to the convicted killer, "You held my fifteen-year-old daughter captive and killed her, but you will not hold me captive. I forgive you." It hit me so hard. I was a victim of my anger. I had been in captivity for nearly four years. I will free myself.*

We break through the brick wall and free ourselves by letting go and letting Christ in. We strive to form a partnership with Him to walk through the wall of anger. As we strive to improve our relationship with God and Christ, we should recognize our inadequacies. Even though *we* are imperfect, *God* and *Christ* are not. Elder Jeffrey R. Holland said:

> *I am a father, inadequate to be sure, but I cannot comprehend the burden it must have been for God in His heaven to witness the deep suffering and crucifixion of His Beloved Son in such a manner. His every impulse and instinct must have been to stop it, to send angels to intervene—but He did not intervene. He endured what He saw because it was the only way that a saving, vicarious payment could be made for the sins of all His other children from Adam and Eve to the end of the world. I am eternally grateful for a perfect Father and His perfect Son, neither of whom shrank from the bitter cup nor forsook the rest of us who are imperfect, who fall short and stumble, who too often miss the mark"* (Ensign, May 1999, 14).

List ways you can strive to walk in His paths. List items that will help you to stretch, but are also achievable.

_____

_____

_____

_____

_____

_____

TAKE RESPONSIBILITY FOR FEELINGS AND EMOTIONS

When our spouses are the ones who are engaged in the compulsive sexual behaviors, it is important that we let them know in an appropriate way the pain and sorrow we feel. Our first reaction may be to pretend that it does not hurt. However, this pretense is like building up pressure inside, and in a sudden instance our emotions might gush out like an erupting volcano, damaging all of those around us.

To avoid such eruptions, we must give expression to the emotions we are feeling. Timing is important. We want our loved ones' full attention. One woman speaking to her husband said:

> *I just want you to know how hurt I am. I cannot express the pain I feel right now. I have cried and cried until I don't think I can cry anymore. It's*

been uncontrollable sobbing. I don't understand why you did what you did, but I want you to know that I am hurting inside and at times feel so helpless.

There are several key points to note: (1) The wife took responsibility for how she felt; (2) She did not blame her husband for his behavior; and (3) Her openness provides an opportunity for the husband to see the consequences and the hurt his behavior has caused. This is very important for the husband to see because often addictive behavior is accompanied by a lack of empathy for others. Beginning to see the consequences of his behavior can be a catalyst to helping him develop empathy toward others once more. It is a starting place—somewhere to begin, even though some loved ones will not respond favorably to openness.

In most relationships, our spouses' problems started long before we knew them. Regarding our children, siblings, or other loved ones, the problem usually started long before it was made known to us. In other words, our loved ones were entrenched with the problem long before we discovered it. The problem may have escalated over time. But the situation we are in has been building up pressure slowly—just like the volcano we spoke of before—and now we have experienced a huge explosion.

Sometimes we wish that all of our shattered dreams and hopes could be put back together to make life as it used to be. But things will never be just the same. We would not want them to be. We want these relationships to grow beyond the shackles of the past toward a more joyful future. The Atonement of Jesus Christ can heal us from the pain and redeem our loved ones from their sins, but life will be different because of what we have experienced. The Atonement provides healing for each person as well as the relationship if there are two partners who are willing to try. Even if our loved ones do not want to try, we can still receive all that God intends for us personally. "Learn that he who doeth the works of righteousness shall receive his reward, even peace in this world, and eternal life in the world to come" (D&C 59:23).

It is true that the memories of the past will always be with us, but they do not need to dictate our ability to find joy and peace. The pain is not forgotten, but the healing power of the Atonement allows us to move forward, stay connected, and fulfill the covenants we have made with the Lord. Even though there are many external events that do impact us, we need to remember that there are many important internal choices that we can still make.

External Events	Internal Choices
My loved one does not want to go to counseling.	I can choose to go and get the help I need—whether my spouse goes or not.
My loved one lapsed and looked at pornography again.	I can choose to tell him how it makes me feel when he looks at pornography. I can also say that it must be very difficult to stop. I can assure him that I love him, if I do, but his behavior is not acceptable, because looking at pornography is sinful.
My loved one tells me I am making such a big deal out of looking at naked woman on the Internet. He says, "After all, they are just pictures!"	I don't have to agree with my husband's opinion, debate, or argue about it. I am entitled to my own opinion. It does not matter what my husband or anyone else thinks about pornography, only what the Lord thinks matters. I know it is wrong and unacceptable behavior. Period.
If my husband does not get sex as often as he wants, he becomes moody, mean and angry.	I can choose when to have sexual intimacy too! It's not just one-sided. It's true I should be sensitive and understanding, but I recognize that I still have a choice. I can suggest to my husband when we are both calm and willing to discuss it, that we have a mature discussion about our sexual intimacy. I can also suggest that we go to counseling. My husband's pouting and sulking when he does not get sexual intimacy is not a mature way to handle his unmet desires. I am even less interested in sexual intimacy when he behaves this way. He is therefore sabotaging his own desires.
My husband keeps asking me when I will forgive him.	I can say, "I'm sorry I do not know when; it is a process, not an event. However, I will promise you that I will continue to work on it, as you continue to work on being forgiven."

External Events	Internal Choices
My husband keeps asking when I will trust him again.	Trust is based on actual evidence that shows improved behavior. It has to be earned; it can't be demanded. I can say, "I will begin trusting again, when I see that changes have taken place and there is progress being made toward improvement."
My husband tells me I should accept him and his looking at pornography just like he accepts me and my weaknesses.	Accepting my husband's sinful behavior enables him to continue the behavior and destroys our relationship. Being an enabler postpones my loved one's healing. There is a big difference between a weakness like one's lack of patience and a sinful behavior such as pornography or any other compulsive sexual behavior that violates covenants.

POSITIVE REPLACEMENTS

Dealing with the emotional pain is much easier when we balance our day and work hard to stay busy doing productive things to occupy our time and energy. Some days we will not feel like doing much, and that is okay. But other days we will have more energy and can do more. President Gordon B. Hinckley encouraged:

> Brothers and sisters, look above your trials. Try to forget your own pain as you work to alleviate the pain of others. Mingle together as opportunity affords. It is important that we do so. We need others to talk with and to share our feelings and faith with. Cultivate friends. Begin by being a good friend to others.
>
> Share your burdens with the Lord. He has said to each of us: "Come unto me, all ye that labour and are heavy laden, and I will give you rest. Take my yoke upon you, and learn of me; for I am meek and lowly in heart: and ye shall find rest unto your souls. For my yoke is easy, and my burden is light" (Matt. 11:28-30).
>
> May I suggest that you go to work on your family history. You will become enthralled with it. (*Ensign*, Mar. 1997, 63).

President Hinckley encourages us to "look above our trials" by implementing the following six suggestions:

1. Reach out and help others who may be in pain.

2. Mingle with others as opportunity affords.

3. Talk with and share our feelings and faith with others.

4. Be a good friend to others.

5. Share your burdens with the Lord.

6. Go to work on your family history.

Finding a positive replacement and achieving balance in our lives will not be easy. Elder Marvin J. Ashton offered this advice:

> *Change is hard. Rather than going through the struggle to overcome a bad habit or rectify a mistake, some of us choose to make excuses for inactivity. Progress comes as we are able to give up something for something we want more. Honesty with oneself and setting of desirable but attainable goals day by day can determine the paths we follow. One might make a list of goals and then a price list for each goal. One day at a time the price of change can be paid. The cost will then not be overwhelming (Ensign, May 1979, 68).*

How can you apply Elder Ashton's suggestion in your healing?

_____

_____

_____

_____

_____

_____

_____

SELF-CARE

We may not get from our loved ones what we really desire or need. They may not have the ability to provide or even to understand what we are asking of them. Or they may not feel like meeting our needs; they may purposely *not* meet them. This leaves us with a choice regarding self-care when our desires or needs are not fulfilled by our loved one. Here are some questions to ask yourself to *engage in self-awareness:*

- How well do your know yourself and your innermost thoughts?

- Are you in touch with your emotions—with what you are feeling?

- Have you decided what improvements you need to make?

- Have you decided what improvements need to be made in the relationship?

- What desires or wishes do you have that are not being met? Have you discussed these desires or wishes with your spouse?

- Are there ways you can be more assertive in order to get more of your desires met?

- If your needs are not going to be met, what choices do you have?

- If your loved one chooses not to change, what choices do you still have?

A co-worker of mine was going through a very difficult divorce. She had been in tears many times while at work. She had shared openly with me and with others how difficult and painful the divorce process had been. She and her estranged husband had both made issues about several joint possessions. After they had been in the divorce process for about a year, their last day before the judge was scheduled. I thought about her when I got to work that day. Late that morning a dozen long-stemmed roses were delivered to our office. They were delicate and fresh and carried a beautiful scent. I thought to myself how wonderful it was that someone (I assumed it might be her father) remembered this co-worker on such a difficult day.

Early in the afternoon she returned and announced joyfully that the divorce was final.

I was the one who got to tell her about the flowers. She exclaimed, "That's wonderful!" She acted very surprised that someone would send her flowers. She read the card, started laughing, and extended it toward me. She said, "You have got to read this!"

The card read, "Lorna, you are an awesome person. Way to go! You did it!"

I was a little puzzled because there was no signature on the card. I inquired, "Who sent these to you?"

Laughing even more than before, she exclaimed, "I sent them to myself!"

She knew herself well enough to know that she needed something to help her celebrate that last day in court. She loved flowers and knew how special it was for her to receive them. She knew that no one else would be sending flowers, and so she sent them to herself.

There may be many things we would like our loved ones to do for us, but they may not be willing or able to provide those things. We know ourselves better than anyone else, and sometimes we need to be the ones to extend the tenderness and nurturing we need so much but may not be getting from those around us.

APPLYING THE SURRENDER PROCESS TO PAINFUL EXPERIENCES

How do we surrender our trials? How do we give up the hurt and pain of the past? Here is one process that provides self-reflection, inner peace, and eventual healing. We surrender by turning our painful plight over to the Lord. We let Him carry the load. Here is one way to begin this process:

1. Write down the experience.

2. Identify unrealistic expectations or irrational thinking errors.

3. Write irrational thoughts that you have had throughout the experience.

4. Work to replace the irrational thoughts with rational thoughts.

5. Write divine affirmations to remind you of God's love for you.

6. Share honest feelings with your loved one when appropriate.

7. Know that there are times when it's important to confront your loved one.

8. Know that this whole experience is very difficult, but you can get through it.

Write Down the Experience

By writing the experience, we can begin to see it from a third-person viewpoint. This helps us to be more objective and look for "truth." Our writing also diffuses some anger, resentment, pain, and hurt.

Our goal is to develop a more realistic and workable viewpoint about the trials and difficulties we face in life. This does not mean in any way that we minimize the seriousness of our present condition or our loved ones' behaviors, but we begin to adopt new thinking patterns that allow us to stay on the healing path. By changing our thinking patterns, we begin to see solutions to our problems rather than just staring at them and remaining emotionally frozen.

Some time ago, a wife whose husband had a history of compulsive sexual behaviors sent me an e-mail explaining her painful situation. I read this woman's e-mail, divided up the paragraphs, and suggested responses that were more rational and that might help her view her situation from a perspective that would facilitate her healing. I wrote each response in first person so that she could relate to them and repeat them to herself as though they were her own words.

I recommend as you go through this workbook that you read this dialogue when you are alone and can read the first-person responses out loud. When we verbalize something, we retain it longer and it begins to become part of our belief system. I generally recommend reading the responses out loud for a number of consecutive days.

The normal text that follows is her e-mail; the text in italics shows the responses that I prepared for her in an effort to be helpful:

> We both grew up in good families, strong in the Church. He served a mission, and we married in the temple.

> *These were wonderful choices. However, our continuing happiness depends on choosing to live the commandments each day, repenting when necessary, and becoming truly converted to the gospel of Jesus Christ. I thought we were both doing this, but I was wrong. Though my own obedience to the gospel can give me strength to endure trials, it does not make it possible to avoid having trials.*

> One day my husband came to me and told me he had something to tell me. When the words came out of his mouth, "I have an addiction to pornography and masturbation," I was COMPLETELY and TOTALLY shocked.

> *I had every right to be COMPLETELY and TOTALLY shocked when my husband told me, "I have an addiction to pornography and masturbation." This is a natural response. My husband had kept this secret for a long time and had been living a lie. Even though I was shocked, I am glad that he told me so that he has the opportunity to begin facing the addiction and not hiding it anymore. Even though it is so hard to hear, I would rather know the truth. I'm glad he trusted me enough to tell me—that's a compliment to me. Hopefully he will choose to get the help he so desperately needs.*

> He told me that it all began when he was a young boy. The problem would come and go, but it started up again one day when he found pornographic materials in the recycling dumpster outside our apartment shortly after we were married.

This behavior, like most compulsive behaviors, often begins during the adolescent years or even earlier. Often Satan lies to children and young adults by saying, "Once you get married you will have the real thing so you won't even want to look at pornography anymore, but for now it's okay." Unfortunately this is one of Satan's traps. Getting married does not solve one's addiction to lust. It's the addiction to lust that is the problem, not the lack of sexual intimacy.

I am still in shock, and especially in shock that this has been going on for 14 years—my whole marriage! And all this time I knew nothing about it.

He was actually addicted to masturbation and pornography long before he ever met me. My husband chose to hide this behavior from me. This was deceitful, but it was his choice, not mine. Yes, I wish he had not made the choice to keep it hidden from me, but now that it is out in the open I can choose how I want to respond. This will be difficult, but I will get through it. I can get the help I need too!

There were things in our marriage that bothered me. When being intimate, I didn't feel like much love was involved. He would make comments to me about my body quite often, and at times he would tell me that he thought about sex all the time. I thought this was a "man" thing—that all men were this way. But I pretty much was fooled all these years.

There were things about our sexual relations that didn't feel right to me. I was uncomfortable with some things that occurred during intimacy. I now understand better the reasons my husband said certain things or acted a certain way during sexual intimacy since his viewpoint about intimacy has been greatly impacted by his pornography usage. Pornography distorts reality. Pornography takes God-given intimacy and diminishes it to lust and makes it solely for personal gratification.

Here is one reason I was completely shocked: I had always greatly admired my husband because anytime a TV commercial came on that had a woman dressed immodestly, he immediately looked at me to avoid watching the woman.

My husband acted a certain way when I was with him. When he was alone, he acted completely different. No wonder I am so shocked! However, his behavior with me may have mirrored his determination never to get caught up in pornography again. This is quite common for the person in an addiction to say, "I'm never going to do it again." He may be successful in avoiding any kind of temptation for a while until the next time he gives in and acts out.

As I said, his confession last October changed my life. I am a very sensitive person—very, very sensitive—and now I wonder if I will ever find happiness again.

This whole thing has been so painful and hurtful. It will take time to work through all these issues. However, as I continue to deal with my own issues, I can find happiness regardless of what my husband chooses to do. This will not be easy to go through. It will be very hard, but I CAN get through this and continue to heal. My happiness cannot be based solely on what my husband chooses to do. My joy and happiness need to be centered on Christ. Christ will never fail me!

I hope you can help me out. I will share some of our story with you, share my feelings and how my emotions are right now, and I hope with all my heart that you can give me some counsel to help me heal.

I want to get help for my own healing. I know I can only be responsible for me. Agency allows me to seek help and to make choices. My spouse has his own agency. He may not choose to get the help he needs, but I can meet with my bishop, follow his counsel, and perhaps meet with a professional counselor too.

He confessed in October. We were due to have our fifth baby in December. I felt sure inside it was going to be another son—we already had one boy and three girls. After he told me, I felt devastated and wondered what I should do. I didn't want to be married to him anymore. However, one day as I was driving and thinking about things, the Spirit told me very strongly that my husband really did love me and that it was meant to be that we got married. This changed everything for me, but it was still hard to adjust to this new reality.

This situation is so painful. I have days when I want to stay in the marriage and work it out and then I have days when I want to leave. This is natural. These feelings are normal. I will continue to have "roller coaster" days with my emotions.

I need to continue to stay close to the Spirit so that I can be guided and directed. It will take a great deal of effort to know when the Spirit is guiding me. In fact, a common thought is "I am so confused that I don't know if it is the Spirit talking to me or if it is just my emotions."

I felt the Atonement working in my life so powerfully.

This is the most important sentence I have written. This is where I find help. This is where I get hope to continue on. "And he cometh into the world that he may save all men if they will hearken unto his voice; for behold, he suffereth the pains of all men, yea, the pains of every living creature, both men, women, and children, who belong to the family of Adam" (2 Ne. 9:21).

We show our faith by accepting His Atonement and recognizing that our sins and our loved ones' sins can be forgiven. Elder Boyd K. Packer explained: "I know of no sins connected with the moral standard for which we cannot be forgiven. I do not exempt abortion. The formula is 'Behold, he who has repented of his sins, the same is forgiven, and I, the Lord, remember them no more'" (Ensign, May 1992, 68).

After his confession in October, my husband seemed to be doing very well. He felt really good about himself and how things were going for him. Then in the middle of February I started having feelings inside that things were not going so well. As I mentioned, it was incredibly painful for me to learn of his addiction, but I decided that I didn't want my husband to know just how painful it really was for me, because I wanted him to be completely honest with me. I worried that if he knew how much it hurt me, he would be too afraid to tell me if he had a slip-up and I would never know. So I hid my pain.

My husband can benefit by seeing my pain. I need to show him that I am human and it does hurt. It might help him to see my emotional pain so that he can see the negative consequences of his behaviors. Satan tells individuals who view pornography that there are no consequences—that it's a natural thing to do.

I need to be more open with my husband regarding my feelings and emotions about his masturbation and pornography addiction. If I choose not to be more open but continue to veil my feelings, eventually I will emotionally explode on him. I want to choose an appropriate time to discuss my feelings, but I do not want to hide them anymore.

I cannot control whether my husband will be emotionally open with me, but I can make it clear to him what I am feeling and experiencing. Compulsive sexual behavior often has its roots in emotional and spiritual problems, not sexual problems. Compulsive sexual behaviors are used to cover up emotional hurt and spiritual inadequacies.

When my husband deals with his emotions in a healthy way and increases his spirituality, he can surrender his compulsive sexual behaviors. It will not be easy, but it can be done.

Another reason I didn't tell him how hurt I was is that I wanted my husband to adore me. I could see how happy he was that he had confessed the truth to me and I was there for him. Quite often he would say how very blessed he was to be married to me. That would make me feel so happy. I wanted him to adore me so much that he would never have the desire again to look at pornography or to masturbate.

No amount of adoration for me would solve his underlying emotional and spiritual problems, and I do not have the power to control my husband by being a certain way. He must choose his own behavior. He is accountable for what he does and cannot blame others for his actions.

It's true that it would be nice to be admired and adored by my spouse, but realistically that will not happen all the time. There are certainly times when I do not adore my husband. This all-or-nothing attitude about wanting to be adored 24/7 sets me up for discouragement and depression. I do not need my husband's nonstop adoration in order to feel good about myself.

Furthermore, overcoming his sexual problem does not depend on me, my appearance, or whether he adores me. His problem is addiction to lust, and I can never satisfy lust. My husband needs to surrender lust and accept my love.

There are some things that I might be contributing to our overall marriage problems, and I am willing to learn what they are and make an effort to change them. However, my husband is responsible for his own behavior. I will not allow my feelings of worth to be wrapped up in his behavior.

I will focus on the knowledge that I am a daughter of God. God loves me perfectly. I will remind myself daily of His perfect love.

As I said in February, I felt like things were not going as well.

"And by the power of the Holy Ghost ye may know the truth of all things" (Moro. 10:5).

I did not want to accuse him, and so I prayed fervently that he would talk to me. Sometimes he did. He would share some of his struggles with temptation. He was hanging in there to be strong, but on a couple of things he could not and had given in. I tried to give him a lot of support and love and encouragement, but I still felt that he was not telling me the whole story.

Yes, it would be nice if my husband were more open all the time, but I cannot control that. However, I can tell him how it makes me feel when he is not open with me. For example, I can say, "I feel like you are so distant right now because we are not talking or sharing our feelings."

There will be times when it is important to confront him and be direct.

We rarely get to date. One day we finally decided that we could leave our oldest in charge, take the baby, and go out for lunch.

Making time for each other is healthy. What can we do as a couple to make this more of a priority in our lives? Let's brainstorm and see what we can discover. Does a walk or just a short drive to get a cold drink count? What are our choices?

A good marriage does not just happen. It takes work, prioritizing what we want in our marriage and working hard to improve our communication with one another.

This time together was very exciting for us since we so seldom go on dates. I tell you this because I was shocked at what happened the day after we finally went out together. I felt so hurt!

The very next day I had to do some things at the church to get ready for an activity, and I took our kids with me. My husband was home alone working at the house.

While I was at the church, I felt something bad was happening. I felt strongly that I should call my husband. I tried our home telephone number, but it was busy and so I called his cell phone. He answered, and at the end of the phone call he told me that he loved me.

I hung up, called the home phone again, and it was still busy. I kept calling and kept getting the busy signal. I went into the church and just shrunk down. I knew my husband was on the Internet looking at pornography.

I was still determined to be happy. I came home, and in our conversation I said to him, "So you're not nervous to be alone in the house anymore?"

He said, "No." When I told him of the strange thing that had happened with trying to call him, he told me that he had been outside getting some things from his car.

Later that night he admitted that he had been on the Internet looking at women while I was talking to him. I was hurt. We had just had a date the day before! He had told me he loved me while looking at someone else, and he still stayed on the computer looking even after we hung up.

My husband made unhealthy choices while I was away from the house. There are two sides to my husband. There is the nice guy who is attentive to my needs and the family's needs most of the time—and then there is the guy who is addicted to pornography.

It is not women he is looking at; it is pornography. I do not like my husband's behavior when he looks at pornography. I will remind my husband of how hurt I feel because of his behavior. It's good to be direct and say, "I feel so hurt because we went out to lunch and had a wonderful time, and then the very next day you were looking at pornography. I want you to know that your behavior really hurts me. I love what we did yesterday going to lunch, but I hate your pornography usage."

I have to be careful and decide how long I want to carry hurt. I cannot be my best self when I am feeling hurt. By telling him about my hurt it will help to diffuse it and I need to continue to find other healthy ways to address the hurt.

I want to focus on what I can do and what I have control over. I don't have control over what my husband chooses to do. I can only control my response. I will recognize that my husband needs help, and I will do my part to work through issues that jointly apply to our marriage. But I will no longer be responsible for my husband's behavior or allow it to make me feel hurt for extended periods of time.

After that happened in February, we had the computer fixed so that you had to know the password in order to log on to the Internet. I was the only one who knew the password. I felt so much better, knowing he could not get on the computer. However, our daughter loves the computer and was getting frustrated by it, and so I let her know the password.

May came along, and one night I returned home after a Relief Society meeting and my husband told me that while our daughter was on the computer, he saw the password. It was late, and so we didn't make the change that night. We went to bed.

The next morning I was tired and stayed in bed; my husband got the girls off to school. I wasn't asleep, but I was lying there resting. My husband came into the room, stood by the door, and asked if I was asleep. I faked sleep, wondering what he would do.

I heard him log onto the computer and then go into the bathroom. I stayed still, pretending that I was asleep. He then came into the room, and gently nudged me. I pretended to wake up. He kissed me goodbye and told me he loved me.

Once again, my husband can choose to keep the behavior going or he can choose to stop it. This is his choice and he must be responsible. Passwords may help in the short-term, but eventually my husband has to choose to give up the compulsive behaviors.

He acted as if nothing had gone wrong—acted normal and happy but I knew he had been viewing pornography. The next day as he got up to get the children off to school, he first turned on the computer. After they left the same things happened while I faked being asleep. This went on for three days.

My husband has to choose not to do it anymore. No one can make that choice for him. I do not have the power to change my husband. This would take away his agency. There would be no salvation for my husband if I could change him. He has to choose to change, connect with the Savior and His Atonement, and continue on the healing path.

I was prepared that when he came to me and reported his lapse, as he promised he would, I would still be supportive, and we would be more determined to fight this thing.

Having someone to be accountable to can be helpful in the short-term, but in the long-run we all need to be accountable to God. I am not my husband's mother. I am his wife. I have to be careful that his reporting to me does not become like a little boy reporting to his mother. We should really discuss this as a couple and see what will work for us. Usually it is helpful to let the bishop handle my husband's slip-ups. This is the way the Lord has outlined repentance. Confessing to the wife is important too so that she knows the seriousness of the situation, but how often do I really want to know? By letting the bishop be the one to hear the confession, I can focus on being a wife and a mother to my children. It is not healthy for me to play the role of wife, mother to my children, and mother to my husband. I will only be a wife to my husband and a mother to my children. Again, my husband and I need to discuss what we will do when there is a slip-up.

Let me back up. When all this happened, I knew I still loved my husband, but my feelings for him were not deep anymore. I didn't feel that special love for him I used to feel. So during all this time I had been praying hard that I could love him deeply again—I wanted that so badly. It took six months, and then one night in April we were talking about when we met and about our courtship. As I heard him share how he felt, my love for him finally deepened and I was in love again!

My husband's behavior has made me wonder about my feelings for him from time to time. This is normal and natural. Some days I will be madly in love with him and other days I will want to pack up the kids and leave. It is good for me to write down my feelings when I am having a good day so that I can refer back to them when I am having a bad day.

Anyway, back to what happened in May. I tried so hard to be patient waiting for my husband to come forward and tell me what happened—that he had been looking again at pornography—but he didn't. It was getting so hard for me and I did not want to be upset with him. So when I finally couldn't take it anymore, I decided to take the kids and go home and visit my parents. It had been a while since we had visited, and school was getting out for summer.

I focused so much on my husband's behavior that I lost the emotional, spiritual, and physical strength to go on. This is what Satan wants. I could no longer talk rationally to my husband because I had let things build up to the point that I lost emotional control. I recognize that my husband has chosen a behavior that would be very hard for any wife to understand. It is so painful at times. However, I am an important person. I am a child of God. I have wishes, dreams, and desires too. I will not allow my husband's behavior to control my emotional well-being. Taking a break away from my husband may be good for both of us, but if I can discuss my feelings with him sooner, rather than later, it will usually help to diffuse emotions before they get out of control.

So I decided to go. My husband stayed and worked. During the time I was at my parent's home, I worried about what was going on with my husband. One night I had a strong feeling come over me that things were happening while I was gone. After almost a week he came to my parents' house. (We live several hours away from both our parents.) He came that weekend because a relative was getting married. Shortly after he arrived at my parents' house, he seemed irritated at me for no reason at all. And that's what did it for me. I had been patient long enough. We had been apart for nearly a week, but instead of being sweet he was upset at me. I exploded that night, something I DID NOT want to have happen. It was bad.

Although I want to avoid doing it again, I can accept the fact that I emotionally exploded. I am human. I have emotions. I have feelings. When I do not choose to deal with my emotions in a healthy way, they build up and I explode. I want to continue to learn about myself and keep focused on my issues and what I can control. However, I can't beat myself up every time I do not do as well as I would like. I can accept my humanness, leave for a while, and see where to go from here.

I told him I knew things were happening and he didn't follow through with our deal that he would tell me. At first he denied it all and was not honest as I brought things up. Finally he began telling the truth, that he did have problems while I was gone. Our daughter has a computer in her room just for typing—she is writing a book. It is not hooked up to the Internet. He found a long phone cord and hooked it up and was able to go on the Internet with her computer. It was the worst weekend of my life. I told him that I hated him, that he just lost his family, and that I was leaving him. It was a bad night!

These are things that my husband needed to hear. I could not go on any longer and hold my emotions in. This is exactly how I felt at the time and I said it. I want my husband to understand where I am coming from so he does not have any questions in his mind. However, I want to learn what I can do now and in the future to diffuse my resentment and anger. Can I discuss these issues with my husband before I explode? Can I initiate a conversation with him early on and tell him how I feel? Can I say, "I really feel hurt inside." When you choose to stay in the addiction, I feel unloved and have feelings of low self-worth. If I use the word "I," then I am taking responsibility for me instead of saying to my husband, "when you view pornography you make me feel hurt."

We made it back home Sunday night. Monday morning I called my brother—he was the only person I confided in about the whole deal. He is a bishop. He talked to me for a long time and I decided not to leave. But I still was not feeling happy. I invited my husband to talk and tell me more things about his problems. It was all very hard to take in all at once. I still am in shock over this whole thing. So here I am. I stayed, but I'm not happy. We are having a hard time. My brother gave me a blessing. In it he told me that it would be a "long-term endurance."

I need to recognize that my brother is a very important part of my support. Are there any other family members that can give me support? Have I talked with my bishop? Do I need a stronger support system? This blessing is wonderful that I received. These words "long-term" are important for me to remember. It will take long-term endurance. Endurance is not self-pity and it does not need to be done alone. I have a support system. I have a bishop. I have my relationship with the Savior. Together we can endure. Healing is a process. My husband can change over time, but only by surrendering to the power of Christ and His Atonement. President Ezra Taft Benson counseled, "You do change human nature, your own human nature, if you surrender it to Christ. Human nature has been changed in the past. . . . And only Christ can change it" (Ensign, July 1989, 4).

I really don't think my husband realizes how much I am hurting. I have such low self-esteem. He keeps talking about how his low self-esteem has caused it all. But, you know, I always have had low self-esteem. My father was very mean and abused us emotionally. While growing up some of my peers were mean to me quite often and made comments about how I looked, but I never resorted to this kind of thing. Why did he?

It's hard to know why he chose those behaviors. It is important to remember that he did choose to become involved with pornography. It was not thrust upon him. Regarding myself, I have self-value because I am a daughter of God and He loves me perfectly. This is where I can feel secure. This is where I can feel loved and cared for. I admit that I have my own issues that I need to work on. As I work on my issues and connect with God and Christ, I can have inner peace. I will remind myself of these divine affirmations.

The scriptures have numerous examples of divine affirmations. These verses include true statements about who we are and the love that God and His Son have for us:

I will have compassion upon you (D&C 64:2).

For ye are all the children of God by faith in Christ Jesus (Gal. 3:26).

I have forgiven you your sins (D&C 64:3).

He has brought them into his everlasting light, yea, into everlasting salvation; and they are encircled about with the matchless bounty of his love (Alma 26:15).

He hath filled me with his love, even unto the consuming of my flesh (2 Ne. 4:21).

I am with you to bless you and deliver you forever (D&C 108:8).

But behold, the Lord hath redeemed my soul from hell; I have beheld his glory, and I am encircled about eternally in the arms of his love (2 Ne. 1:15).

I have loved thee with an everlasting love: therefore with loving kindness have I drawn thee (Jer. 31:3).

Verily, thus saith the Lord unto you whom I love (D&C 95:1).

And the great and wonderful love made manifest by the Father and the Son in the coming of the Redeemer into the world (D&C 138:3).

I will encircle thee in the arms of my love (D&C 6:20).

And he will love thee, and bless thee (Deut. 7:13).

As the Father hath loved me, so have I loved you: continue ye in my love (John 15:9).

I believe it has to do with being truly converted to the gospel of Jesus Christ.

This is truly the key for my husband and me. My husband has to choose to be converted to the gospel of Jesus Christ and not follow after the false god of lust.

I have read where other men read the scriptures, prayed, and fulfilled their callings in the Church and yet still had this problem. That is true for us. We read our scriptures, we pray, we have family home evening, and this still happened.

We can choose to pray. We can choose to fulfill our church calling. We can choose to read the scriptures. But my husband also has to choose not to look at pornography, to learn what emotions he is trying to cover up, to get counseling, and to apply what he learns.

I really don't think I could handle another slip-up. I seriously don't.

I cannot deal with carrying my husband's sins any longer. I am not supposed to carry them. As my husband repents, the Savior will carry his sins so my husband can be free of this behavior. I need to stop trying to be my husband's Savior and let the Savior Himself carry and atone for my husband's sins. The Savior has the power to carry my husband's sins. I do not have that power.

I am having the hardest time with this. I feel so ugly and so unattractive. I feel that I couldn't satisfy my husband. I keep thinking that if I were prettier, he wouldn't have looked at other women. If I satisfied him more while being intimate, he would have never done this. I hurt so badly.

The issue is not about me. It is about my husband's addiction. The issue is his addiction to lust. Lust can never be satisfied. It would not matter to whom my husband was married—he would still be likely to have the problem.

Satan wants men to think exactly the way I am thinking—that their wives are not pretty enough and so they will have to leave the wife and family and go on an endless hunt to find the perfect woman who will fill all their lustful desires. No woman can ever satisfy the lustful wants of a man who is addicted to masturbation and pornography. Even the women who pose for pornography cannot do it. These women are paid to look and talk a certain way to get men addicted. They are led by Satan.

I am in love with my husband. Love and lust are not the same. Love is from God. Lust is from Satan. I will not think less of myself because my husband is addicted to lust. He is not addicted to women. He is addicted to lust. If my husband chooses to surrender lust and give it up, he can be healed. I will be the best I can be, but my goal is to give love to my husband and receive love. Lust kills love.

I prayed for six months to love my husband again deeply, and a month later he hurt me again. How can he tell me he loves me and act like everything's normal right after he has a relapse? He must not love me deeply. I never would have done this to him.

Since I never would have done this to my husband, it makes sense to me that he never should have done this to me. However, that thought process is NOT rational because it takes away my husband's agency and assumes that he should think like I think.

Maybe I would not have done this exact thing (view pornography) to my husband. However, there might be other things that I do that make my husband feel unloved. I should ask my husband and see what I discover.

My husband has two sides. One side of him is kind and loving, and the other side seeks pornography and the drug of lust. I cannot imagine how hard it must be for my husband to try to live both lives. The Savior made it clear how serious this problem is: "No man can serve two masters: for either he will hate the one, and love the other; or else he will hold to the one, and despise the other. Ye cannot serve God and mammon" (Matt 6:24).

Over and over I read that this problem never leaves men even after they have stopped—that it's always there. How can I live with that? I struggle that he's seen so many women throughout our whole marriage. I struggle that he has had so many sexual fantasies about other women.

There is no question that my husband has viewed a lot of pornography, which is very unhealthy for him and our relationship. There is no question that this does affect our relationship. However, my husband CAN choose to surrender the compulsive behavior and be healed. This is not easy. It will take a substantial amount of work, faith, prayers, and self-discovery.

The Savior does have the power to heal my husband, if he will allow it. The Savior said, "Will ye not now return unto me, and repent of your sins, and be converted, that I may heal you?" (3 Ne. 9:13) When I remind myself of this scripture, I realize that my husband can be healed. But he has to choose the healing path. As much as I desire that he would, he must make the choice.

Satan wants me to think that my husband cannot change so that I can have an excuse to be discouraged, feel unloved, and be depressed. When there is a slip-up, all of this negative thinking comes back. I will not allow Satan to put these thoughts into my mind anymore. However, I will also be realistic, know the seriousness of the problem, and follow the Spirit to make future decisions that are best for my children and me.

I can't even go out in public anymore without getting depressed. I see so many women who dress immodestly, so many beautiful women. I see the magazines by the checkout counter. I feel so incredibly inferior; I even struggle at church.

My husband has been caught in the pornography trap, and I need to be careful not to get caught in the "comparison trap." The world stresses the importance of outside appearance. Satan wants me to compare myself to other women on this basis alone so that I will be discouraged and have no feeling of self-worth. When I am discouraged, I cannot be the best wife or mother that I can be. Elder Jeffrey R. Holland gave a masterful talk on this subject in the April 2002 General Conference. He said:

> *One observer has written, "In a world that constantly compares people, ranking them as more or less intelligent, more or less attractive, more or less successful, it is not easy to really believe in a [divine] love that does not do the same. When I hear someone praised," he says, "it is hard not to think of myself as less praiseworthy; when I read about the goodness and kindness of other people, it is hard not to wonder whether I myself am as good and kind as they; and when I see trophies, rewards, and prizes being handed out to special people, I cannot avoid asking myself why that didn't happen to me." If left unresisted, we can see how this inclination so embellished by the world will ultimately bring a resentful, demeaning view of God and a terribly destructive view of ourselves. Most "thou shalt not" commandments are meant to keep us from hurting others, but I am convinced the commandment not to covet is meant to keep us from hurting ourselves (Ensign, May 2002, 63–64).*

How can I ever be happy again? How can I get over this? Every day, tapes play back in my mind of things he has told me. I think of all the women he's seen and the fantasies he's had with them. I am having a very, very, very hard time.

I need to play a different tape in my head. I need to remind myself that, as a couple, we are now addressing certain issues for the first time. Our marriage is broken. Also, my husband is now identifying, perhaps for the first time, the underlying emotional issues that drive his compulsive sexual behaviors. This is wonderful to finally start addressing real issues; resolution of those issues can make a positive difference for each of us and our marriage.

If I choose to stay focused on my husband and his problem, I will stay depressed, particularly if I replay the hurt over and over again in my mind. If I choose to focus on my own issues and the way I respond to my husband's problem, then I can find peace because my efforts are being spent on the area I can control.

Increased stress and anxiety come when I attempt to control my husbands behavior and can't. My husband has to choose his behavior; I can only choose and control my response to his behavior.

How can I get through this? I'm staying because we have a family. If we didn't have kids, I'm sure I would leave him. I do love him, but I'm so scared to get close to him again. I'm scared to love him deeply again. I'm scared of being hurt again—just so, so scared of being hurt all over again.

My husband's problem has hurt me deeply. I am fearful about my relationship with him. However, the Atonement can heal my husband if he truly wants to be healed. The Atonement can make me less fearful and I can feel close to my husband and he to me. This will take time. There are no easy fixes.

I must remember that fear does not come from God. Fear and faith cannot exist in my mind at the same second. I am free to choose whether I will listen to the Spirit and feel faith or listen to the adversary and feel fear.

I feel so ugly.

When I compare myself to other women, I feel ugly. This is again what Satan wants me to think. When I stop and reflect that I am God's creation and He loves me and created this body for me to come to earth, I feel beautiful. I need to remind myself of my relationship with God frequently.

Again, it's not about me and what I look like; it's about my husband's addiction to pornography. If there are things I can change and improve within myself, then I should identify them and work to change them. If my husband wants to view pornography and lose the Spirit, that is his choice, but I do not have to let my husband's behavior take me away from the Spirit by getting me to compare myself to other women. Eventually, if my husband's behavior does not change, I will need to make a decision as to what is best for me and for our children.

Since October this is always on my mind. My husband seems to get very upset whenever I get depressed, and that's really hard on me. That's why I think he does not understand how much he has hurt me. I have been open with him this time—boy, have I shared it all with him. He knows full well how I feel, and I have told him how badly I hurt. I am worried!

I have every right to be hurt. I have every right to be depressed. I am a human being with feelings and emotions. Now that I have had my "hurt" and my "depression," where do I want my life to go? I can control what I choose to do and what I choose to feel, although it is not easy.

I will no longer allow my husband's behavior to map out my destiny. I will stand up as a daughter of God and be accountable for who I am and what I can do. With God's help I can become who He wants me to become. I will learn what I can do to make our marriage better, but I will not buckle under because of my husband's behavior. No more. Enough is enough!

The Savior and His Atonement will heal me if I allow Him to do so, regardless of what my husband chooses to do.

This was a long dialogue between this woman and me. She was in pain and reaching out so desperately for help. I wanted her to see paragraph-by-paragraph that she had many choices that she could make. She did not have to be held captive. She could take action and get into counseling. She could set boundaries and let her husband be responsible for his behavior. But most importantly, I wanted her to know that God loves her perfectly and that through the Atonement of Jesus Christ she could be healed from a broken heart.

A Broken Heart and Christ's Power to Heal

One mother whose husband had chosen an alternative lifestyle and divorced her had three of her four children turn their backs on the Church. She expressed, "My heart was broken by the decisions of my children, and in a very real sense my life fell apart." What can a mother learn from this painful experience? What can we learn from the experiences of this mother? In her own words, she reflects on what she has learned:

Lesson number one was the realization that I cannot change others; I can only change myself.

As I have matured in facing the lifelong challenge with independent children, I find that my prayers are different than they used to be. I used to try to exercise faith by saying, "Heavenly Father, please help my children to change. Help them to become aware of the harmful effects of alcohol or sexual promiscuity, and help them to recognize the truths of the gospel." But now I am more likely to exercise faith in the Lord Jesus Christ by saying, "Heavenly Father, I know thou lovest my children. Help me to feel about them the same way that thou dost. Help me to love them better. Help me to understand thy plan as it applies to them. And help me to be patient."

Lesson number two, for me, was that becoming completely stripped of pride freed me to make spiritual progress.

It was humiliating when I divorced to go from being a strong member of the ward to someone who suddenly needed help. I was embarrassed when people learned that my fourteen-year-old daughter had elected to live with her father, who had chosen a homosexual lifestyle, instead of with me. (What was I doing wrong? I was a good mother. I paid tithing, fasted, and prayed, attended the temple. What more could I do?) Later it was even more embarrassing to admit that my daughter had chosen her father's lifestyle for her own.

But as I learned more about exercising faith in the Lord Jesus Christ, my broken heart became not a crushed heart but a broken heart and a contrite spirit (D&C 59:8)—a heart broken open to receive help, guidance, and wisdom. I was open to learn, to grow, and to change; pride was no longer a barrier. During that time when my heart was so tender, I couldn't sit through a sacrament meeting without weeping. People saw my tears and felt sorry for me, but those tears were more than tears of grief. I was overwhelmed with many feelings—including feelings of gratitude, joy, and love. The Lord was aware of my plight, and His grace was at work in my heart.

Lesson number three was that Christ will never stop loving His Father's children and neither should I.

Loving my children will never be inappropriate, no matter what they may have done to cut themselves off from the Church. I take comfort in reading any scripture that helps me understand the profound love that Christ has for all of His Father's children. One of my favorites is found in Isaiah 49:15-16. "Can a woman forget her sucking child, that she should not have compassion on the son of her womb? Yea, they may forget, yet will I not *forget thee. Behold, I have graven thee upon the palms of my hands; thy walls are continually before me."*

While Christ hung on the cross, I feel He symbolically was engraving the image, the names of my children and me in the palms of His hands.

Faith is a belief that through fasting and prayer all things are possible—even a change of heart in our children so that they will repent and return to the Church. For me, the additional dimension of faith in the Lord Jesus Christ is trusting in the reality and the power of Christ's love for all God's children regardless of our mistakes. Faith in Christ is knowing that His Atonement makes repentance possible (*Ensign*, Feb. 2004, 47-48).

This mother learned several important principles. Without faith in Christ, we naturally experience prolonged unhealthy emotions that pull us down. With faith in Christ, we view our situation from an eternal perspective.

The Savior has promised us that we will never fall if we put our trust in Him:

Behold, ye are little children and ye cannot bear all things now; ye must grow in grace and in the knowledge of the truth.

Fear not, little children, for you are mine, and I have overcome the world, and you are of them that my Father hath given me;

And none of them that my Father hath given me shall be lost.

And the Father and I are one. I am in the Father and the Father in me; and inasmuch as ye have received me, ye are in me and I in you.

Wherefore, I am in your midst, and I am the good shepherd, and the stone of Israel. He that buildeth upon this rock shall never fall (D&C 50:40-44).

Outcome with Increased Faith in the Lord Jesus Christ

How We Naturally View Our Situation	How We View Our Situation If We Have Increased Faith in Christ
Crushed heart	"A broken heart and a contrite spirit" (D&C 59:8).
Abandoned	"For the Lord will not forsake his people" (1 Sam. 12:22).
Afraid	"I will trust, and not be afraid; for the Lord Jehovah is my strength" (2 Ne. 22:2).
Betrayed	"I will not leave you comfortless: I will come to you" (John 14:18).
Alone	"Whosoever shall put their trust in God shall be supported in their trials, and their troubles, and their afflictions" (Alma 36:3).

RESOLVE TO WORK ON OUR OWN ISSUES

Since we cannot change our loved ones' behaviors, even though we so desperately would like to, the best use of our emotional energy is to work on ourselves. We can control how we respond to their behaviors and we can work to improve ourselves. Elder Joseph B. Wirthlin gave us some practical advice:

> *Great sculptors and artists spend countless hours perfecting their talents. They don't pick up a chisel or a brush and palette, expecting immediate perfection. They understand that they will make many errors as they learn, but they start with the basics, the key fundamentals first.*
>
> *So it is with us.*
>
> *We become masters of our lives in the same way—by focusing on first things first. We all have a pretty good idea of the most important decisions we need to make—decisions that will improve our lives and bring us greater happiness and peace. That is where we should start. That is where we should place our greatest effort.*
>
> *Each night before I go to bed, I take out a small card and write a list of the things I need to do the next day in order of their priority.*
>
> *When I arrive at the office in the morning, I check my card and put all my efforts into the first item on the list. When I accomplish that item, I move on to the second and so on. Some days, I finish every item on my list. On other days, some tasks are not completed. I don't become discouraged, however, because I'm focusing my energies on the things that matter most.*
>
> *In most cases, growth comes slowly—one step at a time. We understand this when it comes to mastering a musical instrument, becoming an accomplished athlete, or flying a jet aircraft. Yet, we often can scarcely forgive ourselves when we don't make the progress we expect in all areas of our own lives* (*Ensign*, Nov. 2003, 80).

How can you apply Elder Wirthlin's advice to your situation? When will you begin to use it? How will his advice help you?

PROGRESS, NOT PERFECTION

We want to accept who we are and work gradually to improve ourselves. Demanding perfection now can work against us. President Ezra Taft Benson suggested, "We must be careful, as we seek to become more and more godlike, that we do not become discouraged and lose hope. Becoming Christlike is a lifetime pursuit and very often involves growth and change that is slow, almost imperceptible" (*Ensign*, Oct. 1989, 5). One perceptive wife realized her absolute demand for perfection was not helpful:

> *I now understand that I developed a "perfection or nothing" mentality. I had to be perfect to be okay. If I were perfect, my husband would be defenseless and have no excuse for his behavior. If I were perfect, how could he justify his infidelity?*
>
> *Even society reinforced my faulty thinking. Often, when I was with a group of women and the topic of someone getting a divorce because of infidelity came up, the women talked about what was wrong with the wife. Comments like, "Perhaps if she had lost weight, he would not have cheated. Maybe she was frigid or just a nag." As I listened to these comments I thought, "I have to be perfect in everything so that my husband will not be unfaithful."*
>
> *It was years later, after much studying about sexual addiction, that I realized that my husband's behavior was not about me. It was about him and his issues, and his addiction began long before we were married. He did not know it was an addiction and neither did I.*
>
> *Even if I could have reached some state of perfection, my husband would have still acted out because it was not about me. He had to be the one to stop the behavior.*
>
> *The struggle I am faced with now is how do I defeat the dragon I have created in believing I have to be more than I am? I want my emotional energy spent on improving myself rather than picking myself apart.*

REVIEW OF PRINCIPLES

In what ways can you increase your faith in Jesus Christ?

_____

_____

_____

_____

_____

_____

_____

How will you benefit by having increased faith in Jesus Christ?

_____

_____

_____

_____

_____

_____

_____

_____

How will patience help you during this trial?

_____

_____

_____

_____

_____

_____

_____

How does one become converted to the gospel of Jesus Christ?

_____
_____
_____
_____
_____
_____
_____

How will focusing on progress rather than perfection help you?

_____
_____
_____
_____
_____

Why is it important, for the most part, to keep your loved one's behavior confidential?

_____
_____
_____
_____
_____

If your loved one is lying to you, how can you best deal with the deception?

_____
_____
_____
_____
_____

How can you provide self-care so that your desires and wishes are met in healthy ways?

_____

_____

_____

_____

_____

How can you surrender this trial to the Lord?

_____

_____

_____

_____

_____

What has He promised you?

_____

_____

_____

_____

_____

Record any other insights or thoughts that have occurred to you as you have read this chapter.

_____

_____

_____

_____

_____

_____

What is the single most important principle or concept you have learned from this chapter?

_____

_____

_____

_____

_____

_____

_____

With whom can you share this important principle or concept in the next week?

_____

_____

_____

CALMNESS BREAK

Consider a new hobby or one that you have not done for a while. Plan time each week to work on your hobby or learn about a new hobby, even if just for a few minutes. Get your mind on something else for a while.

Needlepoint	Hiking	Stamp collecting	Woodworking
Aquariums	Snow skiing	Cross-stitch	Hunting
Gardening	Bowling	Drawing	Scrapbooking
Family History	Puzzles	Coin collecting	Sewing
Motorcycles	Doll collecting	Fishing	Knitting
Water skiing	Crochet	Quilting	Painting
Dancing	Swimming	Jogging	Aerobics

Which hobby have you selected? When will you get started? Will you take a class? Does someone you know already have this hobby? Will you ask them to help you?

_____

_____

_____

_____

_____

MESSAGES OF HOPE

Elder M. Russell Ballard: "When we completely surrender ourselves to the Lord, then He will cause a mighty change in us and we will become a new person, justified, sanctified, and born again with His image in our countenances" (*Ensign,* Oct. 1998, 13).

Elder Richard G. Scott: "Don't say, 'No one understands me; I can't sort it out, or get the help I need.' Those comments are self-defeating. No one can help you without faith and effort on your part. Your personal growth requires that. Don't look for a life virtually free from discomfort, pain, pressure, challenge, or grief, for those are the tools a loving Father uses to stimulate our personal growth and understanding. As the scriptures repeatedly affirm, you will be helped as you exercise faith in Jesus Christ. That faith is demonstrated by a willingness to trust His promises given through His prophets and in His scriptures, which contain His own words. You may not fully understand how to do this yet, but trust that He will help you use your agency to open the doors for His healing to occur. Faith in Christ means we trust Him; we trust His teachings. That leads to hope, and hope brings charity, the pure love of Christ—that peaceful feeling that comes when we sense His concern, His love, and His capacity to cure us or to ease our burdens with His healing power" (*Ensign,* May 1994, 8).

PRINCIPLE 5

Our Only Hope Is Christ's Atonement and Its Power to Heal—Spiritually, Emotionally, Mentally, Socially, and Physically

CHAPTER OVERVIEW

We usually think of the Atonement as a way to cleanse us from our sins. It can! But it can also cleanse us from bitterness, resentment, loneliness, the anger we turn toward ourselves, and the anger we harbor toward our loved ones. We certainly have experienced much pain, and the Atonement covers all pain! The spiritual, emotional, mental, social, and physical challenges that burden us as a result of our loved ones' behaviors can be lightened through the Savior and His Atonement as He lifts the weight from our shoulders, and "strengthens (our) feeble knees."

Elder Robert D. Hales explained the process: "'And then may God grant unto you that your burdens may be light, through the joy of his Son' (Alma 33:23). Through faith and trust in the Lord and obedience to His counsel, we make ourselves eligible to be partakers of the Atonement of Jesus Christ so that one day we may return to live with Him" (*Ensign*, Nov. 1998, 16–17).

Negative feelings and thoughts that go unchecked lead to unhealthy choices that keep us from the healing path. To escape this trap, we begin with the core issue—our thoughts and feelings. By altering our thoughts and managing our feelings, we can usually choose a healthier emotional response. This often means we need to change our perspective or viewpoint of our loved ones' behaviors.

Agency applies to all choices in mortality. Beyond the choices we make between right and wrong, agency also includes our choices to view things that have happened to us in helpful or unhelpful ways.

Can we choose to view our experience from a spiritual perspective and develop healthier feelings and attitudes? How long do we want to carry the pain and hurt alone? Can we change our beliefs about a difficult experience so our response will include healthier feelings? Where does Christ and His Atonement fit into our healing process?

"We believe that the first principles and ordinances of the Gospel are: first, Faith in the Lord Jesus Christ" (A of F 4).

"We believe that through the Atonement of Christ, all mankind may be saved, by obedience to the laws and ordinances of the Gospel" (A of F 3).

"We believe in the gift of . . . healing" (A of F 7).

 ## CHAPTER OBJECTIVES

At the conclusion of this chapter you should—

1. Know that the Atonement can heal all pain—spiritual, emotional, mental, and physical.
2. Know that the Atonement can heal the pain of abuse and feelings of anger.
3. Know how to apply the Atonement in your life.
4. Know that the Atonement can heal you and your loved one.
5. Know the difference between a feeling and an emotion.
6. Recognize how to identify feelings and to find the best words to describe them.
7. Realize that it is okay to have the feelings you experience, but then you have the responsibility to decide how to deal with them in a self-enhancing way.
8. Identify unhealthy patterns of behavior between you and your loved one and replace them with healthy patterns.
9. Identify unhelpful beliefs about your loved one's behaviors that you need to change.
10. Be willing to work hard to embrace new beliefs that are helpful and healing.
11. Learn to make choices through the Spirit that will keep you emotionally balanced.

WORKBOOK EXERCISES

The exercises in this chapter may bring up unwanted and buried feelings such as resentment, bitterness, jealousy, abandonment, guilt, anxiety, anger, and more. One woman shared the following experience:

> *I have to be so careful when I work on my issues that I don't get over-whelmed. I read about things in the workbook that I should be doing and seem to do all the wrong things. My husband is trying to overcome his sexual addiction and I'm trying just to hold myself together. I worry about our children and wonder what all of this is going to do to them. The more I learn about my own issues, the more I see that I have to work on, and I don't know that I can do or try one more thing. I'm just so burdened and depressed. I seldom got depressed before, but now it seems that I can't pull myself out of it.*

These feelings and emotions are real and common. We have been hurt and it will take time to work through the pain. Depression is real. Once we recognize that we are depressed, we can make choices to deal with it in a self-enhancing way. It's very important to recognize when we need medical attention. Our diet, exercise, and many other factors can impact our emotional well-being and our level of depression. If there is a prolonged period of depression (This could be several days or a few weeks) where daily tasks are difficult to accomplish, please seek medical advice. It's important for a medical professional to properly diagnose each person and provide the necessary care.

As we continue the healing journey, things can improve. Each exercise in this chapter can improve your current relationships and equip you with skills to effectively deal with your emotions now. You will also learn to engage the power of the Atonement to heal painful, emotional experiences of the past. The process is powerful—yet it works only when we do our part: "For we know that it is by grace that we are saved, after all we can do" (2 Ne. 25:23).

Some days we are capable of doing more work on our emotional issues than on other days. Dealing with our emotions can be uncomfortable, and healing is a process. We can't demand that it be a quick event. Elder Boyd K. Packer remarked, "We seem to demand *instant* everything, including instant solutions to our problems" (*Ensign,* May 1978, 93). There are no quick twenty-four-hour emergency clinics for emotional pain.

Keeping in Balance

Keeping balance in our lives is important. We need to give appropriate emphasis and time to our relationships with God and Christ and our families, co-workers, friends, church responsibilities, work, recreation, and other responsibilities. If we give too much time and energy in one area and don't have any left for other important areas, it is easy to feel overwhelmed and start to sink. If we do not reach out to others and to the Lord, we can lose control of our emotions, and submerge ourselves in the waters of isolation and self-pity. Then, in a very real way, we can capsize just as the great ship *"Vasa"* did in 1628.

On August 10, 1628, the *Vasa* set sail on its maiden voyage. The *Vasa* was the premier warship for Sweden's Navy. It took 1,000 oaks to construct the hull. The masts were more than fifty meters high, and on board were sixty-four large guns and hundreds of sculptures.

The *Vasa* was the most expensive and richly ornamented naval vessel built in Sweden at this time. When the *Vasa* sailed forth on her maiden voyage, Stockholmers stood along the shore to wish her good luck. They were eyewitnesses to the disaster.

The ship capsized in the Stockholm harbor. Why did it sink? A small gust of wind—just a breeze—caused it to capsize. The ship was top-heavy. To counterbalance a ship in those days, rocks were placed in the bottom to offset the masts and force of the wind. In the 1600's it was difficult to calculate the amount of weight needed to balance a ship, and most ships were designed according to what had been learned in the design of their predecessors. Since the *Vasa* was much larger than other vessels that had been built, the measurements and counter-balance methods used in previous ships did not work.

Between four and five o'clock in the afternoon, the great new warship *Vasa* keeled over and sank. "For a magnificent ship that sank on her very first voyage, this could have been the end. Instead, it was the beginning of an adventure that is still in progress. The *Vasa* was found almost intact, standing on the seabed, after three centuries. The ship was salvaged and is now one of the foremost tourist attractions in the world" (*The Vasa Catalogue,* Vasa, 1-3).

When we are not balanced with our life, we too can capsize. It takes a lot of effort to get us back to the surface, but it can be done. Through the Atonement of Christ, we can be rescued. Much like the *Vasa,* we still have great work to do. As we learn and do the works of righteousness, we can be salvaged, begin a new and productive stage of life, and be blessed with peace.

Elder M. Russell Ballard expressed this concern:

As most of you know, coping with the complex and diverse challenges of everyday life, which is not an easy task, can upset the balance and harmony we seek. Many good people who care a great deal are trying very hard to maintain balance, but they sometimes feel overwhelmed and defeated (*Ensign,* May 1987, 13).

"But learn that he who doeth the works of righteousness shall receive his reward, even peace in this world, and eternal life in the world to come" (D&C 59:23).

Reflect on the following areas of your life:

Relationship with God
Relationship with Christ
Moments when you feel the promptings of the Holy Ghost
Relationship with your spouse
Relationships with your extended family
Relationships with your children
Social relationships
Work
Pleasure
Hobbies
Time for yourself
Service

Are there areas of your life that are currently out of balance and need to be changed?

_____

_____

_____

What can you do to change these unbalanced areas of your life and become more balanced?

_____

_____

_____

_____

🌿 When will you make these changes? How can these changes benefit you?

_____

_____

_____

_____

UNDERSTANDING OUR CAPACITY AND RELYING ON THE ATONEMENT

Developing self-awareness—knowing what we are capable of doing now or within the next few hours or days—is very important so that we do not get "burned out." When left to our own abilities and resources, we run out of emotional energy quite soon. Whenever we think or feel that we are alone, we should remind ourselves that at the very least we can travel through life in a foursome: (1) Ourselves; (2) God, our Heavenly Father; (3) Christ, our Savior; and (4) The Holy Ghost. As we stay connected with Christ, our Savior, our own natural abilities are greatly enhanced through His Atonement and perfect love. With Christ and His Atonement we can keep going even when our situation is very difficult. It is much easier to share our burdens and go through life in a foursome! We need to choose to join the Godhead!

🌿 What relationships do you have or can establish that would help you during your time of need?

_____

_____

_____

_____

_____

If we stay isolated and alone, we run the risk of making choices that are not helpful in dealing with our pain—such as staying overly busy. It's usually best to avoid being too busy; otherwise, we don't have time to recognize and feel the hurt, deal with it, and walk through it. Staying too busy allows us to walk *around* the hurt, instead of dealing with it in a helpful, healing way because we never make time to face it.

On the other hand, if we do not have a set schedule and regular routine, we might have too much time available and may try to deal with too much pain at once, trying to rush the healing process. Instead, we simply need to accept the reality that it will take time and energy to deal with our pain. It is not helpful to attempt to rush through it in several weeks or even a few months. Sometimes we set ourselves up for more emotional turmoil by trying to work through our pain more rapidly than we are capable of handling. When we experience emotional challenges, we can choose to either cover them up or clear them up. To clear them up, we can rely on the merits of the Atonement and allow the Savior to dictate our individual healing plan and timetable. Attempting to do too much at once or locking ourselves into expectations of a certain timetable for recovery can burden us down. Part of healing is accepting the Lord's timetable.

How can you benefit by accepting the Lord's timetable for healing?

_____

_____

_____

_____

_____

Often we try to deal with more emotional issues than we can handle for now. I have no intention of trivializing our emotional hurt, but I see a parallel in a situation with one of my grandsons who is a toddler. When he comes to visit, he plays with a toy that has several connecting plastic tracks that extend more than two feet high. After connecting the track, my grandson places marbles on the top track and watches as they traverse back and forth down the tracks until they reach the bottom. My grandson is intrigued with the noise, movement, and number of marbles. His little hands cannot hold all the marbles when they reach the bottom of the track, but he continues to try. He wants to pick up all the marbles at once, but his hands are too small. When he tries, he begins dropping them. When he tries to pick them up with hands already full of marbles, he drops more marbles. He gets frustrated, but has not yet learned that he is only capable of picking up a few marbles at a time. Consequently, he often spends his time dropping marbles instead of seeing the marbles go down the track. If he continues to focus on the marbles he cannot pick up, he will further frustrate himself and eventually he will not enjoy playing the game.

We, like my grandson, should focus on what we *can* do rather than on what we cannot do. Sometimes my grandson in a moment of frustration will drop all the marbles and walk off. He's had enough! We can easily be tempted to do the same—get overwhelmed because there is too much emotional work to do. In desperation and hopelessness we may decide not to do anything or get paralyzed so that we cannot do anything. Over time my grandson will figure out what he is capable of doing. Over time we can do the same. Elder Marvin J. Ashton shared:

> One of life's eternal pursuits is learning to know oneself. Dr. Thomas Harris shares this worthy thought with us: "Most people never fulfill their human promise and potential because they remain perpetually helpless children overwhelmed by a sense of inferiority. The feeling of being okay does not imply that the person has risen above all his faults and emotional problems. It merely implies that he refuses to be paralyzed by them. He is determined to accept himself as he is but also to assume more and more control of his life" (*Ensign*, Nov. 1976, 84).

Our only true freedom lies in choosing our thoughts, feelings, and behaviors and determining how we will take charge of the events of life and how they affect us.

THE ATONEMENT CAN HEAL US AND OUR LOVED ONES

The Atonement is so much more than a healing balm for sin! We believe in the Atonement and know that it has worked for others, but do we really believe that it will heal us? We personally embrace the Atonement when we believe and accept that it will heal us.

> For the natural man is an enemy to God, and has been from the fall of Adam, and will be, forever and ever, unless he yields to the enticings of the Holy Spirit, and putteth off the natural man and becometh a saint through the Atonement of Christ the Lord, and becometh as a child, submissive, meek, humble, patient, full of love, willing to submit to all things which the Lord seeth fit to inflict upon him, even as a child doth submit to his father (Mosiah 3:19).

What can we do to accept the Atonement? Form a partnership with Christ and work as a team. Frequently consult with our Partner. Become teachable. Listen to the Spirit. Try to be more understanding of others. Develop compassion. Submit to the words of the prophets and apostles. Be more gentle. Be humble. Work to be more patient. Try to develop a loving spirit. Develop a willingness to move forward even though we do not have all the answers. Repent and try to change our weaknesses by relying on the Savior. Recognize that the pain we feel now will decrease over time as we "stay connected" with the Savior. Begin to see what the Lord wants us to learn from this experience. Recognize that when we feel all alone, we are not alone. Have hope that we, through Christ's perfect love and watchful care, can get through this even though it is very difficult. Be willing to submit to all things that the Lord permits to happen.

The Atonement can heal us from *all* pain. What pain do we have? Is our pain spiritual, emotional, mental, social, or physical? Think about the pain you have suffered and then reflect on this scripture: "For, behold, the Lord your Redeemer suffered death in the flesh; wherefore he suffered the pain of all men, that all men might repent and come unto him" (D&C 18:11).

How does this scripture apply to your pain?

_____

_____

_____

_____

_____

_____

The above scripture states that Christ "suffered the pain of all men." A similar scripture is found in the Book of Mormon: "And he cometh into the world that he may save all men if they will hearken unto his voice; for behold, he suffereth the pains of all men, yea, the pains of every living creature, both men, women, and children, who belong to the family of Adam" (2 Ne. 9:21). This scripture includes the plural word *pains*. As mortals we suffer more than one "pain." What is included in the word *pain*? Under the word *pain* in the Topical Guide we are referred to other words that are synonymous—affliction, anguish, distress, grief, sorrow, suffering, and torment.

As you think about the issues regarding your loved one, circle the word or words that most accurately describe your pain.

Affliction   Anguish   Distress   Grief   Sorrow   Suffering   Torment

From your perspective, as you think about your loved one and his behaviors, what words most accurately describe his pain?

Affliction   Anguish   Distress   Grief   Sorrow   Suffering   Torment

The Atonement is universal. It can cover our pain and our loved ones' pain. Now let's go back to that same scripture and include all these words in the scripture: "For, behold, the Lord your Redeemer suffered death in the flesh; wherefore he suffered the pain [affliction, anguish, distress, grief, sorrow, suffering, and torment] of all men, that all men might repent and come unto him" (D&C 18:11).

📓 With these additional words added to the scripture, what are your thoughts regarding the Atonement and how it can be used in your situation?

_____

_____

_____

_____

_____

_____

_____

_____

THE ATONEMENT HEALS MORE THAN SIN

When we repent, the Atonement covers our sins. But that is only the beginning of the Atonement, not the ending. If we visualize the Atonement as a pie sliced into pieces, repenting and receiving forgiveness for our sins is only one piece.

The remaining slices cover the emotional, mental, physical, interpersonal, and spiritual anguish that we experience as mortals. The Atonement is all-encompassing. It not only covers sin and a sinful heart; it heals an afflicted heart, a heart full of anguish, a distressed heart, a grieving heart, a sorrowful heart, a suffering heart, a heart full of torment. It covers a lonely heart, a broken heart, a shattered heart, a resentful heart, an angry heart, an unforgiving heart, and much, much more.

What is required of us to receive the blessings of the Atonement? "That all men might repent and come unto him" (D&C 18:11). "If they will hearken unto his voice" (2 Ne. 9:21). Yes, the Atonement covers "the pains of all men, yea, the pains of every living creature, both men, women, and children, who belong to the family of Adam" (2 Ne. 9:21). Why does the Atonement cover children? Children are not accountable for sin until the age of eight. Why would they need the Atonement before the age of eight? Because children need a way to heal from any emotional, mental, physical, or spiritual pain. A child who suffers peer rejection can be healed through the Atonement. Children who are caught in the middle of their parents' divorce are covered with the Atonement. Children who are emotionally hurt because of abuse in any form, whether emotional, mental, physical, or sexual, are included in the Atonement.

CHILD ABUSE AND THE ATONEMENT

The healing power of the Atonement can heal the wounds of child abuse. Child abuse can stifle and kill the human spirit and bring feelings of inferiority. The Atonement restores the human spirit and gives those who have been abused a reason to live and move forward. Here is an experience of how one woman dealt with abuse and how she used the healing power of the Atonement:

> One member, plagued for years with depression, fear, anger, and feelings of suicide, recalled the turning point in her healing journey when she realized the Atonement was applicable in her life. "I was stunned at how loved I must be," she wrote. "Indeed, I stood all amazed at the love Jesus offered me. This new knowledge of how the Atonement applied to me and how I was truly within the bounds of it gave me the courage to try life once again. It has been 10 years since that crossroad of my life. That one gospel principle of the Atonement and how it applied to my situation made all of the difference" (*Ensign*, Sept. 1997, 20).

 How does the Atonement apply to your situation?

_____

_____

_____

_____

ANGER AND THE ATONEMENT

Sometimes our emotions get the best of us and we lash out at our loved ones. Afterwards, we often feel guilty for such behavior. This guilt can foster feelings of despondency, hopelessness, and depression. As we repent, the Atonement covers our anger too! The Atonement allows us to forgive ourselves. A man who was angry at his alcoholic father for how he treated him while he was growing up developed self-anger for treating his own children the way he was treated. While reflecting on his behavior he wrote:

> *I realized that besides forgiving my father, I needed to forgive myself* (see Alma 36:19-21). *This more difficult task takes much longer—in fact, I'm still working on it. But progress is being made, and the Spirit helps me and brings me comfort. Meanwhile, I remind myself that there is One who descended below all things, and that no matter how hard or terrible I think my experiences were, they pale pathetically against the suffering of the Son of God. When I fully accept the reality of the Atonement and make it a living power in my life, then I know my true and complete worth as Heavenly Father sees it* (*Ensign,* Aug. 1994, 25).

PAIN AND THE ATONEMENT

The Atonement is called the Infinite Atonement because it covers all pain—infinitely. The kind of emotional pain we suffer in regard to our loved ones' sexual addiction seems so devastating and difficult to handle that we often wonder if we can continue living with this much pain. Nothing seems to ease it. The best (and only truly effective) prescription is the Atonement. Elder Robert D. Hales noted:

> *As we put our faith and trust in the Lord, we must battle our pain day by day and sometimes hour by hour, even moment by moment; but in the end, we understand that marvelous counsel given to the Prophet Joseph Smith as*

he struggled with his pain of feeling forgotten and isolated in Liberty Jail: 'My son, peace be unto thy soul; thine adversity and thine afflictions shall be but a small moment; And then, if thou endure it well, God shall exalt thee on high; thou shalt triumph over all thy foes' (D&C 121:7–8) *(Ensign, Nov. 1998, 17).*

🖋 **What have you learned from the painful experiences regarding your loved one's behaviors?**

_____

_____

_____

_____

The following scriptures affirm the importance of understanding the Atonement and accepting the healing power by trusting the Lord, being diligent in keeping His commandments, and continuing in the faith:

I say unto you, if ye have come to a knowledge of the goodness of God, and his matchless power, and his wisdom, and his patience, and his long-suffering towards the children of men; and also, the Atonement which has been prepared from the foundation of the world, that thereby salvation might come to him that should put his trust in the Lord, and should be diligent in keeping his commandments, and continue in the faith even unto the end of his life, I mean the life of the mortal body—

I say, that this is the man who receiveth salvation, through the Atonement which was prepared from the foundation of the world for all mankind, which ever were since the fall of Adam, or who are, or who ever shall be, even unto the end of the world (Mosiah 4:6-7).

🖋 **According to the last sentence, who is covered under the Atonement? Are you covered? Can your loved one be covered?**

_____

_____

_____

_____

This scripture should give us great hope. This scripture is for you! Write your name in the blanks below.

> *I say unto you,_____, if ye have come to a knowledge of the goodness of God, and his matchless power, and his wisdom, and his patience, and his long-suffering towards the children of men; and also, the Atonement which has been prepared from the foundation of the world, that thereby salvation might come to him that should put his [her] trust in the Lord, and should be diligent in keeping his commandments, and continue in the faith even unto the end of his [her] life, I mean the life of the mortal body—I say, that_____ receiveth salvation, through the Atonement which was prepared from the foundation of the world for all mankind, which ever were since the fall of Adam, or who are, or who ever shall be, even unto the end of the world* (Mosiah 4:6-7).

Here is a summary of this scripture: The Atonement becomes effective in our lives as we: (1) Put our trust in the Lord; (2) Are diligent in keeping His commandments; and (3) Continue in the faith even unto the end of life. We put our trust in the Lord as we surrender our feelings and emotions to His will.

What other ways can you put your trust in the Lord?

_____

_____

_____

_____

_____

"Diligent in keeping his commandments" means that we are making a real effort to obey His word. What other ways can you be diligent in keeping His commandments? How would repentance apply?

_____

_____

_____

_____

_____

🖋 "Continue in the faith" means that we keep moving forward with faith in Christ and His Atonement. What are some other ways you can continue in the faith?

_____
_____
_____
_____
_____

Elder M. Russell Ballard declared: "And when mistakes are made, the wondrous Atonement of the Lord Jesus Christ must be understood and accepted so that through the complete and sometimes difficult process of repentance, forgiveness and continued hope for the future can be obtained. We must never give up our individual and family quest for eternal life" (*Ensign,* May 1999, 86).

🖋 What is the difference between understanding the Atonement and accepting the Atonement?

_____
_____
_____
_____

🖋 How can you accept the Atonement and apply its healing power to your pain?

_____
_____
_____
_____
_____

How can you ask for His redeeming power in your life each day?

_____

_____

_____

_____

_____

SMALL AND SIMPLE THINGS BRING HEALING

Often we look for some miracle to heal us and our loved ones. Or perhaps we think the right book, a meeting with an experienced counselor, or the latest research study on how to change human behaviors will give us the answers. Even though these things can and do help, we should be aware that some elements for healing are already within us and just need to be tapped. To illustrate this point please read the following quote:

> I WILL STRIVE TO GET THE MOST OUT OF LIFE
> BY BECOMING MY BEST SELF, FOR I AM A
> UNIQUE WORK OF ART FILLED WITH
> UNTAPPED RESOURCES OF STRENGTH.

Now read the quote again and count how many times the letter "F" appears in the quote. How many did you count? Three, four, five? Actually, the letter "F" appears seven times in the quote. Which letter "Fs" did you miss? Generally, we train our minds to skip over the short words. You probably missed the "Fs" in the small words, such as *of*. Sometimes we do this in our healing—look for some big miracle to occur in our loved ones' lives or our own lives and skip over the little miracles just as we missed some of the letter "Fs" in this quote. Miracles do happen, but often they are found in the small and simple things we do each day. By small means, salvation is brought to many souls:

> *Now ye may suppose that this is foolishness in me; but behold I say unto you, that by small and simple things are great things brought to pass; and small means in many instances doth confound the wise.*
>
> *And the Lord God doth work by means to bring about his great and eternal purposes; and by very small means the Lord doth confound the wise and bringeth about the salvation of many souls* (Alma 37:6-7).

What are some small and simple things that couples can work on to improve their relationship? Here are some ideas:

- Do wholesome recreational activities together.

- Take a class together.

- Read an article from the *Ensign* or other Church magazine and discuss it.

- Read a book together.

- Read the scriptures together and discuss what you learn and feel.

- Review letters or cards you may have sent one another.

- Look at pictures you took during your courtship and discuss them.

- Take a walk and just listen to each other.

- Do something nice for each other once a day.

- Start a new hobby together—one that neither one of you do now.

- Do a weekend retreat together—just the two of you.

- Discuss where you would like your marriage to be in one year, five, or ten years.

- Surprise each other with a gift each week that costs less than $2.

- Give each other encouragement.

- Give each other your full attention when one is talking.

- Do a candlelight dinner.

- Wash the car together.

- Do household chores together.

- Fix a favorite meal.

- Ask your spouse what you could do to show you really care.

Another important area is to identify the unhealthy patterns and practices in a couple's relationship that have developed over time and replace them with healthy patterns and practices. With help from a therapist, here are the unhealthy patterns that one couple replaced with healthy alternatives. (Not their real names*)

Unhealthy Patterns and Practices	Healthy Replacements
Jack* continues to discuss a point when Janice has had enough. However, Janice does not say anything but becomes resentful, upset, and angry. She may eventually spout off or withdraw emotion-ally when Jack insists on continuing the conversation.	Janice* takes an assertive position and says, "I have reached my limit for now for discussing this issue; can we talk about it later? What day and time will work for you?" It's important to decide when the talk will continue so each spouse knows that further discussion will take place.
When Jack initiates sexual intimacy and Janice is not interested, he withdraws emotionally, becomes sulky, or goes into another room. He does not share his feel-ings with Janice.	When Jack initiates sexual intimacy and Janice is not interested, he is asser-tive and takes responsibility for how he feels. He says something like, "Janice, I need to share how I feel right now. I'm telling you this to take responsibility for my own feelings and not to manipulate you into having sex with me. Right now I feel unloved, hurt, and rejected. These feelings have been trigger points for me in the past, so I want to discuss them and learn to deal with them in a positive way." In return Janice says, "Jack, I want you to know how much I love you and care for you. I appreciate how hard you work for the family. You keep up with school and work and really try hard. [Janice gives a warm embrace and Jack and Janice hold each other as the conversation continues.] Physically, I just am not up to having sex tonight, but I want you to know that does not in any way mean that I do not care for you and love you." This healthy pattern replacement allows both partners to share feelings, be responsible for what they feel, and learn to deal with feelings in a healthy way that brings them closer together, even without sexual intimacy.

Unhealthy Patterns and Practices	Healthy Replacements
Both Jack and Janice use the words "always" or "never" to describe the other partner's actions. This sets in motion a thought pattern that the other person will never change or will always do the same thing. This allows both partners to hold onto resentment, self-pity, and anger. For example, Jack may say to himself, "Janice always asks me too many questions." Janice may say, "I always have to pull information out of Jack. He never tells me anything on his own."	Both Jack and Janice decide to use the words "often," "sometimes," and "usually," instead of the absolute words such as "always" and "never." This is a reminder that their partner is not always that way. It also keeps a rational perspective regarding the ability of the partner to change. This is another way of looking for the good in each other.
Jack and Janice say, "As a couple, we will get over this problem and won't have to deal with it anymore or work at it anymore. Our lives will be back to normal and life will go on just like it does for other couples."	Jack and Janice say, "As a couple, we can choose to use the healthy pattern replacements and continue our spiritual and emotional fitness program for the rest of our lives so we will not succumb to temptation." It's just like staying in shape by maintaining a healthy diet and exercise. We need to maintain healthy pattern replacements in order to keep our marriage in shape.
Jack thinks, "If Janice would just stop asking so many questions, she would be so much easier to live with. In fact, I got involved with another woman in the first place because I was not happy at home."	Jack says, "I made the choice to get involved with another woman. I am totally responsible for my choices. If I manipulate Janice by purposefully withholding information, she will keep asking questions so I can justify getting mad and indulge my lustful feelings. I need to share my thoughts and feelings so Janice can feel emotionally connected to me. When Janice feels emotionally close to me she is a lot more interested in having sexual intimacy."

Unhealthy Patterns and Practices	Healthy Replacements
Janice wants to control Jack's use of the drug of lust. She does this by asking lots of questions and double checking the information that he gives to her. She even talks to other people about where Jack has been or what he has been doing. Because she cannot control him, she becomes angry and upset; then Jack does not want to be around her.	Janice says, "I will give up the idea that I can control Jack and his use of the drug of lust. This would take away his agency. I will accept that it is Jack's responsibility to give up the drug, not mine. I will now focus on myself and what I need. I need to help myself and our children. This new focus will be much better for me, and actually a relief not to wear myself out emotionally."
Jack thinks, "I have caused so much pain to my wife and children and have been excommunicated from the Church. God has punished me for what I have done."	Jack thinks, "I am a son of God. He loves me perfectly. I have made choices in the past that caused me to engage in compulsive sexual behaviors. It's my behaviors that have caused my wife and sons pain, not who I am as a person. God has disciplined me so He could teach me what I need to know to change my behaviors. I love God and He loves me. I will continue to stay connected with God so I can continue to change my behaviors."

After reading these healthy pattern replacements, let's go back to the paragraph with all the letter "Fs." If we keep reading the way we always read—left to right—we may not be able to discover all the letter Fs. This time read the paragraph backward, starting with the word *strength* and see if it is any easier to find the seven letter "Fs."

> I WILL STRIVE TO GET THE MOST OF LIFE
> BY BECOMING MY BEST SELF, FOR I AM A
> UNIQUE WORK OF ART FILLED WITH
> UNTAPPED RESOURCES OF STRENGTH.

Like Jack and Janice, if we want to improve our relationship with our loved ones, we may have to change our approach. One place to begin a new approach is to identify our own unhealthy patterns and replace them with healthier patterns. Our loved ones may not have a desire to change or identify unhealthy patterns, but we can still identify our own. If we use our inner strength and begin to make some progress, it may spark our loved ones to self-assessment and motivate them to change. If our loved ones see that we are becoming more healthy, they may be motivated to change. If not, in our more healthy state, we will have achieved some degree of peace and we will be better equipped to deal with our situation. At first this may seem uncomfortable, too simple, or even backward, but it can make a big difference in our relationships with our loved ones. The idea is to catch ourselves doing the unhealthy pattern and then quickly change it to the healthier pattern. Write a healthy pattern replacement for each unhealthy pattern that you have discovered.

Unhealthy Pattern

_____

_____

_____

_____

Healthy Pattern Replacement

_____

_____

_____

_____

Unhealthy Pattern

_____

_____

_____

_____

Healthy Pattern Replacement

_____

_____

_____

_____

Unhealthy Pattern

_____

_____

_____

_____

Healthy Pattern Replacement

_____

_____

_____

_____

Unhealthy Pattern

_____

_____

_____

_____

Healthy Pattern Replacement

_____

_____

_____

_____

FEELINGS AND EMOTIONS

Our feelings and emotions are usually very volatile. One moment we can feel one way and the next moment feel the opposite. This roller coaster ride is very difficult and draining. What is the difference between a *feeling* and an *emotion?* Let's consult the dictionary: "*Feeling* is a general term for a subjective point of view as well as for specific sensations: to be guided by feeling rather than by facts; a feeling of sadness, or rejoicing" (*Webster's Encyclopedic Unabridged Dictionary*, 521).

"*Emotion* is applied to an intensified feeling: agitated by emotion" (Ibid, 521).

One of the keys to healing is properly identifying our feelings and emotions and then monitoring them so that we can deal with them in healthier ways.

Our spirit self in the pre-earthly life had agency and was capable of all the emotions. *The Encyclopedia of Mormonism* states:

> Inherent in the makeup of their intelligent nature, spirits have agency and are able to make choices. The scriptures teach that spirits are capable of all the emotions, passions, and intellectual experiences exhibited by mortals, including love, anger, hate, envy, knowledge, obedience, rebellion, jealousy, repentance, loyalty, activity, thought, and comprehension. Using their agency, some of God's children rebelled in the premortal life, and war in heaven ensued. The rebellious spirits followed Lucifer and with him were cast down to the earth and became devils or evil spirits, never to receive physical bodies on earth (Moses 4:1-4; D&C 76:25-27; cf. Rev. 12:4, 7-9; D&C 29:36)(3:1404.)

IDENTIFY FEELINGS

We really cannot change our feelings unless we know what they are. To begin healing, one of the first choices we can make is to identify our feelings. A feeling is usually one word, whereas a thought is usually several words. For example, let's say that we feel lonely. If we look at the word *lonely* from our list (on the next page), we find several other words that might more accurately describe our feelings. Do we feel resentful? Enraged? Angry? Explosive? More accurately defining our true feelings allows us to have a starting place to begin our healing. If we cannot decide what we are feeling, we might feel confused and need to check the words under the column "Confused" in order to identify the feelings.

How do you really feel right now? What feeling is deep down inside of you? Do you have pleasant feelings of warmth, value, and compassion? How did you really feel about the difficult situation regarding your loved one's behaviors? Think of one experience and then try to identify the feeling word you would attach to the experience. If you choose a pleasant experience, were you positive, radiant, delighted, or content? If you choose a difficult situation, were you angry, bitter, resentful, tense, edgy, or explosive? Is there one word that would better describe how you felt? If so, what word is it?

Love	**Hatred**	**Angry**	**Sad**
charity	spite	explosive	grief
appreciation	aversion	resentful	depressed
cherish	distrust	enraged	despondent
adoration	bitterness	mad	sorry
affection	envy	agitated	unhappy
intimacy	hostility	upset	discouraged
admiration		annoyed	down
warmth		furious	melancholy
value		irate	disappointed
fondness		livid	
infatuation		mean	
respect		offended	
kindness		testy	
tenderness		bitter	
reverence		tense	
compassion		edgy	

Happy	**Confused**	**Scared**	**Lonely**
positive	unsettled	afraid	alone
pleasant	uncertain	anxious	isolated
radiant	topsy-turvy	nervous	desolate
perky	foggy	upset	bleak
beaming	disorganized	worried	forsaken
sunny	clouded	spooked	friendless
blessed	boggled	startled	lonesome
cheerful	blinded	horrified	secluded
content	groggy	shocked	withdrawn
delighted	complicated	alarmed	abandoned
ecstatic	hectic	fearful	
optimistic	baffled	frightened	
vivacious	stunned	intimidated	
glad	mixed-up	panicked	
fortunate	mystified	terrified	
joyful	disarranged	paralyzed	
lively	dazed	apprehensive	
merry	flustered		
devotion			

We are entitled to feel emotions. We are human. We do feel. Each feeling we have is ours and we can take ownership. After we have labeled our feelings and emotions, we can pursue the process of changing the unhelpful ones to healthier ones.

VIEWING LIFE'S EXPERIENCES
FROM A HEALTHIER PERSPECTIVE

It's very easy to say, "Let's choose the right emotional response," but how do we do that? One wife commented, "I am so angry all the time at my husband ever since his affair, and I just can't stop my feelings. I feel guilty for being so angry at him, but as hard as I try, I can't stop the feeling." Feelings of anger toward our loved ones and their behaviors are common. We certainly have the right to feel anger. Once we recognize the anger, is there a way to direct it so we can use it to our advantage? Can we use anger to help us in our healing? Is it possible to look at the experience from a different perspective and begin to choose a more helpful emotional response? It's true our loved ones' betrayal (behavioral and emotional withdrawal) does emotionally impact us, but do we want to disturb ourselves even more by our choices of how we view the experience? Elder Joseph B. Wirthlin observed:

> *We all are going through different life experiences. While some are filled with joy today, others feel as though their hearts could burst with sorrow. Some feel as though the world is their oyster; others feel as though they were the oyster itself, plucked from the ocean, cracked open, and robbed of all that is precious to them* (Ensign, Nov. 2001, 25).

Life experiences are different for each of us. How we *view* our life's experiences will in great measure determine our emotional response and level of disturbance. If we view our situation as though we are the oyster, cracked open and robbed of our pearls, we will have an emotional response that is counterproductive. On the other hand, if we view the world as our oyster and us as the pearl becoming more refined and spiritually beautiful with each hard experience, our emotional response is likely to be more helpful.

🌿 How can you use Elder Wirthlin's analogy in your present situation?

_____

_____

_____

_____

_____

_____

The Prophet Joseph Smith described the refinement from his trials: "I am like a huge, rough stone rolling down from a high mountain; and the only polishing I get is when some corner gets rubbed off . . . Thus will I become a smooth and polished shaft in the quiver of the Almighty" (*Teachings of the Prophet Joseph Smith*, 304.)

🌿 How can you view your present situation as an opportunity to become "a smooth and polished shaft in the quiver of the Almighty?"

_____

_____

_____

_____

_____

BINOCULAR VISION

With "binocular vision" we attempt to see a distinction or separation between our loved ones and their behaviors. When we look through a pair of binoculars, we can focus the lens to see one image or two images. If we adjust the lens so there is only one image, we have lumped our loved ones and their behaviors together. This single-lens approach often increases our negative emotions to unhealthy levels. When we adjust the binoculars so we can see two images through the lens, our loved one is one image and their compulsive behaviors that we dislike is the other image.

If we charted our feelings on paper, we would discover that healing for us and our loved ones is not a straight line. The line is usually squiggly, jagged, erratic, unpredictable, and temperamental, with an occasional upward movement. If we demand positive upward movement all the time, we will make ourselves very unhappy and quite often disappointed and depressed. Over time we hope that the line symbolizing our progress will have fewer jagged low points and eventually begin to move more consistently upward. Moving upward toward God is *our* goal, but it may not be our loved ones'. We can only work on our own goals and perhaps influence our loved ones in positive ways.

Over the "long haul" we hope that our chart would show feelings of love, but on a day-to-day basis feelings of bitterness, resentment, hatred, and anger during our healing are commonly recognized. In addition, we often experience feelings of being used, deceived, and manipulated. Our goal is to direct these volatile emotions *toward our loved ones' behaviors* rather than at *our loved ones*. Alma used this perspective when he talked to his son, Corianton, about his sexual sins:

> *And now, my son, I would to God that ye had not been guilty of so great a crime. I would not dwell upon your crimes, to harrow up your soul, if it were not for your good.*
>
> *But behold, ye cannot hide your crimes from God; and except ye repent they will stand as a testimony against you at the last day.*
>
> *Now my son, I would that ye should repent and forsake your sins, and go no more after the lusts of your eyes* (Alma 39:7-9).

Alma was adamant that Corianton's crimes were sins, but he still called him "my son." He did not disown him. By calling him "my son," Alma separated the crime from the fact that Corianton was his son. Alma did not call Corianton a criminal, but he clearly declared that his son's crimes could not be hidden from God and that his son was personally responsible to repent and forsake his sins.

This is not easy because we usually see our loved ones and their behaviors as one and the same—which I call single vision. To create helpful, binocular vision, take a piece of paper and draw a vertical line down the middle. Draw a stick figure of your loved one on the left side and label it "son or daughter of God." On the right side list the behaviors you dislike about your loved one that are connected with his compulsive behaviors. Realize that the negative *behaviors* on the right side of the page are what we hate, not the person on the left side.

▶ Has this exercise helped you to create binocular vision—an ability to separate your loved one from his behaviors?

_____

_____

_____

_____

This idea of developing binocular vision will take a substantial amount of work and effort to become part of our healing. When a spouse has been involved with inappropriate sexual behavior, it is so difficult not to take it personally. In these situations we are trying to separate ourselves from our loved ones' behaviors.

> *I knew intellectually I could separate my husband's behaviors from me, but it was very difficult to do so emotionally. The volatile emotional experience was so painful it seemed to attack me from all sides. I knew in my mind and on paper I could separate all of this out, but how could I separate all of this from my heart? I had committed my mind, heart, and soul to my husband, and now was I supposed to just cut out my emotions like some kind of surgery? This was so difficult for me to do.*

When our spouse is the one involved in inappropriate behavior, we attempt to use binocular vision to separate us from them and recognize that they are responsible for their own behavior. In addition, we attempt to use binocular vision to separate our loved ones from their compulsive behaviors. This way we can see our loved ones as sons or daughters of God and their behaviors as sinful acts that need to be changed. The day-to-day picture may look bleak. During our healing, we benefit by looking at the big picture and our long-term relationship with our loved ones. To teach this principle, President James E. Faust shared an excerpt from a letter he had received:

> *An anonymous Church member wrote about the continuous heartache her brother caused her parents. He got involved in drugs. He resisted all efforts at control and discipline. He was deceitful and defiant. Unlike the prodigal, this errant son did not come home of his own accord. Instead he got caught by the police and was forced to face the consequences of his actions. For two years his parents supported Bill's treatment program, which brought about his eventual*

recovery from drugs. In summary, Bill's sister observed: "I think my parents are extraordinary. They never wavered in their love for Bill, though they disagreed with and even hated what he was doing to himself and to their family life. But they were committed enough to their family to support Bill in any way necessary to get him through the tough times and onto more solid ground. They practiced the deeper, more sensitive, and extensive gospel of Christ by loving one who had gone astray (Ensign, May 2003, 67-68).

The helpful binocular approach is to separate our loved ones from their behaviors. Our loved ones certainly have positive qualities and talents, but they also have these behaviors that pull them down and tear us apart. The sentences I wish to emphasize from this letter are, "I think my parents are extraordinary. They never wavered in their love for Bill, though they disagreed with and even hated what he was doing to himself and to their family life." The parents loved Bill but hated Bill's behaviors. We can do the same. We can see the person as a son or daughter of God and see the behaviors as separate. President N. Eldon Tanner taught this principle: "Sometimes the ones who need to be loved most are the ones who seem to deserve it the least. Though we may not appreciate or approve of what someone does, we must still show love for the individual" (*New Era*, June 1977, 5). Bill had a change of heart! He chose to turn himself around. Sadly, not all of our loved ones will follow Bill's repentant course.

🔯 How can you separate your loved one from his behaviors?

_____

_____

_____

_____

_____

🔯 Why is it important to separate the two?

_____

_____

_____

_____

_____

By reminding ourselves to use binocular vision, we can see two images as we look through the lens. One image is a loved one, who is a son or daughter of God, and the other image is a loved one's behaviors that need improvement. We will greatly reduce our emotional disturbance by seeing two images.

OPPOSITION IN ALL THINGS

We know that there is opposition in all things, and we often think about opposition as the difference between good or bad. Opposition in all things is not only the difference between righteousness and wickedness, but it is also the difference between happiness and misery. We have opposition in our emotions too! The prophet Lehi taught:

> For it must needs be, that there is an opposition in all things. If not so, my firstborn in the wilderness, righteousness could not be brought to pass, neither wickedness, neither holiness nor misery, neither good nor bad. Wherefore, all things must needs be a compound in one; wherefore, if it should be one body it must needs remain as dead, having no life neither death, nor corruption nor incorruption, happiness nor misery, neither sense nor insensibility (2 Ne. 2:11).

Seldom do we think about "opposition in all things" as the difference between happiness and misery, even though happiness and misery was an example provided by Prophet Lehi. Is it possible to move our emotions from misery to some degree of happiness? The scriptures teach this principle:

> [We are] troubled on every side, yet not distressed; [we are] perplexed, but not in despair;
> Persecuted, but not forsaken; cast down, but not destroyed (2 Cor. 4:8-9).

Our experiences impact us and our emotions. Our loved ones' behaviors affect us too! But how much will we allow their behaviors to control us and escalate our emotions to increasingly unhealthy levels? Can we choose where our anger is directed and to what level it climbs? Can we eventually respond with strength and power rather than anger?

WE CHOOSE OUR EMOTIONAL RESPONSE

We all want to feel accepted, calm, and secure. We do not like to see ourselves as lonely, frustrated, or insecure. When we begin to feel emotional pain, the natural tendency is to simultaneously and unconsciously attempt to cover up the unwanted emotion by running away, getting defensive, being angry, or making poor choices. Healing begins when we accept the pain as part of real life and deal with it in a healthier way, that means dealing with the pain directly instead of letting it turn to anger. President Ezra Taft Benson taught: "There is a tendency to think of fitness solely in terms of physical, in terms of bodily strength. But to be truly fit, truly equal to the demands of life, requires much more than bodily strength. It involves the mind and the training of the mind, the emotions and their use and control. Yes, and it involves the soul and the spiritual growth, too" (*Teachings of Ezra Taft Benson*, 239).

Hymn 336, "School Thy Feelings," by Charles W. Penrose reinforces this principle:

School thy feelings, O my brother;
Train thy warm, impulsive soul.
Do not its emotions smother,
But let wisdom's voice control.
School thy feelings; there is power
In the cool, collected mind.
Passion shatters reason's tower,
Makes the clearest vision blind.

Chorus

School thy feelings, O my brother;
Train thy warm, impulsive soul.
Do not its emotions smother,
But let wisdom's voice control.

We sing in church, "Choose the right when a choice is placed before you." While singing, we usually think about choosing to obey the Word of Wisdom, to keep the Sabbath day holy, or to pay our tithing—the commandments and how well we live them. Let's sing the first line of the song with a different approach, "Choose the right emotional response when the choice is placed before you." What do you think of the new version? Can we sing these new words to ourselves? Can we implement these new words in our lives? If we have agency to choose between right and wrong, don't we also have agency to choose a helpful emotional response to our loved ones' behaviors? Elder Neal A. Maxwell observed, "The defining moments in the 'life of the soul' continue to turn on whether we respond with self-indulgence or self-denial in our daily, individual decisions, as between kindness and anger, mercy and injustice, generosity and meanness" (*Ensign,* May, 2003, 70). Can we actually choose between kindness and anger, mercy and injustice, and generosity and meanness? Yes, we can, but it takes new thoughts and a new perspective.

This does not mean that negative emotions are always bad—it's the way we choose to respond and deal with them that might make them unhealthy. President Brigham Young taught: "Do not get so angry that you cannot pray: do not allow yourselves to become so angry that you cannot feed an enemy—even your worst enemy, if an opportunity should present itself. There is a wicked anger, and there is a righteous anger. The Lord does not suffer wicked anger to be in his heart; but there is anger in his bosom" (*Journal of Discourses,* 5:229-30, Sept. 13, 1857). For example, we may use anger in unhelpful ways if we use it as a weapon, become more unhappy, create more self-pity, lose self-respect, make our emotions worse, and feel guilty for being angry. On the other hand, we may use anger in helpful ways if it motivates us to solve our problems, take assertive action, maintain our rights, protect ourselves, decline unreasonable demands, and solve our problems.

It is easy to write about what we should do on paper, but it is difficult to do it. President Gordon B. Hinckley stated: "Anger is not an expression of strength. It is an indication of one's inability to control his thoughts, words, his emotions. Of course it is easy to get angry. When the weakness of anger takes over, the strength of reason leaves. Cultivate within yourselves the mighty power of self-discipline" (*Ensign,* Nov. 1991, 51). Choosing the right emotional response is very difficult because it requires us to rise above the natural man, and "the natural man is an enemy to God" (Mosiah 3:19).

 What are your thoughts about our ability to choose our emotions?

The natural man response is to get even with our loved ones or try to control them so that they will never act out again. The natural man response is to display anger toward our loved ones and want them to hurt as much as we do. We can actually choose a better way to respond to our loved ones' behaviors. Why is it so important to respond in a healthier way? Because the "life of our soul" will be impacted by our choice! Satan may have succeeded for now in leading our loved ones away, but we cannot let him lead us away too! We can easily be led away, not by breaking obvious commandments, but by choosing an unrighteous emotional response. Satan has many ways to trap us; he doesn't care how—he just wants us trapped and miserable.

For our loved ones, the trap may have been being tempted and finally violating the law of chastity. For us, Satan's trap may be tempting us to choose emotions of bitterness, resentment, hatred, and anger. Satan has many cunning avenues to approach us and get to our weaknesses. Elder George Q. Cannon taught how Satan works: "By this we see the power of Satan, the knowledge of Satan, and his cunning. He understands the avenues through which he can approach us best; he knows the weaknesses of our character, and we do not know the moment we may be seduced by him, and be overcome and fall victims to him" (*Journal of Discourses*, 11:173-74, Oct., 1865).

We need to be aware and alert so our responses to our loved ones' behaviors include helpful ways to deal with our own pain. Unhealthy emotions such as bitterness, resentment, hatred, revenge, and anger separate us from God and keep us from becoming like Him. They also blind our spiritual eyes so that we cannot see what God wants us to do and become. If we want to remove these slow-growing emotional cataracts from our spiritual eyes, we need to make a conscious choice to use the healing power of the Atonement moment by moment. Otherwise, we may choose an unhealthy response to our emotions during one of our "defining moments."

What can you do to avoid the power of Satan and his cunningness?

REDUCING EMOTIONAL DISTURBANCES

We can diffuse our emotional disturbances in several different ways. There is a link between our thoughts, feelings, and behaviors. Proverbs says, "For as he thinketh in his heart, so [is] he" (Prov. 23:7). In essence, what we think is what we become. If we constantly have feelings of being hurt by our loved ones, and the hurt turns to anger, we usually act in angry ways. Following in the wake of anger, we may experience feelings of guilt for being angry. How do we begin to change our thoughts, feelings, and behaviors toward our loved ones? We begin by realizing that we have our agency to *choose* our thoughts, emotions, and behaviors just as they do. This awareness leads us to take responsibility for these thoughts, feelings, and actions and see that we can change them. Let's look at the scriptures again:

> *[We are] troubled on every side, yet not distressed; [we are] perplexed, but not in despair;*
> *Persecuted, but not forsaken; cast down, but not destroyed* (2 Cor. 4:8-9).

We Choose Our Emotions	
Troubled	Not distressed
Perplexed	Not in despair
Persecuted	Not forsaken
Cast down	Not destroyed

We can choose our emotional responses. The emotional responses on the left side of the chart are confining and unhelpful, but we do feel them at times and need to have self-awareness. The emotional responses on the right side are healthier because they empower us to continue. In essence we learn over time how to manage our emotions better and respond in ways that are productive.

If we recognize that we have our agency and others have theirs, we begin to see that choice and accountability are the answers to diffusing the unhealthy emotional habits that can victimize us. To stop the pattern of being victims of distress or despair or having feelings of being forsaken or destroyed, we need to exercise our God-given agency and choose to seek the power of the Atonement to help us see the situation through His eye, with eternal lenses that will mend and heal our broken heart. We begin this journey by laying our negative feelings on the altar in order that He may perform the altering miracle within our hearts. Elder Joseph B. Wirthlin counseled:

> *We must let go of the negative emotions that bind our hearts and instead fill our souls with love, faith, and thanksgiving.*
>
> *Anger, resentment, and bitterness stunt our spiritual growth. Would you bathe in impure water? Then why do we bathe our spirits with negative and bitter thoughts and feelings? . . .*

He further explained:

> *You can cleanse your heart. You don't have to harbor thoughts and feelings that drag you down and destroy your spirit. . . . Every day drain from your heart the feelings of resentment, rage, and defeat that do nothing but discourage and destroy. Fill your heart with those things that ennoble, encourage, and inspire* (*Ensign,* Sept. 2001, 11).

It will take work, but it can be done. How often does Elder Wirthlin recommend that one cleanse the heart? What does he suggest as replacements?

_____

_____

_____

_____

_____

_____

How can you begin the journey of letting go of negative emotions?

_____

_____

_____

_____

🌿 As you pray for the strength and insight to let go of negative emotions, record the thoughts and feelings that come into your mind and heart.

_____

_____

_____

_____

_____

We heal by letting go, diffusing our negative emotions, and moving on. Here is one way to approach it: (1) Recognize what we are feeling and realize that it is okay; (2) Realize that we can choose a healthy response to what we are feeling; (3) Manage our emotional response the best way we can; and (4) Let go of unhealthy response habits by changing our viewpoint or perspective.

In the past we wanted to heal, but we also wanted to keep our rage and anger toward our loved ones. Since these two responses are contrary to one another, one or the other must go. We decide. We choose which one to let go. If we accept and respect the eternal principle of agency, our emotional responses to our loved ones will be more helpful to them and will advance our own healing.

THE GREAT PLAN OF HAPPINESS

The great plan of happiness provides a way for us to return to live with our Heavenly Father. Since we all would sin, we needed a Savior. In the pre-earthly life our Father, referring to a Savior, said, "Whom shall I send?" (Abr. 3:27) Two of our brothers responded to the question. One said, "Father, thy will be done, and the glory be thine forever" (Moses 4:2). The other brother said, "Behold, here am I, send me, I will be thy son, and I will redeem all mankind, that one soul shall not be lost, and surely I will do it; wherefore give me thine honor" (Moses 4:1). Our Heavenly Father's response was, "I will send the first" (Abr. 3:27). How did Satan respond? "And the second was angry, and kept not his first estate" (Abr. 3:28). Satan demanded that all obey and return to live with Heavenly Father. No one must be lost. Every one must return. Because his demand was not accepted he became very angry and "many followed after him" (Abr. 3:28). If our demands are not met, we often become angry too. Unhealthy emotions are usually created because we have a "must" or a demand. We must have it. We demand it. Life must change. Our loved ones must change. Our loved ones must not do this to us.

Our Father responded to Satan's plan, "Wherefore, because that Satan rebelled against me, and sought to destroy the agency of man, which I, the Lord God, had given him, and also, that I should give unto him mine own power; by the power of mine Only Begotten, I caused that he should be cast down" (Moses 4:3). God's plan provided for choice and accountability. With agency, we choose to obey or disobey. Giving ourselves and our loved ones permission to use agency to make choices is the only healthy way to approach life, because agency is the eternal principle that God operates under and so must we. Here is a summary of the pre-earthly life:

Demand or Must	Agency or Choice
I will redeem all mankind.	Father, thy will be done.
One soul shall not be lost.	[Every person may choose to come back.]
Surely I will do it.	I, the Lord God, had given [them–Agency.]
Wherefore give me thine honor.	The glory be thine forever.
Sought to destroy the agency of man. (Moses 4:1, Moses 4:3)	[Protect agency.] (Moses 4:2-3)

There were two responses to the plan presented by our Heavenly Father in the pre-earthly life. Agency or choice is the Christ-centered plan for healing.

DEMANDS OR AGENCY

When we demand something and don't get it, we usually have emotions similar to those on the left side of the chart (page 238). In addition, we usually think that happiness is an outside event—something that happens *to* us, rather than something that happens *inside* us. A demand is often part of a search for someone or something external to make us happy. Sometimes we tell ourselves we must have happiness, and we demand that our loved ones give it to us. That kind of happiness is always elusive.

When we recognize that we have agency to choose, we realize that happiness is what we become—it's what we choose on the inside—not because of what happens on the outside. Elder L. Tom Perry stated, "Given that there must be opposition in all things (see 2 Ne. 2:11), with agency comes the need to choose good from evil. Moreover, agency also opens the possibility for sin" (*Ensign,* Nov. 1999, 77). Because of agency our loved ones can choose to sin if they so desire. Even though we may demand their abstinence, they may choose to act out. This brings us great sorrow, similar to what Lehi recorded about Nephi's experience with Laman and Lemuel, "He hath suffered much sorrow because of you" (2 Ne. 1:24). Jacob, Nephi's younger brother, had a similar experience, "And behold, in thy childhood thou hast suffered afflictions and much sorrow, because of the rudeness of thy brethren" (2 Ne. 2:1). We too have suffered afflictions and much sorrow because of our loved ones' behaviors!

Still, accepting agency is the only wise path. We only increase our emotional turmoil and experience more emotional distress when we make demands. We decrease our distress when we embrace God's gift of agency—the right to choose. We can ask the Lord to help us begin to see others as God sees them—as children who have the right to choose.

> *Wherefore, men are free according to the flesh; and all things are given them which are expedient unto man. And they are free to choose liberty and eternal life, through the great Mediator of all men, or to choose captivity and death, according to the captivity and power of the devil; for he seeketh that all men might be miserable like unto himself* (2 Ne 2:27).

We are free to choose for ourselves and so are our loved ones. Even though we may not like our loved ones' behaviors, which violate God's laws, we cannot override our loved ones' agency.

This new way of thinking and behaving will take time to learn and live; but agency not only allows our loved ones to make poor choices, it also empowers us to choose healthier emotional responses.

🔖 Review the feelings listed on the chart again (Page 238). Are your thoughts, emotions, and behaviors usually attached to the left side of the chart or the right?

_____

_____

_____

_____

_____

_____

How would it help your healing to embrace the right side of the chart?

_____

_____

_____

_____

_____

_____

When we set a demand or must, rather than allowing agency or choice, we usually set ourselves up for unhealthy, emotional volatility that eventually wears us out.

AVOID DEMANDS OR MUSTS

We are talking about avoiding the idea or belief that our loved ones must not behave the way they do. We are working to give up the demand that they behave a certain way. Why? Because when it comes right down to decision time, they will do what they *choose* to do, what they desire. If that is not what we want, where will that leave us? We will be less emotionally disturbed if we accept their agency and use the Spirit to guide our decisions.

Operating under agency and choice does not mean we let our loved ones "walk over" us. Instead it *does* mean that we can set firm boundaries and make those boundaries known to our loved ones. (Boundaries are discussed in Principle 7.) We make sure that we protect ourselves! Furthermore, accepting their agency does not mean we approve of their unrighteous behaviors. We do not approve, and we make that clear when we feel impressed to do so. By operating under eternal laws and honoring the agency of our loved ones, we receive healing. We want to heal from the hurt regardless of the choices of our loved ones. When we embrace the reality of God's universal gift of agency and choice, we are more likely to respond in ways that move us toward our own healing.

Another danger to consider is this: If we continue our patterns of "musts or demands" with those around us, we usually use this same pattern when dealing with God—we demand things. This is not helpful and is contrary to God's eternal plan for us. Elder Boyd K. Packer expressed,

It is not wise to wrestle with the revelations with such insistence as to demand immediate answers or blessings to your liking. You cannot force spiritual things. Such words as compel, coerce, constrain, pressure, demand, do not describe our privileges with the Spirit. You can no more force the Spirit to respond than you can force a bean to sprout, or an egg to hatch before its time. You can create a climate to foster growth, nourish, and protect; but you cannot force or compel: you must await the growth (*Ensign*, Jan. 1983, 53).

Shouldn't we try to create a climate where we can grow, nourish, and protect ourselves? Why is this so important to our healing and salvation? Elder Boyd K. Packer continued: "Do not be impatient to gain great spiritual knowledge. Let it grow, help it grow, but do not force it or you will open the way to be misled" (*Ensign*, Jan. 1983, 53).

What are some of the demands you have made on others or God?

Why is it so important that you give up the idea or belief that you can demand answers or blessings from the Spirit?

Elder Neal A. Maxwell gave us more wise counsel: "And when we are given thorns in the flesh, let us not demand to see the rose garden! (see 2 Cor. 12:7)" (*Ensign*, Nov. 1980, 15). Even though we may have a thorny path to trod, we can choose to view our situation from a healthy perspective, one that allows us to regain hope and empowers us to draw on the powers from Heaven. The principle of agency extends to all aspects of our lives. We can choose to heal without demanding that our circumstances be different.

CHANGE IRRATIONAL BELIEFS ABOUT THE EVENT; GET HEALTHIER EMOTIONS

If we do not like the feelings we are having regarding our loved ones' behaviors, we need to backtrack and discover what *irrational beliefs* we hold about those behaviors. We cannot change their behaviors, but we can change our irrational beliefs or perspectives about their behaviors. What is an irrational belief? One that usually includes a demand or must. Here is an example from the scriptures about how two people viewed the same incident. Because of their viewpoints or beliefs about the incident, each one created a different set of emotions and corresponding behaviors. The Parable of the Prodigal Son (Luke 15:11-32) illustrates a three-step process: (1) Our irrational beliefs about an event (how we choose to interpret it); (2) The emotions created because of our irrational beliefs about the event; and (3) Our behavioral choices because of our emotions—our response.

To change our emotions and generate healthier ones that facilitate healing, we need to change our irrational belief about the event. Here is the event and each person's perspective.

> *A certain man had two sons:*
> *And the younger of them said to [his] father, Father, give me the portion of goods that falleth [to me]. And he divided unto them [his] living.*
> *And not many days after the younger son gathered all together, and took his journey into a far country, and there wasted his substance with riotous living* (Luke 15:11-13).

The younger son spent all of his inheritance and, in the words of his elder brother, "devoured [his] living with harlots" (Luke 15:30). While the younger son was away, after he wasted his inheritance and lost it, he became a servant for another man and fed his swine. Speaking of the younger son, the scriptures record:

> *And when he came to himself, he said, How many hired servants of my father's have bread enough and to spare, and I perish with hunger!*
> *I will arise and go to my father, and will say unto him, Father, I have sinned against heaven, and before thee* (Luke 15:17-18).

When the younger son returned, the father had an entirely different emotional response than the older son because of their differing beliefs about the return of the younger son. Here is the father's response to the younger son's return:

> But when he was yet a great way off, his father saw him, and had compassion, and ran, and fell on his neck, and kissed him.
>
> For this my son was dead, and is alive again; he was lost, and is found. And they began to be merry (Luke 15:20, 24).

Here is the older brother's response:

> Now his elder son was in the field: and as he came and drew nigh to the house, he heard musick and dancing.
>
> And he called one of the servants, and asked what these things meant.
>
> And he said unto him, Thy brother is come; and thy father hath killed the fatted calf, because he hath received him safe and sound.
>
> And he was angry, and would not go in: therefore came his father out, and intreated him. (Luke 15:25-28).

The incident was the same. The younger brother returned home, and a party and celebration followed. However, the father (row 1 below) and the elder brother (row 2 below) created two entirely different sets of emotions because of how each viewed the incident. Their behaviors (column 3 below) were a reflection of the emotions that were created because of their beliefs about the event.

Father's Belief about the Event	Father's Emotional Response	Father's Behavior
[Son] was dead, and is alive again; and was lost, and is found (Luke 15:31-32).	His father saw him and had compassion and ran and fell on his neck and kissed him (Luke 15:20).	Father killed the fatted calf because he hath received him safe and sound (Luke 15:27). And they began to be merry (Luke 15:24).
Elder Son's Irrational Belief about the Event	**Elder Son's Emotional Response**	**Elder Son's Behavior**
Father, Lo, these many years do I serve thee, neither transgressed I at any time thy commandment: and yet thou never gavest me a kid, that I might make merry with my friends: (Luke 15:29).	He was angry. (Luke 15:28).	Would not go in [to party]: therefore came his father out, and intreated him. (Luke 15:28).

Father's Response

The father's emotions included compassion:

> *But when he was yet a great way off, his father saw him, and had compassion, and ran, and fell on his neck, and kissed him.*
>
> *For this my son was dead, and is alive again; he was lost, and is found. And they began to be merry* (Luke 15:20, 24).

Elder Son's Response

The elder son's emotions were filled with self-pity, resentment, and anger. He would not participate in the welcome home party and stayed outside. He pouted and waited until his father came out to find him. How did the elder son respond to his father?

> *And he answering said to [his] father, Lo, these many years do I serve thee, neither transgressed I at any time thy commandment: and yet thou never gavest me a kid, that I might make merry with my friends:*
>
> *But as soon as this thy son was come, which hath devoured thy living with harlots, thou hast killed for him the fatted calf* (Luke 15:29-30).

The elder brother was angry because the younger brother was getting all the attention, and no such party had ever been thrown for him, even though he was the obedient son and had lived the commandments. How did his father respond?

> *And he said unto him, Son, thou art ever with me, and all that I have is thine.*
>
> *It was meet that we should make merry, and be glad: for this thy brother was dead, and is alive again; and was lost, and is found* (Luke 15:31-32).

The elder son was so angry that he missed the reason the party was thrown in the first place. The father said, "This thy brother was dead, and is alive again; and was lost, and is found." The party was not thrown as a reward for the younger son's bad behaviors and choices, but because the son had returned. That was reason to celebrate! But the elder son's irrational belief and anger blinded him. How do we know this? By his response:

> *These many years do I serve thee, neither transgressed I at any time thy commandment: and yet thou never gavest me a kid, that I might make merry with my friends:*
>
> *But as soon as this thy son was come, which hath devoured thy living with harlots, thou hast killed for him the fatted calf* (Luke 15:29-30).

In summary, the father was happy because of his younger son's return. The elder brother was miserable and angry; he had always been faithful, while the younger son wasted his inheritance on riotous living. He couldn't change his brother's choices or the fact that his father chose to give him a party—but he could change his response.

In a way we are in the same situation as the elder son. We cannot change the choices our loved ones have made in the past, but we can work to change our emotional response. How? By changing our irrational beliefs about the incident. If we read between the lines, the irrational belief that the elder son held appears to be:

> *My father should throw a party for me too. I have lived the commandments and my brother has not. My father ought to reward me with a party. Life isn't fair. Life must be fair. I should be treated the same as my brother—or better. This can't go on. I can't endure such a terrible injustice. No one should ever be treated this unfairly.*

The elder son carried a very irrational belief about the return of his younger brother, and only he had the power to change his irrational belief. He needed to recognize that the irrational belief he so desperately clung to was unhealthy and he needed to be willing to change it. Why was his belief irrational? Because his father could choose to throw a party for whomever he wants.

Since when is life always fair? When are two siblings always treated the same? When does one human being need to meet another human being's definition of fairness? Why can't we be treated unfairly? Was Joseph Smith treated fairly? Was the Savior treated fairly? Why can't we go on with life even when it is not fair? By identifying and changing our irrational beliefs, we can create healthier emotions.

If we want to change our emotions and have a helpful response for ourselves and our loved ones, we need to go back to step one and change how we are choosing to interpret the event. Why do we work hard to change our perspective? Because how we interpret the event creates the disturbed emotional feelings, not the event itself. We are working toward seeing the truth—not fooling ourselves or talking ourselves out of what seems true to us. Our interpretations that cause us grief are almost always distortions of the truth—not at all the way the Lord sees things. Peace comes only as we bring our perspective in line with His. The Spirit can help us: "For the Spirit speaketh the truth and lieth not. Wherefore, it speaketh of things as they really are, and of things as they really will be; wherefore, these things are manifested unto us plainly, for the salvation of our souls" (Jacob 4:13). We can change our irrational belief by strongly embracing agency and the right to choose. We rewrite what we tell ourselves and then work hard to embrace the new belief using the principles from the chart.

Agency and Choice
Father, thy will be done.
[Choose to come back.]
I, the Lord God, have given [them agency].
The glory be thine forever.
[Protect agency.] (Moses 4:2-3)

How will we choose to view our loved ones' behaviors? If we work hard to change our irrational belief and recognize that our loved ones have their agency and can choose, we will experience less emotional turmoil even though we still feel pain. If we say their behaviors *must* change or we *demand* that they change, we will increase our emotional disturbance if they do not. Why? We are not getting what we wanted or what was promised, which often results in anger and more upset feelings. When we have an extreme emotional disturbance, we usually have irrational beliefs about the event. Our beliefs usually have the following:

Must or Demand
I will redeem all mankind.
One soul shall not be lost.
Surely I will do it.
Wherefore give me thine honor.
Sought to destroy the agency of man. (Moses 4:1, Moses 4:3)

CREATING HEALTHIER EMOTIONS

We can change unhealthy emotions to healthier emotions if we are willing to change our irrational beliefs regarding the incident. The elder son's distress was not the fact that the father threw a party for the younger son. It was about his irrational belief that "life must be fair according to my definition of fair." The elder son's irrational belief about what a party represented created his anger and then he made choices to inflame his anger by not discussing it with his father and choosing not to attend the party. Anger is healthy when we choose to recognize it and use it to further our healing. It is what we choose to do with the emotion of anger that either makes it healthy or unhealthy.

Suppose you were the elder brother and your younger brother returned home after riotous living. How could you change your irrational belief about the purpose of the party in order to create a healthier emotional response? What would you need to say to yourself? Study and ponder the chart below before you write what you would need to say to yourself (your new rational belief about the event). Our goal is to move away from the left side of the chart, since it's unhelpful in dealing with our loved ones' behaviors, and move toward the right side of the chart. The more we can use the principles from the right side of the chart to establish our new belief and really strive to live by them, the healthier our response will be to our loved ones' behaviors. Please use the words *agency* and *choice* in your response.

Must or Demand	Agency or Choice
I will redeem all mankind.	Father, thy will be done.
One soul shall not be lost.	[Choose to come back.]
Surely I will do it.	I, the Lord God, had given [them agency].
Wherefore give me thine honor.	The glory be thine forever.
Sought to destroy the agency of man (Moses 4:1, 3).	[Protect agency.] (Moses 4:2–3).

My new belief: What do I need to tell myself to create healthier emotions about my loved one's behaviors? I will choose to incorporate this new belief so I will respond in a healthier way.

How would this new rational belief about the party help you in your healing and dealing with your younger brother?

🌿 Would this new rational belief about the party help you to draw closer to your younger brother?

_____

_____

_____

_____

_____

🌿 How would this new rational belief about the party be helpful in your relationship with your father?

_____

_____

_____

_____

_____

🌿 After evaluating your present situation regarding your loved one's behaviors, how could you change any irrational beliefs about the incidents in order to experience healthier emotions? What would you need to tell yourself? Please use the words *agency* and *choice* in your response.

_____

_____

_____

_____

_____

Often it is what we tell ourselves that gets us in trouble. It is not the incident nor event that upsets us, but what we say or tell ourselves about it.

CHANGE THINKING WHEN STUDYING THE NEW TESTAMENT

We usually have to adjust our own beliefs about the upsetting incident in order
to find the happiness and peace we desire. Why? Because that's the only part we
can control. Adjusting our thinking to change our emotions and behaviors is not
a new idea. It parallels the adjustment it takes when studying the New Testament
versus the Old Testament. President James E. Faust explained:

> The Apostle Paul was well acquainted with the adjustment in thinking
> needed when moving from the Old Testament to the New Testament. It is a
> journey from the rigid formality of the letter of the law taught by Moses to
> the spiritual guidance found in the Holy Spirit.
>
> In his epistle to the Hebrews, Paul described this adjustment: "For the
> law [of Moses] made nothing perfect, but [was only] the bringing in of a
> better hope . . . ; by the which we draw nigh unto God. . . . [And] by so much
> was Jesus made [the] surety of a better testament" (Hebrews 7:19, 22; see
> also *Joseph Smith Translation*, Hebrews 7:19—20) (*Ensign*, Sept. 2003, 3).

Many examples in the scriptures show how individuals changed their beliefs
to correlate with divine perspective and by so doing experienced healthier emotions—new emotions that allowed them to feel the Spirit and become more
Christlike. President James E. Faust continued:

> The New Testament is "a better testament" because so much is left to the
> intent of the heart and of the mind and the promptings of the Holy Spirit. This
> refinement of the soul is part of the reinforcing steel of a personal testimony of
> Jesus Christ. If there is no witness in the heart and in the mind by the power of
> the Holy Ghost, there can be no testimony (*Ensign*, Nov. 2003, 6).

CHANGE IRRATIONAL BELIEFS ABOUT OUR LOVED ONES' BEHAVIORS

Our goal is to follow the example of Paul and diffuse distress, despair, and feelings of being forsaken or destroyed by aligning our views with God's eternal
perspective. We want to manage our emotions and move them from the left side
of the chart to the right side of the chart. How do we do this? By changing our
irrational belief about the event. What are our irrational beliefs about our love
ones' behaviors? Are our beliefs helpful or unhelpful?

Unhealthy Emotions: Usually generated by setting musts or demands on ourselves or others.	Healthy Emotions: Usually generated by accepting agency and choice for ourselves and others.
Troubled	Not distressed
Perplexed	Not in despair
Persecuted	Not forsaken
Cast down (2 Cor. 4:8-9)	Not destroyed (2 Cor. 4:8-9)

We can either set demands for our loved ones and attempt to override their agency, or we can change our irrational beliefs about their behaviors by listening to the Spirit and following the promptings as they come. What is our irrational belief about a loved one's indulgence in pornography or other wayward behaviors? When we have uncomfortable emotions, such as misery, we often have some work to do in changing our *irrational belief* regarding the incident that is causing our emotions. Why? Because that is what we can control—the way we view or interpret the incidents that happen in life. Only seeking the truth sets us free from the misery of our false beliefs.

We cannot control what another person decides to do. The father could not control his younger son's decision to leave and waste his inheritance. If our loved ones leave with their inheritance, we, like the father, should recognize that it is their choice and natural consequences will follow their use of agency. Accepting a new belief about our loved ones' decision will have less impact on our happiness and contentment. "[He that is] slow to anger [is] better than the mighty; and he that ruleth his spirit than he that taketh a city" (Prov. 16:32).

VOCALIZING OUR PREFERENCES

We have every reason to believe that the elder son would have liked to have a party thrown for him. However, he never states his preference, wish, or desire, but was a talented hint dropper. The wishes of the elder son were not likely to be met as long as he sat outside, pouted, and never expressed them. He may even have become more angry when he did not get attention for being angry. The more the elder son replayed the hurt, the more angry he was likely to become. Similarly, the more we replay and practice our hurt, the more angry we are likely to become. It is better to face our hurt, experience it, deal with it, and walk through it. One way to walk through the hurt is to clearly tell our loved ones what we prefer, wish, or desire.

What feelings or emotions are you experiencing that you would like to share with your loved one?

_____

_____

_____

_____

When is an appropriate time and place to share your feelings and emotions?

_____

_____

_____

_____

OUR NEW BELIEFS ABOUT OUR LOVED ONES' BEHAVIORS

When we embrace agency and choice, we actually have more control over our emotional response and eternal destiny. We can quit *reacting* to the events of life and begin *acting*. We stop being passive and become assertive and proactive. We are no longer tossed to the wind and blown around like a tumbleweed. We are more likely to assert our thoughts and feelings and make them known. We let our loved ones know what we desire in the relationship. We state our boundaries. We tell them our desire for them to get help.

There are three parts to this new belief: (1) I can choose; (2) My loved one can choose; and (3) I will continue my healing even if I do not like my loved one's choices.

When we respect their agency to choose something other than what we desire, we have less emotional disturbance and can therefore make better decisions for ourselves. By honoring agency we invite the Spirit into our lives.

Let's review. Part one (next page) is using our agency to clearly state our choice—what we prefer, wish, or desire. This includes statements that involve agency and choice.

(1) Our new belief that "I can choose" includes:

I wish . . .

It would be nice . . .

I desire . . .

My choice is . . .

I prefer . . .

The second part to this new belief is recognizing that our loved ones may make choices different from our preferences and different from our own choices. This includes statements which involve agency and choice for our loved ones.

(2) Our new belief that "My loved one can choose" includes:

My loved one can choose . . .

He is an adult and can choose . . .

She is accountable for her choices . . .

He made that decision . . .

He exercised his agency . . .

The third part to this new belief is using "I will" statements that empower us to use our agency and stay on the healing path. We need to see ourselves being able to walk through the dark and lonely tunnel, coming out the other side into the daylight with only a few bruises, and knowing that the Atonement will heal our bruises.

(3) Our new belief that "I will" includes:

I do not accept my loved one's behaviors, but "I will" continue to deal with my emotions in helpful ways so that I may experience healing.

It hurts me when I see him making destructive choices, but "I will" focus on what I can do and continue my healing even though it is very difficult.

I feel such deep pain because of my loved one's choices, but "I will" get through this even though it is hard.

My loved one sometimes chooses terrible behaviors, but "I will" seek the help that I need and find a helpful way to deal with the pain even though it really hurts.

I do not condone my son's behaviors, but "I will" stay connected with him and try to help and influence him even though it is so difficult.

Using the "I will" statements reminds us that we do have a choice to continue on even though it is very hard. The "I will" statements remind us that we can get through this experience and deal with our loved ones' behaviors, even though we don't like it. This does not in any way mean we condone our loved ones' behaviors, but we recognize they have agency and can choose what they desire. Here are some examples of this new three-part way of dealing in a more healthy way with our loved ones' behaviors.

I wish that this had not happened, but it did. My spouse made some terrible choices. I do not like it, but "I will" get through it as I listen to the promptings of the Spirit and follow them.

It would have been nice to have had a better relationship with my spouse, but I didn't. I prefer that we learn and grow and try to improve our marriage. But if my spouse chooses not to, "I will" seek the Spirit and choose what is best for me.

I desire that my husband would not have had another affair, but I cannot control what he does. "I will" continue to follow the Spirit and make the best decisions and choices for me and the children, which may mean we eventually separate or divorce.

My choice is that this behavior of indulging in pornography cease, but I know my loved one has his agency. I do not like it when I see agency used to violate God's laws and for self-gratification, but "I will" choose to stay on the healing path, even though he may not choose the same. This is difficult, but "I will" get through it and make the best possible choices for me in the future.

I prefer that we go to counseling and get help, but if my loved one chooses not to, "I will" go and get the help that I need anyway.

CHOICES AND ACCOUNTABILITY

The power with this new way of thinking and believing is that we are living by the eternal principle of choice and accountability. We make our choices and are accountable. Our loved ones make their choices and are accountable. We release ourselves from condemning and handing out sentences for misbehavior. We give up our judgeship. We let Christ take care of that. We want to make sure that we are protected and we take care of ourselves. Our loved ones will experience the natural consequences for their sins. They cannot escape them, even though it may look like they are for a while. We let our loved ones know our own boundaries and stick to them. (Boundaries are discussed in Principle 7.) By embracing this new way of thinking and believing, we reduce our emotional disturbances, have the Spirit in our lives, and make better choices for ourselves. One wife expressed:

> It is such a relief not to be worrying about what my husband may be doing and to stop the detective work. I have more energy now to deal with my husband's pornography addiction than ever before. I recognize now that in order for him to stop, he must choose to stop. In the past I have worked so hard to get him to stop, but now I realize it was wasted energy and made me more upset when he acted out. When I talk to him I am able to express quite calmly how I feel about his viewing pornography. I let him know it really hurts me when he views pornography and it creates a wedge in our relationship. I cannot give myself to him when he views pornography. Before I changed my beliefs about his pornography usage, I attacked him. I told him what a bad person he was for using pornography and breaking his covenants. This did not motivate him to change and just made me more angry.

We are more likely to get what we want—healing—when we truly embrace the principle of agency in the way we think, feel, and behave.

AVOID BLAMING OTHERS

In order for our loved ones to heal, they need to stop blaming others, including us, for the emotions they feel and the behaviors they choose. We should be careful not to fall into the same trap of blaming our loved ones for the emotions *we* feel and the behaviors *we* choose, or blaming our spouse for the way our children turned out. We need to accept responsibility for our own thoughts, feelings, and behaviors and encourage others to do the same.

It is very natural to think that our loved ones caused us to feel the way we do. Our thoughts are usually, "If my loved one stopped acting out, I wouldn't feel and act this way anymore." It may seem difficult to accept and very foreign to say, "I choose my own thoughts and emotions by how I interpret and respond to my loved one's acting out."

Does our loved ones' acting out *create our* troubled feelings or distressful feelings? Does the problem seem very perplexing or cause us to fall into the depths of despair? We can choose the emotions we want to feel, but it starts with changing our irrational beliefs about the events of life.

By deciding to view our loved ones' acting out as use of agency and choice and by avoiding our tendency to demand that they change, we can generate healthier emotions. We can stay connected to the spiritual conduit that will lead us safely through the "mists of darkness" generated by our loved ones' poor choices. This course allows us to stay connected with them, have some influence, and continue to encourage them to change their behaviors. If they choose to act out, we will usually feel troubled or perplexed by their behaviors, but we don't have to feel "in despair" or "cast down."

When we choose unhealthy emotions, we use up our emotional energy, often replay the hurt in our minds, and have little or no emotional energy left to deal with the problem. In this helpless state we often have feelings of self-pity and hopelessness, and we distance ourselves from our loved ones. By choosing healthier emotions, we have emotional energy left to deal with our situation in spiritually sound ways. We then have emotional energy left to take care of our own needs and the needs of other family members. We focus on controlling our own thoughts, emotions, and behaviors rather than controlling our loved ones. We may certainly feel that we have been stepped on, but we do not have to feel that we are being destroyed.

This emotional self-control allows us to see the big picture and empowers us to find solutions and to make choices that are most helpful for us. This new emotional energy can sustain us and actually help us feel renewed. "For which cause we faint not; but though our outward man perish, yet the inward [man] is renewed day by day" (2 Cor. 4:16).

REPLAY POSITIVE EMOTIONS

We often dwell too long on the negative feelings or thoughts we have. The Prophet Joseph Smith taught us how to use the process of "feelings to thoughts" in an uplifting way:

> *Never did any passage of scripture come with more power to the heart of man than this did at this time to mine. It seemed to enter with great force into every feeling of my heart. I reflected on it again and again* (JS-H 1:12).

First, the Prophet had the feeling in his heart. Then he reflected on it again and again. He thought about it and pondered it over and over in his mind.

Think about an experience where you had strong feelings and emotions that were uplifting. How much time did you spend thinking about the experience?

Did you record the experience in your journal? Unfortunately we spend so much time thinking about and replaying the bad experiences in our lives that we get stuck. We forget or don't realize we can reflect, ponder, and replay the uplifting experiences. A wife shared:

My thirteen years with my husband had been filled with pain and anguish because of his addiction to pornography and continued adultery. On one occasion, I spent days on my knees pleading with God for comfort and direction. His answer was simple and direct, "Be still my child, all is well." The answer gave me great peace. My husband was two weeks away from finishing graduate school and we were ready to begin our new life together with our four children. We purchased a home, enrolled the children in school, and made new friends in the community when my husband revealed (after a series of events which are too lengthy to discuss) he had never ceased being unfaithful. He was now going to choose this life over our eternal family. He moved into the home we had purchased, while the children and I moved into my sister's basement. My world had once again been shattered. My life and the lives of my children were turned upside down. I had spent so many years hiding the truth from our children, family, and friends. Now it was out in the open. No more hiding. Our lives were about to change forever—deep emotional scars and broken hearts.

I went back to God and pleaded for understanding, but this time I was angry with Him. Did He not tell me just three months ago that "ALL WOULD BE WELL!" Had I not trusted that answer and been obedient? I prayed fervently, angrily for an answer. I was hurting emotionally and so were my children! The thought that our family would not be together and the family unit had disintegrated right before my eyes was unbearable. This was not fair. Had I not been patient, loving, and endured long-suffering? How could God promise that all would be well when it was not well at all? Nothing was well, everything was in a mess, and nothing would be okay again. I demanded an answer from God.

My answer came in the same sweet tone it had before. The same peaceful feeling I had received three months earlier. "Be still my child, all is well. This was not your test, it was your husband's test. I am sorry life is not fair, but if it were fair you would not need the Savior or the Atonement. The Atonement is here because life is not fair." My anger melted away and with new understanding, I embraced the Lord's comforting words, "Be still my child, all is well." I asked God to forgive me because of my anger and thanked Him for my Savior.

Describe an experience where you had strong feelings and emotions that were uplifting:

_____

_____

_____

_____

_____

How can you benefit by reflecting on the uplifting experience?

_____

_____

_____

_____

_____

Elder George Q. Cannon taught the following:

> *Our only preservation is in living near to God, day by day, and serving him in faithfulness, and having the light of revelation and truth in our hearts continually, so that, when Satan approaches, we will see him and understand the snare that he has laid for us. . . .Can we do this without the light of the Spirit? No; we cannot see where the path upon which we have entered will lead to; we cannot tell what the results will be; but when the light of the Spirit of God illuminates our minds and we are enlightened by it, we plainly see the results; and if we do not see them at the time, the Lord soon reveals them to us, and shows us that if we continue to take that course we will grieve his Spirit and fall victims to the adversary* (Journal of Discourses, 11:173-74, Oct. 8, 1865).

It is important to note the beginning words used by Elder Cannon, "*Our only preservation.*"

How are we going to survive? What is the secret to healing? Living near to God, day by day, every day—one day at a time. How can you focus on healing one day at a time?

_____

_____

_____

_____

_____

_____

_____

Elder Boyd K. Packer taught about the workings of the Spirit:

Enos, who was "struggling in the spirit," said, "Behold, the voice of the Lord came into my **mind***" (Enos 1:10; bold added.) While this spiritual communication comes into the* **mind***, it comes more as a feeling, an impression, than simply as a thought. Unless you have experienced it, it is very difficult to describe that delicate process (Ensign, Nov. 1991, 21).*

Summary

In summary, the Atonement covers our sins when we repent. In addition, the Atonement covers the pain and heartache that our loved ones' sins have caused us. In other words, the Atonement covers what we do, and it also covers what our loved ones do to us—whether they choose to repent or not. Why? Because the Atonement covers ALL pain. Speaking of the Savior: "He shall go forth, suffering pains and afflictions and temptations of every kind; and this that the word might be fulfilled which saith he will take upon him the pains and the sicknesses of his people" (Alma 7:11).

This means whatever pain we are experiencing because of our loved ones' behaviors has already been paid through the Atonement of Jesus Christ. We can choose to carry the hurt or we can let the Savior, through His Atonement, carry the load. We have agency and can choose to stay burdened down with the pain caused by our loved ones' behaviors, or we can decide to let the Atonement work for us. Once we realize and accept that the Savior suffered our pain through His

Atonement, we don't have to continue to suffer and carry it any more. We begin to heal at a much faster pace. Why? Because "He will take upon him the pains and the sicknesses of his people" (Alma 7:11).

REVIEW OF PRINCIPLES

What have you learned about the power of the Atonement to heal you and your loved one?

_____

_____

_____

_____

_____

_____

_____

How does knowing that the Atonement heals abuse and feelings of anger benefit you?

_____

_____

_____

_____

_____

How can you accept the Atonement in your life?

_____

_____

_____

_____

_____

As you reflect on the spiritual, emotional, mental, and physical pain that you experience from your loved one's behaviors, how can your knowledge and acceptance of the Atonement be used to heal the pain?

What is the difference between a feeling and an emotion?

What are some unhelpful beliefs about your loved one's behaviors that need to be changed?

How will you go about changing the unhelpful beliefs you hold regarding your loved one's behaviors?

What have you learned about your own feelings and emotions and how to deal with them in a healthier way?

_____

_____

_____

_____

_____

What are some skills or techniques you have learned in this chapter that you will try to implement in your relationships with others in the next thirty days?

_____

_____

_____

_____

_____

As you reflect on this chapter, what principle or concept stood out and had the most impact on your healing?

_____

_____

_____

_____

_____

_____

Calmness Break

Take a moment for some aerobic exercises, a brisk walk, jog, or bike ride. Get some fresh air. Breathe deeply. Think about the beauty that surrounds you—the sky, trees, birds, flowers, rain, and all of God's creations. While exercising, realize that you are one of His creations! You have your own God-given talents. Decide to find out what they are if you don't already know and use them to help you surrender *your* own obsessive thoughts and/or compulsive behaviors. Then return from your aerobic exercises and have a refreshing glass of water.

This chapter may have been emotionally difficult because of the exercises that require emotional digging. In a way we discover great treasures as we search and learn who we are and how we arrived at this point in life. We strive to accept where we are and begin to make emotionally healthier choices that get us out of unhealthy responses. Our goal for this chapter is summarized by President Ezra Taft Benson's statement: "This means he [or she] is restrained in his emotions and verbal expressions. He does things in moderation and is not given to overindulgence. In a word, he has self-control. He is the master of his emotions, not the other way around" (*Teachings of Ezra Taft Benson*, 446).

Messages of Hope

Elder Jeffrey R. Holland: "Claim the promises of the Savior of the world. Ask for the healing balm of the Atonement for whatever may be troubling you or your children. Know that in faith things will be made right in spite of you, or more correctly, because of you" (*Ensign,* May 1997, 36).

President James E. Faust: "All of us benefit from the transcendent blessings of the Atonement and the Resurrection, through which the divine healing process can work in our lives. The hurt can be replaced by the joy the Savior promised. To the doubting Thomas, Jesus said, 'Be not faithless, but believing.' Through faith and righteousness all of the inequities, injuries, and pains of this life can be fully compensated for and made right" (*Ensign,* Nov. 1996, 52).

PRINCIPLE 6

Your Bishop Is Called of God; Work Hard to Build a Strong Support System with Him and Other Trusted Individuals

CHAPTER OVERVIEW

Bishops, branch presidents, stake presidents, and district presidents are valuable resources in our situation with wandering loved ones. Besides the capacity to help our loved ones through the repentance process, these Church leaders have the God-ordained power to offer priesthood blessings, hope, and encouragement.

If our loved ones are sincerely trying to repent, *they* will be meeting with the bishop. Similarly, we can benefit by working together with the bishop as he offers spiritually discerned advice and counsel. Because grief often shrouds tidbits of help, hope, and direction, he may be able to open our eyes to things we might have missed. Emotionally we might not be ready, able, or willing to listen to promptings. The bishop can help us recognize these spiritual promptings and encourage us to follow them.

> "We believe that a man must be called of God, by prophecy, and by the laying on of hands by those who are in authority, to preach the Gospel and administer in the ordinances thereof" (A of F 5).

> "We believe in the gift of tongues, prophecy, revelation, visions, healing, interpretation of tongues, and so forth" (A of F 7).

CHAPTER OBJECTIVES

At the conclusion of this chapter you should—

1. Recognize that the bishop can be a source of support and strength.
2. Realize that the bishop is there for people who need to repent, but he is also available for people who need support, guidance, and spiritual direction.
3. Be willing to meet with the bishop and accept his inspired counsel and advice.
4. See how others have benefited by meeting with their bishops.
5. Discover ways you can build a support system.
6. Know the advantages and disadvantages of attending a support group.
7. Learn why it is important to tell people who are in your support system what you need.

MEETING WITH THE BISHOP

In a letter dated November 14, 1991, Elder Dallin H. Oaks encouraged us to reach out with love and understanding to loved ones who are struggling and also to seek counsel from our bishop, branch president, stake president or district president. After reaffirming the sinful nature of *"fornication, adultery, and homosexual and lesbian behaviors,"* Elder Oaks added:

Individuals and their families desiring help with these matters should seek counsel from their bishop, branch president, stake or district president. We encourage Church leaders and members to reach out with love and understanding to those struggling with these issues. Many will respond to Christlike love and inspired counsel as they receive an invitation to come back and apply the atoning and healing power of the Savior (See Isa. 53:-5; Mosiah 4:2-3.) (Ensign, Oct. 1995, 12-13).

MEETING WITH THE BISHOP HELPED

Many who have tried to help loved ones have sought for and received counsel and direction from their bishop. Here is what others have said about the help they received.

One wife, whose husband left her with the responsibility for a large family, said:

I came to appreciate my bishop's guidance in helping me make a number of sound decisions. He checked on our family often and made sure I was all right and my family was well cared for. He was my support both temporally and spiritually.

One day the bishop called me into his office and discussed with me each of my children, one by one, to see how they were doing. We came up with a plan to make sure each of my boys received priesthood support through their quorum and auxiliary leaders. He also discussed my financial situation and made sure we had food in the house, and when Christmas came he checked again to be sure we had something to go under our tree.

Besides helping my children, he gave me priesthood blessings and helped me explore my new role as a single sister. What a comfort it was to know I had his backing (Ensign, June 2000, 54).

A wife whose husband had been excommunicated because of adultery commented:

Through all of this, a kind and loving bishop and a close friend helped me greatly. Following my husband's confession and excommunication, our bishop regularly counseled with us, sometimes separately, sometimes together (Ensign, Aug. 1988, 22).

Another wife recounted:

My worst Mother's Day was more than five years ago. That was when I told my husband, Jim, that I could not bear his addiction to pornography any longer, that it was as if he had a mistress in the house. I also told him I had sought counsel and a priesthood blessing from the bishop (Ensign, Feb. 2001, 57).

These are some of the blessings that others have received by meeting with their bishop.

How helpful would it be for you to meet with your bishop? What would you want to talk about?

_____

_____

_____

_____

SMALL DAY-TO-DAY FAITHFULNESS—
NOT SOME GREAT THING

The success of our encounter with our ecclesiastical leader largely depends on our willingness to listen, ponder, and prayerfully consider the advice we receive from him. Like Naaman, hoping to be healed from his leprosy, we may go into the bishop's office with expectations of some great advice or counsel that in our minds would solve our problems—the perfect solution directly from the Lord. We might be a little surprised when the counsel from the bishop is pretty basic—personal prayer, reading scriptures, paying tithing, fasting, and so forth. We might even be tempted to discount that advice, complaining, "I already know that. Tell me something that I don't know."

President James E. Faust's words at a priesthood session apply to all Church members:

> We are all familiar with the Old Testament story of Naaman, the captain of the Syrian hosts, who was a leper. A little Israelite servant told Naaman's wife that there was a prophet in Israel who could heal him. Naaman came with his chariot and horses to the house of Elisha, who sent a messenger to instruct Naaman, "Go and wash in Jordan seven times, and thy flesh shall come again to thee, and thou shalt be clean."
>
> You younger boys know how it is when you show your hands to your mother: she'll tell you to go and wash! But Naaman was not a young boy. He was the captain of the Syrian hosts, and he was offended by Elisha's instruction to wash in the Jordan. So he "went away in a rage." One of Naaman's servants with a wise head remonstrated with him and said: "If the prophet had bid thee [to] do some great thing, wouldest thou not have done it? How much rather then, when he saith to thee, Wash, and be clean?" Naaman then repented and followed the counsel of the prophet. The leprosy disappeared, and "his flesh came again like unto the flesh of a little child, and he was clean." "Some great thing" in this instance was extraordinarily simple and easy to do. . . .
>
> We do not prove our love for the Savior only by doing "some great thing." If the prophet personally asked you to go on a mission to some strange and exotic place, would you go? You would probably make every effort to go. But what about paying tithing? What about doing your home teaching? We show our love for the Savior by doing the many small acts of faith, devotion, and kindness to others that define our character. . . .
>
> May we all be faithful in doing the day-to-day, ordinary things that

prove our worthiness, for they will lead us to and qualify us for great things (*Ensign,* Nov. 2001, 46, 48-49).

The counsel we receive from the bishop, branch president, or stake/district president may not be anything new, but we need to remember that the counsel is for *us right now in our present situation.* As we prayerfully ponder the counsel given, we will be guided by the Spirit and directed by the Lord.

📖 **What counsel have you received from the bishop? Have you followed his counsel? In what specific ways have you followed his counsel?**

_____

_____

_____

_____

_____

_____

_____

Ecclesiastical Leaders and Others Who Are Helping

This book was written for any loved one who is trying to help a family member or friend find his or her way out of compulsive sexual behaviors. However, you may be reading this book because you are in a position to provide emotional and spiritual support to a person who is reaching out to a family member who is stuck in the behavior. It is a difficult time for loved ones who are trying desperately to keep their own heads above water as they reach out to help family members.

A comment or remark from someone, although given in the spirit of helping, can turn out to be very unhelpful and can make life even more difficult. Loved ones have commented, "Just when I felt I was getting some air, I was pushed under the water again by that remark." It is therefore important for those who we are trying to help to tell us what they need. Sometimes, however, the pain is so great and they are still in such shock that they cannot even sort through their emotions. It is best if they can state their needs, but if not, here are some statements or suggestions from loved ones that were very hurtful and caused more pain. We want to avoid such statements or suggestions as we work with loved ones who are trying to help their family members or friends.

If we are in a position to provide emotional and spiritual help to a person who is trying to help a family member get out of the behaviors, here is a list to review called "Please Don't." (Loved ones might wish to share these lists with friends and family that want to be part of their support system.)

"Please Don't":

- Don't tell me I need to forgive him. I'm not ready to begin to even think about forgiveness. Over time I can and will.

- Don't say it could be worse or compare my situation with someone else's situation. No two situations are the same. Comparisons usually hurt more than heal.

- Don't give my spouse all of the attention. I have needs and want to be able to talk and discuss my feelings, share my concerns, and deal with my emotions in a positive way.

- Don't tell me you know what it's like. If you haven't been there, you have no idea what it is like. Even if you *have* been there, no two situations are alike.

- Don't tell me how I should feel or how I should be responding to this situation.

- Don't tell me I'll get over it and everything will be back to normal again.

- Don't tell me how I should feel about my spouse's compulsive sexual behaviors. Quite often I don't even know how I feel. Sometimes I'm angry and resentful. I feel guilty for feeling this way, but please let me work through these very real feelings.

- Don't set a timetable for where I should be. I need to work through my feelings at my own pace.

The following statements or suggestions validated the loved one's pain and feelings. This made them feel connected and free to express themselves—they felt safe. This is a "Please Do" list of responses that loved ones have said were very helpful.

"Please Do":

- Do let me be angry, upset, and cry. I only have a few people I can open up with who know the whole situation.

- Do call and initiate an appointment with me. I need regular contact too.

- Do be attentive to my needs. Because of my guilt, shame, and embarrassment, I am not able right now to be assertive and ask for help.

- Do keep our situation confidential. Only those that absolutely need to know should know. Please no one else!

- Do show me genuine love and concern.

- Do compliment me for the strengths and talents that I have.

- Do say, "It must be difficult."

- Do say, "I can't imagine how hard this must be."

- Do let me talk.

- Do listen to me.

- Do try to understand me.

Questions to ask people as they reach out to help family members are:

- "What can I do to be most helpful to you during your time of need?"

- "What needs do you have that are not being met right now?"

- "How can we help you to meet those needs?"

However, loved ones might not know what they need. During these moments only the Spirit can guide and direct you to know what can be done to help.

AFFILIATION AND A SUPPORT SYSTEM

Having a strong support system is critical to help us during our healing. A support group can consist of family members, a bishop, and friends who provide a good influence. By affiliating with others, we are less likely to feel isolated and alone. Unwanted feelings of isolation and loneliness can be diffused with a strong support system.

We cannot underestimate the value of a strong support system. Family, friends, and Church leaders are usually our best resources.

BUILDING A SUPPORT SYSTEM

We need and should want to have a place where we can just talk about our emotions, anger, and frustration without being judged, criticized, or trying to have someone fix us. At the same time we want gentle love and guidance to keep us focused when our thinking is irrational.

Elder Henry B. Eyring explained the power of friendship: "All of us will be tested. And all of us need true friends to love us, to listen to us, to show us the way, and to testify of truth to us so that we may retain the companionship of the Holy Ghost. You must be such a true friend" (*Ensign,* May 2002, 29).

Without having a support system and being surrounded with others who genuinely care about us, it is easy to feel abandoned. Elder Russell M. Nelson expressed: "How sorrowful must a brother or sister feel when they think they are abandoned, when they think no one cares! Perhaps it was this feeling that caused the psalmist to write, 'I looked on my right hand, and beheld, but there was no man that would know me: refuge failed me; no man cared for my soul'" (Ps. 142:4) (*Ensign,* Jan. 1987, 72).

What support system do you have in place, or what support system do you need to establish?

_____

_____

_____

_____

_____

How can you maintain a strong support system?

_____

_____

_____

_____

_____

When we have enjoyed good relationships with family members in the past, we would be wise to recognize the likelihood that strained relations now do not mean that they have withdrawn from us. More than likely *we* are the ones who have withdrawn from *them*. When we need support the most, we want to work hard to stay connected to family members who can listen and help.

🖋 One way to assess our extended family situation is to compare the quality of the relationships we have now with the relationships we had one year ago. Has there been a change? What can you actively do to restore any family relationships that have become distant because of your withdrawal due to your loved one's behavior?

_____

_____

_____

_____

_____

_____

_____

_____

_____

Here are some additional ideas that can help to build a support group:

- Make it a priority to stay in touch with family, friends, and others with whom you have developed healthy relationships.

- Decide which members of your support system can most likely help you. Let them know that it is a difficult time and that you need extra support. Tell them what you need.

- Promote healthy relationships by remembering birthdays and other special events.

- When it is appropriate, be willing to share your thoughts, feelings, and emotions so that others can feel connected.

- Choose a support group that is in line with the teachings and doctrines of the Church.

SUPPORT GROUPS (Refer to page 454)

There are support groups for loved ones who are trying to help wayward family members escape their sexual addictions. Some support groups can be very worthwhile and extremely helpful, but other so-called support groups may be designed to get loved ones to accept their family members' behaviors. We want to accept our family members, but not their inappropriate behaviors.

Most support groups for spouses remind their members about the "C" Rules, which are: (1) I did not *cause* it; (2) I cannot *control* it; and (3) I cannot *cure* it. These simple "C" Rules remind us of where our responsibility ends and where our loved ones' responsibility begins. Our loved ones are responsible for their behaviors.

SUPPORT GROUP ADVANTAGES

- Each support group has its own personality—some can be positive.

- Support groups are anonymous fellowships that foster openness and make it easier to share inner feelings without the threat of being emotionally "stepped on." Participation in support groups says to the person who struggles with a loved one "I'm not in this alone."

- Support groups provide an opportunity to associate with others who share the same problems. Participants can learn to be more open and cease being so isolated and closed off from the world. They "get out of their own heads."

- Participants may recognize in others the pain, guilt, hurt, and anger connected with their loved ones' compulsive sexual behaviors and see positive ways they are dealing with it.

- Participants may recognize the irrational thinking patterns that others use when trying to help their loved ones, and this may help identify their own irrational thinking patterns. (Most irrational thinking patterns are identified outside the person. In other words, some have to see the patterns in others before they will believe that they practice the same irrational thinking.)

- Support groups may provide a sense of reality especially needed because we often think we can control or get others to change. Our loved ones need to decide they *want* to change. We may influence them, but ultimately they have to decide.

SUPPORT GROUP CONCERNS

- Each support group has its own personality—some can be negative.

- A support group may become a participant's main source for spiritual guidance. Instead of praying to God, who has all power, they may be encouraged to call a member of the support group first. In other words, the support group becomes their first line of defense in helping loved ones to overcome compulsive sexual behaviors.

- Spending more and more time away from family to be with members of the support group may lead to relationships detrimental to marriage.

- Listening to members of the group who begin spouse-bashing and only dwell on the negative can dishearten us and postpone our healing.

- Relying more on statements made by members of the support group than statements made by living prophets can be counterproductive.

- A group member may use interaction with the group as a substitute for closeness with spouse, family, and church.

By attending a support group, we can learn how others are dealing with their pain and we can receive ideas on how to deal with ours. If you choose to attend a support group, be very selective. Do your homework so that you know something about the goals, mission statement, or objectives of the group. If you can find out what others who have attended the support group have learned, this can be a tremendous help in making a decision. If you choose a support group, it is recommended that you attend a few times before making a decision on whether or not the support group can help you.

REVIEW OF PRINCIPLES

What blessing can you receive by meeting with your bishop?

_____

_____

_____

_____

_____

_____

What have you learned from others who have tried to help loved ones get out of compulsive sexual behaviors?

_____

_____

_____

_____

_____

_____

_____

What are some ways you can get through the emotional ups and downs and maintain a spiritual foundation?

_____

_____

_____

_____

_____

_____

Who will you include in your support system?

_____

_____

_____

_____

_____

Do they have the capacity, resources, time, and understanding to effectively provide you with the support you need?

_____

_____

_____

_____

_____

How will you let your support system know what you need? Have you decided what you need?

_____

_____

_____

_____

_____

Record any other insights or thoughts that have come as you have read this chapter.

_____

_____

_____

_____

_____

What is the single most important principle or concept you have learned from this chapter?

_____

_____

_____

_____

_____

_____

_____

With whom can you share this important principle or concept in the next week?

_____

_____

_____

CALMNESS BREAK

Go for a walk and get in touch with what you are feeling deep down inside of you. Think about the people in your support system. Review the names of each one. Who is helping you and who is hindering your progress and healing? How can you spend more time or solicit more help from those who are supportive? How can you limit the amount of time or set boundaries for those who are trying, but not helping? Think about the word *gratitude* and what it means to you. Say a silent prayer for every member of your support system. Pray that they may know how much you appreciate them, and also commit to verbally express your appreciation next time you talk with each other. Enjoy the walk and the warm feelings of gratitude.

Messages of Hope

Elder Neal A. Maxwell: "Genuine support and love from others—not isolation—are needed to sustain this painful forsaking and turning" (*Ensign,* Nov. 1991, 31).

Elder Joseph B. Wirthlin: "Though you may feel weary, though you sometimes may not be able to see the way, know that your Father in Heaven will never forsake His righteous followers. He will not leave you comfortless. He will be at your side, yes, guiding you every step of the way" (*Ensign,* Nov. 2001, 27).

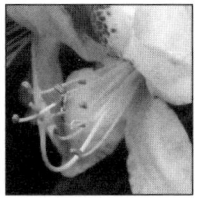

PRINCIPLE 7

Personal Honesty with Ourselves and Others Is Essential to Learn How to Set and Keep Boundaries

CHAPTER OVERVIEW

"We believe in being honest, true, chaste" (A of F 13).

"We believe in being subject to kings, presidents, rulers, and magistrates, in obeying, honoring, and sustaining the law" (A of F 12).

So much of our progress depends on being honest with ourselves and others. Learning to be honest with our emotions, feelings, decisions, and behaviors may be challenging, but this sort of unguarded honesty is the launch pad for our spiritual journey towards healing and wholeness. As we take an honest inventory of the outcome of past decisions and behaviors, personal strengths and weaknesses become apparent. We then have the opportunity to evaluate our views, beliefs, and current course, and grow beyond those barriers. As we become more authentic human beings, we become more comfortable with ourselves and others.

We need to set boundaries with our loved ones. One important aspect of taking an honest inventory of our behaviors and decisions is setting boundaries regarding how far we will allow others to impact our lives. Liquid boundaries that flow with the current situation or our loved ones' moods drown healing. Boundaries do not restrict us, but actually give us more choices and freedom because we realize that we have agency and can choose to say "yes" or "no."

As we experience the Lord's healing power, we find that we do not have to force a smile around others and *pretend* to be happy. We simply *are* happy because of our increasing level of inner peace and joy and not because of the choices of others. Expressions of empathy or sympathy flow freely when we are in tune with the Spirit. These expressions are a natural part of us and flow reflexively. We do not act one way at home and another way in public. We live authentically in both our private and public lives.

The degree of inner peace we feel is directly proportional to our degree of honesty with ourselves and others. We cannot achieve one without the other. The freedom generated by authentically owning our emotions, decisions, and behaviors allows us to love ourselves for who we are—sons or daughters of God. We learn to accept ourselves as a total package—faults and fallacies, and strengths and virtues. Challenges and burdens can then be shared with those around us who possess a genuine concern for our well-being. If someone close to us senses our pain or concerns and asks if we are "down," we can say yes! We see that our strengths, virtues, good qualities, and weaknesses are intertwined as part of our divine potential. Knowing and accepting ourselves where we are now in relation to our divine potential is the key to catching the vision of what one day can and will be if we so choose.

God sets boundaries with us—His commandments. Also, when we pray and ask for things, God sometimes tells us "yes," other times, "no." He knows when to say "yes" and when to say "no." God permits or says "yes" to some experiences of life that we do not like and don't want to go through, so we can grow and progress. These difficult experiences help us become more like Him if we turn to Him and not away from Him.

Countries, states, and cities have laws and boundaries in order to maintain order and protect the rights of their citizens. "We believe in being subject to kings, presidents, rulers, and magistrates, in obeying, honoring, and sustaining the law" (A of F 12).

The laws of the land are designed to protect the rights of each individual. Similarly, we have the right to set boundaries or "laws" regarding our mental, emotional, physical, spiritual, sexual, and financial well-being. We have the responsibility to set boundaries in each of these areas for our own protection. By setting and keeping boundaries, we generate the emotional energy to keep focused on the healing process and to stay on the pathway to inner peace.

 **CHAPTER OBJECTIVES**

At the conclusion of this chapter you should—

1. Know the value of being honest with yourself, others, and God.
2. Know the definition of a boundary.
3. Understand the different types of boundaries.
4. Understand the benefits you receive by setting boundaries.
5. Understand why it may be difficult to set and keep boundaries.
6. Strive to earnestly set boundaries.
7. Learn ways to strengthen your determination and ability to keep boundaries.
8. Take time to ponder and write your boundaries.
9. Refer frequently to your boundaries worksheets so you can remind yourself of your commitments.

HONESTY WITH SELF AND OTHERS: DEFINING BOUNDARIES

We see and set physical boundaries all the time in regard to real estate. For example, inside our homes we have walls that form boundaries, but we also have doors that allow people to come and go. We choose who enters, and we can also ask them to leave. Outside our homes we have fences, sidewalks, flower beds, hedges, rock gardens, retaining walls, and driveways that separate our property from the next-door neighbor's. We are responsible for our home and yard, but not the neighbor's. For example, it's not our responsibility to go into any of the neighbors' yards and try to bring their flowers back to life. We might notice that they are dying, but realize it is their responsibility to take care of their own flowers. We might wonder why they don't take care of them and feel sorry that they do not, but it's their yard and their responsibility. Do we have any responsibility to our neighbor? Yes. If we see something suspicious going on at their house when they are out of town, we can investigate or call the police. If they ask us to water the flowers while they are away on a trip and we choose to say yes, then we are responsible to follow through. Though we want to be a good neighbor, we know where our responsibility begins and ends. We avoid overstepping our bounds, let go of our desire to solve the neighbor's problem, and let them be responsible for their own property.

Boundaries associated with property lines generally make sense to us and we are grateful for them. The need for personal boundaries within a relationship may seem less obvious, defined, necessary, or valid. The first step in setting appropriate boundaries with those around us begins with knowing where our responsibility begins and ends. Knowing where our responsibilities end tells us where our loved ones' responsibilities begin. Whether or not our loved ones are ready or willing to take on their own responsibilities is irrelevant. It is their business, not ours. Does that mean we just abandon our loved ones? No! We have a responsibility to be there for them in healthy ways, but not in unhealthy ways. If our boundaries are too rigid, we might drive our loved ones away. If we have no boundaries, then our wishes and desires are usually not met and eventually we just get too tired and stop trying. Either extreme is not good for relationships. We have a responsibility to help our loved ones become independent, not dependent on others or us.

We are not responsible for our loved ones' dying flowers. They are responsible and should be held accountable. As long as we keep watering their flowers, we enable them to avoid their own responsibility and accountability. If we stop watering their flowers, they might realize that they do not like dead flowers in front of their home and decide to do something about it or they may choose to ignore the situation entirely. The bottom line is that it is their choice whether to water them or not. We may not like their choice, because of the impact on the neighborhood, but it is their choice! By running to their rescue and saving the flowers, we eliminate the natural consequences our loved ones should experience and make them less responsible. Sadly, when we unwisely take over their responsibilities, we often become resentful and angry over their *irresponsibility*—while at the same time rewarding and enabling it! Once we begin understanding the need for appropriate boundaries, we may also become angry at ourselves for not allowing our loved ones to experience the consequences of their behavior.

BOUNDARIES: WHAT ARE THEY?

The value of appropriate boundaries may become more apparent if we liken them to a pasta strainer. The strainer is a metal or plastic boundary for the pasta. Imagine the mess if we just dumped the pasta into the sink, ran cold water over it, and then picked up the pieces one-by-one and placed them into a bowl. Some of the pasta would become mangled or undoubtedly go down the drain. However, when we pour the pasta into a strainer, the pasta stays in one place and is much easier to manage. Likewise, our mental, emotional, physical, spiritual, and sexual lives are easier to manage when we maintain appropriate boundaries.

A pasta strainer has holes in the container to let the hot water flow out and cold water to flow over the pasta. Similarly, we want to let the good in, but drain the unhealthy aspects of our relationships. We want to limit the impact our loved ones' negative behaviors have on our lives. We no longer want to be held captive.

Boundaries free us! They empower us when we begin to truly recognize our God-given power to choose. We can choose to say "no" or we can choose to say "yes" to any request or demand. The choices for our own lives center in *our* agency and no one else's! Firm boundaries give us emotional strength and energy to say "no" when we need to, empowering us to choose situations and places that are safe for us—emotionally and physically.

Boundaries help us avoid self-talk filled with guilt such as, "Why did I agree to do that when I really didn't want to?" Boundaries give us order and a sense of direction in our lives that restores our self-respect and empowers us to take charge of our lives—to be in control of our own healing process. When we realize we have agency and the power to choose, we can act by making the necessary changes. We then will generally feel good inside even when those around us choose to remain stuck in unhealthy patterns and test our boundaries. These good, warm feelings empower us to keep setting reasonable boundaries.

On the flip side, a boundary should not be a brick wall shutting others out. Such a stance is not generated by healthy decisions, but usually a fear-based response to trauma or pain. We want healthy relationships and support systems that can enter our space and provide us with needed help. These are the times when we need to say "yes." By setting boundaries we choose who is invited into our lives and can legitimately help and support us and who is not. Boundaries enhance our personal integrity as our desires, emotions, and behaviors become more congruent. Many times we need to say "yes" to others who can help us; we need to let them into our space. Though we want to "drain" away the unhealthy aspects of the relationship, it is wise to maintain a way for the good to enter in. Our boundaries become a gate that we are in charge of.

✍ Write your definition of a boundary:

_____

_____

_____

_____

What benefits might you receive by setting boundaries? Would you have less stress? Would you have fewer days when you feel emotionally out-of-control or that your world is caving in?

_____

_____

_____

_____

_____

Is it possible that your loved one would benefit from your boundaries? How?

_____

_____

_____

_____

_____

In what circumstances and/or with whom would it be important for you to have firm boundaries and say "no?"

_____

_____

_____

_____

In what circumstances and/or with whom would it be important for you to have firm boundaries and say "yes?"

_____

_____

_____

_____

THE BENEFITS OF SETTING BOUNDARIES

We set boundaries to limit our contact with certain people who are manipulative, hurtful, and emotionally damaging. Appropriate boundaries are not a way to avoid a situation, but rather a way to enable us to take control and be responsible for our own "yard."

- Boundaries allow us to take control of only the areas we are responsible for and can control. They lighten our load because we realize that we aren't responsible for our loved ones' behaviors. We are only responsible to take care of our own flower beds.

  For whatsoever a man soweth, that shall he also reap. For he that soweth to his flesh shall of the flesh reap corruption; but he that soweth to the Spirit shall of the Spirit reap life everlasting (Gal. 6:7-8).

- We establish our own identity by setting boundaries and we reap the positive blessings from the law of the harvest. Boundaries make us unique and tell us and others what is important in our lives. We discover our own humanness and what makes us tick inside. We begin to like what we see in ourselves and accept the whole package.

- Boundaries allow us to be better stewards over what God has given us because we are more responsible.

- Boundaries set us free because we no longer feel we are being controlled by outside forces. We take control of our lives from the inside and set limits.

- Boundaries give us freedom and space to move about because we are not cumbered by the need to control those around us. Boundaries leave us free to grow, progress and reach our divine potential.

- Boundaries stop us from getting pulled in every direction because we know how and when to say "NO!"

- Boundaries remind us that we need others in our lives who can help us, so we need to know how and when to say "YES!"

- Boundaries allow us to be individuals. They allow us to be more human as we embrace those feelings and emotions that are uniquely ours.

- Boundaries reduce the possibility of our loved ones being able to manipulate or use us.

- Boundaries give us more emotional energy to give out of choice rather than out of an unhealthy sense of obligation.

- Boundaries allow us to take ownership of the part of the problem we can control and to do something about that part.

- Boundaries allow the natural consequences from our loved ones' choices to play out. Boundaries remind us where our stewardship and responsibilities end so we are no longer enabling our loved ones to continue their immature behavior.

- Boundaries bring our relationships more into balance since we have set limits on what we will and won't do, or what we will and won't put up with. We have taken a stand.

- Boundaries reduce the possibility of us becoming resentful because we recognize that it is our choice to say yes or no. We no longer make our choices because we feel controlled or manipulated by our loved ones.

- Boundaries remind us that we can make an inner-directed choice without caving into external pressure and manipulation of our loved ones.

- Boundaries reduce the possibility of nagging, screaming, or becoming angry because we realize that as we set boundaries our loved ones will experience natural consequences for their behavior. They may or may not choose to change, but we are freed from the responsibility for their decision.

- Boundaries give us more emotional energy to take care of our own needs. We are not using our strength to try to solve our loved ones' problems. We don't waste our time trying to control them or trying to control situations that are not within our ability or responsibility to control. We are not wearing ourselves out trying to do the impossible.

- Boundaries remind us what we are responsible for. Boundaries are a choice to let our loved ones take responsibility for *their own* area of stewardship. Reasonable and firm boundaries let our loved ones be responsible for their own lives. It's not possible to keep doing what we are responsible for plus what others are responsible for—eventually we run out of gas and just can't do it anymore.

- Boundaries remind us when we need to stop and say "no." Service to others is good and right, but not to the point that we cannot take care of ourselves and our own needs. To set boundaries is not selfish. It shows wisdom and is essential for self-preservation. "And see that all these things are done in wisdom and order; for it is not requisite that a man should run faster than he has strength" (Mosiah 4:27). "Do not run faster or labor more than you have strength" (D&C 10:4).

- Boundaries empower us to be appropriately assertive so we don't give into our loved ones just to avoid conflict or to get their approval.

- Boundaries are a way to show self-respect. When we are able to make and keep boundaries, it also becomes easier for us to respect the boundaries of others when they say "no."

BOUNDARIES HELP TO PREVENT BECOMING ENMESHED

Without boundaries it is very easy to go along with our loved ones just to appease them or smooth things over. We might have the false idea that caving in is the way to be a peacemaker when in reality a healthy, peaceful relationship requires each participant to be assertive and to set and keep boundaries. Firm boundaries reduce the possibility of becoming enmeshed with our loved ones. Enmeshment means we have lost our individual identity and become absorbed in our loved ones' agenda to the point that we no longer see that our own desires or needs are important. (At least we do not try to get them met.) We can become so entangled in a relationship that we make no clear distinction between ourselves and the other person. It's like two different colors of string, one green and one yellow, becoming entangled and full of knots until they are one big mess. They can become totally enmeshed to the point that you cannot see where the yellow string begins or ends; you cannot tell it apart from the green. When we are enmeshed to this point, we decide our own needs or opinions are not important; we don't want to "rock the boat," so we agree with our loved ones to their face even though deep down inside we feel hurt, pain, and a yearning to be ourselves. Enmeshment is not intimacy. Real intimacy can be defined as emotional and physical closeness brought about by sharing, working together, having the right to disagree, being equal, having individual responsibilities, and being unified in purpose. We want real intimacy with our spouse while maintaining our uniqueness. The *Proclamation of the Family* states:

> *By divine design, fathers are to preside over their families in love and righteousness and are responsible to provide the necessities of life and protection for their families. Mothers are primarily responsible for the nurture of their children. In these sacred responsibilities, fathers and mothers are obligated to help one another as equal partners.*

We all want to know that our own needs and opinions are valid. Clear boundaries allow us to create that kind of individual identity. If each string keeps its
individual color by setting distinct boundaries, it can be wrapped around the
other color in a way that forms a beautiful design. An onlooker can see the
clear distinction between the two colors (green and yellow) and see how the
two colors enhance one another. Each color is unique. That uniqueness needs
to be maintained in order for the individual beauty of each color to enhance the
other. How can the beautiful design be maintained if the yellow color becomes
so tangled with the green that you can't see it as a separate color?

President Gordon B. Hinckley, who is famous for encouraging his wife to
"maintain her own color," eloquently reminds us:

> *The women in our lives are creatures endowed with particular qualities,*
> *divine qualities, which cause them to reach out in kindness and with love*
> *to those about them. We can encourage that outreach if we will give them*
> *opportunity to give expression to the talents and impulses that lie within*
> *them. In our old age my beloved companion said to me quietly one evening,*
> *"You have always given me wings to fly, and I have loved you for it" (Ensign,*
> Nov. 2004, 84–85).

When we respect each others' individuality, each person in the relationship
benefits and the resultant synergy strengthens the relationship beyond the individual capacities of the individuals.

Elder L. Tom Perry counseled:

> *Since the beginning, God has instructed mankind that marriage should*
> *unite husband and wife together in unity. Therefore, there is not a president*
> *or a vice president in a family. The couple works together eternally for the*
> *good of the family. They are united together in word, in deed, and in action*
> *as they lead, guide, and direct their family unit. They are on equal footing.*
> *They plan and organize the affairs of the family jointly and unanimously as*
> *they move forward (Ensign, May 2004, 71).*

President Gordon B. Hinckley has taught: "In this Church the man neither
walks ahead of his wife nor behind his wife but at her side. They are coequals"
(*Ensign,* Nov. 1996, 49).

Boundaries allow us to keep our identities, be coequals, and enhance our relationship. When we do this, everyone benefits! If not, we run the risk of becoming
codependent.

Codependency

Codependency has many definitions. Here is one: Feeding someone else's weaknesses in order to get approval which we feel desperately in need of because we aren't getting approval from ourselves and most importantly from the Lord. For example, a son is angry at his father and the two do not get along. The father desperately wants his son's approval. The son loses his job at work because he was viewing pornography there. The son can't pay his rent. The father gives the son money hoping the son will like him more and do more with him.

Son's weaknesses: pornography and interpersonal relationships.

Father's weaknesses: interpersonal relationships and dire need for approval.

By feeding each others' weaknesses neither the father nor the son got healthier. How did they feed each others' weaknesses? The son did not experience the natural consequences of losing his job because his Dad stepped forward and paid the rent. The father is hoping that his son will now approve of him since he helped him out. Neither one has addressed the core issues in the relationship that prevent them from talking, listening, and resolving conflict. In the relationship they are dependent on each other in an unhealthy way.

The son is dependent on the money because he lost his job, and the father is dependent on the son's approval. Neither dependency heals the relationship nor makes the relationship or the individuals better. Healthy boundaries help to reduce codependent relationships.

Why Boundaries Are Hard to Set

- We may fear that the person will leave us and talk behind our back—in essence betray us.

- We may fear that the person will not like us, or that they will leave us.

- We may think it is selfish or unchristian to set boundaries.

- We may feel guilty for setting boundaries because we are taught to be forgiving and Christlike and give our loved ones a second, third, fourth, or fifth chance. This may make us feel we have to continue this pattern for a lifetime.

- We may be afraid that our loved one will become angry with us, and we can't stand the thought of someone being angry with us.

- We might be afraid that our loved one will punish us and try to get even with us.

- We may be too dependent on our loved ones and afraid we may want something or need something from them later on and they will not give it to us.

- We might feel guilty for saying "no" because we are taught to give service and to be kind. We think saying "no" is being unkind. We sometimes think we are being mean if we say "no."

- When someone told us "no," we remember how bad it made us feel, so we don't want our loved one to feel the way we felt at that time.

- We are people pleasers and we want everyone to think how nice we are, so we keep saying "yes" to get their approval.

- We avoid getting our own desires or wishes met under the belief that "I'm sacrificing for my family." We may even believe it is not right to have our desires or wishes met.

What are your own personal stumbling blocks to setting appropriate boundaries?

_____

_____

_____

_____

_____

How will you deal with these stumbling blocks so you can move forward and set your boundaries?

_____

_____

_____

_____

_____

WHY BOUNDARIES ARE HARD TO KEEP

One of the most common reasons it is difficult to keep boundaries once we have set them is that our loved ones are used to the way we have responded in the past and expect us to keep responding that way. They may unconsciously like the fact that we do not have boundaries because it means we will usually give in to what they want. If we attempt to take a stand, they know what to say to blame us, confuse us, manipulate us, or to get us so emotionally charged up that we will question our position. They know how to take our words and twist them around to their benefit. In short, they know how to talk us out of keeping our boundaries or to manipulate circumstances to make it difficult for us to do so. In most cases our loved ones will not like the "new" person with healthy boundaries. They will not like the fact that they cannot control us or push our buttons. In the short term, our new position may further agitate them or make them angry, but it is important for us to be consistent and firm with our boundaries. It is especially difficult to keep righteous boundaries that emotionally upset our loved ones. We may have learned that it is mean to make someone else angry, and when we do, we are responsible for how they feel. This belief may have been reinforced by statements from our caretakers when they said, "See what you have done now? You have made your sister cry." If our new boundaries upset our loved ones, we can feel sorry that they are upset; but realize we have the right to do what is best for us and stay firm in our decision. By sticking with our boundaries, we gain emotional power that enables us to keep setting appropriate boundaries generating increased self-respect and healing.

Childhood issues involving the way our caretakers treated us and whether or not they validated our feelings may prove to be a stumbling block in setting and maintaining personal boundaries in our adult relationships. If we were raised in homes where our caretakers tried to make everything all better by smoothing over situations and sweeping them under the rug, we may believe it is not okay to feel sad, lonely, afraid, or angry. We may have observed our mother giving in to our father so that he would not become angry. We may have learned to just go along and endure whatever is thrown at us so another family member wouldn't be angry. When we tried to share feelings as a child, our caretakers may have said, "You should not feel that way . . . " and quickly discounted what we were feeling. We may have learned that it was not okay to have or express feelings.

We may discover many reasons to explain our difficulty in setting and keeping boundaries. However, even with our backgrounds and families of origin, we can choose to set boundaries now in order to maintain our own individuality, have more backbone, and increase our self-respect. Lack of self-respect keeps us from standing up for ourselves and what we feel is right. Lack of emotional control of our own life keeps us enmeshed with our loved one.

☙ Identify specific ways your loved one tries to keep you from setting or maintaining healthy boundaries.

_____

_____

_____

_____

_____

_____

☙ How will you deal with your loved one when he/she complains or tries to change your boundaries?

_____

_____

_____

_____

_____

_____

☙ How can you get support from others to help you keep your boundaries? Who will be your support? Family, or friends, a support group, bishop, or therapist?

_____

_____

_____

_____

How have I taken my loved one's problem from him, so he does not have to be responsible for it, carry it, work through it, and eventually resolve it?

_____

_____

_____

_____

_____

Why does taking on my loved one's problem burden me?

_____

_____

_____

_____

How does trying to solve my loved one's problem put me at risk?

_____

_____

_____

_____

Do I feel guilty when I let my loved one resolve his or her own problems? What can I do to be supportive, but not assume my loved one's responsibility to resolve his or her own problem?

_____

_____

_____

_____

■ If I set boundaries, what am I afraid will happen?

_____

_____

_____

_____

TYPES OF BOUNDARIES

Mental Boundaries

We are unique in our thoughts, ideas, opinions, and the way we choose to express them. We should take responsibility for our own, but not for others' mental well-being. Mental boundaries allow us to set limits on the types of questions we will answer from family members or others who may be inquiring about our loved ones. We can respond with, "I'm sorry, you will need to ask that question to my husband." Or "That's a very personal question and I choose not to answer it." We have a choice whether we answer a question or not. We should let our loved ones be responsible for their own actions and behaviors by letting them be the ones to answer specific questions or requests from others.

We have the right to express ourselves and share our thoughts, ideas, and opinions with our loved ones and others. We do not force our opinions on others, but recognize that we are equals. Each person, including our loved one, is entitled to his or her own opinion. By setting boundaries we take ownership of our opinions and share them, if we choose, even though our loved ones may not agree with them. The boundary is this, "I have a right to share my opinions even though you may not agree." Their disagreement should not cause us to hold back, withdraw, or stop sharing our true thoughts, ideas, or opinions.

We decide what we say and when we say it and we also choose to limit what we let in. We do not have to agree with the opinions of our loved ones and they do not have to agree with ours. These mental boundaries remind us of the importance of being assertive, so there is less chance that our loved ones will mentally or verbally keep us in a corner and silence our opinions. By setting mental boundaries we recognize that we are responsible for our thoughts, feelings, and opinions and should not change them or modify them just to please the person we are talking to at the time. Furthermore, we recognize that we have a responsibility to share our thoughts and opinions appropriately and should not become passive just because our loved ones may be angry or upset at our opinions. Our mental boundaries should keep us from withdrawing or remaining silent and thereby maintain our authenticity and uniqueness. If we share what is on our mind with our loved ones, they do not have to guess what we are thinking. This is the only path to true communication and trust. We should decide to speak the truth to our loved ones and to tell them what we really feel inside, knowing that our loved ones do not have to agree with our thoughts and opinions. Here is a simplified example:

Before Mental Boundaries Were in Place

Husband: "I'm going to vote for Mr. Hansen for the city council. I know him personally and think he would be the very best choice."

Wife: "I think I will too!"

She agrees with her husband without even considering what she really thinks or intends to do. She has had reservations about voting for Mr. Hansen, but did not say anything to her husband about her concerns. Without boundaries she has become enmeshed with her husband's thinking and no longer thinks for herself.

Over time this wife was manipulated and feels that her thoughts or opinions do not matter, so she just goes along with her husband. She has not set a mental boundary or decided to say "yes" to her own thoughts and opinions and to be responsible for them. She does not realize she can say "no" or is afraid to say "no" to her husband's opinion and vote for the candidate of her choice. Yet she needs to give herself that right; she has that choice. She has the right to be an equal and to share her own thoughts and feelings. Here is an example of the same conversation when the wife uses her agency, sets mental boundaries, and expresses her own thoughts and opinions:

After Mental Boundaries Were in Place

Husband: "I'm going to vote for Mr. Hansen for the city council. I know him personally and think he would be the very best choice."

Wife: "I'm not sure yet how I will cast my vote. I have read a lot of information concerning each candidate and right now I am actually leaning toward Mr. Jensen."

With a mental boundary firmly in place, she recognizes that she is an equal. She is an individual with the right to think on her own and decide for herself how to cast her own vote. She respects her husband's choice and asks that he do the same for her.

What benefits will you receive by being responsible for your own thoughts and opinions and being willing to share them?

EMOTIONAL BOUNDARIES

Each of us is a unique human being. Our reactions to life's challenges are ours alone. No one else responds exactly as we do. No one else feels the pain exactly as we do. No one else feels the joy as we do either. Our feelings belong to us and we should take ownership of them. Only when we emotionally connect with ourselves, can we connect with others. Emotional boundaries allow us to set limits on acceptable or unacceptable ways for others to interact with us. In other words, we set emotional boundaries to disengage from our loved ones' abilities to emotionally pull our strings or push our buttons. For example, one husband often instigated arguments with his wife. Here is a simplified example before emotional boundaries were set:

Before Emotional Boundaries Were Set

Husband: "You are never interested in sex."

Wife: "That's not true, I *am* interested in sex—just not as often as you."

Husband: "You never initiate sex and I can't remember the last time you appeared to be interested—probably on our honeymoon."
    (Husband is upset and angry and keeps adding more words and digs to keep the argument going.)

Wife: "I've been interested in sex lots of times; you just don't choose to remember any of them!"

Without an emotional boundary in place the wife gets emotionally charged up, defends herself, counterattacks, and continues to argue with her husband about their sexual intimacy.

Compare the same discussion after emotional boundaries were set and the wife decides she will no longer argue with her husband about the frequency of sexual intimacy and go through the emotional trauma each time the subject surfaces.

After Emotional Boundaries Were Set

Husband: "You are never interested in sex."

Wife: "There *are* times when physically, mentally, or emotionally I prefer not to engage in sexual intimacy."
     (Wife focuses on her own feelings rather than on what he said, and shares these feelings with her husband.)

Husband: "You never initiate sex and I can't remember the last time you appeared to be interested— probably on our honeymoon."
     (Husband is upset and angry and keeps adding more words and digs to keep the argument going.)

Wife: "I'm so sorry you feel the way you do and I sense that you are getting upset about this. I'm more than willing to discuss our sexual intimacy, but I choose not to argue about it. You can either lower your voice so we can talk civilly to each other or I will end the conversation. What would you prefer?"

With an emotional boundary in place, the wife knows where she will end the conversation. She can be kind and avoid verbally attacking her husband, but can make it clear what her limits are. In the example, the wife has set an emotional boundary for herself that she will no longer argue about sexual intimacy and become angry. When we set emotional boundaries, we are less likely to buy into or be manipulated by our loved ones' arguments or accusations and become emotionally upset in the process. More than likely our loved ones will not like our new response. In fact, they may say things that are hurtful and mean to try to get us back in the argument. They know what has worked in the past to manipulate us and they will continue to use these methods. We can respect our spouse's viewpoint even though we do not agree with it. He is entitled to his viewpoint and we are entitled to ours, and we determine what our boundaries are in regard to sharing those viewpoints.

Instead of verbally striking out at us in an attempt to battle our boundary-setting, our loved ones may withdraw or become silent, refusing to even discuss the issue when we try to hold that boundary. This type of response—or lack of response—is a common passive-aggressive maneuver. Because there are not angry words or shouting, the unhealthiness of this type of response may be very confusing and often results in a very powerful and effective blockade to true communication. Silence can be just as powerful as angry words in causing us to question our stance.

If our loved ones continue their immature behavior, we can choose a place to go where we can emotionally reconnect with ourselves. For example, we may take a short walk. During this time we take ownership of how we feel and protect ourselves against becoming enmeshed. This is very different from a silent, passive-aggressive response mentioned above. When our loved ones withdraw to prove a point or get something from us, we are being manipulated by them through passive-aggressive behavior. Setting an emotional boundary is not running away, but rather taking a "time out" to reconnect with ourselves in a healthy way. By doing so, we let others know that inappropriate, unhealthy, or hurtful behavior or words will no longer be tolerated. We cannot force them to change, but we can choose not to respond, leave the room, go to another part of the house, take a walk, or go for a drive. We remain willing to discuss the real issues if and when an emotionally healthy boundary is in place and mutual respect governs the process.

By setting and keeping boundaries we remind ourselves that we do have several choices when our emotional boundaries are crossed or ignored by others. We want to know ourselves well enough to know when the behavior of others begins to impact us emotionally, so we can implement and enforce our boundaries. To do this we need to set our boundaries long before the actual situation or circumstance occurs. It's too late in the heat of the battle. Derogatory or disparaging comments from our loved ones, displays of anger, unhealthy silence or withdrawal, and manipulation do impact us emotionally, but we can choose our response to such assaults. For example, an insensitive remark by a loved one can be responded to with, "I would appreciate it if you would not say that; those words are very hurtful." Our response tells our loved one about our boundary. If our loved one responds with passive-aggressive silence, we can state our willingness to discuss the issue in a healthy way and then leave the decision in their court. If our loved one repeats the insensitive remark, we remind them again of our boundary. When our loved one becomes angry we can say, "I feel scared," or "I feel manipulated because of your angry voice. I ask that you lower your voice or I will end the conversation until you can talk in a normal tone of voice." If our loved ones continue the anger, we can remind them again that we wish to discuss the matter calmly. If they do not, we can say, "I choose not to discuss this matter under these circumstances. If you cannot talk calmly, I will leave the room." If our spouses do not control their anger, it's important that we follow through and leave the room. By setting and keeping boundaries, we are less likely to be manipulated because we recognize that our loved ones' anger is not a reason to change *our* boundaries, and we also avoid escalating the conflict and becoming angry ourselves. If we decide to change our boundaries, it will be by our own choice and not because of someone's anger.

Our loved ones will only know if we are serious about boundaries if we *keep* them. Words have little impact without action—they need to see that we mean business and that we will keep our boundaries. If we do not keep them, our loved ones might think they can continue to emotionally push us around.

PHYSICAL BOUNDARIES

Physical boundaries may also include sexual boundaries, but I have chosen to show these as two separate boundaries. Physical boundaries establish a limit on how close we want people to stand next to us, whether we want them to touch or hug us, and under what conditions or circumstances physical contact is acceptable. We set the physical limits. We decide who can get closer and who needs to stay further away. With these boundaries in place, we are more at ease because we realize that we have agency and can choose to say "yes" or "no." We can say "no" to adults who may initiate inappropriate physical contact or encroach on our space. On the other hand, with our children and grandchildren we want to say "yes" to physical contact with lots of nurturing. By listening, letting them express themselves, validating their feelings and providing lots of nonsexual hugs, kisses, and cuddling, we enhance their emotional, mental, and physical development.

Boundaries are all about when to say "yes" and when to say "no." Physical boundaries can release us from feeling socially pressured or manipulated by our loved ones to respond a certain way or to change our boundaries. We recognize that we have the choice to set boundaries, and we have the right to maintain them. In addition to the physical boundaries we might set when interacting with others, there are also physical boundaries that define what we will accept in our homes, the places we will visit, and any other items that may impact us in a negative way. Here is a simplified dialogue between a husband and wife where the wife had not set a firm boundary about pornography in the home:

Before Physical Boundaries Were Set

Husband: "You are making such a big deal out of nothing. So what if I view pictures of naked women on the computer? *National Geographic* magazines show naked women too."

Wife: "I don't think it is a good idea to be looking at naked women."

Husband: "Like I say, you are blowing something so minor into this huge problem." (Husband's voice is raised and his body language shows he is becoming very angry.)

Wife: "Well fine, let's not talk about it anymore."

Without physical boundaries, the wife began questioning herself and wondered if maybe she was blowing this matter out of proportion. She also felt guilty for making her husband angry. Because she had not set a clear boundary, she backpeddled on her position, and compromised her own ethics and values about having no pornography in the home. She also took responsibility for her husband's anger. In the process she was losing her own identity—what she stands for—and was becoming enmeshed with her husband. She was almost dissolving herself by accepting his position on pornography even though deep down inside she knew it was wrong.

After Physical Boundaries Were Set

Here is a simplified dialogue between a husband and wife where the wife had set a firm boundary about no pornography in the home:

Husband: "You are making such a big deal out of nothing. So what if I view pictures of naked women on the computer? *National Geographic* magazines show naked women too."

Wife: "This *is* a very important issue for me and for our children. I will not accept any pornography in our home."

Husband: "Like I say, you are blowing something that is so minor into this huge problem." (Husband's voice is raised and his body language shows he is becoming angry.)

Wife: "I'm so sorry that you seem to be angry about this, but it is not right to bring pornography into our home, affecting the children and me. So if you bring Internet pornography into our home, I will install a filter and password on the computer. I do not want pornography from any source in our home."

By setting boundaries and sticking with them, we have more inner strength and recognize that we do have the right and the ability to take a stand. We also realize that we are not helpless in this matter and that there are many choices we can make. In the second example the wife had set firm boundaries on what she expected in the home. She was firm and direct with her comments to her husband. She recognized that he was angry and told him that she was sorry that he felt that way. However, she also recognized that she is not responsible for his anger. He is responsible for his own anger. Her husband's anger at her boundaries is not a reason to change them. By setting boundaries, she does not take on the responsibility and guilt for her husband's anger.

SPIRITUAL BOUNDARIES

We determine our own relationship with God and Christ and what we need to do to stay connected with Them. We have the divine opportunity to our own spiritual direction through the Holy Ghost. We want to open our boundaries and allow the words of our prophets and apostles to flow in so that we have their inspired counsel to guide and direct our lives. Our local leaders give inspired counsel as well. Spiritual boundaries remind us to determine for ourselves the sources of spiritual direction we will accept.

We can be reminded of spiritual sources of direction by keeping a spiritual journal of impressions and feelings that enter our minds and hearts. By reviewing our spiritual writings, we will be reminded of what the Spirit directed us to do and can recommit to follow that direction. By setting a spiritual boundary and deciding whom we will listen to for spiritual guidance and direction, we avoid the risk of being talked out of our spiritual standards or a decision we made according to the guidance of the Holy Ghost. The Savior encouraged, "Learn of me, and listen to my words; walk in the meekness of my Spirit, and you shall have peace in me" (D&C 19:23). Here is a simplified example of spiritual boundaries:

Before Spiritual Boundaries Were Set

Friend: "I have really been praying and thinking about what you should do. I know I have received an answer for you."

Wife: "Well I am very interested in what you have received."

Friend: "I think you should separate from your husband and teach him a lesson. He needs to get the message and so far he has not."

Wife: "That's probably a good idea. I think I will do that."

After Spiritual Boundaries Were Set

Friend: "I have really been praying and thinking about what you should do. I know I have received an answer for you."

Wife: "Well I'm interested to hear what you think, but I have to make my decisions according to the spiritual direction I receive for myself."

Friend: "I think you should separate from your husband and teach him a lesson. He needs to get the message and so far he has not."

Wife: "Thanks for your opinion."

When we have clear boundaries, we will not find it necessary to explain why we are doing something or not doing something. We know inside why we have set the boundary, but we should not feel obligated to share every thought or reason with others. Because she had set her own spiritual boundaries, this wife was not unduly influenced by her friend's advice. She knew her source of spiritual direction. She had set her spiritual boundary and knew that her friend was not the source of her spiritual direction.

FINANCIAL BOUNDARIES

Financial boundaries mean we set a boundary on our own finances. A budget is a financial boundary. By setting and maintaining a budget, we are more likely to enjoy peace of mind by living within our own means. Financial boundaries also mean we determine how much financial help, if any, should be given to loved ones, family members, and others. Here is a simplified example:

Husband has spent a lot of money on pornography in the past so the family is now short on money for food and other necessary items.

Before Financial Boundaries Were Set

Wife: "I was just reviewing our bank statement and noticed that you cashed a $200 check that came out of our grocery money. What did you do with the money?"

Husband: "I had a slip-up and used the money for pornography." (This assumes that her husband is actively repenting and is willing to tell the truth.)

Wife: "That's really hard on the family not to have the money for groceries like I had planned, but maybe I can find a way to get through until next pay day."

Husband: "I'm sorry; I feel really bad."

Wife: "It's okay; we'll get by somehow."

After Financial Boundaries Were Set

Wife: "I was just reviewing our bank statement and noticed that you cashed a $200 check that came out of our grocery money. What did you do with the money?"

Husband: "I had a slip-up and used the money for pornography." (This assumes that her husband is actively repenting and is willing to tell the truth.)

Wife: "That's really hard on the family not to have the money for groceries like I had planned. Using the family money for pornography is not acceptable. I need the $200 deposited back into the account. How will you do that?"

Husband: "I don't know because I don't get paid for another week or so."

Wife: "I'm sorry about that, but I need the money in the account. We need groceries and I plan to go shopping on Thursday. Please make arrangements to get the money in the account." (Perhaps the husband could borrow money from the bank, his parents, siblings, or a friend, but let him be responsible to replace the money.)

By having firm boundaries the wife lets the natural consequences follow her husband's actions. She lets her husband find the solution to his own problem. She sets a deadline by planning to do her shopping on Thursday. The husband has a couple of days to resolve his problem and bear the consequences of his behavior. Even though it is painful for the wife to have her husband lapse, she does not enable him by assuming the responsibility for his behavior.

Questions we might ask ourselves to help us set financial boundaries are these:

- If we assume the consequences of our loved ones' behavior, are we postponing the day when they have to become financially responsible?

- If we resolve the financial burden created by our loved ones, will they expect us to bail them out each time?

- How will our financial assistance hurt or help our loved one in the long run?

- Are there consequences that our loved ones should experience and be responsible for, but are not experiencing because we came to their rescue?

- Are we considering changing our budget to smooth over their bad behavior because we want to please them and want them to think we are kind and generous?

Financial boundaries, like all boundaries, are important to set and keep for our own emotional well-being.

SEXUAL BOUNDARIES

Because sexual boundaries are so often violated when our loved one has a sexual addiction, I have chosen to discuss this subject at length. Our bodies are exactly that—ours! They were created in the image of God. God has given us our bodies as the grand prize for following His plan and choosing to come to this earth. We should cherish and respect our bodies and require that others do the same–especially our spouses. Just being married to us does not give our spouses the right to interact sexually with us whenever or however they may choose. We should set sexual boundaries that work for us and share them with our spouse. During intimacy if those boundaries are crossed, we should remind our spouse of our boundaries, stop the behavior, and continue intimacy only when the behavior is consistent with our boundaries. We respect our bodies and ourselves by setting sexual boundaries. We ask that our spouse respect our bodies too! Here is a simplified dialogue taking place during sexual intimacy:

Before Sexual Boundaries Were Set

Husband: "I want you to . . . "

Wife: "Okay, I guess so."

Even though the wife felt uncomfortable with her husband's suggestion, she went along with it because she had not set any sexual boundaries. Afterwards, she felt that she had violated her own personal integrity because she had gone against her own feelings. This is an important area to consider—particularly when a husband has been addicted to pornography. Sometimes the wife thinks that going along with her husband's requests will stop him from viewing pornography. The husband might even imply that it would. This is not true. Fulfilling every lustful act that a husband may have seen in pornography only reinforces, rewards, and enables his inappropriate desires and cravings to continue. Instead of being supportive, the wife is enabling him to stay in lust rather than cultivating the kind of loving intimate relationship she really wants.

After Sexual Boundaries Were Set

Husband: "I want you to . . ."

Wife: "I'm sorry, I am very uncomfortable with that."

It is more likely that we will set sexual boundaries if we clearly understand how damaging it is to the marriage for the husband to continue in lust. Only lust-free love and tenderness truly enhance intimacy rather than taking away from it. Studying and pondering what our prophets and apostles have said about intimacy can help us as we set sexual boundaries.

SEXUAL INTIMACY IN MARRIAGE

God created man and woman in His image. Sexual intimacy for a man and a woman within the marriage covenant is ordained of God. "Therefore shall a man leave his father and his mother, and shall cleave unto his wife: and they shall be one flesh" (Gen. 2:24). Whether sexual relations enhance or put a wedge in our marriage relationship depends on: (1) How we view sexual intimacy; (2) Whether we seek guidance and direction through the Spirit; and (3) Our sensitivity to and understanding of our spouse.

One of the great challenges for anyone who has been addicted to pornography is to understand the difference between love and lust. Pornography in all of its different forms promotes pure lust. There is no love or relationship involved. Elder Russell M. Nelson speaks out about the harmful affects of pornography:

> *Hence, I warn against pornography. It is degrading of women. It is evil. It is infectious, destructive, and addictive. The body has means by which it can*

*cleanse itself from harmful effects of contaminated food or drink. But it can-
not vomit back the poison of pornography. Once recorded, it always remains
subject to recall, flashing its perverted images across your mind, with power
to draw you away from the wholesome things in life. Avoid it like the plague!*
(*Ensign*, May 1999, 39).

Choosing the drug of lust is deadly to loving relationships, but in our society
many choose it before they know anything about real love. One of the puzzling
realities of human sexuality is that young people are physically able to engage
in sexual intimacy long before they are ready mentally, emotionally, and spiritually to do so in a mature way. When compulsive sexual thoughts or experiences occur during the adolescent years, the physical aspects and physiological
responses often occur with no mental, emotional, or spiritual connection.

Following marriage one of the challenges for a person who has been involved
in early compulsive sexual behaviors is to begin to connect mentally, emotionally, physically, and spiritually during sexual intimacy. A truly loving relationship
includes them all. Pornography, lust, and fantasy—the counterfeits of love—thwart
intimacy.

THE DRUG OF LUST AND ITS NEGATIVE IMPACT ON A MARRIAGE RELATIONSHIP

On the left side of the chart, I have shown the lies and deceptions that Satan
wants our loved ones to believe. These Satanic lies are told in videos, books,
magazines, songs, Internet websites, and wherever other media can find an
audience. The left side of the chart shows the lies Satan tells men about women
through pornography. On the right side of the chart, I have shown the eternal
truths that God wants us to believe because they will bring joy and happiness to
our lives.

Pornography, lies, fantasy, lust—Attitudes that are carnal and degrading	Purity, truth, reality, love—Attitudes that are caring and uplifting
Women are willing and ready at any time.	Emotional exchange, tenderness, and caring marital relation first—then sexual intimacy.
Women always want sex and initiate it.	Most women enjoy holding and touching their spouse, feeling emotional close-ness; sexual intimacy is secondary.

Pornography, lies, fantasy, lust—Attitudes that are carnal and degrading	Purity, truth, reality, love—Attitudes that are caring and uplifting
If she has a nice body, she has it all, and it's hers to do with whatever she wants.	Talents, attributes, and our bodies come from God and we should strive to use them according to His guidelines.
Human bodies are toys so we can play with them any way we desire.	Our bodies are temples of God, and so we achieve sexual fulfillment only within the boundaries He has set.
Sexual arousal is the main reason for living.	Sexual intimacy allows a husband and wife to have sexual fulfillment, but it is only one of many facets of a couple's relationship.
A person can get or take sex when he wants it regardless of how he gets it.	Abstain from masturbation, illicit sexual activities involving another person, and all other inappropriate activities. Sexual intimacy is to be within the marriage covenant only.
There are no boundaries. If it feels good, do it.	The Lord has set boundaries. Boundaries are important; they enhance self-mastery and marital bonding.
Do anything you want—whenever you want.	Wait; be patient; express love in many ways.
Sex is the only way to express love.	There are many ways to express love and many women prefer other ways, although they do enjoy sexual intimacy.
Every sexual fantasy can and should be fulfilled.	Sexual intimacy within marriage is ordained by God. Caring and concern for one's spouse are true expressions of love even though there may be no sexual intimacy at the time.
If your spouse doesn't want to do what you want to do when you want to do it, or if she resists in any way, there must be something wrong with her.	By divine nature most women are not carnal. They want to know that they are more than just a body and that they are respected.
Leave your spouse, divorce your spouse, and find someone who can fulfill your sexual wants and fantasies.	Stay, seek help from your bishop and/or a professional counselor who is gospel-centered, and support your spouse so you can both have joy and sexual fulfillment in your marriage.

The left side of the chart explains why lust creates a wedge in the marital relationship. The drug of lust changes our spouses' behaviors and can generate confusion, discouragement, and hopelessness for us and our spouses. We may wonder if we can ever get back to a "normal" attitude about sexual intimacy again. One woman wrote this about her husband, "I have felt so betrayed and have lost trust over and over. I'm afraid to be with him intimately. How can we ever have a normal healthy sexual relationship again?"

Satan depicts his false doctrine of lust on the left side of the chart as love. Speaking about Satan and his agents, Elder Richard G. Scott warns:

> *Satan's agents speak of love, but it is really lust. It is the increasing gratification of personal appetites at the expense of another person. It leads to serious violation of the commandments of God. Why does Satan concentrate so intently on sexual transgression? Because he knows that immorality feeds upon itself. It numbs spiritual sensitivity and neutralizes the will to resist. There is never any place for Satan's kind of love in your life* (*Ensign,* June 1997, 54).

Lust does not come into a person's life all at once. It happens ever so slowly without the user realizing how far it has penetrated the mind and soul. Elder Marvin J. Ashton shared how tricky and deceptive Satan can be and what consequences a user of lust may face:

> *How does the adversary wage this battle? What are his tactics? Those who are fighting pornography and obscenity have helped us recognize some of his battle plans. They tell us that a person who becomes involved in obscenity soon acquires distorted views of personal conduct. He becomes unable to relate to others in a normal, healthy way. Like most other habits, an addictive effect begins to take hold of him. A diet of violence or pornography dulls the senses, and future exposures need to be rougher and more extreme. Soon the person is desensitized and is unable to react in a sensitive, caring, responsible manner, especially to those in his own home and family. Good people can become infested with this material and it can have terrifying, destructive consequences.*
>
> *One such young man who became a casualty of this conflict was a respected husband and community member. Someone with whom he worked brought lurid bits of pornography and passed them around the office. At first it was treated as a joke, and those who viewed them kidded each other about such things of the world. This young man, however, mainly out of curiosity, thought he should study them carefully in case he might have occasion to*

help others combat such evils of the world. As he looked at the items more and more frequently, he was overcome by a spirit of the adversary that he did not recognize. Soon he sought more pornographic materials from his fellow employee, and the two of them began to spend more time discussing these evil things.

Still thinking he was becoming enlightened as to the ways of the world so that he could be a stronger influence for good among his friends, this young man became trapped by his own ignorance of the enemy's ways. His associate convinced him that he should experiment with the actions portrayed in the materials he was viewing. With his spiritual sensitivity dulled, he agreed, and he approached his wife with the idea. She was surprised and shocked by his suggestions, and when he continued his insensitive pleas, she finally refused to have anything to do with him. In his distorted condition he sought gratification elsewhere, and in the end he lost her, his family, and his self-respect (Ensign, Nov. 1977, 71-72).

If our loved ones choose to repent, the end result can be different—much different.

Sexual Intimacy Within the Marriage Covenant

President Spencer W. Kimball said:

Divorces often occur over sex, money, and child discipline. If you study the divorces, as we have had to do in these past years, you will find there are one, two, three, four reasons. Generally sex is the first. They did not get along sexually. They may not say that in the court. They may not even tell that to their attorneys, but that is the reason. . . . Husband and wife . . . are authorized, in fact they are commanded, to have proper sex when they are properly married for time and eternity. That does not mean that we need to go to great extremes. That does not mean that a woman is the servant of her husband. It does not mean that any man has a right to demand sex anytime that he might want it. He should be reasonable and understanding and it should be a general program between the two, so they understand and everybody is happy about it (The Teachings of Spencer W. Kimball, 312).

The Church has a wonderful booklet called *A Parent's Guide*. This book summarizes what are age-appropriate discussions to have with children regarding sex education. It also provide wonderful counsel for married couples:

Both husbands and wives have physical, emotional, psychological, and spiritual needs associated with this sacred act. They will be able to complement each other in the marriage relationship if they give tender, considerate attention to these needs of their partner. Each should seek to fulfill the other's needs rather than to use this highly significant relationship merely to satisfy his or her own passion.

Couples will discover differences in the needs or desires each partner has for such a relationship, but when each strives to satisfy the needs of the other, these differences need not present a serious problem. Remember, this intimate relationship between husband and wife was established to bring joy to them. An effort to reach this righteous objective will enable married couples to use their complementary natures to bring joy to this union.

The intimate relationship between husband and wife realizes its greatest value when it is based on loving kindness and tenderness between the marriage partners. This fact, supported by valid research data, helps newly married couples recognize that the so-called sex drive is mostly myth. Sexual intimacy is not an involuntary, strictly biological necessity for survival, like breathing and eating. Sexual intimacy between a husband and wife can be delayed or even suspended for long periods of time with no negative effect (for example, when the health of one or the other requires it). Husbands and wives are not compelled to mate because their genes or hormones order them to do so. Sexual powers are voluntary and controllable; the heart and mind do rule. While sex drive is a myth, husbands and wives do have physical and emotional needs that are fulfilled through sexual union. If they perceive and appreciate their masculine and feminine natures as important, complementing, but not controlling, parts of their lives, becoming as one flesh can be one of life's richest and most rewarding experiences (A Parent's Guide, 47–49).

Sexual intimacy, between a husband and a wife, is ordained of God and can be rewarding and uplifting, but there are times when abstinence may be helpful and necessary.

SEXUAL ABSTINENCE

When our loved ones have been involved with compulsive sexual behaviors, their attitude and desires toward intimacy can be very distorted. It may be necessary for the couple to abstain from sexual intimacy while one or the other begins to give up the drug of lust. This decision should be made mutually because both parties involved feel it would be beneficial to the relationship. Here is a suggestion from *A Parent's Guide:*

> *There are times within the marriage when complete abstinence is appropriate for extended periods of time, such as during ill health, difficult pregnancy, separation due to employment away from home, or a need to restore respect and mutually decent emotional and spiritual relationships. There also are times when a spouse's emotional and physical needs would make it desirable for the other to be especially affectionate (A Parent's Guide, 49).*

Sexual boundaries enhance sexual intimacy and allow the Spirit to refresh us as we develop strong bounds of love, tenderness, and care towards our spouse.

How to Set Boundaries

- Determine the areas in which we need to set boundaries. In order for us to set boundaries, we have to decide that we are in charge of our lives. We must know where we want to go and what we want to become. We have to take responsibility and ownership for our boundaries.

- List the boundaries you wish to set on a piece of paper.

- Define how each boundary will allow the opportunity for agency, peace, and wholeness. If we can see how the boundary will give us more choices and actually reduce emotional turmoil, we are more likely to keep them. After all, they are *our* boundaries. Consider setting boundaries in the following areas:

Mental   Emotional   Physical   Spiritual   Sexual   Financial

Write a detailed explanation of where you will set boundaries in each of these areas and why these will help you.

Mental Boundaries (This is where I will set my boundaries. This is where my responsibility ends and my loved one's responsibility begins.)

_____

_____

_____

_____

How will these boundaries benefit me by giving me more choices and making my life easier?

_____

_____
_____
_____
_____

Emotional Boundaries (This is where I will set my boundaries. This is where my responsibility ends and my loved one's responsibility begins.)

_____

_____
_____
_____
_____

How will these boundaries benefit me by giving me more choices and making my life easier?

_____

_____
_____
_____
_____

Physical Boundaries (This is where I will set my boundaries. This is where my responsibility ends and my loved one's responsibility begins.)

_____

_____
_____
_____
_____

How will these boundaries benefit me by giving me more choices and making my life easier?

_____

_____

_____

_____

_____

_____

Spiritual Boundaries (This is where I will set my boundaries. This is where my responsibility ends and my loved one's responsibility begins.)

_____

_____

_____

_____

_____

How will setting these boundaries generate the opportunity for me to develop a clearer vision of my personal agency, wholeness, and my relationship with God?

_____

_____

_____

_____

_____

_____

Sexual Boundaries (This is where I will set my boundaries. This is where my responsibility ends and my loved one's responsibility begins.)

_____

_____

_____

_____

_____

How will these boundaries allow me to separate love from lust and restore peace?

_____

_____

_____

_____

_____

Financial Boundaries (This is where I will set my boundaries. This is where my responsibility ends and my loved one's responsibility begins.)

_____

_____

_____

_____

_____

How will these boundaries help me exercise personal agency in an appropriate way and ease any financial burdens?

_____

_____

_____

_____

_____

BOUNDARIES REVIEW

If we have been living a life without boundaries, setting and holding them will be very challenging at first. Similarly, the transition will be challenging for our loved ones as they learn to live with someone who has set boundaries. It will be new for us and new for our loved ones. It will take a lot of emotional and spiritual energy with consistent effort to change our attitudes and understanding of appropriate boundaries. It may be advisable to begin slowly by setting boundaries in one area at a time and learning how to maintain those boundaries. Small glimpses of success in one area will encourage us and motivate us to keep trying because we will see firsthand the advantages of setting and maintaining boundaries. Even small steps of positive change can bring us progress and personal satisfaction. Elder Russell M. Nelson said: "The enormous effort required to attain such self-mastery is rewarded with a deep sense of satisfaction. More importantly, spiritual attainments in mortality accompany us into eternity" (*Ensign,* Nov. 1995, 86). The benefits for setting boundaries far outweigh any cost, work, or effort on our part.

Here are some important points about setting and maintaining boundaries: (1) Determine where the boundaries need to be set and why this will help you. (2) Firmly set the boundary. Also, when it is appropriate and if circumstances warrant it, be willing to brainstorm with your loved one and discuss other possibilities regarding your boundaries that might be mutually acceptable. (3) Make sure that your loved ones and others know where the boundaries have been set. (4) Follow through with the consequences if the boundaries are crossed. (5) Pray for help to keep your boundaries. (6) Have a support system in place that will help you to keep your boundaries.

If our loved ones' speech or behavior is not acceptable and is outside the boundaries we have set for ourselves, we have several choices (1) We can tell the person how the statement or behavior makes us feel. (2) We can ask the person to change the way they are talking or otherwise behaving and let them know we will terminate the conversation or follow up with other consequences if they do not. (3) We can limit the amount of information we share with the person. (4) We can choose to limit our contact with the person. (5) We can choose to physically leave the room or area whenever the person does not respect our boundaries.

Boundaries and Self-mastery

By setting boundaries we develop more self-mastery. Boundaries and self-mastery are rarely possible if we try to accomplish them alone without the Savior's help. The Savior said: "Abide in me, and I in you. As the branch cannot bear fruit of itself, except it abide in the vine; no more can ye, except ye abide in me. I am the vine, ye [are] the branches: He that abideth in me, and I in him, the same bringeth forth much fruit: for without me ye can do nothing" (John 15:4-5). The apostle Paul taught: "I can do all things through Christ which strengtheneth me" (Philip. 4:13).

If we turn to the Lord and not away from Him, the experiences we have in life can help us develop self-mastery. There is only one way for developing self-mastery—good old hard work and effort, asking every step of the way for the Lord's help. President Thomas S. Monson explained this process: "The battle for self-mastery may leave a person a bit bruised and battered, but always a better man or woman. Self-mastery is a rigorous process at best; too many of us want it to be effortless and painless" (*Ensign,* Mar. 1988, 4).

By setting boundaries we are achieving self-mastery even though it will be difficult. Knowing up-front that it will be difficult makes us less surprised when we discover the difficulty on our own. Even with the difficulty, the blessing of inner peace and self-mastery are well worth the effort we pay.

How will setting boundaries help you to develop self-mastery?

_____

_____

_____

_____

How will you know you are making progress in your quest for self-mastery? What will be the gauge? How will you keep score?

_____

_____

_____

_____

_____

REVIEW OF PRINCIPLES

Why is it important to be honest about where you are in the healing process?

_____

_____

_____

_____

How would you define a boundary to a child?

_____

_____

_____

_____

How would you teach a child about boundaries?

_____

_____

_____

_____

_____

How will your life be more manageable when you set boundaries?

_____

_____

_____

_____

_____

In which area(s) of your life have you decided to set boundaries?

_____

_____

_____

_____

How can you get support from others to help you to keep your boundaries?

_____

_____

_____

_____

Record any other insights or thoughts that have come as you have read this chapter.

_____

_____

_____

_____

_____

What is the single most important principle or concept you have learned from this chapter?

_____

_____

_____

_____

With whom can you share this important principle or concept in the next week?

_____

_____

What are some skills or techniques you have learned in this chapter that you will try to implement in your relationships with yourself and others in the next thirty days?

_____

_____

_____

_____

_____

_____

CALMNESS BREAK

Consider purchasing a child's coloring book and coloring the pictures with crayons. Spend about an hour and see how you feel at the end.

What have you discovered, and what choices can you make to rediscover some of the simple things in life?

_____

_____

_____

_____

_____

_____

_____

_____

MESSAGES OF HOPE

Elder Gordon B. Hinckley: "Begin with yourself. Reformation of the world begins with reformation of self. It is a fundamental article of our faith that 'We believe in being honest, true, chaste, benevolent, [and] virtuous'" (A of F 13) (*Ensign,* Nov. 1975, 38).

President James E. Faust: "Who are good parents? They are those who have lovingly, prayerfully, and earnestly tried to teach their children by example and precept 'to pray, and to walk uprightly before the Lord.' This is true even though some of their children are disobedient or worldly. Children come into this world with their own distinct spirits and personality traits. Some children 'would challenge any set of parents under any set of circumstances. . . . Perhaps there are others who would bless the lives of, and be a joy to, almost any father or mother.' Successful parents are those who have sacrificed and struggled to do the best they can in their own family circumstances" (*Ensign,* May 2003, 61).

PRINCIPLE 8

God's Words Have Healing Power;
Search and Ponder His Words Daily

CHAPTER OVERVIEW

The news of a loved one's compulsive sexual behaviors often launches a sense of uncertainty regarding the future. We wonder if the destructive patterns and habits of our loved ones can ever be overcome. This state of sudden chaos and uncertainty may even cause us to lose our sense of direction and purpose in life, leaving us vulnerable to the destructive forces of fear and frustration. We often find ourselves riddled with questions for which answers seem elusive, thus increasing our sense of uncertainty and fueling our downward, spiraling crash-and-burn descent.

One spouse commented, "I just want to know how everything is going to work out. If I just knew that things would eventually be okay, I could deal with the pain I have right now." Such feelings are typical and normal.

Is there a way out of this downward spiral? Yes! There is hope regardless of the choices of those around us, "For whatsoever things were written aforetime were written for our learning, that we through patience and comfort of the scriptures might have hope" (Rom. 15:4).

The scriptures can provide the spiritual and emotional anchor we need during this time of healing. They can assure us that since the Lord is in charge, if we just keep turning to Him and trusting in Him, everything will be okay for us. We can learn from the examples of men and women in the scriptures who dealt with some of life's most daunting challenges and found courage, tenacity, and hope as they turned toward the Light and walked in His way toward wholeness and safety.

Perhaps initially focusing on the scriptures sounds more like a "Sunday School" answer than the kind of help you may be seeking. The truth, however, is that the scriptures are the perfect foundation for finding our footing because: (1) They contain all the basic truths necessary to weather even hurricane-force challenges; (2) The view is often clearer watching someone else face challenges; (3) The scriptures are filled with accounts that parallel our own lives, and (4) When we sup directly from the pages of scripture, we feast straight from the source rather than settling for the watered-down version of someone else's persuasions.

The opinions of friends and immediate family members are just that—opinions. Daily scripture study affords one-on-one time with the Spirit as our teacher, opening the way for personalized, specific instruction and insight. However, the scriptural insights of others may initially help us gain our spiritual eyes and ears. In Acts we read how Philip offered that kind of help to the Ethiopian who was struggling to read Isaiah. It is important to note that the Ethiopian was reading the scriptures, and because of his efforts, Philip was prompted to offer help:

> *Then the Spirit said unto Philip, Go near, and join thyself to [the Ethiopian's] chariot.*
>
> *And Philip ran thither to him, and heard him read the prophet Esaias, and said, Understandest thou what thou readest?*
>
> *And he said, How can I, except some man should guide me? And he desired Philip that he would come up and sit with him* (Acts 8:29-31).

As Philip sat in the chariot and taught this humble man "of great authority" about the Savior's mission, the Ethiopian's heart was touched and he was converted and "went on his way rejoicing" (Acts 8:39).

Developing ears to hear and eyes to see, however, may take some time and considerable concerted effort. Gradually, as our hearts and minds remain open and receptive to the verses we read, the Spirit will proffer counsel, nudge us in a particular direction, or simply wrap us in a blanket of peace amid the turmoil.

CHAPTER OBJECTIVES

At the conclusion of this chapter you should—

1. Understand that the scriptures can enlighten your mind and fill your heart with eternal truths.
2. Learn from the accounts of men and women in the scriptures who faced formidable obstacles; ponder how to respond in "like manner" in your own life.
3. Recognize the value of recording in a journal the thoughts and feelings you receive while reading the scriptures.
4. Recognize that your personal journal can become scripture for you.
5. Realize that reading and reflecting on your personal journal will illuminate the insights you gained, reminding you that the Lord hears your prayers and is aware of your circumstances.
6. Increase your trust in future endowments of knowledge and direction as a result of past spiritual experiences recorded in your journal.
7. Recognize that when you receive inspiration and direction from reading the scriptures, you should act on it.
8. Know the value of sharing your written record with your immediate family and others when appropriate.

SCRIPTURES GIVE US SPIRITUAL EYES TO SEE THE WORLD

Satan wants us to look at the world through the world's eyes. He wants us to shape our viewpoints, opinions, and beliefs by the doctrines of men. As we read the scriptures, gleaning truth and light, our view of life's challenges is altered to more closely approximate that of our Heavenly Father.

When we allow the insights and truths found in the scriptures to be the guide and standard by which we judge all other philosophies and doctrines of men, we are able to distinguish truth from error. When viewed through this lens of pure truth, even popular yet incorrect ideologies of the day are exposed for what they truly are. Then will our "confidence wax strong in the presence of God; and the doctrine of the priesthood shall distil upon (our) soul as the dews from heaven" (D&C 121:45). With such vision, we do not embrace what the world tells us to believe about sexuality, relationships, and marriage, for we are built upon a more sure foundation of eternal truths and divine direction.

President Joseph Fielding Smith taught: "Our conscience and the scriptures tell us what to live by—and they tell us what habits we should change for our eternal welfare and progress" (*New Era,* Jan. 1971, 5). This statement reaffirms an eternal truth: We can learn from the scriptures the habits we need to change in order to progress.

Through the scriptures we learn of Christ: "Search the scriptures; for in them ye think ye have eternal life: and they are they which testify of me" (John 5:39). To the degree we come to Christ for help and healing, we find wholeness and peace, regardless of our circumstances.

THE SCRIPTURES GIVE US DIRECTION, COMFORT, AND ANSWERS

Studying and pondering the scriptures is a positive choice we can make when we are struggling with our emotions, feelings, or problems. This spiritual practice is just as important when things seem to be going our way as when we are facing major challenges.

Most of us have given a note or written a letter to a family member or close friend who was going away for a while. We wanted to record on paper our thoughts and feelings about this person so that during the absence he or she would feel our love. This is what the Lord did for us when He gave us the scriptures. Since we would be out of His presence for a while, He wanted us to have a written record of His thoughts, His feelings, His counsel, and His perfect love.

President Gordon B. Hinckley said:

> *Recently while wrestling in my mind with a problem I thought to be of serious consequence, I went to my knees in prayer. There came into my mind a feeling of peace and the words of the Lord, "Be still and know that I am God." I turned to the scripture and read this reassuring statement spoken to the Prophet Joseph Smith 150 years ago: "Let your hearts be comforted concerning Zion; for all flesh is in mine hands; be still and know that I am God" (D&C 101:16)* (Ensign, May 1983, 6).

Just as President Hinckley found spiritual counsel and comfort through a particular verse from the Doctrine and Covenants, the scriptures can proffer insight and vision beyond our own as we read the accounts of earlier Saints who dealt with anger, rejection, loneliness, trials, fear, and success. Like us, they struggled to "stay connected" with the Savior and to follow counsel contrary to mortal reasoning. Like us, they sometimes faltered.

By contrast, the Savior never faltered. He is our Exemplar, Foundation, and Hope. The triumphs of the Savior and many others, together with the failures of some as recorded in the scriptures, provide important insights and tutoring as we "liken all scriptures unto us, that it might be for our profit and learning" (1 Ne. 19:23).

You may be wondering just how to go about a study of the scriptures to glean the direction and insights necessary for your successful journey through the challenges before you. There are as many answers to this question as there are individuals. Each of us must find our own best way and time for this type of pondering and study of the scriptures. When we read with "real intent" as Moroni suggests, the answers *will* come, along with peace and the assurance that we are not alone in our struggles.

The Lord has promised, "Come unto me all ye that labour and are heavy laden, and I will give you rest. Take my yoke upon you, and *learn of me;* for I am meek and lowly in heart; and ye shall find rest unto your souls" (Matt. 11:28-29). Learning how others in the scriptures dealt with emotional pain and made positive choices that drew them closer to God can renew our hope.

The Lord can and does speak to us through the scriptures. While we are studying and pondering, our minds are usually more open to spiritual direction and guidance. While pondering the scriptures, the Lord can tell us what we need to do to stay on the healing course. The scriptures are a true friend. President Gordon B. Hinckley explained the power that we can glean from the scriptures:

> *I am grateful for emphasis on reading the scriptures. I hope that for you this will become something far more enjoyable than a duty; that, rather, it will become a love affair with the word of God. I promise you that as you read, your minds will be enlightened and your spirits will be lifted. At first it may seem tedious, but that will change into a wondrous experience with thoughts and words of things divine (Ensign, May 1995, 99).*

THE SCRIPTURES PROVIDE A SUPPORT SYSTEM

The scriptures, if fully utilized, provide the ultimate support group—available any time, day or night. The vital nature of the scriptures is illuminated in the account of Nephi and his brothers returning to Jerusalem to obtain the plates of brass because *contained on these plates were the revealed scriptures.* Considering the many things they left behind in Jerusalem, including all their riches, they were instructed to get only one item—the scriptures.

The Lord knew that Nephi and his family would survive without their wealth and all else they left behind, but the scriptures were a must. A spiritual support system had to be in place in order for Lehi and his family to get through the difficult times ahead as they established a new nation in a new land. Without the anchor and illumination of the scriptures, precious truths and pivotal doctrines give way to the philosophies of men. Consider the array of hope-filled passages found in scriptures, including the following:

> *The LORD [is] my strength and my shield; my heart trusted in him, and I am helped: therefore my heart greatly rejoiceth; and with my song will I praise him* (Ps. 28:7).

> *He healeth the broken in heart, and bindeth up their wounds* (Ps. 147:3)

> *O all ye that are pure in heart, lift up your heads and receive the pleasing word of God, and feast upon his love; for ye may, if your minds are firm, forever* (Jacob 3:2).

> *Then they cried unto the Lord in their trouble, and he delivered them out of their distresses* (Ps. 107:6).

We can receive spiritual direction from the scriptures and other sources. One wife chose temple attendance and scripture study for her spiritual and emotional support. She shared,

> *Right after [my husband's] confession, I began attending the temple each week, trying to find comfort and answers. There was some relief there, but sometimes those hours spent within the temple were painful. All the reminders of covenants that had been broken broke my heart. But I determined that I would keep going often because I didn't want to give up my righteous goals and ideals. I poured over the scriptures, searching for direction, comfort, and answers. I memorized D&C 58:2-5 and committed to myself that I would qualify as one who "keepeth the commandments"* (Ensign, Feb. 1997, 41–42).

SCRIPTURES CAN SUSTAIN US
DURING OUR EMOTIONAL FAMINE

Like accounts of famines and droughts in the scriptures, we may find ourselves in a famine—not a famine of food or drink, but of the emotional reserves to continue on.

At times of emotional emptiness, we can draw understanding and strength from scriptural accounts. To replenish our spiritual and emotional reserves, we should review the encounter between Elijah and the widow of Zarephath. She learned to step out into the unknown, trusting that she would find solid ground beyond her present vision. The prophet Elijah had been at the brook Cherith, but it had dried up as a result of his sealing the heavens in an attempt to turn the hearts of the people back to God.

> *And the word of the LORD came unto him, saying,*
> *Arise, get thee to Zarephath, which [belongeth] to Zidon, and dwell there: behold, I have commanded a widow woman there to sustain thee.*
> *So he arose and went to Zarephath. And when he came to the gate of the city, behold, the widow woman [was] there gathering of sticks: and he called to her, and said, Fetch me, I pray thee, a little water in a vessel, that I may drink.*
> *And as she was going to fetch [it], he called to her, and said, Bring me, I pray thee, a morsel of bread in thine hand* (1 Kgs. 17:8-11).

The widow was down to her last handful of meal and precious drops of oil. Not only her own life, but the life of her young son stood in jeopardy, adding to her burden. Why would the Lord ask a widow in dire, life-threatening circumstances to give up the last of her food? Yet this faithful widow received a commandment to "sustain" the prophet.

> *And she said, [As] the LORD thy God liveth, I have not a cake, but an handful of meal in a barrel, and a little oil in a cruse: and, behold, I [am] gathering two sticks, that I may go in and dress it for me and my son, that we may eat it, and die.*
> *And Elijah said unto her, Fear not; go [and] do as thou hast said: but make me thereof a little cake first, and bring [it] unto me, and after make for thee and for thy son* (1 Kgs. 17:12-13).

This widow did not know beforehand what the outcome would be if she used the last of her supplies to provide food for Elijah. Reality told her that she and her son would die. Aren't we in a similar situation with our lives? Haven't we been to the point when reality tells us one thing, but the Spirit tells us something else? The widow walked strictly by faith! The prophet Elijah said unto her, "Fear not; go and do!" She found the strength to follow the prophet's command. Standing at death's doorway, she surrendered her fear and walked by faith.

> *For thus saith the LORD God of Israel, The barrel of meal shall not waste, neither shall the cruse of oil fail, until the day [that] the LORD sendeth rain upon the earth.*
>
> *And she went and did according to the saying of Elijah: and she, and he, and her house, did eat [many] days.*
>
> *[And] the barrel of meal wasted not, neither did the cruse of oil fail, according to the word of the LORD, which he spake by Elijah* (1 Kgs. 17:14-16).

The widow's faith and her willingness to follow the words of the Prophet Elijah brought the miracle of the meal, which never wasted, and the cruse of oil, which never failed, throughout the duration of the drought and famine. Her faith brought down the blessings of heaven in a way she never could have imagined. The barrel and cruse were not filled to overflowing, but rather granted the necessary meal and oil sufficient for the day at hand—one day at a time. The life-sustaining miracle dictated a day-to-day walk in trust and faith. The Savior will require no less of us as He provides soul-sustaining sustenance for us one day at a time during our season of emotional famine.

📖 **Read 1 Kings Chapter 17 again. How does the account of the widow of Zarephath apply to your own situation?**

_____

_____

_____

_____

_____

Another tutoring scriptural account is found in Genesis 21:14-20 concerning Hagar, Sarah's handmaid, given to Abraham as a second wife.

> *And Abraham rose up early in the morning, and took bread, and a bottle of water, and gave [it] unto Hagar, putting [it] on her shoulder, and the child, and sent her away: and she departed, and wandered in the wilderness of Beersheba.*
>
> *And the water was spent in the bottle, and she cast the child under one of the shrubs.*
>
> *And she went, and sat her down over against [him] a good way off, as it were a bowshot: for she said, Let me not see the death of the child. And she*

sat over against [him], and lift up her voice, and wept.

And God heard the voice of the lad; and the angel of God called to Hagar out of heaven, and said unto her, What aileth thee, Hagar? fear not; for God hath heard the voice of the lad where he [is].

Arise, lift up the lad, and hold him in thine hand; for I will make him a great nation.

And God opened her eyes, and she saw a well of water; and she went, and filled the bottle with water, and gave the lad drink.

And God was with the lad; and he grew, and dwelt in the wilderness, and became an archer (Gen. 21:14-20).

Did you notice the action words woven into this account? When the angel addressed the reasons for Hagar's distress, he told her that God had heard the prayers of her son. Then he told her to "arise" and "lift up the lad and hold him in thine hand." She must have promptly obeyed the angel's instructions, for God "opened her eyes and she saw a well of water." To her credit, she then "went" and "filled the bottle with water" and finally "gave the lad drink." Once her eyes were opened to the reality of the life-sustaining well, she got up and moved toward it and filled the bottle with that precious water. As a result, they survived the ordeal, and Ishmael went on to become a great nation. The well was always there. She just couldn't see it.

Similarly, there is a well of living water in the scriptures for us to drink from during our own times of spiritual and emotional famine. We can drink deeply of the truths contained in accounts such as this one about Hagar when we make the scriptures an integral part of our healing and journey toward wholeness.

Personal Journals Can Be Scripture for Us

Recording our thoughts and feelings on paper gives us a place to vent our feelings and to receive promptings. We should write down what we feel when we feel it so that later we can see the progress we have made. Some days we will record little successes; other days we will record failures. This is mortality—we have the good and the bad. President Spencer W. Kimball encouraged:

Get a notebook, my young folks [older members too], a journal that will last through all time, and maybe the angels may quote from it for eternity. Begin today and write in it your goings and comings, your deepest thoughts, your achievements and your failures, your associations and your triumphs, your impressions and your testimonies. Remember, the Savior chastised those who failed to record important events (New Era, Oct. 1975, 5).

We can learn so much about ourselves when we take the time to express our thoughts and feelings on paper. Writing our life experiences and problems on paper allows us to work through them and access the Spirit as we seek solutions. The power of a personal journal is exemplified in the following:

> *During the initial few days following the disclosure of my husband's compulsive sexual behaviors, as I prayed for direction, a thought entered my mind and heart: "Keep a journal of your journey. Record every insight, experience, and revelation which comes."*
>
> *The purpose was not immediately apparent. However, a few weeks later, when I found myself overwhelmed with feelings of failure, hopelessness, and despair, I felt prompted to read through my spiritual journal. I realized how many times heavenly insight filled my mind, lending strength, direction, or simply assurance of His Love. I was reminded of insights received. I realized I was indeed moving forward though my husband chose to remain stuck in his compulsion.*
>
> *My recovery journal has become a powerful part of my own journey over the past fourteen years. During all that time, my husband chose to remain stuck, but reading back through the pages from time to time, I witness again that Heavenly Father does hear my prayers; that the Savior can and does send the promised peace, comfort, direction, and healing.*
>
> *Some time later, while reading in the Doctrine and Covenants, I came across a powerful passage which lent a second witness to the importance of keeping a journal. In Section 6, Oliver Cowdery was seeking another witness of the things he had previously received from the Lord concerning the translation of the Book of Mormon, and the Lord's response is recorded in verses 22, 23, and 24 as follows:*
>
> > *Verily, verily, I say unto you, if you desire a further witness, cast your mind upon the night that you cried unto me in your heart, that you might know concerning the truth of these things.*
> >
> > *Did I not speak peace to your mind concerning the matter? What greater witness can you have than from God?*
> >
> > *And now, behold, you have received a witness; for if I have told you things which no man knoweth have you not received a witness?*

Once we have received revelations from God, it is important that we remember them and act on them. By keeping a spiritual healing journal, we can reread what the Holy Ghost has inspired us to do and continue to act on that inspiration.

ACT ON THE INSPIRATION AND DIRECTION

Studying the scriptures in a quiet place is only the beginning. The real inspiration and changes in our hearts take place as we ponder the scriptures, record our thoughts, and then act.

In order to continue our healing, we must act on the inspiration and direction we receive as we study and ponder the scriptures. President Ezra Taft Benson taught that certain blessings are only available in the scriptures: "However diligent we may be in other areas, certain blessings are to be found only in the scriptures, only in coming to the word of the Lord and holding fast to it as we make our way through the mists of darkness to the tree of life" (*Ensign,* May 1986, 82).

🖋 **Where is a quiet place you can study the scriptures? What time is the best for you?**

_____

_____

_____

_____

_____

🖋 **How will you apply the principle of pondering to your scripture study?**

_____

_____

_____

_____

_____

President Ezra Taft Benson reminded us of the blessings that we receive from studying the scriptures:

> *Success in righteousness, the power to avoid deception and resist temptation, guidance in our daily lives, healing of the soul—these are but a few of the promises the Lord has given to those who will come to His word. Does the*

Lord promise and not fulfill? Surely if He tells us that these things will come to us if we lay hold upon His word, then the blessings can be ours. And if we do not, then the blessings may be lost (Ensign, May 1986, 82).

One of the blessings that President Benson listed was "healing of the soul." What is the most important thing we are seeking? It is the healing of our soul through Christ the Lord. What more could we want?

How does President Benson's promise regarding scripture study apply to you and your healing process?

_____

_____

_____

_____

_____

CONTINUE FORWARD EVEN WITH OUR WEAKNESSES

The scriptures can provide us with hope and encouragement to continue to try even when we might not do all the right things. Since all of us have weaknesses and fall short, we should not let that reality burden us. Instead we should recognize that we are doing the best we can at this time. Hopefully we will be able to do even better in the future. President Brigham Young taught:

You may inquire—"Do you think we are doing right?" Yes, as well as you know how. If you do not fully live up to the knowledge you have, I can say that you have done about as well as you could. We have a warfare on our hands. Evil is here; the Devil reigns on the earth, and has held dominion on it for thousands of years. That reign we have to break and cast him out, with the help of God; but we cannot do it at once. Thousands of temptations assail, and you make a miss here and a slip there, and say that you have not lived up to all the knowledge you have. True; but often it is a marvel to me that you have lived up to so much as you have, considering the power of the enemy upon the earth (Journal of Discourses, 8:285, June 7, 1860).

The scriptures record remarkable accounts of others who have been made whole. We too can receive the same blessing. The scriptures record:

And Jesus arose, and followed him, and [so did] his disciples.

And, behold, a woman, which was diseased with an issue of blood twelve years, came behind [him], and touched the hem of his garment:

For she said within herself, If I may but touch his garment, I shall be whole.

But Jesus turned him about, and when he saw her, he said, Daughter, be of good comfort; thy faith hath made thee whole. And the woman was made whole from that hour (Matt. 9:19-22).

What impressions come to your mind from these verses? How do these verses apply to you?

_____

_____

_____

_____

_____

_____

_____

_____

REVIEW OF PRINCIPLES

What is the difference between just reading the scriptures and pondering the scriptures?

_____

_____

_____

_____

_____

How can you apply and act on divine advice from God and Christ found in the scriptures?

_____

_____

_____

_____

_____

_____

_____

How can the story about the widow of Zarephath be applied to your healing?

_____

_____

_____

_____

_____

_____

_____

What did you learn from Hagar, a woman in the Old Testament? How can you apply the principle in the story to your own healing?

_____

_____

_____

_____

_____

_____

_____

What are some skills or techniques you have learned in this chapter that you will try to implement in your relationships with yourself and others in the next thirty days?

_____

_____

_____

_____

_____

_____

_____

_____

What is the single most important principle or concept you have learned from this chapter?

_____

_____

_____

_____

_____

_____

_____

_____

With whom can you share this important principle or concept within the next week?

_____

_____

_____

_____

_____

Calmness Break

Go to a pet store or zoo and just look around. See the birds, fish, and animals. Watch how they nap, eat, or play with others. Think about their daily routine. What control do they have over their lives? Watch the puppies or kittens. How playful are they with each other? How curious are they about their world? What have you discovered?

Messages of Hope

Elder Richard L. Evans: "You who stay with loved ones in loyalty—you who are discouraged in your work—you who are disappointed in others, in yourselves, in circumstances—you who feel you have little of the brightness of life—trust; have faith; do the best you can. Don't give up" (*Ensign,* Jan. 1971, 26).

Elder Robert D. Hales: "My message today is how to aid the healing process of the soul. It is a message to lead you and me to the Great Healer, the Lord and Savior Jesus Christ. It is a plan to read the scriptures, pray, ponder, repent if necessary, and be healed with the peace and joy of His Spirit" (*Ensign,* Nov. 1998, 14).

PRINCIPLE 9

Personal Revelation Is Available through Prayer and Fasting; We Can Embrace the Revelations from Our Prophets

CHAPTER OVERVIEW

Personal revelation means exactly that—*personal*. What does God want *me* to do? What is His will for *me*? How can *I* prepare myself to listen and obey His will?

Most relationships in today's world seem so *impersonal*. The days of enjoying personal relationships with doctors, pharmacists, mechanics, or grocery store owners are pretty much over. Few still experience one-on-one personal service where long-lasting relationships span generations. We may feel like nothing but a number or a name on a list at the doctor's office, discount store, credit card company, or in a variety of other situations. We live in a corporate world, and the individual, personal touch seems almost non-existent.

We may wonder if anyone "at the top" knows who we are or even cares. However, Elder Jeffrey R. Holland assures, "I bear personal witness this day of a personal, living God, who knows our names, hears and answers prayers, and cherishes us eternally as children of His Spirit. I testify that, amidst the wondrously complex tasks inherent in the universe, He seeks our individual happiness and safety above all other godly concerns" (*Ensign,* Nov. 2003, 72).

God and Christ do know us personally and will come to our aid! Elder Russell M. Nelson admonished, "Faith can be fortified through prayer. Prayer is the powerful key to making decisions, not only concerning your physical body, but concerning all other important aspects of your life. Humbly seek the Lord in prayer with a sincere heart and real intent, and He will help you" (*Ensign,* Nov. 1990, 75).

What a blessing and a promise to know that we can and will get divine help as we seek it. We have been promised:

> *Draw near unto me and I will draw near unto you; seek me diligently and ye shall find me; ask, and ye shall receive; knock, and it shall be opened unto you.*
>
> *Whatsoever ye ask the Father in my name it shall be given unto you, that is expedient for you* (D&C 88:63-64).

In addition to divine help, we should also receive spiritual direction from our apostles and prophets. To embrace the revelations from our prophets means that we willingly accept their counsel and direction. We learn their counsel and advice through the scriptures and conference talks. These talks are a tremendous source of spiritual direction.

> *We believe in the same organization that existed in the Primitive Church—namely, apostles, prophets . . .* (A of F 6).

> *We believe in the gift of tongues, prophecy, revelation, visions . . .* (A of F 7).

> *We believe that the first principles and ordinances of the Gospel are . . . fourth, Laying on of hands for the gift of the Holy Ghost"* (A of F 4).

> *We believe all that God has revealed, all that He does now reveal, and we believe that He will yet reveal many great and important things . . .* (A of F 9).

CHAPTER OBJECTIVES

At the end of this chapter you should—

1. Know that God knows you personally and will listen to your prayers and help you.
2. Pray for strength to give up unhealthy emotions, such as inappropriate guilt.
3. Identify how Satan and his associates work to keep you down and discouraged.
4. Determine how to rely on Christ and His associates to keep you focused on your healing.
5. Realize the benefits of recording personal promptings that come to you from the Spirit.

6. Recognize that God has a timetable and that with patience and faith you can accept His will.
7. Understand that the words of the prophets are the same as if they came directly from the Lord.
8. Have confidence that the Lord will bless you as you embrace the revelations from His prophets.

PRAYER—A SACRED PRIVILEGE

Prayer keeps us connected with God and Christ. President James E. Faust said:

> *I have learned from countless personal experiences that great is the power of prayer. No earthly authority can separate us from direct access to our Creator. There can never be a mechanical or electronic failure when we pray. There is no limit on the number of times or how long we can pray each day. There is no quota of how many needs we wish to pray for in each prayer. We do not need to go through secretaries or make an appointment to reach the throne of grace. He is reachable at any time and any place* (Ensign, May 2002, 59).

We *can* communicate with God through prayer. It is an honor for us to communicate with God. He always listens to our prayers. When it appears that all of our support is gone, God is still there and we should remind ourselves that He will give us the direction and guidance we need. Elder Richard G. Scott reminds us: "Communication with our Father in Heaven is not a trivial matter. It is a sacred privilege. It is based upon unchanging principles. When we receive help from our Father in Heaven, it is in response to faith, obedience, and the proper use of agency" (Ensign, Nov. 1989, 30).

The *Bible Dictionary* states:

> *Prayer is the act by which the will of the Father and the will of the child are brought into correspondence with each other. The object of prayer is not to change the will of God, but to secure for ourselves and for others blessings that God is already willing to grant, but that are made conditional on our asking for them. Blessings require some work or effort on our part before we can obtain them. Prayer is a form of work, and is an appointed means for obtaining the highest of all blessings* (752-53).

👉 What blessings do you want from God?

_____

_____

_____

_____

_____

_____

👉 What amount of work are you willing to do or what effort are you willing to put forth to receive these blessings?

_____

_____

_____

_____

_____

_____

Praying sincerely is a part of our lives that is vitally important to our spiritual well-being. President Gordon B. Hinckley said: "Be prayerful. I hope that every one of you gets on your knees every morning and every night and expresses gratitude to the Lord, that you share with Him the righteous desires of your hearts, that you pray for those in need and distress wherever they may be" (*Ensign,* Mar. 1997, 62–63).

We cannot expect to heal from the painful effects of our loved ones' behaviors without reaching out in prayer to God. Our problems will take more than our own wisdom to solve. We cannot rely solely on our own will power or strength. President James E. Faust said: "Each of us has problems that we cannot solve and weaknesses that we cannot conquer without reaching out through prayer to a higher source of strength. That source is the God of heaven to whom we pray in the name of Jesus Christ. As we pray we should think of our Father in Heaven as possessing all knowledge, understanding, love, and compassion" (*Ensign,* May 2002, 59).

According to President Faust, how does prayer help us to solve our problems?

_____

_____

_____

_____

_____

Through prayer we can receive personal revelation and know what the Lord wants us to do. Elder Russell M. Nelson said, "Prayer provides communication with your Heavenly Father and invites the promptings of personal revelation" (*Ensign*, Nov. 1990, 74).

PRAY FOR OURSELVES, OUR LOVED ONES, AND OTHERS WHO ARE HELPING

Alma had some loved ones, the Zoramites, who had fallen away from the truth. The scriptures record that "they [the Zoramites] had fallen into great errors, for they would not observe to keep the commandments of God" (Alma 31:9). Doesn't this describe some of our loved ones? Alma prayed for his loved ones. We can learn many principles from Alma's recorded prayer.

Prayer for Strength

> O Lord, wilt thou give me strength, that I may bear with mine infirmities. For I am infirm, and such wickedness among this people doth pain my soul (Alma 31:30).

When our loved ones choose iniquity, it does cause us pain and we need the omniscience and omnipotence of our Creator in meeting and overcoming the challenges brought to the family circle by the addictions of our loved ones.

> O Lord, my heart is exceedingly sorrowful; wilt thou comfort my soul in Christ. O Lord, wilt thou grant unto me that I may have strength, that I may suffer with patience these afflictions which shall come upon me, because of the iniquity of this people (Alma 31:31).

Prayer for Our Own Souls and Others
Who Are Trying to Help Our Loved Ones

> *O Lord, wilt thou comfort my soul and give unto me success, and also my fellow laborers who are with me . . . even all these wilt thou comfort, O Lord. Yea, wilt thou comfort their souls in Christ.*
>
> *Wilt thou grant unto them that they may have strength, that they may bear their afflictions which shall come upon them because of the iniquities of this people* (Alma 31:32–33).

Prayer for Success: Respect God's Will and Our Loved Ones' Agency

> *Lord, wilt thou grant unto us that we may have success in bringing them again unto thee in Christ.*
>
> *Behold, O Lord, their souls are precious, and many of them are our brethren; therefore, give unto us, O Lord, power and wisdom that we may bring these, our brethren, again unto thee* (Alma 31:34–35).

Record your impressions as you read these verses:

_____
_____
_____
_____
_____
_____
_____
_____
_____
_____

Even though we may want our loved ones to change, they may choose not to. In such circumstances, we can, as Alma did, pray to have the strength to bear with patience our afflictions and continue to seek and do the Lord's will. The Lord did strengthen Alma and those who were preaching the word: "The Lord provided for them . . . gave them strength, [and they] were swallowed up in the joy of Christ. Now this was according to the prayer of Alma; and this because he prayed in faith" (Alma 31:38).

What success did Alma and the others have in preaching to the Zoramites? The humble had a change of heart and were converted. In other words, those who wanted to change and made an effort to change did so.

We pray, as Alma did, to know the Lord's will. We truly want to know what is the Lord's will for us. What would the Lord have us do in this situation with our loved ones? Here is a very sobering reminder about seeking the Lord's will rather than our own interests. The *Bible Dictionary* states the importance of becoming one with Christ:

> *We pray in Christ's name when our mind is the mind of Christ, and our wishes the wishes of Christ—when his words abide in us (John 15:7). We then ask for things it is possible for God to grant. Many prayers remain unanswered because they are not in Christ's name at all; they in no way represent his mind, but spring out of the selfishness of man's heart* (753).

Pray to Give Up Inappropriate Guilt

We are taught to pray for many things and to be grateful for what we have. Can we pray to accept ourselves as humans who have weaknesses and frailties? Can we pray for strength to do better? Can we pray to give up feelings of unearned guilt regarding our loved ones' behaviors? Can we pray to stop saying to ourselves the words, "If only?" A single mom came to this realization:

> *I have decided not to wallow in guilt and misery. I could torture myself with so many "if only's"–if only I had married someone else, if only I had been a stronger influence when my children were young, if only I had recognized some of their concerns earlier. But "if only" doesn't make any difference now and berating myself doesn't accomplish anything either. Rather, if I truly believe that the gospel of Jesus Christ is the plan of happiness, then it is my responsibility to be happy. The best way I can be a missionary to my children is to radiate the joy of the gospel by the way I live (Ensign, Feb. 2004, 49).*

Continual focus on "if only" statements usually produces feelings of guilt, anxiety, and depression. Instead, we need to catch ourselves when we say "if only" and quickly change to "what now" statements. *What* can I do *now* to stay connected with my Heavenly Father? *What* can I do *now* to feel the Spirit more often in my life? *What* can I do *now* to be supportive to my loved ones, to deal with this problem, but also to make them responsible for their choices?

Record a few "what now" thoughts and statements in place of the counterproductive "if only" sentiments:

_____

_____

_____

_____

_____

_____

_____

FASTING

Combined prayer and fasting puts us in a prime position to be receptive to spiritual promptings. As we continue in these spiritual practices, we receive many blessings that will strengthen us and allow us to find solutions and joy regardless of what our loved ones choose to do.

> *Nevertheless they did fast and pray oft, and did wax stronger and stronger in their humility, and firmer and firmer in the faith of Christ, unto the filling their souls with joy and consolation, yea, even to the purifying and the sanctification of their hearts, which sanctification cometh because of their yielding their hearts unto God* (Hel. 3:35).

Through prayer, fasting, humility, and faith in Christ, we can eventually yield everything unto God—even our hearts, pains, sorrows, and fears. As we do, we will be able to listen to His answers.

LISTENING FOR ANSWERS

Through prayer we can receive direction and guidance from the Holy Ghost. Receiving direction and inspiration from the Holy Ghost is a daily challenge. Elder Henry B. Eyring gave this assurance: "The words of confirmation into the Church are an invitation: 'Receive the Holy Ghost.' And that choice must be made not once, but every day, every hour, every minute. . . . With faith and obedience practiced long enough, the Holy Ghost becomes a constant companion, our natures change, and endurance becomes certain" (*Ensign,* May 2002, 28).

 How can you seek direction and guidance from the Holy Ghost?

_____

_____

_____

_____

_____

_____

_____

A real effort to listen for answers while we pray is so vital. President Thomas S. Monson explained this process:

> *We left our heavenly home and came to earth in the purity and innocence of childhood. Our Heavenly Father did not launch us on our eternal voyage without providing the means whereby we could receive from Him guidance to ensure our safe return. Yes, I speak of prayer. I speak, too, of the whisperings from that still, small voice within each of us* (*Ensign,* June 1993, 5).

Elder Russell M. Nelson gave this counsel: "Carefully listen to learn from the Lord through the still small voice—the Holy Spirit—which leads to truth. . . . Listen to learn in prayer, for He will answer the humble who truly seek Him" (*Ensign,* May 1991, 24–25).

One sister wrote:

> *At times, watching our three grown children struggle in their personal lives tends to generate feelings of regret and sorrow. I find myself wishing I could turn the clock back and change all the abuse and unhealthiness they experienced growing up in a home with an abusive, pornography-addicted father. One particularly painful night, I pled with the Lord to help me know how to help them. The answer came into my heart and mind, "Model a perfect brightness of hope." I turned to the scriptures and read several verses dealing with hope. I cling to those verses during the really difficult times, remembering my example of hope will eventually lead them to drink from the well, whether in this life or the next.*

How can you listen for answers to your prayers?

_____

_____

_____

_____

_____

Prayer can help us to make sure we are listening to the right voices. We need to watch our thoughts and make sure we are not listening to Satan and his committee.

SATAN'S COMMITTEE

Letting go and letting God into our lives will bring us joy! How do we let go of inappropriate guilt and other negative emotions that pull us down? Here is one suggestion: We can visualize two separate committees that operate inside our minds. Christ is the chairman of one committee and Satan is the chairman of the other. The adversary's committee members introduce continual statements into our minds designed to bring us down and make us believe lies.

Let's suppose Satan has assigned five committee members to us. Here is an example of how Satan and his committee might work inside our minds. We often carry out this dialogue with his committee without consciously realizing what is happening. We may give very good rational responses as this example illustrates, but it takes our energy to keep responding.

Committee Member 1: "You should have been a more responsive wife and this never would have happened."

Your response: "I was a good wife. I did take care of my husband's needs."

Committee Member 2: "If you were taking care of your husband's sexual needs, he would not be looking at pornography."

Your response: "I was sexually responsive. I can't help it that my husband decided to look at pornography."

Committee Member 3: "Let's get real. Why would he be looking at pornography if all his sexual needs were being met?"

Your response: "Well, I don't know all the reasons, but he has his agency and he has to decide. I can't control what he chooses to do."

Committee Member 4: "Sure that's true, you can't control what he decides to do, but you *are* his wife. You *are* married. Other couples don't have this problem—just you two do."

Your response: "Sure we are married, but I'm still not responsible for what he does. Besides, I know of other couples that have struggled with these same issues, and so we are not the only ones."

Committee Member 5: "You've got to admit that you are the problem. It is not your husband. It is you. You have to change and do what he wants in order to save this marriage."

Your response: "I know there are things I need to work on and try to change and I am willing to work on them. However, my husband's addiction to pornography is not acceptable and I will not take responsibility for it nor condone it in any way."

Satan and his five-member committee make it six on one. While we are debating one of Satan's committee members, the next committee member has time to think up a new reason why we are to blame for our loved ones' behaviors. We do not have time to think up strong rebuttals because one of the committee members is always engaging us in conversation.

We might be strong at first and not believe what they are saying, but eventually, if we keep listening to this committee, we can get worn out, give in emotionally, and lose the debate. The end result is that we start believing the lies and deceptions the members of Satan's committee are telling us.

 In what ways have you been listening to Satan and his committee?

_____

_____

_____

_____

_____

_____

_____

We do not have an unlimited supply of emotional energy. It is entirely possible to beat ourselves up with the comments of Satan's committee until we believe we are no good. We can even be persuaded to take total blame for our loved ones' behaviors and to become discouraged and depressed.

🖋 Identify some of the untruths generated by Satan's "committee" that you may be listening to:

_____

_____

_____

_____

_____

We can get trapped by Satan if we entertain his committee and let down our defenses. We are always outnumbered when we try to withstand the comments of this committee by ourselves. This is why it is so important that we choose to seek help by tuning in to the other committee headed by Christ. He communicates with us through His co-chairman, the Holy Ghost.

When we are emotionally down, we should always ask ourselves, "Have I been listening to and debating Satan's committee? Have I become so worn out that I cannot face the mental debate anymore? Is this why I just want to give in or give up?"

Satan surely knows all the angles. He will customize a temptation committee to get us down and discouraged. We can decide now to say the following:

"I will choose not to talk to the committee. I will look to God (Alma 37:47).*"*

"I will choose not to listen to the committee. I will look to God."

"I will choose not to debate the committee. I will look to God."

"I will choose not to entertain the committee. I will look to God."

"I will choose to leave the 'room' when I hear their voices. I will look to God."

"I will choose to listen to Christ's committee instead."

We need to catch ourselves whenever we are listening to Satan's committee and then make a firm decision not to listen to it and pray to have the strength to follow through. "Watch and pray, that ye enter not into temptation: the spirit [indeed] is willing, but the flesh [may be] weak" (Matt. 26:41). We want to look to God and live (Alma 37:47).

Whether it comes as an obvious temptation to disobey God's commandments or a less obvious temptation to feel guilty and to beat ourselves up, we need to watch and pray. We need to be on the lookout, catch ourselves whenever we are listening to the wrong committee and immediately say, "I will not listen to that committee."

We may have to change the channel 1,000 times a day. We cannot be listening to Satan's committee when we are praying or repeating the sentence, "I will not listen to the committee." Why? Because we cannot have two thoughts occupying our minds at the same time. Think about watching a news channel that has printed news bulletins running across the bottom of the screen while the anchor person is speaking. Have you tried to read the news bulletins and at the same time concentrate on what the anchor person is saying? As powerful as the mind is, it is next to impossible to have two thoughts going on simultaneously. Our mind focuses on either one or the other.

What negative committees have been operating in your mind and how will you turn them off?

_____

_____

_____

_____

_____

CHOOSE CHRIST'S COMMITTEE

Every hour of the day and night the Lord's committee is available to influence our thoughts and feelings. Our thoughts do influence our emotions. If we want a healthy emotional response, we need to watch out for any irrational thinking or thoughts from Satan's committee that might produce unwanted emotions.

The Holy Ghost will speak to our hearts from Christ's committee and tell us that our emotional energy should be spent on reducing our own weaknesses and building our strengths rather than worrying about our loved ones' weaknesses. We can appropriately learn about dealing with our weaknesses and strengths through prayer. We do not need Satan's committee to magnify weaknesses, minimize our strengths, distort them, and tell us lies about them. We learn in Psalms, "The LORD [is] my light and my salvation; whom shall I fear? the LORD [is] the strength of my life; of whom shall I be afraid?" (Ps. 27:1)

In Ether 12:27 we read, "If men come unto me I will show unto them their weakness." What is the purpose of showing us our weakness? It's not to beat us down, but to make us humble so we will come to Him for strength. We cannot improve on a weakness if we do not even know it is there.

President Ezra Taft Benson taught: "He knows our weaknesses and He knows our strengths. By personal revelation, we may discover some of our strengths through careful and prayerful study of our patriarchal blessing. In prayer we can ask Him to reveal to us our weaknesses so that we can amend our lives" (*Ensign*, Sept. 1988, 2).

We must always choose to listen only to God's committee in our minds—the one where the Savior is the chairman. The scriptures exemplify the messages of this committee:

I will have compassion upon you (D&C 64:2).

He hath filled me with his love, even unto the consuming of my flesh" (2 Ne. 4:21).

I am with you to bless you and deliver you forever (D&C 108:8).

I have loved thee with an everlasting love: therefore with loving kindness have I drawn thee (Jer. 31:3).

I will encircle thee in the arms of my love (D&C 6:20).

We have to work tirelessly at times to listen to the committees that God has set in place for us. We have to catch ourselves when we are listening to Satan and his committee and quickly "change the channel" to listen to God's committee:

And I now give unto you a commandment to beware concerning yourselves, to give diligent heed to the words of eternal life.

For you shall live by every word that proceedeth forth from the mouth of God.

For the word of the Lord is truth, and whatsoever is truth is light, and whatsoever is light is Spirit, even the Spirit of Jesus Christ.

And the Spirit giveth light to every man that cometh into the world; and the Spirit enlighteneth every man through the world, that hearkeneth to the voice of the Spirit.

And every one that hearkeneth to the voice of the Spirit cometh unto God, even the Father (D&C 84:43-47).

We have many positive members of God's committee that we can listen to and receive direction from. The prophets and apostles are a powerful part of that committee, and their words of inspiration and direction can lead us and guide us. Our local leaders, branch president or bishop, and stake president are part of God's committee. We decide which committee we will listen to, agree with, and work with.

🌿 How can you tune into God's committee and invite it to work in your mind?

_____

_____

_____

_____

_____

🌿 What will you do if members of Satan's committee begin a meeting in your mind?

_____

_____

_____

_____

_____

RECORD PERSONAL REVELATIONS

As we take time to ponder the principles outlined in this chapter, the Spirit will direct our thoughts, impressions, and actions. Many times during our healing we may feel overwhelmingly impressed to respond to the Spirit and follow its direction—even though that direction may be counter to what others close to us have advised.

Recognizing and following the Spirit is important to our joy, happiness and success in this life and the world to come. We should take time to record spiritual "nudgings" in our journals. As we write, more thoughts and insights may come. Record those too. These entries will be invaluable in the days, weeks, and months to come. When we feel discouraged or disheartened by the struggles, we can read our journals and recall those promptings and whisperings of the Spirit again. Our journals will chronicle those experiences, weaving the delicate spiritual strands into a unique tapestry of faith. Elder Richard G. Scott counseled:

> *Write down in a secure place the important things you learn from the Spirit. You will find that as you write down precious impressions, often more will come. Also, the knowledge you gain will be available throughout your life. Always, day or night, wherever you are, whatever you are doing, seek to recognize and respond to the direction of the Spirit. Express gratitude for the help received and obey it. This practice will reinforce your capacity to learn by the Spirit. It will permit the Lord to guide your life and to enrich the use of every other capacity latent in your being. . . . What you write down from the impressions you feel will be the most valuable help you can receive* (Ensign, June 2002, 32, 34).

One wife recorded:

> *After bringing child sexual abuse charges against my husband on behalf of our daughter, I felt alone, frightened, uncertain, and extremely fearful of the future as a single mother and sole provider for the family.*
>
> *My father called and offered to send plane tickets for us to come to their home and spend the summer with them. Logically, his plan made sense. I wanted desperately to accept the offer and flee the confines of our ward and neighborhood in light of our circumstances. But the Spirit strongly countered that plan. I tried to explain that to my father. He told me I was not thinking clearly. I knew it didn't make sense, but I also knew I was being directed to stay where I was.*
>
> *Following that prompting ultimately proffered one of the grandest views of God's mercy, love, willingness, and ability to strengthen our feeble knees and heal our broken hearts. If I had accepted the offer to escape our embarrassing and challenging circumstances, I would have missed the most important tutoring time of my life. I would have missed the ultimate "support group."*
>
> *The journal pages recording this event have become important, priceless personal scriptures guiding me through other prostrate moments.*

It is important to note that this wife felt strongly about staying put. Her husband was no longer living at home, so she knew her daughter was in a protected environment. However, another wife may feel impressed to accept a family member's offer to get out of the environment for a while. Each of us needs to follow the promptings of the Spirit that come into our own minds and hearts.

🔯 How can you benefit by recording these spiritual promptings?

_____

_____

_____

_____

GOD'S TIMETABLE

Not every prayer we offer will be answered immediately. Immediate answers to all our prayers would take away the necessary requirement to build our faith. Because prayers may not be answered right away, we have ample opportunities to increase our faith. Elder Richard G. Scott explained: "It is a mistake to assume that every prayer we offer will be answered immediately. Some prayers require considerable effort on our part. True, sometimes impressions come when we have not specifically sought them. They generally concern something we need to know and are not otherwise able to find out" (*Ensign,* Nov. 1989, 30).

🔯 How can you continue with faith even though your prayers may not be answered immediately?

_____

_____

_____

_____

_____

Elder Neal A. Maxwell taught: "Faith also includes trust in God's timing, for He has said, 'All things must come to pass in their time' (D&C 64:32). Ironically, some who acknowledge God are tried by His timing, globally and personally!" (*Ensign,* May 1991, 90).

🖎 Identify some specific timing issues in your own life. How can you begin to trust in God's timing?

_____

_____

_____

_____

_____

_____

WORDS OF THE PROPHETS ARE THE SAME AS FROM THE LORD

The words from our prophets are the same as if given from the Lord. This means general conference addresses by those whom we sustain as "prophets, seers, and revelators" should be of paramount importance in our lives. These talks give us current direction from the Lord on what we can do now to improve our healing and spiritual well-being. This principle is clearly taught: "What I the Lord have spoken, I have spoken, and I excuse not myself; and though the heavens and the earth pass away, my word shall not pass away, but shall all be fulfilled, whether by mine own voice or by the voice of my servants, it is the same" (D&C 1:38).

EMBRACE THE REVELATIONS FROM PROPHETS

What does it mean to embrace the revelations from our prophets? To embrace is to "take or receive gladly or eagerly; accept willingly"(*Webster's Encyclopedic Unabridged Dictionary*, 466). How gladly do we receive the conference talks? Do we willingly accept the words of the Brethren and earnestly try to apply them in our lives? One man commented:

> *I gain so much from the Brethren and their insights. After working through the issues of trying to help my wife deal with her compulsive sexual behaviors, I have found many answers in the words from the Brethren. Even though their talks may not be specifically on how loved ones can help family members who struggle with compulsives sexual behaviors, the principles are universal and do apply.*

With today's advances in technology, the words from these apostles and prophets are delivered in several formats. We may want to evaluate the way we learn best and choose that format.

Elder James E. Faust suggested that we do a self-evaluation on where we stand with the Brethren:

> *We should ask ourselves: What are the Brethren saying? The living prophets can open the visions of eternity; they give counsel on how to overcome the world. We cannot know what that counsel is if we do not listen. We cannot receive the blessings we are promised if we do not follow the counsel given* (*Ensign*, Mar. 1988, 70).

🖉 **How can you best learn of the counsel from the Brethren and then follow it?**

_____

_____

_____

_____

_____

_____

We eliminate emotional turmoil as we strive to follow the Brethren and draw closer to the Savior. This happens because we begin to understand the doctrines of the kingdom and our divine destiny more fully. We learn that our healing and our loved ones' behaviors are not outside the healing power of the Atonement—that the Atonement applies to us personally and to our loved ones.

There is help for us as we reach out and use the resources that the Lord has provided. Elder Dallin H. Oaks explained these resources:

> *Through Christ and His church, those who struggle can obtain help. This help comes through fasting and prayer, through the truths of the gospel, through church attendance and service, through the counsel of inspired leaders, and, where necessary, through professional assistance with problems that require such help* (*Ensign*, Oct. 1995, 13-14).

 **REVIEW OF PRINCIPLES**

In what ways can you receive personal revelation? How will personal revelation enhance your healing?

_____

_____

What are the spiritual blessing you can receive through fasting?

_____

_____

Record any other insights or thoughts that have come as you have read this chapter.

_____

_____

What is the single most important principle or concept you have learned from this chapter?

_____

_____

CALMNESS BREAK

Choose something that is fun for you and plan to do it. Set the day and time. Learn how to take care of yourself. Be gentle and kind to yourself. Give yourself this special moment. You deserve it. You have earned it. One woman commented, "I enjoy going to movies but had not been to one in a long time. I called my daughter, scheduled the time, and we went a couple of days later in the afternoon. The movie was okay, but we had so much fun together—no kids, no interruptions, just the two of us in an air-conditioned theater on a hot summer afternoon."

 What can you plan that is fun for you? What day and time will this event take place?

_____

_____

_____

_____

_____

_____

MESSAGES OF HOPE

Elder Marvin J. Ashton: "Satan will do his best to deter us and let discouragement impede our progress. . . . 'And ye shall know the truth, and the truth shall make you free' (John 8:31–32). Paul Harvey, news analyst and author, said, 'Some day I hope to enjoy enough of what the world calls success so that someone will ask me, 'What's the secret of it?' I shall say simply this: 'I get up when I fall down'" (*Ensign,* Nov. 1981, 89).

President James E. Faust: "Peace in this life is based upon faith and testimony. We can all find hope from our personal prayers and gain comfort from the scriptures. Priesthood blessings lift us and sustain us. Hope also comes from direct personal revelation, to which we are entitled if we are worthy. We also have the security of living in a time when a prophet who holds and exercises all of the keys of God's kingdom is on the earth" (*Ensign,* Nov. 1999, 60).

Being Kind and Forgiving to Self and Others Is Healing—So Is Giving Service without Reward

CHAPTER OVERVIEW

Forgiving our loved ones who have caused us so much pain may be the furthest thought from our minds right now. At this time in our lives, there are so many other emotions we are dealing with that we usually do not want to add one more.

Speaking about forgiveness, a wife said, "I don't even know what the word means." A husband commented, "I'm not even ready to think about forgiveness at this point." That's okay because forgiveness cannot be rushed nor achieved when we feel pressure by our loved ones or others.

Forgiveness is also very elusive. At times we may think we have forgiven, and then we are hit again with bitterness, resentment, and anger. When we feel confused by our tendency to revisit those feelings, we must realize that forgiveness is an ongoing process that takes time. We should apply patience to this process and give ourselves credit for every small degree of success, knowing we'll have more later on. Over time we come to realize that an unforgiving heart hurts us more than it hurts the person who may have offended us. We learn that forgiveness is not about them, it's about us!

We can only forgive when we are ready. Forgiveness cannot be rushed, but at the same time we should not purposely keep pushing it back. We often hear advice on how to forgive, but somehow it does not seem to apply to our situation. Because of this we may find ways to justify our lack of forgiveness.

To help us choose the forgiveness path, we can remember that forgiveness does not mean that we condone or forget what happened and it does not mean that we let our loved ones walk all over us. It does not mean that we can avoid having feelings of anger and resentment pop up from time to time.

Forgiveness does not mean that our loved ones are not accountable. They are accountable! We can forgive and still set boundaries. We give up the idea that forgiveness should happen within a certain timetable.

 ## CHAPTER OBJECTIVES

At the conclusion of this chapter you should—

1. Identify what forgiveness means to you.
2. Realize how important it is to begin with forgiving yourself.
3. Benefit from the experiences of others who have gone through the forgiveness process.
4. Realize that the exact time line and process that may have worked for someone else to achieve a level of forgiveness may not work for you.
5. Understand that forgiveness is a process that takes time—a different amount of time for each person.
7. Be willing to work hard to stay engaged in the forgiveness process.
8. Ask God in faith that you might be able to forgive.
9. Understand, believe, and accept the blessings that can come through forgiveness.

FORGIVENESS

As youngsters in the Church, we are taught the importance of forgiveness. Most parents try to teach their children about forgiveness when something goes wrong by asking them to tell a friend or sibling, "I am sorry."

We are counseled, "Judge not, and ye shall not be judged: condemn not, and ye shall not be condemned: forgive, and ye shall be forgiven" (Luke 6:37). Forgiveness is not an absolute science. We cannot expect that by doing 1+1 we will get 2 as the result. Our emotions are not some mathematical formula. Only we and the Lord can arrive at a formula that will work for us!

What is forgiveness? Forgiveness has many interpretations. It is important that we accept the interpretation and definition that works for us. If we are unrealistic in our interpretation, we can quickly become discouraged. For example, one woman said, "As long as I have moments when I still become very angry and bitter, I have not forgiven him." Her absolute, 100% interpretation may cause feelings of guilt because she has not forgiven according to her high standard and then she questions herself by asking, "What is wrong with me? Why can't I forgive him?"

A more realistic approach is helpful, such as, "I have fewer moments when I am angry or bitter than I had before." This more realistic definition gives us inner peace. With inner peace we are actually able to do more because our emotional energy is not spent in achieving the impossible and then beating ourselves up for not achieving it. Forgiveness is usually achieved in stages. Stage One of forgiveness is doing what we can now—what we are capable of doing, nothing more—and accepting it. Maybe later we can expand the definition to include a little bit more—Stage Two. Perhaps later we can add more—Stage Three—and so forth.

We do not have to forgive perfectly to forgive our loved ones. Forgiveness does not mean that all trust has been restored in our relationship. Forgiveness and trust are not the same. We might forgive our spouse for past transgressions, but we may still wonder if we trust him when he says, "I need to work late tonight at the office."

Trusting our loved ones may take more time than forgiving them. Others who have reached a level of forgiveness toward their loved ones have made these forgiving statements as they continued to forgive:

"I'm not blaming her anymore for what she did."

"I'm less emotionally sensitive to what my husband did."

"I no longer think of ways to get revenge."

"I no longer have a desire to seek revenge."

"I have more empathy for him and the environment in which he was raised."

"I have been able to just let my anger and resentment go."

"I'm focusing more on me and my own spiritual progress than on what he did."

"It no longer occupies my mind every waking hour."

"I have less bitterness and anger toward my spouse."

"I'm not going back and replaying the event in my mind again and again."

"I stopped trying to control my forgiveness and just let it happen."

"I decided to let God serve justice."

"I don't dwell on the emotional pain anymore."

It might be easier to think of forgiveness in terms of a measuring cup. We can forgive 1/4 of a cup right now, and we will continue to work on forgiving more. Maybe months later, after more trust has developed, we might be able to forgive 1/2 of a cup. We should realize that it is okay to be where we are on the forgiveness measurement scale, keeping in mind that it is okay if we never completely get to a full cup.

We are blessed for trying, and Christ will accept our offering. As long as we stay engaged in the forgiveness process, the Lord's blessings and Spirit will strengthen us so that we can do more.

FORGIVING OURSELVES

Forgiveness of self and our own imperfections is one place to begin. We are mortals and have weaknesses. We make mistakes. There is usually a parallel between our willingness to forgive ourselves and our ability to forgive others. We may be guilty of setting the bar so high for ourselves that we could never jump over it and then making ourselves feel depressed when we fail. Accepting the bar at a lower height, one that is achievable some of the time, is more realistic. This gives us the opportunity to accept ourselves for where we are in the healing process. Forgiving ourselves means we grant ourselves permission to be human and make some mistakes. We accept that we will not always make the best decisions, be the best spouse, parent, brother, sister, breadwinner, homemaker, or whatever else we attempt to do.

By accepting ourselves and forgiving ourselves, we are empowered to change. At the end of the day, we still have energy left to keep trying and progressing. We take our mistakes in life and use them as learning experiences rather than as ways to punish ourselves, feel guilty, or create feelings of shame or depression. Then, after we forgive ourselves for our own weaknesses, we can work on forgiving others.

Forgiving ourselves means that we go from self-blaming to self-forgiving. We no longer hold ourselves as prisoners in the jail of self-blaming. We give up self-blaming thought patterns such as:

"I should have said more or been there for him when he was struggling."

"If I had kept my physical appearance up, this would not have happened."

"I've been so caught up in all the emotional issues regarding my spouse's behaviors, I was not there for my children."

"I've withdrawn from family and friends because I tried to protect them from knowing everything that was going on with our marriage."

"I've felt unacceptable by comparing myself to other women who are more attractive or in better shape."

Self-forgiving means we forgive ourselves for self-blaming thought patterns that have pulled us down. It will be easier to forgive ourselves if we recognize and accept the fact that our loved ones are accountable for what they chose to do. We did not make their decisions for them, so why should we blame ourselves?

As we forgive ourselves for our own infirmities, it will be easier to forgive others. How can we give away something that we do not possess ourselves? Furthermore, we often discover that if we cannot forgive others, it usually means that we have not forgiven ourselves for our own imperfections, decisions, and weaknesses. God and Christ are perfect and are the only ones who can give perfect love. Can we cleave to God as Jacob taught? "Wherefore, my beloved brethren, I beseech of you in words of soberness that ye would repent, and come with full purpose of heart, and cleave unto God as he cleaveth unto you. And while his arm of mercy is extended towards you in the light of the day, harden not your hearts" (Jacob 6:5).

If we cleave to God, we are less likely to place conditions on loving and forgiving ourselves. We are more likely to accept His mercy and avoid a hardened heart. When we cleave unto God, we do not use things, people, or situations to tell us that we have value. We have value simply because we are sons or daughters of God. Because we have been created in His image, we have infinite value and can love ourselves. No other conditions are necessary.

Love for ourselves should not be based upon whether we perceive our marriage as "good" and all our children as active and righteous. It cannot be based on the good deeds we might have done for others either. Nor does our current calling in the Church determine our value. Elder Neal A. Maxwell emphasized: "Mistakenly regarding our present assignments as the only indicator of how much God loves us only adds to our reluctance to let go. Brothers and sisters, our individual worth is already divinely established as great; it does not fluctuate like the stock market" (*Ensign*, May 2002, 36).

If we had to be living the gospel perfectly to love and forgive ourselves, no one could do it. We must avoid the all-or-nothing attitude where we have to reach a level of perfection in order to satisfy ourselves. Constantly telling ourselves that we are not measuring up, or refusing to talk about anything because we are so unhappy with our lack of perfection are both unhealthy alternatives. Rather, we should accept ourselves as humans with weaknesses and strengths and work to become genuine and real. Accepting this truth and loving ourselves because we are sons and daughters of God frees us from the notion that we have to do everything perfectly *now* in order to have value.

We need a spirit of humility and a willingness to repent and strive to continue to do the best we can each day. One wife realized:

> *It is such a relief not to be trying so hard to be everything to everyone. I have spent so many depressed days because I could not do all that I expected of myself and what I thought others expected of me. I now accept that I am mortal and do have weaknesses. It's okay if I don't get everything done and if I make some mistakes along the way. Tomorrow is another day and I will continue to try. I recently held my own party—just for me. I called it "Welcome Home to the Human Race!"*

ACCEPTING OURSELVES

If we are only willing to accept ourselves when we achieve and perform well, we will have many miserable days when we cannot meet our own expectations. Why? Because we are mortals who may accomplish much on some days and little on other days. Whether we accomplish a lot or very little each day, can we still love ourselves the same?

The secret is to separate our performance or behavior from our value. By accepting our imperfections and forgiving ourselves for the decisions, thoughts, emotions, and behaviors that may not be good, we actually empower ourselves to overcome our weaknesses because we build on a foundation of self-acceptance. We are comfortable and at peace with ourselves. With love and acceptance for ourselves, we are more likely to follow the Spirit and continue to work on our weaknesses with hope and encouragement.

We can be our best "cheerleader" if we accept ourselves as a total package. We can also teach our loved ones by example so they too will accept, love, and forgive themselves. Nephi gave us an example of how to love ourselves with our weaknesses and yet stay focused on Christ as we work to overcome them:

> *Behold, my soul delighteth in the things of the Lord; and my heart pondereth continually upon the things which I have seen and heard.*

> *Nevertheless, notwithstanding the great goodness of the Lord, in showing me his great and marvelous works, my heart exclaimeth: O wretched man [woman] that I am! Yea, my heart sorroweth because of my flesh; my soul grieveth because of mine iniquities.*
>
> *I am encompassed about, because of the temptations and the sins which do so easily beset me.*
>
> *And when I desire to rejoice, my heart groaneth because of my sins; nevertheless, I know in whom I have trusted.*
>
> *My God hath been my support; he hath led me through mine afflictions in the wilderness; and he hath preserved me upon the waters of the great deep.*
>
> *He hath filled me with his love, even unto the consuming of my flesh* (2 Ne. 4:16-21).

Acceptance of self is a Christ-centered virtue that leads and empowers us to stay on the healing path. We can dislike our behaviors and still love ourselves! Working to change what needs to be changed, accepting the progress we have made, and forgiving ourselves for our weaknesses are eternal principles. Elder Boyd K. Packer stated: "That great morning of forgiveness may not come at once. Do not give up if at first you fail. Often the most difficult part of repentance is to forgive yourself. Discouragement is part of that test. Do not give up. That brilliant morning will come" (*Ensign,* Nov. 1995, 20).

By forgiving ourselves, we are no longer held hostage by the past. We have been liberated. Forgiving ourselves allows us to look to the future with hope.

FORGIVENESS: IS IT POSSIBLE?

In the early stages, there is so much emotion surrounding our loved ones' behaviors that we are not usually ready to even consider forgiveness. One wife explained how painful it was when a friend said to her, "I guess you realize that you are going to need to forgive your husband?" This was not what she needed to hear at that time. She had so many other emotions going on that having a friend tell her she needed to forgive just made her angry.

We may feel the same way; however, as we stay engaged in the healing process, forgiveness will find us. We do not have to go find it, but we do need to be ready to receive it. Forgiveness comes as a gift from our Heavenly Father through the Atonement of Christ. It usually comes, here a little and there a little, when we least expect it. Each time it arrives, we usually feel better mentally, emotionally, spiritually, and physically. We can still experience some level of forgiveness even though we are emotionally pulled between feelings of love one moment and feelings of hate toward our loved ones' behaviors the next moment. We usually vacillate back and forth.

Forgiveness does not work like a college class. We do not enroll in the "forgiveness class" at the beginning of a semester and then plan to learn and complete the course by the end of the semester. If this were the case, many of us would get an "incomplete." Why? We cannot place a timetable on our emotions and the forgiveness process. There is no final exam at a set time. Human beings do not work that way. Christ is our Teacher. We are the students. He will give us private tutoring.

Still, while we cannot repent for our loved ones, we can eventually forgive them. Basically our loved ones took something from us and have incurred a debt. Often we want the debtor to repay the debt before we forgive. Forgiveness is not really about whether the loan is repaid or not. Forgiveness is really not about two human beings. It's about us. It's about our peace. We really only need one party to act in order to achieve forgiveness and that is us. We do not need the other party who offended us to do anything. Yes, it would be nice if they made amends and repaid the debt, but many will not and may even be arrogant. By not choosing forgiveness, we are allowing our loved ones to continue to hold us captive. We are allowing our loved ones to control us if we choose not to forgive. Forgiveness is releasing our loved ones from the debt they incurred. The slate is wiped clean. We are no longer the creditor and they are no longer the debtor. We have forgiven the debtor; however, we are the ones who are free.

We want to stay engaged in the forgiving process, because an unforgiving heart prevents us from becoming one with Christ and puts distance between us and others who need our love. We pay a high price when we choose not to forgive others. Unhealthy negative emotions come with a cost—they are not free.

What is the emotional cost you pay when you choose not to forgive your loved one?

⚡ What is the physiological cost you pay when you choose not to forgive your loved one?

_____

_____

_____

_____

⚡ What is the spiritual cost you pay when you choose not to forgive your loved one?

_____

_____

_____

_____

We usually do not realize the heavy load of an unforgiving heart until it is lifted. We really cannot have an unforgiving heart for one person and show love with the same heart to another person. The heart goes one way or the other. It cannot go both ways at once. "No man [heart] can serve two masters: for either he will hate the one, and love the other, or else he will hold to the one, and despise the other. Ye cannot serve God and mammon" (Matt. 6:24).

We realize that for our own healing, regardless of what our loved ones decide to do, we need to decide that we will forgive. Some of our loved ones will choose to change; others may not. There is a way back from the deepest compulsion if our loved ones will only choose the path, but only they can decide.

Alma the Younger before His Conversion

There are many accounts in the scriptures of those who were deep in sin and later changed their behaviors. Alma the Younger had chosen to do much evil. The scriptures use the following words to describe Alma the Younger and his evil activities:

- Wicked and an idolatrous man.

- Spoke many words, and did speak much flattery to the people.

- Led many of the people to do after the manner of his iniquities (Mosiah 27:8).

- A great hinderment to the prosperity of the church of God.

- Stealing away the hearts of the people.

- Causing much dissension among the people.

- Giving a chance for the enemy of God to exercise his power over them (Mosiah 27:9).

- Going about to destroy the church of God.

- Led astray the people of the Lord, contrary to the commandments of God, or even the king (Mosiah 27:10).

If we had lived during the time of Alma the Younger and had been assigned to visit teach or home teach him, what hope would we have in his ability to change? Would we have thoughts such as:

"Why would we even consider going to this man's house? He will never change."

"This man is so evil that he deserves exactly what he gets."

"He made his choices and now he has to pay the consequences."

"He is so negative; I don't even want to be around him."

"He just wants to argue with me. He doesn't want to learn anything."

Regardless of how many people thought Alma the Younger would never change, he did have a complete change of heart and was fully converted to the gospel of Jesus Christ. After that his countenance and behavior changed remarkably, and he became a great missionary and a prophet of God.

THE VILEST OF SINNERS

It is important to note that the scripture states that Alma the Younger and the four sons of Mosiah were not only sinners but "were the very vilest of sinners" (Mosiah 28:4). Could anyone have been more vile than the "very vilest of sinners?" What does the word vile mean? The dictionary definition is "wretchedly bad, highly offensive, unpleasant, repulsive, disgusting, morally debased, depraved, despicable, foul, or filthy" (*Webster's Encyclopedic Unabridged Dictionary,* 1593).

Over the years when I have met with parents or a spouse concerning their loved ones' compulsive sexual behaviors, they often use some of the words in this definition to describe how they feel about their loved ones' behaviors. Here are some examples.

> *A wife lamented, "It is so disgusting to me that my husband views pornography."*

> *A husband said, "I am repulsed by what my wife has done with another person."*

> *Parents of a son who engaged in homosexual behaviors expressed, "It's just despicable to think our son has had homosexual relations with another man."*

We do not need to know what acts were included in the phrase, "the very vilest of sinners." We do not want to focus on the vile things that Alma the Younger and the sons of Mosiah may have done to destroy the church and to lead the people away. Instead, our focus should center on their transformation to great servants of God. This story proves that, regardless of one's vile behaviors, there is hope.

Any sinner can begin to respond to the Spirit of the Lord, accept the mercy and love from God and Christ, pay the consequences for past choices, fully repent, and overcome the fear of being cast out. This is important for us to remember since at times we may lose hope for our loved ones. We may think their condition is so "wretchedly bad, highly offensive, unpleasant, repulsive, disgusting, morally debased, depraved, despicable, foul, or filthy" that it can never change. This is not true, although Satan wants us to think our loved ones will never change.

The Satanic thought is, "If our loved ones are not going to change, why should we even try to make things work out? It would be so much easier to just give up on them." The story of Alma the Younger illustrates that all of us can change if we begin to respond to the Spirit and act on the promptings we receive. Alma the Younger made a choice to change, and the Spirit worked through him. Sadly, some of our loved ones will not choose to change. In such cases those who are in a marital situation will have some very important decisions to make about the future.

Alma the Younger after His Conversion

We know that Alma the Younger and the four sons of Mosiah engaged in many evil acts. The scriptures record their condition:

And thus did the Spirit of the Lord work upon them, for they were the very vilest of sinners.

And the Lord saw fit in his infinite mercy to spare them; nevertheless they suffered much anguish of soul because of their iniquities, suffering much and fearing that they should be cast off forever (Mosiah 28:4).

Here are the important points from this verse for us to remember:

- The Spirit of the Lord worked upon them.

- They were the very vilest of sinners.

- The Lord in His infinite mercy spared them.

- They suffered much anguish of soul because of their iniquities.

- They feared that they would be cast off forever.

As we read through the passages that describe the wicked Alma the Younger, we might wonder how those words could be referring to the same person we read about after his mighty change of heart. How can a person go from one extreme point on the spectrum to another? How could he have been so lost and yet still find his way back? The answer is simple: Through the Atonement of Jesus Christ.

The third Article of Faith states: "We believe that through the Atonement of Christ, all mankind may be saved, by obedience to the laws and ordinances of the Gospel." This Article of Faith explains a very important part of our doctrine: "ALL mankind may be saved." The word ALL includes our loved ones too. Christ extends to ALL the invitation to turn and live—to be forgiven and to be saved. Our part is to choose (at any point) to come to Christ and begin to obey the laws and ordinances of the gospel.

Alma the Younger stated:

I have repented of my sins, and have been redeemed of the Lord; behold I am born of the Spirit.

The Lord said unto me: Marvel not that all mankind, yea, men and women, all nations, kindreds, tongues and people, must be born again; yea, born of God, changed from their carnal and fallen state, to a state of righteousness, being redeemed of God, becoming his sons and daughters (Mosiah 27:24-25).

Nevertheless, after wading through much tribulation, repenting nigh unto death, the Lord in mercy hath seen fit to snatch me out of an everlasting burning, and I am born of God (Mosiah 27:28).

My soul hath been redeemed from the gall of bitterness and bonds of iniquity. I was in the darkest abyss; but now I behold the marvelous light of God. My soul was racked with eternal torment; but I am snatched, and my soul is pained no more (Mosiah 27:29).

I rejected my Redeemer, and denied that which had been spoken of by our fathers; but now that they may foresee that he will come, and that he remembereth every creature of his creating, he will make himself manifest unto all (Mosiah 27:30).

Speaking about Alma the Younger and others who changed, President Ezra Taft Benson taught:

We must be careful, as we seek to become more and more godlike, that we do not become discouraged and lose hope. Becoming Christlike is a lifetime pursuit and very often involves growth and change that is slow, almost imperceptible. The scriptures record remarkable accounts of men whose lives changed dramatically, in an instant, as it were: Alma the Younger, Paul on the road to Damascus, Enos praying far into the night, King Lamoni. Such astonishing examples of the power to change even those steeped in sin give confidence that the Atonement can reach even those deepest in despair.

But we must be cautious as we discuss these remarkable examples. Though they are real and powerful, they are the exception more than the rule. For every Paul, for every Enos, and for every King Lamoni, there are hundreds and thousands of people who find the process of repentance much more subtle, much more imperceptible. Day by day they move closer to the Lord, little realizing they are building a godlike life. They live quiet lives of goodness, service, and commitment. They are like the Lamanites, who the Lord said "were baptized with fire and with the Holy Ghost, and they knew it not" (3 Ne. 9:20) (Ensign, Oct. 1989, 5).

For us and our loved ones, the process of healing is day by day. Often we cannot see the progress we or our loved ones are making. We should keep our spiritual eyes open so that we can remind ourselves of the progress that is being made.

Where have you seen spiritual growth in your life in the last 60 to 90 days?

_____

_____

_____

_____

THE SPIRIT OF THE LORD WORKS UPON US

God wants all of His children to come back into His presence—including our loved ones. The Savior said, "For behold, this is my work and my glory—to bring to pass the immortality and eternal life of man" (Moses 1:39), and He has worked tirelessly and will continue to do so in order to bring to pass the immortality and eternal life of every man and woman.

The Spirit of the Lord works upon each of us, prompting us to do good and to make choices that will turn us toward God. Our loved ones may not feel the Spirit right now or respond immediately because of past choices. However, the encouragement we gain from this scripture is knowing that the Spirit of the Lord continues to work with even the vilest of sinners. In the meantime, the Spirit will work with us to help us continue our own process of forgiving.

FORGIVENESS IS A PROCESS, NOT AN EVENT

If we are looking for a specific time or event that will cause us to forgive, we will probably never experience forgiveness. If we try to force forgiveness, it usually does not happen. When we try too hard to forgive, we can get frustrated at the results.

Forgiveness does not happen just because someone says we should forgive. One wife made this comment: "My blood just curdles when someone says to me 'You must forgive your husband.' My response is, 'Oh, no I don't! Why do I have to forgive him? I didn't do anything wrong. He injured me and should pay a price for what he has done.'" These initial feelings are natural—after all, we have been badly hurt.

The emotional pain is often so great that forgiveness may sound utterly impossible. Nevertheless, if we do not harden our hearts against the Spirit, forgiveness happens over time. We cannot cite a day or event when forgiveness happens because forgiveness is a process. How do we go about forgiving our spouse, child, or others? President Gordon B. Hinckley explained:

> *If there be any who nurture in their hearts the poisonous brew of enmity toward another, I plead with you to ask the Lord for strength to forgive. This expression of desire will be of the very substance of your repentance. It may not be easy, and it may not come quickly. But if you will seek it with sincerity and cultivate it, it will come. And even though he whom you have forgiven continues to pursue and threaten you, you will know you have done what you could to effect a reconciliation. There will come into your heart a peace otherwise unattainable. That peace will be the peace of Him who said: "For if ye forgive men their trespasses, your Heavenly Father will also forgive you: But if ye forgive not men their trespasses, neither will your Father forgive your trespasses" (Matt. 6:14–15) (Ensign, June 1991, 5).*

Forgiveness does not mean that we give in or that we are the weaker one. It means that we keep dealing with our emotions in a healthy way, focusing on our issues, and eventually achieving a state of inner peace. Forgiveness is an essential part of that peace. When we work hard and strive to live the gospel principles, forgiveness happens, even though at first we did not seek it. We must keep an open heart, even though it may be only slightly open. We must save a place for forgiveness, allowing it to stay when it shows up. Forgiveness cannot stay if there is still too much anger residing in our hearts.

To forgive is to succeed spiritually. To forgive is to have inner peace. Even after we have feelings of forgiveness, there may still be moments when we wonder how well we have done at forgiving. We are imperfect. We have weaknesses. How can we forgive perfectly with such weaknesses?

Maybe in some way forgiveness means we can occupy our minds with uplifting thoughts. We are no longer controlled or obsessed by what happened to us, and hence we can move forward with our lives. We have more days when we feel joy and we experience more restful nights. We harbor fewer ill feelings and have learned much about ourselves and the Spirit.

As we do our best and stay focused on spiritual things, forgiveness shows up like a friend who has been gone from our lives for a while and has now returned. Just when we think we cannot forgive or that it is just not going to happen to us, we are surprised by the welcome return of our friend. We can have a welcome home party, welcoming forgiveness with open arms and a warm embrace!

President Gordon B. Hinckley said: "A spirit of forgiveness and an attitude of love and compassion toward those who may have wronged us is of the very essence of the gospel of Jesus Christ. Each of us has need of this spirit. The whole world has need of it. The Lord taught it. He exemplified it as none other has exemplified it" (*Ensign*, June 1991, 2).

It is interesting to note that President Hinckley said we have the need to forgive. President John Taylor taught, "Forgiveness is in advance of justice where there is repentance; and . . . to have in your heart the spirit of forgiveness and to eliminate from your hearts the spirit of hatred and bitterness, brings peace and joy" (*CR*, Oct. 1920, 5-7).

It makes no difference if our loved ones make amends or not. We have the need to forgive. An unforgiving heart, though it does not appear to do too much damage at first, quickly spreads throughout the spirit like some terminal cancer. It can kill our ability to hear and follow the Spirit.

Several warning signs reveal an unforgiving heart, such as spending a lot of time replaying the hurt and pain our loved ones caused. We may make it the topic of our conversations with those who are closest to us, or we may notice an inability to stay focused on our responsibilities.

At times we set requirements on when we will be ready to forgive. We say things like:

"I'll forgive if he agrees never to do it again."

"I'll forgive once she has suffered as much as I have."

"As long as I can still remember the hurt and pain, I cannot forgive."

"Some things people do are forgivable, but this transgression is not."

"If I forgive, I will be condoning his behaviors, and I can't do that."

"I can only forgive once my spouse has paid for all the pain she caused."

"I'll forgive him some time, but for now he must pay for what he has done."

"I'm afraid to forgive because then I won't know what to do with all my anger and resentment."

These initial responses are quite common. They are very human. President Gordon B. Hinckley recognized the difficult task of forgiving and counseled:

> *How difficult it is for any of us to forgive those who have injured us. We are all prone to brood on the evil done us. That brooding becomes as a gnawing and destructive canker. Is there a virtue more in need of applica-*

tion in our time than the virtue of forgiving and forgetting? There are those who would look upon this as a sign of weakness. Is it? I submit that it takes neither strength nor intelligence to brood in anger over wrongs suffered, to go through life with a spirit of vindictiveness, to dissipate one's abilities in planning retribution. There is no peace in nursing a grudge. There is no happiness in living for the day when you can "get even" (Ensign, June 1991, 4).

When we read scriptures on forgiveness or think of the Savior's forgiveness of His accusers while on the cross, we may feel that we will never reach forgiveness. President Gordon B. Hinckley expressed:

> *In the time of his agony on the cross of Calvary, with vile and hateful accusers before him, those who had brought him to this terrible crucifixion, he cried out, "Father, forgive them; for they know not what they do"* (Luke 23:34).
>
> *None of us is called on to forgive so generously, but each of us is under a divinely spoken obligation to reach out with pardon and mercy. The Lord has declared in words of revelation: "My disciples, in days of old, sought occasion against one another and forgave not one another in their hearts; and for this evil they were afflicted and sorely chastened"* (D&C 64:8)(Ensign, June 1991, 2).

Why do we want to strive to forgive? So we can heal from the pain and sorrow. It is an amazing principle. We heal by giving a gift of forgiveness—a gift we receive through the Atonement. Normally, we think that we heal by receiving from others. But as we give forgiveness, we receive so much more, such as an improved relationship with God and Christ. We not only feel Their Spirit more often, but we feel Their love.

Forgiveness and Empathy

As we strive to forgive, it may be helpful to develop more empathy for the person we are trying to forgive. Empathy does not mean that we condone our loved ones' behaviors, but it does mean that we try to see what life must be like for them. We try to look at the circumstances that our loved ones' choices have placed them in and recognize that natural consequences follow.

We can develop empathy by recognizing that our loved ones are in difficult circumstances and it will take a great deal of work to get out. We can empathize because we know how hard it is for us to work through our issues. Our loved ones have their own issues to work through too. This process can work even when our loved ones do not want to show how much they hurt inside. Many times our loved ones will try to cover up their hurt and pretend that they do not hurt. One wife commented:

> *I started to forgive when one day I realized what my husband's behaviors and choices must have done to him. For so long I looked at what my husband's choices did to me—how much he hurt me and what impact his choices had on our children and our eternal family. Then one day almost out of no where I thought, "What must my husband feel like at times?" I can't imagine how torn up he must be inside. I can't imagine what it is like to go through a church disciplinary council and tell that many men what he had done. I could not change what had happened, but I caught a glimpse of what life might be like for him.*

Avoid Judging Loved Ones

We might be quick to rush to judgment concerning the reasons our loved ones engaged in compulsive sexual behaviors. Even though we feel the pain and hurt, we should be careful about judging. Elder Dallin H. Oaks said:

> *We must refrain from making final judgments on people because we lack the knowledge and the wisdom to do so. We would even apply the wrong standards. The world's way is to judge competitively between winners and losers. The Lord's way of final judgment will be to apply His perfect knowledge of the law a person has received and to judge on the basis of that person's circumstances, motives, and actions throughout his or her entire life (see Luke 12:47–48; John 15:22; 2 Ne. 9:25)* (Ensign, Aug. 1999, 8).

Even though we work to avoid judging our loved ones, we still need to set appropriate boundaries to protect ourselves from mental, emotional, spiritual, and physical abuse.

How does knowing that the Lord will judge you and your loved ones based on your circumstances, motives, and actions throughout your life and by applying His perfect knowledge of the law make you feel?

_____

_____

_____

_____

⚒ Who should be the one to judge your loved one?

_____

_____

_____

_____

FORGIVING OUR CHILDREN

As parents, we may have children who do not make choices that draw them closer to the Savior and the plan of happiness. A child may have offended us because of his choices. What should we strive to do in these situations? President Gordon B. Hinckley explained our responsibility:

> *I know of no more beautiful story in all literature than that found in the fifteenth chapter of Luke. It is the story of a repentant son and a forgiving father. It is the story of a son who wasted his inheritance in riotous living, rejecting his father's counsel, spurning those who loved him. When he had spent all, he was hungry and friendless, and "when he came to himself" (Luke 15:17), he turned back to his father, who, on seeing him afar off, "ran, and fell on his neck, and kissed him" (Luke 15:20).*
>
> *I ask you to read that story. Every parent ought to read it again and again. It is large enough to encompass every household, and enough larger than that to encompass all mankind, for are we not all prodigal sons and daughters who need to repent and partake of the forgiving mercy of our Heavenly Father and then follow His example?*
>
> *His Beloved Son, our Redeemer, reaches out to us in forgiveness and mercy, but in so doing He commands repentance. A true and magnanimous spirit of forgiveness will become an expression of that required repentance* (*Ensign*, June 1991, 5).

Forgiveness may be a difficult word to hear right now. You may not be ready to deal with it for a while. That is okay. Only you can determine when you are ready. Keep in mind there is no time limit. Try not to feel guilty because you have not had feelings of forgiveness yet, but please keep a small corner of your heart open to the idea. All you need is a place to begin. Alma taught:

> *But behold, if ye will awake and arouse your faculties, even to an experiment upon my words, and exercise a particle of faith, yea, even if ye can no*

more than desire to believe [forgive], let this desire work in you, even until ye believe in a manner that ye can give place for a portion of my words (Alma 32:27).

Leaving a Place in Your Heart to Forgive

We want to be careful that we do not close the door on a relationship. This does not mean that we allow ourselves to be abused by our loved ones. We can reject our loved ones' behaviors and set boundaries for our own well-being without rejecting or hating our loved ones.

When we withdraw emotionally, reject totally, refuse to forgive, even allow hate to harden our hearts, we close the door not only on our loved ones; we also close the door on God. It would be very easy to become hard-hearted right now. It would be very easy to give our loved ones the silent treatment and seal off the relationship. Be careful and work hard to avoid that.

God comes into our hearts the same way that other people come into our hearts. We cannot close our heart to one of God's children and at the same time expect it to be wide open for God. These challenging experiences can draw us closer to Christ only if we choose to allow them to.

We often ask God to take us closer to His Son, and then when we have an opportunity to do just that, we fight it. Let's try not to fight it. Let's allow this experience to take us closer to the Savior, who is all-loving and has outstretched arms for each of us. He will never forsake us! We might think we can learn life's most vital lessons by reading a book or taking a class; however, important principles of the gospel are usually learned in real life by going through hard experiences. We might think we can learn them without stress, difficulty, or emotional pain, but that is not so: "For it must needs be, that there is an opposition in all things. If not so . . . righteousness could not be brought to pass, neither wickedness, neither holiness nor misery, neither good nor bad" (2 Ne 2:11).

A Journey to Forgiving

Forgiveness is a journey. We all know that we must take this journey. Although we do not have a road map, we can learn from the journeys of forgiveness that others have traveled. Knowing that they made it to the end of the journey gives us hope that we can get there too. Here is one wife's journey. As you read and ponder her words, focus on the principles that allowed her to forgive. Sometimes we can get so caught up in being able to forgive someone that we overlook the principles that we need to accomplish forgiveness.

As I climbed toward my goal of forgiving my husband, I knew I was traveling through a refiner's fire. But I was not going alone and unassisted.

My peaceful, 18-year marriage slammed into an almost impossible barrier late one night when my husband confessed to me a long series of moral offenses. I was caught completely by surprise.

The next day we visited the bishop and then the stake president. Within two weeks my husband was excommunicated. Overnight, predictability and contentment left me and was replaced by deep sorrow, rage, and confusion.

I had lost my best friend suddenly and violently. He was still physically beside me, but he had become a stranger. He had thrown our beautiful marriage and all of our dreams away like rubbish.

I had never been seriously wronged before by anyone, and in fact I felt that because I was a good person, I was somehow protected from being hurt. I had obeyed the principles of the gospel as best I could throughout my life. I had married a returned missionary in the temple, we had several children, and both my husband and I held responsible Church callings.

I thought we would therefore have a relatively trouble-free life. But I had misunderstood the realities of being an imperfect person on an earth with other imperfect people and complex problems. No one has a guarantee against pain and injury.

I immediately set about trying to forgive my husband. I thought this was what I needed to do, and I wanted to do it. But somehow I seemed incompetent to do the thing that simply had to be done and had to be done by me. I felt competent in many areas, but forgiving seemed impossible. I could not make my heart change. I felt helpless and desperate.

My struggle to forgive my husband when he broke his covenants was the greatest challenge I have faced in my life. Perhaps sharing my journey to forgiving him might help others.

Several influences contributed to my finally being able to forgive, including maintaining basic ideals and standards. I was so shaken by the abrupt change in my life that I had to take time to reaffirm my basic beliefs, commitments, and values.

Having lofty values is painful when they seem impossible to attain, and during this time my dearest goals were the most frustrating. I reaffirmed my belief in love and happy marriages. I strengthened my desire to attend the temple.

Support from others helped me keep trying to forgive. Both my husband and I had solid support—two stake presidents and three bishops who advised and mourned with us and our parents, brothers, sisters, and friends who listened, prayed for us, and stuck by us.

Another great influence was our counselor. Our stake president had advised us to get regular counseling, and we found a therapist who shared our values and understood our beliefs in a loving Heavenly Father and our desire to work on saving our marriage. I found myself just barely hanging on emotionally each week until we could meet and talk through the emotional stress Sam and I were experiencing.

Initially I wanted our counselor to explain what had gone wrong so that everything then would be clear—my husband would be "cured" and the horror would be over. I wanted the counselor to take charge of my life, create forgiveness, and insert it into my heart.

I learned over the next several years, however, that it is not that easy. I had to be in charge of my own life, no matter how unmanageable it seemed to be.

I had several dreams during this period that I believe were from God and were meaningful and powerful. They helped me discover some truths and clarify my understanding of the forces at work in my life, helping untie some emotional knots.

At one of our meetings the bishop told me that it might take me several years to heal from my hurt and truly feel that I had fully forgiven my husband. I felt tired just thinking of a long-term struggle, but I also felt relieved that I didn't have to do it all overnight.

As it turned out, that process required several years of my utmost commitment, extended effort, and acceptance of the realities of my situation.

Strengthened by the Spirit, I was gradually able to rely less on my bishop and counselor and more on the scriptures, prayer, and the Lord. More than at any other time of my life, I began to find answers and counsel in the scriptures.

I was surprised at how I was given very specific and pointed guidance. One particular selection in the scriptures guided me past an especially confusing conflict. Heavenly Father can indeed speak to us through the scriptures. I was taught (see Isa. 30:20–21), I was lovingly strengthened and guided (see Isa. 41:10, 13–14), and I found courage (see Job 23:10–12). I knew I was going through a refiner's fire, but I was not going alone nor was I unassisted.

My husband's repentance was not a smooth process. There were so many setbacks that after two years we divorced. It was the most difficult decision of my life but, feeling it was right, I went ahead confidently, although worn out emotionally. At this point some support from family and friends crumbled, and so having inner spiritual support was very important to me.

Our divorce, however, did not release me from the obligation to forgive. I truly wanted to do it, but it was as if I had been commanded to do something of which I was simply incapable. This made me even more angry at my husband for putting me in a position to come under God's censure when I had not broken my covenants.

I tried and tried. I knew the doctrine: "I, the Lord, will forgive whom I will forgive, but of you it is required to forgive all men" (D&C 64:10). I felt guilty and miserable, but as I looked honestly into my heart I knew very well that full-grown forgiveness was not there. What more could I do? Was I going to lose my own soul to this horrible mess?

Again some advice from my bishop proved crucial. As we discussed the struggle to forgive one day, he said, "Well, keep a place in your heart for forgiveness, and when it comes, welcome it in." That seemed like weak advice in a way, but the Spirit etched it into my memory and it became a golden rule to me. On bad days when I was angry, I could at least say to myself, "I want to forgive, and I will hang on to that as a goal and desire it and welcome it when it comes."

It is difficult to define what happened to me spiritually through these many months. Some things are too personal to share, but one thing I learned was to pray with all my heart—no pretenses, no self-righteousness and honestly admitting my anger, my fears, my hurt, and my sins.

I had to acknowledge that my husband's sins were great but really were not my problem. My problem was my sins and my seeming inability to forgive.

In the final analysis, what happened in my heart was for me an amazing and miraculous evidence of the Atonement of Christ. I had always viewed the Atonement as a means of making repentance work for the sinner. I had not realized that it also makes it possible for the one sinned against to receive into his or her heart the sweet peace of forgiving.

For me, forgiving is a miracle that we cannot create for ourselves. It is a gift of God to the injured party as well as to the sinner. What sweet relief when the spirit of forgiveness comes! It finally came to me. After a long period of struggle, with help and comfort from Heavenly Father, the full richness of being able to completely forgive my husband came into my heart.

Eventually my husband fully repented, and his repentance added to the joy I felt in having forgiven him. For me, the struggle to forgive was recompensed with rich knowledge. I learned along the way that Heavenly Father lives and that the Atonement is a reality for me, for my husband, for our children, and for all of Heavenly Father's children (Ensign, Feb. 1997, 40-43).

It took several years for this woman to reach the end of her forgiveness journey. She started out like most of us, not knowing whether she could ever forgive. She made a very important observation:

My husband's repentance was not a smooth process. There were so many setbacks that after two years we divorced. It was the most difficult decision of my life but, feeling it was right, I went ahead confidently, although worn out emotionally. At this point some support from family and friends crumbled and so having inner spiritual support was very important to me. Our divorce, however, did not release me from the obligation to forgive.

This woman understood an eternal principle—there are no exceptions when it comes to forgiveness. We need to work hard to forgive everyone. Even though her marriage ended in divorce, she still worked hard and eventually forgave her husband.

Whether one stays married or divorces is an individual choice. At the very least the decision involves the wife, husband, and God. Before making this decision seeking counsel from a bishop, branch president, or stake president is very prudent. As the wife said regarding her divorce, "It was the most difficult decision of my life but, feeling it was right, I went ahead confidently, although worn out emotionally."

As we follow the Spirit, the Lord will direct each of us so we will know what the Lord would have us do regarding our marriage.

Begin the Journey

In order to forgive, we need to begin the process. Elder Joseph B. Wirthlin said:

Sometimes we make the process more complicated than we need to. We will never make a journey of a thousand miles by fretting about how long it will take or how hard it will be. We make the journey by taking each day step by step and then repeating it again and again until we reach our destination.

The same principle applies to how you and I can climb to higher spirituality. Our Heavenly Father knows that we must begin our climb from where we are. *"When you climb up a ladder,"* the Prophet Joseph Smith taught, *"you must begin at the bottom and go on until you arrive at the top; and so it is with the principles of the gospel—you must begin with the first and go on until you learn all the principles of exaltation. But it will be a great while after you have passed through the veil before you will have learned them"* (see *Times and Seasons,* August 15, 1844, 614).

Our Heavenly Father loves each one of us and understands that this process of climbing higher takes preparation, time, and commitment. He understands that we will make mistakes at times, that we will stumble, that we will become discouraged and perhaps even wish to give up and say to ourselves it is not worth the struggle (*Ensign,* Nov. 2001, 25-26).

Elder Joseph B. Wirthlin encouraged:

We know it is worth the effort, for the prize, which is eternal life, is "the greatest of all the gifts of God." And to qualify, we must take one step after another and keep going to gain the spiritual heights we aspire to reach. An eternal principle is revealed in holy writ: "It is not requisite that a man should run faster than he has strength. And again, it is expedient that he should be diligent, that thereby he might win the prize" (*Ensign,* Nov. 2001, 26).

PROPHETS' COMMENTS ON FORGIVENESS

We may have questions and concerns about whether or not our loved ones can be forgiven. Although we recognize that the Atonement is real and that it works for us and our loved ones, we might sometimes wonder whether there is really hope for them to be forgiven. The following pages set forth common questions that others have asked regarding their loved ones and forgiveness, with corresponding answers from prophets of God.

Questions Regarding Loved Ones and Answers by Prophets

Can my loved one ever be forgiven for the immoral behaviors that she has done?

Elder Boyd K. Packer: "I know of no sins connected with the moral standard for which we cannot be forgiven. I do not exempt abortion. The formula is . . . 'Behold, he who has repented of his sins, the same is forgiven, and I, the Lord, remember them no more'" (*Ensign,* May 1992, 68).

My spouse committed adultery. I don't know if forgiveness is possible.

Elder Robert D. Hales: "To the woman taken in adultery, Christ did not soften the commandment to not commit adultery. Rather, He counseled her to 'sin no more' (John 8:11). He promises all of us forgiveness through repentance. It is we who must change, not the commandments" (*Ensign,* May 1996, 37).

How much effort will it take for my spouse to receive forgiveness for committing adultery?

President Spencer W. Kimball: "In the matter of sexual sin and adultery many have likewise been deeply worried. The prophet Joseph Smith gave us many scriptures which state that there is forgiveness; and other holy scriptures attest that repentance can bring forgiveness if that repentance is sufficiently 'all-out' and total" (*Ensign,* Mar. 1982, 5).

My son has been involved in homosexual behaviors. At times I feel like I should isolate myself from him. I'm confused and don't know what to do.

President Gordon B. Hinckley: "We want to help these people, to strengthen them, to assist them with their problems and to help them with their difficulties. But we cannot stand idle if they indulge in immoral activity, if they try to uphold and defend and live in a so-called same-sex marriage situation. To permit such would be to make light of the very serious and sacred foundation of God-sanctioned marriage and its very purpose, the rearing of families" (*Ensign,* Nov. 1998, 71).

My spouse is guilty of child sexual abuse. Can he ever be forgiven?

Elder Richard G. Scott: "Committing physical and sexual abuse are major sins. Such grave sins require deep repentance to be forgiven. President Kimball taught: 'To every forgiveness there is a condition. The plaster must be as wide as the sore. The fasting, the prayers, the humility must be equal to or greater than the sin.' It is unthinkable that God absolves serious sins upon a few requests. He is likely to wait until there has been long, sustained repentance" (*Ensign,* May 1995, 77).

My husband's behaviors have done so much damage to the children. Most of our children know that my husband has been unfaithful to me. How can he ever fix all the pain and hurt he has caused our family?

> Elder Boyd K. Packer: "To earn forgiveness, one must make restitution. That means you give back what you have taken or ease the pain of those you have injured. . . . There are times you cannot mend that which you have broken. Perhaps the offense was long ago, or the injured refused your penance. Perhaps the damage was so severe that you cannot fix it no matter how desperately you want to. Your repentance cannot be accepted unless there is a restitution. If you cannot undo what you have done, you are trapped. It is easy to understand how helpless and hopeless you then feel and why you might want to give up, just as Alma did. The thought that rescued Alma, when he acted upon it, is this: Restoring what you cannot restore, healing the wound you cannot heal, fixing that which you broke and you cannot fix is the very purpose of the atonement of Christ. When your desire is firm and you are willing to pay the "uttermost farthing," the law of restitution is suspended. Your obligation is transferred to the Lord. He will settle your accounts" (*Ensign,* Nov. 1995, 19-20).

I think my husband has some kind of sexual addiction. Can he ever get over this and obtain forgiveness?

> Elder Boyd K. Packer: "I repeat, save for the exception of the very few who defect to perdition, there is no habit, no addiction, no rebellion, no transgression, no apostasy, no crime exempted from the promise of complete forgiveness. That is the promise of the atonement of Christ" (*Ensign,* Nov. 1995, 20).

My son struggles with same-sex attraction. What can we do as a family to help him?

> Elder Dallin H. Oaks: "Through Christ and His church, those who struggle can obtain help. This help comes through fasting and prayer, through the truths of the gospel, through church attendance and service, through the counsel of inspired leaders, and, where necessary, through professional assistance with problems that require such help. Another important

source of help is the strengthening influence of loving brothers and sisters. All should understand that persons (and their family members) struggling with the burden of same-sex attraction are in special need of the love and encouragement that is a clear responsibility of Church members, who have signified by covenant their willingness 'to bear one another's burdens' (Mosiah 18:8) 'and so fulfil the law of Christ' (Gal. 6:2)" (*Ensign,* Oct. 1995, 13–14).

How can I help a loved one who has embraced a so-called gay or lesbian lifestyle, and what can other church members do to reach out and help these sons and daughters of God?

President Gordon B. Hinckley: "People inquire about our position on those who consider themselves so-called gays and lesbians. My response is that we love them as sons and daughters of God. They may have certain inclinations which are powerful and which may be difficult to control. Most people have inclinations of one kind or another at various times. If they do not act upon these inclinations, then they can go forward as do all other members of the Church. If they violate the law of chastity and the moral standards of the Church, then they are subject to the discipline of the Church, just as others are.

We want to help these people, to strengthen them, to assist them with their problems and to help them with their difficulties. But we cannot stand idle if they indulge in immoral activity, if they try to uphold and defend and live in a so-called same-sex marriage situation. To permit such would be to make light of the very serious and sacred foundation of God-sanctioned marriage and its very purpose, the rearing of families" (*Ensign,* Nov. 1998, 71).

My daughter has been involved with necking and petting with her boyfriends, but she has never had sexual intercourse. How difficult is it for her to repent and receive forgiveness?

President Ezra Taft Benson: "Yes, one can repent of moral transgression. The miracle of forgiveness is real, and true repentance is accepted of the Lord. But it is not pleasing to the Lord prior to a mission, or at any time, to sow one's wild oats, to engage in sexual transgression of any nature, and then to expect that planned confession and quick repentance will satisfy the Lord. . . . 'Among the most common sexual sins our young people commit are necking and petting. Not only do these improper relations often lead to fornication, pregnancy, and abortions—all ugly sins—but in and of themselves they are pernicious evils, and it is often difficult for youth to distinguish where one ends and another begins. . . . Too often, young people dismiss their petting with a shrug of their shoulders as a little indiscretion, while admitting that fornication is a base transgression. Too many of them are shocked, or feign to be, when told that what they have done in the name of petting was in reality [a form of] fornication' (see *Miracle of Forgiveness*, 65–66)" (*Ensign*, May 1986, 44–45).

My son and his girlfriend have had sexual intercourse many times. Can they be forgiven?

President Spencer W. Kimball: "Serious as is the sin of fornication (sexual intercourse by the unmarried), there is forgiveness upon condition of total repentance. But first one must come to a realization of the seriousness of his sin. Since the beginning there has been in the world a wide range of sins. Many of them involve harm to others, but every sin is against ourselves and God, for sins limit our progress, curtail our development, and estrange us from good people, good influences, and from our Lord" (*Ensign*, Nov. 1980, 95).

My son has had a problem with masturbation for a number of years. What hope is there for him?

President Spencer W. Kimball: "Masturbation, a rather common indiscretion, is not approved of the Lord nor of his church, regardless of what may have been said by others whose "norms" are lower. Latter-day Saints are urged to avoid this practice. Anyone fettered by this weakness should abandon the habit before he goes on a mission or receives the holy priesthood or goes in the temple for his blessings" (*Ensign*, Nov. 1980, 97).

My husband was sexually involved with one of our daughters. Is there hope for him?

President Spencer W. Kimball: "The early apostles and prophets mention numerous sins that were reprehensible to them. . . . One of the worst of these is incest. The dictionary defines incest as 'sexual intercourse between persons so closely related that they are forbidden by law to marry.' The spirituality of one's life may be severely, and sometimes irreparably, damaged by such an ugly sin. The First Presidency and the Quorum of the

Twelve have determined that the penalty for incest shall be excommunication. Also, one excommunicated for incest shall not be baptized again into the Church without the written permission of the First Presidency. . . . The Lord and his church can forgive. The image of a loving, forgiving God comes through clearly to those who read and understand the scriptures. Since he is our Father, he naturally desires to raise us up, not to push us down, to help us live, not to bring about our spiritual death" (*Ensign*, Nov. 1980, 95).

My husband has a problem with masturbation. Have the prophets said anything regarding the seriousness of masturbation?

President Spencer W. Kimball: "The early apostles and prophets mention numerous sins that were reprehensible to them. Many of them were sexual sins. . . . They included all sexual relations outside marriage—petting, sex perversion, masturbation, and preoccupation with sex in one's thoughts and talking. Included are every hidden and secret sin and all unholy and impure thoughts and practices" (*Ensign*, Nov. 1980, 95).

My husband has a problem with Internet pornography. I'm concerned about him.

President Ezra Taft Benson: "Control your thoughts. No one steps into immorality in an instant. The first seeds of immorality are always sown in the mind. When we allow our thoughts to linger on lewd or immoral things, the first step on the road to immorality has been taken. I especially warn you against the evils of pornography. Again and again we hear from those caught in deep sin that often the first step on their road to transgression began with pornographic materials. The Savior taught that even when a man looks upon a woman to lust after her, or in other words, when he lets his thoughts begin to get out of control, he has already committed adultery with her in his heart (see Matt. 5:28; D&C 63:16)" (*New Era*, Jan. 1988, 6).

I have heard others say that pornography is very addictive. How addictive is it?

President Gordon B. Hinckley: "'Let virtue garnish thy thoughts unceasingly' (D&C 121:45). There is so much of filth and lust and pornography in this world. We as Latter-day Saints must rise above it and stand tall against it. You can't afford to indulge in it. You just cannot afford to indulge in it. You have to keep it out of your heart. Like tobacco it's addictive, and it will destroy those who tamper with it. 'Let virtue garnish thy thoughts unceasingly'" (*Ensign,* Aug. 1997, 6–7).

My son has told me that he has been sexually involved with girls while dating. He tells me that he loves them.

President Gordon B. Hinckley: "While speaking of these matters, let me say that any young man who asks for sexual favors from a young woman whom he may be dating on the basis that he loves her is saying in the strongest terms that he does not love her. Such an expression is one of lust and not of love" (*Ensign,* June 1996, 5).

Can my daughter ever be forgiven for lesbian relationships?

Elder Richard G. Scott: "Committing homosexual acts and other deviations approaching these in gravity are not acceptable alternate lifestyles. They are serious sins. . . . Such grave sins require deep repentance to be forgiven. President Kimball taught: 'To every forgiveness there is a condition. The plaster must be as wide as the sore. The fasting, the prayers, the humility must be equal to or greater than the sin.' 'It is unthinkable that God absolves serious sins upon a few requests. He is likely to wait until there has been long, sustained repentance'" (*Ensign,* May 1995, 77).

Our loved ones do not receive forgiveness and we do not achieve a forgiving heart at a set time or place. It is not something that comes by meeting a checklist. Our hearts do not change overnight. The Lord commands us to forgive others, but He lets us choose how we go about it and how long we take to do it. One man said:

> I had carried hurt and an unforgiving heart for about three years after the incident. I had prayed for the person who had hurt me. I had asked the Lord to help me so that I would be able to forgive the person. My answer came one morning while cooking breakfast. It was a simple answer, but the words just popped into my mind, "The Lord has released you!" This meant that I was released from the pain and hurt.

Even though we reach forgiveness in different ways, the end result is simply this: We are no longer held hostage by the incident and can move forward with our lives. We also have peace in our hearts.

If we look for one huge experience that will allow us to forgive, we may never find forgiveness. Forgiveness, for the most part, is made up of little changes we make over time until one day we find ourselves at peace. We have to be willing to give up the hurt and pain so that forgiveness can take place. That's right—forgiveness replaces the hurt and pain. We do not have room in our hearts for both. At some point we either let forgiveness in or we choose to hold onto the hurt and pain. It really is our choice. We don't have to rush it. We don't have to work on someone's schedule, and forgiveness really does not have much to do with the person who offended us. It is a matter between us and the Lord.

Forgiving is what we can do only when we have the Lord's Spirit in our lives and hearts. Like all other gospel principles, the Lord has not asked us to forgive others without preparing a way for us to forgive. Nephi and his brothers had to keep trying to get the plates. We too have to keep trying to accept the spiritual gift of a forgiving heart. The Lord will help us as we do our part, for we know that it is by "grace that we are saved, after all we can do" (2 Ne. 25:23). After we have put forth our best efforts to forgive someone, the Lord will pick up whatever slack is remaining. He will finish anything unfinished so that we can have the peace He has promised.

THE ATONEMENT IS A PERFECT MATCH

On October 29, 2002, I was on a business trip to Raleigh, North Carolina and sat next to a gentleman who brought on board a small picnic cooler. I thought perhaps the man had brought his supper to eat during the one-hour flight. I introduced myself, and we talked back and forth for a few minutes.

I asked him why he was going to North Carolina, and he told me about his work and the institution that he worked for—a bone marrow transplant company. He explained that the little picnic cooler on the floor between his legs actually contained bone marrow. A donor in Dallas, Texas had made the donation earlier that day and he was on his way to deliver it to a hospital in Raleigh, North Carolina. He went on to explain that once the marrow is taken from the donor, he has twenty-four hours to get it to the recipient.

I asked him how difficult it was to get a match between the donor and donee. He explained that in one set of circumstances, a match might be 1/20,000, in another the match is 1/30,000, and in yet other circumstances the match is 1/100,000.

My next questions was, "How much does it cost for a transplant?"

He said, "About $250,000."

I responded with, "It must be very rewarding to have a profession where you have part in saving another person's life."

He responded, "It is very rewarding, and that's what keeps me here at times. I work for a non-profit company, and the pay is not as good as I would like, but the work is very rewarding."

I continued, "I cannot imagine what it must be like to arrive at a hospital and have the recipient and loved ones waiting for you. In a way there must be a sense of relief when you arrive and they know that the marrow has safely arrived."

"Yes," he responded, "there is a great deal of anticipation when I'm en route to my destination. I confirm with the hospital when I board the plane so that they know exactly where I am and when I should arrive."

We continued to visit until we exited the plane. As we walked together to the luggage carousel, his cell phone rang. It was a person from the hospital informing him that someone was already at the luggage carousel waiting for him and would take him immediately to the hospital. We said our goodbyes and he was on his way.

As I prepared for bed that night, I thought about the bone marrow transplant and all the work, energy, and money that had gone into saving another human being. I imagined the joy recipients must feel once they learn that a bone marrow match has been found. Added joy must come when the recipient learns that the person is actually donating the marrow. The anticipation must be high waiting for the marrow. There must be great concerns about the surgery-transplant and fear that the body will reject the marrow. Yet, all involved are willing to go through all of this to physically save another person's life.

What about those who need spiritual transplants? What about us? Who could not benefit from a spiritual transplant? Spiritual surgery is similar to physical surgery in that much preparation and effort must take place prior to the operation. The Donor and the recipient must be well prepared. The donation has already been made. The Donor has already paid the price. He gave His life. The transplant is His Atonement. Will we accept His Atonement or reject it? The choice is ours!

What is the likelihood of having a perfect match between the Savior's Atonement and us? For bone marrow the likelihood of a match between the donor and the recipient is 1/20,000, 1/30,000, or 1/100,000, depending on different variables. With the Atonement of Jesus Christ the match ratio between Him and us is 1 for 1, and the spiritual transplant is successful 100 percent of the time, if we as the recipients decide to accept it.

Can the Atonement be rejected? Yes, but we must individually choose to reject it. He will not reject us. Jesus paid for our sins and has already provided a spiritual transplant that we can choose to accept. Through repentance, we accept the transplant. This spiritual regeneration occurs not just once, but many times throughout our lives.

As we strive to repent for our own sins and forgive others of theirs, the Lord will heal our hearts and forgiveness will come. "A new heart also will I give you, and a new spirit will I put within you: and I will take away the stony heart out of your flesh, and I will give you an heart of flesh" (Ezek. 36:26). This is His promise.

SUMMARY

Forgiveness does not mean we forget what our loved ones have done. Forgiveness does not mean we are guilty of committing sin too. Forgiveness does not mean we will immediately have warm and tender feelings toward our loved one. Forgiveness is not saying that our loved ones' poor choices are all right. Forgiveness is something that we decide to do. It's our choice. It's for our healing. Forgiveness does mean we need to let go of the hurt, move on with our own progression, and allow the peace that the Savior has promised into our lives.

Another way to look at forgiveness is to compare it to a new sheet that we are about to unfold over a bed. The sheet is folded compactly inside the package. We open the package and begin to unfold the sheet. Unlike the speed of making a real bed, we do not unfold the sheet of our own forgiveness in one big motion; in fact, we cannot unfold it all in a day, a week, or a month. We should take our time. However, as we desire to forgive and continue to work on the process, we unfold the sheet more and more—until one day the entire bed is covered with the clean, bright sheet. The bed full of pain that we have slept on for a long time is now gently covered with the sheet of forgiveness. A forgiving heart that Christ can help us develop is not based on our loved ones' changing or not changing. It's based on our willingness to forgive and on His Divine gift as the Prince of Peace.

REVIEW OF PRINCIPLES

How would you define forgiveness?

_____

_____

_____

_____

_____

In what ways have you experienced forgiveness?

_____

_____

_____

_____

_____

_____

In what ways do you need to forgive yourself?

_____

_____

_____

_____

_____

_____

What has been the most difficult part for you in reaching a level of forgiveness regarding your loved one's behaviors?

_____

_____

_____

_____

_____

_____

_____

What are some specific things you have learned from this chapter that will help you begin the process of forgiving your loved one?

_____

_____

_____

_____

_____

_____

_____

What are some skills or techniques you have learned in this chapter that you will try to implement in your relationships with yourself and others in the next thirty days?

_____

_____

_____

_____

_____

_____

What is the single most important principle or concept you have learned from this chapter?

_____

_____

_____

_____

_____

_____

_____

With whom can you share this important principle or concept in the next week?

_____

_____

_____

_____

_____

CALMNESS BREAK

Think about ways you unwind and relax. Which relaxation methods usually work best for you? When was the last time you engaged in this activity? How would you benefit if you were able to do this activity on a regular basis?

MESSAGES OF HOPE

Elder Marvin J. Ashton: "A warm handshake and a friendly smile can be wonderfully healing medicine. Conversely, how unwise we are when we declare, 'I'll never speak to him again.' Never is a long time, and even those who have caused heartache or shame are not beyond ultimate repentance. Sometimes hurts to the heart are more damaging than physical blows. Yes, they may take longer to heal, but they will heal more quickly if we avoid bitterness and anger and practice forgiveness" (*Ensign,* May 1988, 62).

Elder James E. Faust: "The denial of our own sins, of our own selfishness, of our own weakness is like a crown of thorns which keeps us from moving up one more step in personal growth. Perhaps worse than sin is the denial of sin. If we deny that we are sinners, how can we ever be forgiven? How can the atonement of Jesus work in our lives if there is no repentance? If we do not promptly remove the slivers of sin and the thorns of carnal temptation, how can the Lord ever heal our souls? The Savior said, 'Repent of your sins, and be converted, that I may heal you.' (3 Ne. 9:13) It is most difficult for us to pray for those who hate us, who despitefully use us, who persecute us. But by failing to take this vital extra step, however, we fail to remove some of the festering briars in our souls. Extending forgiveness, love, and understanding for perceived shortcomings and weaknesses in our wives, husbands, children, and associates makes it much easier to say, 'God be merciful to me a sinner'" (Luke 18:13) (*Ensign,* May 1991, 68).

PRINCIPLE 11

We Are Protected when We Obey the Laws of the Land and Seek that which Is Good

CHAPTER OVERVIEW

We are here on earth to learn, grow, and progress. What a wonderful laboratory for learning! When our life's experiences are painful, however, a great deal of pondering and patience may be necessary in order to see through the shards and shrapnel and glimpse the blessings and opportunities for growth. For instance, family members involved in certain compulsive sexual behaviors may experience serious legal and criminal consequences for violating civil, state, or federal laws. We have definite legal responsibilities when we suspect any form of abuse, particularly toward children, the disabled, or the elderly. Failure on our part to report abuse violates the law. Though we definitely must allow our loved ones to experience the consequences of their behaviors and avoid trying to soften the blow—even if it means imprisonment for them—our own security and privacy may be invaded as well.

"We believe in being subject to kings, presidents, rulers, and magistrates, in obeying, honoring, and sustaining the law" (A of F 12).

 ## CHAPTER OBJECTIVES

At the conclusion of this chapter you should—

1. Understand why it is important to allow the natural consequences of your loved one's behaviors to play out.

2. Know why it is important for your loved one to accept total responsibility for any consequences regarding their behaviors (including family, community, church, and criminal or civil liabilities).
3. Understand the definitions of abuse regarding children, the elderly, or disabled.
4. Understand your responsibility to report abuse.
5. Recognize the signs of spouse abuse.
6. Be aware of the choices you can make if you are in an abusive relationship.
7. Become aware of warning signs signaling that your children may be in danger while using the Internet.
8. Know what steps you can take to minimize your children's exposure to unwanted material on the Internet.

Serious Consequences

Sometimes our loved ones may not recognize the seriousness of their problems until they experience the consequences of their behavior. Natural consequences can be their "wake-up call" to get out of denial, stop rationalizing or blaming others, and choose instead to move forward toward wholeness. The longer they stay in the addictive cycle, the harder it is to quit. In the case of pornography addiction, the longer they stay in the cycle, the images they choose to see, fantasize about, or desire will become more intense and explicit. Although they may not like to admit it, each behavior connected with the drug of lust is a choice—a poor use of agency. There are so many examples of the drug of lust, and Satan creates more every day since he is "the author of all sin" (Hel. 6:30).

The compulsive sexual behavior choices Satan provides have no boundaries or limits. Satan does not exclude any person or situation. All compulsive sexual behaviors have serious spiritual consequences. In addition, some behaviors have serious criminal and civil consequences.

One man's compulsive sexual behavior choices resulted in jail time. He wrote:

> I am in a room with about 35 other men. We sleep on bunk beds and I have a bottom bunk. All inmates have only the same few personal items, such as a toothbrush, toothpaste, and other essentials, and that's it. I wear an orange-colored jumpsuit with my jail number on the back, just like all the other inmates. Roll call and bed checks are done by the inmates' jail number. The food is okay, but it's been hard to get used to. Some inmates give their

food to other inmates to score points with them. It's like we have this little city in here with some inmates taking on the role of setting rules, enforcing them, and punishing other inmates who don't follow. It's like a pecking order in the animal world.

There is one bathroom in the room with no privacy—a small area at the one end of the room. There are no windows, so we have no outside light in the room. The lights never go out, but are dimmed at night. This way the guards can always see what's going on inside the room.

I have not told anyone the real reason I am here. If I make progress and don't mess up, it looks like I won't have to go to prison [be incarcerated in a long-term facility]. My attorney tells me I will probably be here for about nine months. I am frightened at times but I know with the Lord's help I can get through this ordeal.

I never thought my behavior would cause me to end up in jail. For the first time I am starting to recognize what I need to change. I realize now that I made some bad choices. I could not see this before, but now I see it clearly.

This man's choices had severe consequences; however, he is beginning to see the steps he needs to take in order to change. The good that is coming from his consequences is his recognition that he personally made the choices that resulted in jail time. Our loved ones can only change when they are willing to see the real problem and do their part to get out of the behavior.

What benefits did this man receive by experiencing the consequences of his behavior?

_____

_____

_____

_____

_____

Abuse

Abuse has many faces and forms, most of which cannot be seen or detected by outsiders. The fact that abuse is not always noticed by others does not mean that it is not serious. Even though emotional abuse produces emotional and spiritual scars and injuries, the consequences of such abuse can be at least as damaging as physical abuse. Any kind of abuse is wrong. President Gordon B. Hinckley said:

> *We condemn most strongly abusive behavior in any form. We denounce the physical, sexual, verbal, or emotional abuse of one's spouse or children. . . .*
>
> *No man who abuses his wife or children is worthy to be a member in good standing in this Church. The abuse of one's spouse and children is a most serious offense before God, and any who indulge in it may expect to be disciplined by the Church (Ensign, Nov. 1998, 72).*

In addition to physical, emotional, sexual, or verbal abuse, neglect of a child or a disabled or elderly person is also abuse. Even more than the above types of abuse are possible in the most intimate of relationships—marriage.

Spouse Abuse

When we hear the word *abuse*, we may think of cuts, bruises, and broken bones. However, abuse is much more than what we may see on the surface. The truth is, abuse may be perpetrated physically, emotionally, verbally, sexually, spiritually, and financially.

The Various Faces of Abuse

Physical Abuse: Physical abuse involves various forms and degrees of violence. It ranges from punching, kicking, hitting, slapping, shoving, choking, biting, pinching, and a multitude of other forms of assault with any object that can cause injury. The aftermath of physical abuse leaves behind both physical and emotional scars.

Physical abuse, like many other destructive behaviors, usually follows a vicious cycle. The cycle begins with a tension buildup often caused by poor choices. As the tension builds, one spouse becomes angry and frustrated and begins to take it out on the other spouse. However, this part of the cycle is usually not violent and is characterized mainly by yelling or acting in a rude or demeaning manner.

Then the anger continues to spin out of control and reaches the point of violence. Here, in the second phase, a serious act of violence may take place. Following this outburst of violent behavior, the abusive spouse begins the last part of the cycle—apologizing and promising to improve. In fact, the abusive spouse may feel badly enough to act extremely kind and generous after the act. This calm demeanor and kind behavior following the storm of abuse is what makes the cycle so dangerous. The abused spouse is often convinced that the abusive spouse is ready to change or has already done so. However, the abusive cycle plays out over and over again with escalating consequences. The longer the abuse cycle is permitted to continue, the more violent it becomes. Like a car with failing shocks, each bump in the relationship road throws the vehicle more out of control and leads to bigger problems on the next bump.

How would you explain the cycle of abuse to a friend?

_____

_____

_____

_____

_____

_____

Verbal/Emotional Abuse: Emotional abuse is extremely dangerous because it is so hard to detect and so harmful to the victim. Common forms of emotional abuse include berating criticism, degrading remarks, name-calling, insulting the beliefs or values of another, withholding appreciation, cursing, and threatening. Threats could come in the form of a threat to leave, to take the children, or to injure or kill another.

This type of abuse should not be overlooked because its occurrence leaves a wake of uncertainty, eroded self-esteem, anger, and hatred. In addition, it may lead to other forms of abuse, including physical and sexual abuse.

Sexual Abuse: Unwanted or undesired sexual attention is abusive, even to a spouse. A woman forced to engage in sexual relations has been raped, whether or not she is married. Most rape victims are raped by someone they know and even love, including their husbands. Such abuse may also consist of unwanted touching, affairs, withholding sex, sexual criticism, or insisting a woman wear specific clothing.

Sexual abuse leads to problems of low self-esteem and psychological trauma. Many women hesitate to discuss sexual abuse because doing so engenders feelings of embarrassment or guilt. As with other forms of abuse, sexual abuse has lasting consequences and may be a precursor to other forms of abusive behavior, including violence.

Spiritual Abuse (Unrighteous Dominion): I choose to list this form of abuse under its own heading even though it may be lumped together with emotional abuse.

A loved one who quotes from the scriptures, the Brethren, or other Church manuals or articles as weapons to get what is wanted instead of using them as the Lord intended is guilty of spiritual abuse. Here are comments from wives who were spiritually abused:

"I have had several spiritual experiences, but when I have shared them with my husband, he makes light of these experiences and discounts them."

"I needed a priesthood blessing and my husband used it to lecture me and impose his own will rather than seeking the will of the Lord."

"My husband uses the scriptures, words of the prophets, or articles from the Ensign as weapons to beat me so I will change my opinion even though I know through the Spirit that he is once again trying to control me."

"My husband met alone with the bishop and lied about our relationship so that he could look good for the bishop."

"My husband told me that I would never receive exaltation without him even though he was abusive in many ways."

Spiritual abuse is very hurtful to the wife as well as the children. The Lord is clear about His standard:

We have learned by sad experience that it is the nature and disposition of almost all men, as soon as they get a little authority, as they suppose, they will immediately begin to exercise unrighteous dominion.

Hence many are called, but few are chosen.

No power or influence can or ought to be maintained by virtue of the priesthood, only by persuasion, by long-suffering, by gentleness and meekness, and by love unfeigned;

By kindness, and pure knowledge, which shall greatly enlarge the soul without hypocrisy, and without guile—

Reproving betimes with sharpness, when moved upon by the Holy Ghost; and then showing forth afterwards an increase of love toward him whom thou hast reproved, lest he esteem thee to be his enemy (D&C 121:39-44).

If there is a need to reprove, then it should be followed by an increase of love.

The person that has been reproved should not feel that love has been withdrawn. They should not feel abandoned.

Financial Abuse: Lastly, we will discuss a form of abuse that is generally intertwined with some of the abusive patterns mentioned above. Financial abuse is used as a method of trapping a woman in an abusive situation. Many times a woman feels that leaving an abusive spouse is impossible because she has been denied the right of earning income, gaining employable skills, or even reviewing the family's financial data. In extreme cases of financial abuse, the victim's assets may have been confiscated, stolen, and even sold by a spouse.

Another less obvious form of financial abuse may be withholding financial support for the spouse's personal needs. It may also be withholding the means needed to purchase the very necessities of life for the victim or the children. A financially abusive husband generally exercises tight control over all financial matters and leaves his wife in the dark, weaving yet another web of abuse to keep her from leaving.

What examples of spouse abuse do you know about or have experienced?

_____

_____

_____

_____

_____

_____

GET HELP NOW!

Any person who is in an abusive relationship should seek immediate help. It is important to let your bishop know about the abuse. In addition, if sexual abuse has occurred, it is important to notify law enforcement personnel.

Professional help will also be needed. Find a counselor that specializes in working with victims of abuse and begin counseling sessions. A strong support system will also be needed. Over a period of time we can choose our own outcome.

Before Seeking Help	After Seeking Help (We choose this outcome and work to achieve it.)
I do not trust anyone.	I have learned to trust when it is appropriate.
My family relationships are all in a big mess.	Progress has been made and my relationships have improved.
I want my loved one to suffer like I have.	I have made some progress toward forgiveness and recognize that I can forgive, but also I need to set appropriate boundaries so that the abuse does not happen again.
I feel so trapped and there is no way to get out.	I have several choices I can make. I can seek help. I can choose to attend a support group. I can read books on the subject. I can choose to separate from my spouse. I can choose to divorce my spouse.
I have closed myself off from the rest of the world.	I recognize the need to let others into my life who are trustworthy and can help me. This I am doing, although it is uncomfortable for me.
I usually feel anxiety and depression and I don't like feeling this way.	I have learned positive ways I can deal with anxiety and depression and have made some progress.
I question the motives of almost everyone I am around.	I have chosen to associate with people who can help me during this difficult time, and I know that they truly care about me.
I am so controlling and want to make sure that everyone does what I say or I become very angry.	I recognize that others can choose for themselves. I respect their agency and their right to choose.
I don't think I can ever heal from such a horrible event.	I am grateful for the inner peace I have. I recognize that it has been a partnership with the Savior. I am grateful for His perfect love.

WHY WOMEN STAY IN ABUSIVE RELATIONSHIPS

Oddly enough, people living in abusive situations often choose to stay and endure further abuse. Why is that the case? While there is not one reason that can possibly answer the motives of millions of people, there are usually a few common characteristics:

- They love their spouse despite the abuse.

- They have low self-esteem.

- They feel ashamed that they are being abused.

- They feel guilty for enduring abuse, or they blame themselves for the abuse.

- They are fearful of leaving the abusive situation.

- They feel socially isolated and unable to share their situation with a close friend or family member.

- They are in denial of the abusive nature of their relationship.

- They feel financially dependent upon their abusive spouse.

- They fail to realize that they have a potential for a healthy relationship.

- They do not realize that help is available and may not have any idea where they could go if they leave.

- They may be following promptings to stay for the present.

Many abused spouses have convinced themselves that they have no other option but to stay in an abusive situation. A strong commitment to temple marriage and the idea that the supreme goal is endurance in that marriage may make the idea of leaving totally unacceptable, no matter how bad the situation.

The thought of leaving a familiar situation, although they recognize the danger of staying, may conjure up feelings of uncertainty and anxiety. Thus, they continue doing what they have always done—failing to admit that the situation will only get worse.

Abuse weaves a web that is hard to escape because it manipulates the physical, social, and emotional aspects of the abused spouse's life. Help and change are possible, however. We need to remember that no one should remain in an environment that is destructive to emotional and spiritual growth or that does not allow physical safety. Admitting the abuse is the first step on the road to a healthy future.

Child Abuse

Child abuse may be physical, emotional, or sexual. In addition, it is child abuse for a parent to neglect a child, fail to supervise children even when the parent is in the home, leave children unattended for extended periods of time, fail to get medical treatment when needed, or not send children to school.

President Gordon B. Hinckley reminds us of the seriousness of abuse:

> *We condemn most strongly abusive behavior in any form. We denounce the physical, sexual, verbal, or emotional abuse of one's spouse or children. Our proclamation on the family declares: "Husband and wife have a solemn responsibility to love and care for each other and for their children. . . . Parents have a sacred duty to rear their children in love and righteousness, to provide for their physical and spiritual needs. . . . Husbands and wives—mothers and fathers—will be held accountable before God for the discharge of these obligations"* (Ensign, Nov. 1995, 102).

Physical Abuse: Signs of physical abuse may include unexplained cuts, bruises, sores, welts, burns, or broken bones. Because of physical abuse, a child may by apprehensive around adults and may show signs of anxiety, withdrawing from others or may be overly aggressive. Being fearful of one or both parents may also indicate physical abuse. We should avoid going on a witch hunt, but we should also be alert, attentive, and aware of the signs of abuse.

Verbal/Emotional Abuse: Emotional abuse includes constant statements that are demeaning, insulting, belittling, criticizing, or that negatively impact a child's self-worth and feeling of value. Emotional abuse not only includes devastating statements, but it also includes withholding love, affection, reassurance, compliments, and guidance.

Sexual Abuse: Sexual abuse occurs when a child is drawn into a sexually stimulating activity involving an adult. It also includes a sexually stimulating activity involving another child who may have power or control over the child because of age, strength, or even trust. President Gordon B. Hinckley gave a stern warning to those who sexually abuse children:

> *Shame on any man or woman who would sexually abuse a child. In doing so, the abuser not only does the most serious kind of injury. He or she also stands condemned before the Lord.*
> *It was the Master himself who said, "But whoso shall offend one of these*

little ones which believe in me, it were better for him that a millstone were hanged about his neck, and that he were drowned in the depth of the sea" (Matt. 18:6).

How could he have spoken in stronger terms?

If there be any within the sound of my voice who may be guilty of such practice, I urge you with all of the capacity of which I am capable to stop it, to run from it, to get help, to plead with the Lord for forgiveness and make amends to those whom you have offended. God will not be mocked concerning the abuse of his little ones (Ensign, Nov. 1994, 54).

It's very important that we know our children's friends as well as their parents. We should make an effort to spend adequate time with our children and provide opportunities for them to talk, ask questions, and share feelings, and for us to teach them about ways to protect themselves from others who might be abusive.

WHAT CAN YOU DO TO MINIMIZE THE CHANCES OF AN ON-LINE EXPLOITER VICTIMIZING YOUR CHILD?

This question was asked on the FBI's website (www.fbi.gov), and the FBI provided these responses.

1. *Communicate and talk to your child about sexual victimization and potential on-line danger.*

2. *Spend time with your children on-line. Have them teach you about their favorite on-line destinations.*

3. *Keep the computer in a common room in the house, not in your child's bedroom. It is much more difficult for a computer sex offender to communicate with a child when the computer screen is visible to a parent or another member of the household.*

4. *Utilize parental controls available from your service provider and/or blocking software. While electronic chat can be a great place for children to make new friends and discuss various topics of interest, it is also prowled by computer sex offenders. Use of chat rooms, in particular, should be heavily monitored. While parents should utilize these mechanisms, they should not totally rely on them.*

5. *Always maintain access to your child's on-line account and randomly check his/her e-mail. Be aware that your child could be contacted through the U.S. Mail. Be up front with your child about your access and reasons why.*

6. *Teach your child the responsible use of the resources on-line. There is much more to the on-line experience than chat rooms.*

7. *Find out what computer safeguards are utilized by your child's school, the public library, and at the homes of your child's friends. These are all places, outside your normal supervision, where your child could encounter an on-line predator.*

8. *Understand, even if your child was a willing participant in any form of sexual exploitation, that he/she is not at fault and is the victim. The offender always bears the complete responsibility for his or her actions.*

9. *Instruct your children to—*

   a. *Never arrange a face-to-face meeting with someone they met on-line;*

   b. *Never upload (post) pictures of themselves onto the Internet or on-line service to people they do not personally know (sometimes even to those they do know).*

   c. *Never give out identifying information such as their name, home address, school name, or telephone number;*

   d. *Never download pictures from an unknown source, as there is a good chance there could be sexually explicit images;*

   e. *Never respond to messages or bulletin board postings that are suggestive, obscene, belligerent, or harassing;*

   f. *Understand that whatever they are told on-line may or may not be true.*

CHURCH DISCIPLINE

Because of certain choices made by our loved ones, their Church membership may be restricted. This could include probation, being disfellowshipped, or being excommunicated. President Howard W. Hunter emphasized the seriousness of abuse by saying: "No man who has been ordained to the priesthood of God can with impunity abuse his wife or child. Sexual abuse of children has long been a cause for excommunication from the Church" (*Ensign*, Nov. 1994, 51).

REPORT TO LAW ENFORCEMENT

If we know or suspect child abuse in any form in the past or present, then we have the legal responsibility to report it to the local law enforcement. While it is true that child physical abuse may be easier to see, all forms of suspected abuse must be reported. In addition, any abuse to those who are disabled or the elderly must also be reported. Failure to do so subjects us to the law; we risk having legal charges filed against us. These are very serious matters.

Even if abuse involves our loved ones, we have a legal responsibility to report it. The local law enforcement and family social services agencies have the responsibility to determine if abuse actually occurred. Working closely with our bishop and making full disclosure to him about what we know regarding a child at risk is also very important. The bishop needs to know so that others can be protected too, but we are the ones who should do the reporting to the legal authorities.

Our loved ones might plead with tearful eyes, assure us that it won't happen again, and beg us not to report the abuse. But it is important that we stay strong, recognize our loved ones' behavior as abuse, and report the abuse. The sooner abuse is reported, the sooner the victim and perpetrator can get the help they need. If our loved ones truly want to change, they need help to do so. They cannot change this behavior without the proper spiritual, emotional, and professional support and guidance. One man reflected:

> *I was so angry at my daughter for calling the police station and turning me in. She was sixteen years old at the time, and I thought she was trying to get even with me because I would not let her drive until she had better grades.*
>
> *I realize now that it was the best thing that ever happened to me. I needed help and got it. I've learned a lot about myself and still have a long way to go. I realize now that I am totally responsible for what I did. I cannot blame anyone but me.*
>
> *My daughter is slowly starting to trust me again. It will take a long time. I hurt her badly. I cannot believe what I did. I have been incarcerated for my actions. I am responsible for the choices I made.*

Not all of our loved ones will respond to help, but it is their choice. We have the responsibility to notify the authorities, and it is our loved ones' responsibility to respond to help. Help is there if our loved ones want to find it and accept it and work very hard to make the necessary changes.

One major way to know that our loved ones are responding to help is that they will take full responsibility for their choices and stop blaming others, their past, the way they were raised, their circumstances, or anything else. Full accountability for their choices means they are on the healing path. Anything less than full accountability, indicated by statements such as, "This would not have happened, if . . . ," means our loved one still has work to do.

🖊 **What benefits did this man receive by having his daughter report him to the police?**

LEGAL CONSEQUENCES

For some of our loved ones, in addition to spiritual consequences for their behavior, there may also be legal and civil consequences. We should not in any way try to prevent or stop the legal consequences. If our loved ones have been involved with child sexual abuse, they should make restitution, serve the required jail or prison time, and meet all other requirements set forth by the judge.

When appropriate, it is okay to testify on behalf of our loved one or write letters to the court so that the judge has viewpoints from others to take into consideration prior to sentencing. However, we should not in any way minimize what happened or fail to give the complete truth. It is very wise to have good legal advice from a competent lawyer who specializes in these matters.

Victims

Whatever the court requires our loved ones to do for the victims should be top priority. If this means paying for counseling, etc., our loved ones should satisfy every requirement laid out by the court. Part of our loved ones' healing requires that restitution be made to those who have been hurt because of their actions. We can be supportive to our loved ones by encouraging them to fulfill all of their legal obligations and by supporting the judge's decision regarding sentences or other legal matters.

There are decisions and requirements set forth by Church disciplinary councils that must also be followed. Our loved ones must be held accountable for their choices—which includes accepting the just consequences of their actions.

Legal Counsel

Both victims and perpetrators have rights, and both need legal counsel and advice. It is wise to seek and obtain counsel from someone who specializes in cases regarding sexual behavior.

HOPE FOR OUR LOVED ONES

Is there still hope for our loved ones to return and receive all the blessings of Church membership? Yes, but they need to choose to return. The scriptures remind us that very serious behavior can eventually be forgiven.

> *Turn, all ye Gentiles, from your wicked ways; and repent of your evil doings, of your lyings and deceivings, and of your whoredoms, and of your secret abominations, and your idolatries, and of your murders, and your priestcrafts, and your envyings, and your strifes, and from all your wickedness and abominations, and come unto me, and be baptized in my name, that ye may receive a remission of your sins, and be filled with the Holy Ghost, that ye may be numbered with my people who are of the house of Israel* (3 Ne. 30:2).

Through repentance and the Atonement, our loved ones' slates can be wiped clean. When justice and mercy meet, the debt is completely satisfied. The Savior has promised this blessing for all those who repent. Elder Boyd K. Packer gave this assurance:

> *I repeat, save for the exception of the very few who defect to perdition, there is no habit, no addiction, no rebellion, no transgression, no apostasy, no crime exempted from the promise of complete forgiveness. That is the promise of the atonement of Christ* (*Ensign*, Nov. 1995, 20).

Our loved ones make choices and must experience the consequences of those choices. There is no such thing as turning the clock back and reliving yesterday. Repentance can cleanse yesterday, but no one can go back and relive it. There are many things that our loved ones cannot replace or fix. However, if they are sincere and truly humble, the Lord will settle their account. Elder Boyd K. Packer said:

> *The thought that rescued Alma, when he acted upon it, is this: Restoring what you cannot restore, healing the wound you cannot heal, fixing that which you broke and you cannot fix is the very purpose of the atonement of Christ. When your desire is firm and you are willing to pay*

*the "uttermost farthing," the law of restitution is suspended. Your obliga-
tion is transferred to the Lord. He will settle your accounts* (*Ensign,* Nov.
1995, 19-20).

DIVORCE

Divorce is a very sensitive issue. President Gordon B. Hinckley gives us this rem-
edy, "The cure for most marital troubles does not lie in divorce. It lies in repentance
and forgiveness, in expressions of kindness and concern" (*Ensign,* Nov. 2004, 84).
President Hinckley also made this poignant observation:

> *The fact is that it is predominantly men who bring about the conditions
> that lead to divorce.*
>
> *After dealing with hundreds of divorce situations through the years, I am
> satisfied that the application of a single practice would do more than all else
> to solve this grievous problem.*
>
> *If every husband and every wife would constantly do whatever might
> be possible to ensure the comfort and happiness of his or her compan-
> ion, there would be very little, if any, divorce. Argument would never
> be heard. Accusations would never be leveled. Angry explosions would
> not occur. Rather, love and concern would replace abuse and meanness*
> (*Ensign,* Nov. 2004, 84).

Some of our loved ones will choose not to admit that they have a problem,
repent, or make necessary changes. The reality of broken commandments and
covenants means that some couples will inevitably choose divorce. This is a
painful decision that only adds to the pain already inflicted because of our loved
ones' behaviors.

Deciding Whether To Divorce Worksheet

What traits or behaviors does your spouse have that make you consider divorce?

If you decided to divorce, would you feel guilty that you haven't tried hard enough to make it work?

Which of these traits or behaviors would your spouse have to change for you to want to stay married?

What are your needs that are not being met in the marriage that make you con-sider a divorce?

Which of these behaviors are serious abuses and marriage violations, and which are just minor irritations?

How, where, and from whom would you get these needs met if you divorced?

Deciding Whether To Divorce Worksheet

Rank problems of your spouse from most to least serious.

Which of these behaviors have been going on for a long time?

Which of these behaviors is your spouse unwilling or unable to change and so will probably continue?

What should your spouse have done to solve problems?

Do you have or will you need proof of your spouse's bad behaviors?

What things has your spouse done to try to solve these problems?

What changes would you have to make for the marriage to be successful?

What things have you done to try to solve problems?

Have you tried your best to make the marriage work?

Have you asked for and pondered the advice of your children, your family, your bishop, other experts, and books on marriage and divorce?

What have you learned from each of these?

What people are in favor of you divorcing? Why?

What people want you to stay married? Why?

What people say it is up to you and your decision?

What religious reasons do you have to divorce or stay married?

Have you considered other options, such as marriage counseling or separation?

Are your reasons for considering divorce valid?

What are you getting from the marriage that has made you stay in the marriage so far and that makes you want to stay married?

Have you been honest with yourself and thought it through logically?

When comparing the logic of your head and thinking with the emotions of your heart and feelings, do you come to the same decision? Or do they conflict and get you confused?

Are you already divorced emotionally, financially, sexually, physically, or spiritually? Who caused these "divorces"?

What is the probability that things would get better, get worse, or stay the same if you stayed in the marriage?

If you were divorced now, would you marry your spouse?

Are your present thinking and feelings real, long-term needs? Or are they just impulsive desires?

Would staying together or divorcing be better for you and your children 5, 10, or 20 years from now?

Who should you tell and consult with about your concerns or decisions about divorce?

Would you be willing to take the time to get the facts about a divorce, particularly about your finances, custody, and visitation rights?

If you divorce, would you want the divorce to be fair or to get as much as you can?

If you divorce, would you be able to take care of yourself financially?

Deciding Whether To Divorce Worksheet

Do you have all the information you need to make your decision? Are there unknown things you still need to find out?

Have you gathered enough facts to make a good decision?

Have you waited long enough to know what you need to know to make the decision?

Are you living a life worthy of answers to prayers?

Have you fasted and gone to the temple to pray?

Have you made a decision and prayed about it? What inspiration or answer did you get?

Do you have copies of all financial papers such as earnings, credit card statements, bank accounts, loans, deeds, and taxes? What do they tell you?

In what ways would staying in the marriage help or hurt your children?

What other people would be affected by the divorce? How would they be affected?

Is fear keeping you from carrying out your decision?

If you divorce, do you know what work changes you would have to make, and are you willing to make them?

If you divorce, what changes would probably be made in home and living arrangements?

If you divorce, would you be willing to accept the judge's decisions on finances, custody, and visitation?

In what ways would your spouse be helped and hurt by a divorce?

How would a divorce, only having one parent, moving, custody, visitation, changes in finances, remarriages, step parents, or step brothers and sisters help or hurt your children?

Are you emotionally ready to make the decision to divorce or stay married?

Are you emotionally ready and strong enough to go through with the decision?

How likely would you be to change your mind or think it was a mistake if you stayed married? If you divorced?

Many times children and other innocent family members are caught in the middle of divorce. President James E. Faust counseled:

> *Far too many families are breaking up. This heartbreaking trend has an endless train of consequences. Happiness in marriage begins with husband and wife living together in love, kindness, and mutual respect, walking righteously and humbly before the Lord. It is contingent on being faithful to all vows and covenants. When families do break up for whatever reason,*

the parents need to try especially hard to sustain and help innocent family members (Ensign, May 2004, 67-68).

When divorce does occur, special effort and consideration should be given to help and support the children. *The Encyclopedia of Mormonism* outlines some of the challenges that a divorced person has within the LDS culture:

> *Church leaders urge members to prepare for marriage, marry within the faith, marry in the temple, live righteously and nurture their marriage relationships, pray for guidance, and counsel with each other and with priesthood leaders to resolve differences and deter divorce. Priesthood leaders are advised to help members strengthen their marriages but, when necessary, to permit divorce and to determine whether disciplinary action should be taken against any spouse guilty of moral transgression, such as infidelity or abuse. Priesthood leaders are to "cast out" (i.e., excommunicate) unrepentant adulterers from among the Saints, but to accept the victims of divorce (D&C 42:74-77).*
>
> *Church members who are divorced and the children of divorced parents sometimes report feelings of isolation or lack of acceptance because of the strong orientation toward two-parent families in the Church (Hulse, p. 17). Church leaders admonish all members to be sensitive to the needs of people in difficult circumstances and to offer help and appropriate encouragement and compassionate service wherever possible (Encyclopedia of Mormonism,* Vol. 1, "Divorce").

It is not easy to find ways to deal with life after divorce. Here is a story of one woman, the mother of ten children, who divorced after a long-term temple marriage. Here are some ways she coped with divorce:

Life after Divorce

When my husband left, I faced life as a single mother with ten children looking to me for answers.

Three and a half years ago, my twenty-nine-year temple marriage ended in divorce. My life up to that time had centered around the Church, my husband, my children—eight still living at home—and two grandchildren. As a result of the divorce, my life changed in ways I could not have imagined.

Since then I have been a single mother trying to meet the needs of five boys heavily involved in sports, a teenage daughter, and two adult children who have been working while going to school. In the first months of our separation, I felt alone, discouraged, and often depressed. I was simply overwhelmed with all the tasks and responsibilities that had fallen to me. How would my divorce affect the children? Would they still have any trust in marriage? Could we ever again be a "forever" family?

My life as a single mother demanded much, and I learned to do things I had never done before. My children, too, learned to accept greater responsibilities that at times I wished they did not have to bear. Among other things, we learned about repairing sprinkling systems, cabinets, and plumbing. One day I took inventory of the many repairs my house still needed and sat down and cried. I didn't have money for repairs, and I didn't know how to do them myself.

Although life as a single mother has been challenging, I have learned that Heavenly Father does not expect me to do it alone. As I've come increasingly to rely on Him, I have found comfort and support through dedicated gospel living, supportive ward members, and a desire to seek for the good in my life.

Setting My Gospel Foundation

Staying active. As additional responsibilities settled on me, I increasingly felt a need to reevaluate where I stood in living the gospel. I made perhaps one of my most important decisions immediately: I would stay active in the Church and attend ward activities even if I had to go alone or felt uncomfortable participating alone.

Reading scriptures. Although I had read the Book of Mormon throughout my life, since the divorce I have been reading it daily. The scriptures have taken on new meaning for me. They comfort and guide me. They bring me closer to Heavenly Father. They give me answers.

Keeping the commandments. Our family's income dropped considerably during the divorce process, and we struggled financially. I faced the dilemma of whether to pay tithing when there clearly was not enough money to feed and care for my large family and to make the essential house repairs. I sought counsel from my priesthood leaders and knew my answer. I decided I would pay a full tithing. I believe this single act of faith opened the windows of heaven, for many blessings were showered on our family.

Accepting a calling. Just before legal papers were filed for divorce, our Relief Society presidency was reorganized, and I was called to be secretary. Our new president later told me that my name came to her while she was meditating in the temple. Looking back, I see that Heavenly Father put me in a position to receive loving help, kindness, and concern from my sisters in the presidency in those stressful days during and after the divorce.

Drawing upon My Ward Family

Counseling with my bishop. I came to appreciate my bishop's guidance in helping me make a number of sound decisions. He checked on our family often and made sure I was all right and that my family was well cared for. He was my support both temporally and spiritually.

Relying on home teachers. When our home teacher and his sons were called to home teach our family, he expressed his desire to serve my family. Over time I came to understand the depth of his commitment. He checked on us often and asked about our week.

Appreciating my ward sisters. For the first two years after my divorce, I was surrounded by supportive and loving friends in the Relief Society presidency. They cried with me and laughed with me, and I felt close to them. Through my calling I became aware of some of the needs of my ward sisters, and giving service to them helped me keep my perspective and find healing within my own heart.

Finding Joy

Surrounding myself with beauty. The 13th Article of Faith suggests we seek after that which is good. Music has been a powerful influence in our home, especially since the divorce. I have felt closer to Heavenly Father and Jesus Christ just by listening to sacred music. I have read good books and attended good plays. Sometimes I go to a movie or play by myself, and I have found that I can have a good time even when I am alone. Other times I find a friend or family member to accompany me.

Developing new friendships. As a newly single sister, I became aware of two widowed sisters in my ward and three others recently divorced, and we became fast friends. We get together often, usually on Friday nights. Our times together have helped us grow close. We support and encourage each other. We have fun together.

Attending the temple. The temple is a place of goodness and beauty, and I know I am welcome there. Although temple attendance can bring painful reminders of broken covenants, I am comforted knowing that all promised blessings of the temple will eventually be mine again if I do my part to remain true and faithful. I realize that I and my children, who were born in the covenant, are still heirs to all the blessings of a covenant people. Because of these sweet assurances, I have learned to feel peace and joy while in the temple.

Experiencing joy. My youngest son and I share a birthday. He was to turn eight, and I was to turn fifty. He wanted to be baptized and confirmed *by his brothers on our birthday, and so our home teacher took time to instruct my older sons how to perform the ordinance and he later attended the service. After the baptism, he was confirmed by the oldest son in our family, a married brother. During the program all ten of my children, along with two spouses and two grandchildren, stood and sang "Families Can Be Together Forever." It was a moment I will always remember. My feelings of gratitude for the gospel and the richness of the spiritual blessings that had come to me to help sustain me and tutor me filled my heart. As I looked at my beautiful family and listened to the words they sang, I knew without a doubt that we were still a "forever" family* (Jackie Witzel, *Ensign*, June 2000, 54–57).

This woman discovered several ways she could deal with her pain. The principles she shared are universal in their application surrounding trials. One of the most important principles she discovered was her responsibility for her own stewardship, not her husband's; that his choices could not keep her from the long-term blessings of the gospel as long as she continued to be faithful. The Prophet Joseph Smith taught:

I am glad I have the privilege of communicating to you some things which, if grasped closely, will be a help to you when earthquakes bellow, the clouds gather, the lightnings flash, and the storms are ready to burst upon you like peals of thunder. Lay hold of these things and let not your knees or joints tremble, nor your hearts faint; and then what can earthquakes, wars and tornadoes do? Nothing. All your losses will be made up to you in the resurrection, provided you continue faithful. By the vision of the Almighty I have seen it (*History of the Church*, 5:362).

What principles have you learned from the Prophet's statement? How can you apply these principles to your own life?

_____

_____

_____

_____

_____

_____

FINANCIAL PREPARATION FOR DIVORCE

If our loved ones choose to repent and come unto Christ, the Atonement will right all the wrongs. However, some of our loved ones will choose not to change. At some point we have to make a decision as to what is best for us and our children—spiritually, emotionally, and physically.

After careful and prayerful consideration, weighing all the pros and cons and closely following the Spirit, we may feel impressed to divorce. I certainly do not advocate divorce, but the reality is that some of us will be directed by the Spirit to divorce our spouse. This is one of the most difficult decisions we will ever make, if not the most difficult.

Many women remain in abusive and unhealthy relationships and stay in the marriage because of financial fear for the future. "If I leave, where will I live and what will I do to support myself?" These financial concerns are valid and very important because many times a woman does not actually know the assets she and her spouse have, where the assets are, or how to get her share of them. It is common for a husband to file the tax returns and keep his other benefits—such as accumulated vacation time and stock options—a secret.

In these cases, it is vital to seek legal advice from a competent lawyer who specializes in divorce. Furthermore, many lawyers who specialize in divorce do so by representing either men or women. If you are a woman, it's not only important to hire a lawyer who specializes in divorce, but one who also usually represents women. It is not wise to hire a lawyer who is an old friend of the family, and has practiced business law most of his career. Your future and your children's future are too important not to have expert legal advice. You must be willing to discuss all aspects of your life and marriage with your lawyer. Make sure you have informed your lawyer about what is important to you.

So how can a woman seeking a divorce prepare for a financial future on her own? The first step to gaining confidence in your financial future is to learn as much as you can now. You cannot claim assets that you don't know exist, and you cannot know how much child support you will need unless you make accurate calculations.

There are several practical ways to determine the value of your family's assets and enable you to secure what you will need to be financially sound. Total the amount of assets that are uniquely yours, such as a trust account, assets purchased before marriage, and gifts given specifically to you. Generally, these assets will not be divided and will be yours following divorce.

Next, call or visit your spouse's work and get documentation of his salary, benefits, stock options, vacation pay, retirement accounts, and other potential earnings. (The employer may or may not be willing to give you this information.) If at all possible, get all of this information in writing before the divorce papers are served. Deceitful spouses, including spouses who are in denial and spouses who are unwilling to confront the truth, have been known to delay salary payments, raises, bonuses, and other benefits until after a divorce is finalized in order to avoid losing assets. By having a clear understanding of your spouse's compensation and employment benefits, you may avoid or lessen these issues. This step will also facilitate the process of claiming assets during court proceedings, because assets are often moved and hidden once the divorce proceedings begin. Having a valuation of total assets at the time the divorce papers are served will be enormously beneficial.

Finally, think of all the assets that you own together—house, cars, boat, artwork, antiques, collections, real estate, time shares, etc. After you have made an all-inclusive list, determine the value of each asset as best you can. The best way to do this is through an official appraisal. The appraiser will provide documentation of the value of the assets, which is crucial in receiving a fair share later on. Appraisals can be expensive. If you have purchased or refinanced the home in the last couple of years, the lending institution has the original appraisal and you could contact them for a copy. Even though the appraisal is outdated, it might give you an approximate price as a starting point. You would want to get the appraisal updated later. If your spouse owns or operates a business, it can also be appraised. Doing your homework, gathering necessary financial information, and receiving competent legal advice is so important to your financial future.

For retirement plans, such as a 401K, you will need to file a Qualified Domestic Relations Order before your husband begins to take distributions to avoid paying a penalty tax if money is withdrawn prior to 59½. If you do not file a QDRO, income taxes and a 10% early withdrawal penalty will be applied to the account if it is withdrawn before 59½. If you file the QDRO, any distribution is only subject to federal income tax.

It is also important to determine debt, since you may be held responsible for debts accumulated by your spouse. Run a joint credit report from all three credit reporting agencies:

Equifax www.equifax.com (800-685-1111) or write:
P.O. Box 740241, Atlanta, GA 30374-0241

Experian www.experian.com (888-EXPERIAN OR 397-3742) or write:
P.O. Box 2002, Allen, TX 75013

TransUnion www.transunion.com (800-888-4213) or write:
P.O. Box 1000, Chester, PA 19022

Some spouses will begin to run up high amounts of debt once divorce is on the horizon. Having the credit reports will provide a snapshot of your financial debt before the papers were served, and you will be able to avoid debts accumulated in last-minute purchases.

Once divorce is imminent, you need to take additional financial measures to protect yourself. Close joint bank accounts and credit cards and establish private accounts. This should be done in writing, clearly stating what you want to have happen to this account. By doing this, you will protect yourself from possible debts and expenses accumulated by your spouse.

An attorney will generally counsel divorcing individuals to take these steps, but if you do not have an attorney, take the initiative and do them on your own while the opportunity is present. Other areas for considerations include medical insurance for dependants, social security, and military benefits. Following the finalization of the divorce, take care of the paperwork involved in changing wills, deeds, titles, insurance, and investment plans.

Prepare yourself for divorce. When you have acquired information, documentation, and appraisals, you are empowered to face the future with less financial fear.

Even more important, prepare yourself spiritually. Furthermore, remembering that the Lord has always watched over you and that He will lead you to the situations that will best serve your family's financial needs is important. In addition to these practical suggestions, faith and trust in the Lord are your most important preparation.

 **REVIEW OF PRINCIPLES**

Why is it important to your loved one's healing to allow the natural consequences to happen?

_____

_____

_____

_____

_____

_____

Are there any legal issues regarding your loved one's behavior that need to be resolved with the proper authorities?

_____
_____
_____
_____
_____
_____

Is there any form of abuse regarding a child, the disabled, or the elderly that you suspect but have not yet reported? If so, it is required by law to report it. Report it today.

_____
_____
_____
_____
_____
_____
_____
_____

If you are being abused in any way, how can you get help? With whom will you talk?

_____
_____
_____
_____
_____
_____
_____

Record any other insights or thoughts that have occurred as you have read this chapter.

_____

_____

_____

_____

_____

_____

_____

What is the single most important principle or concept you have learned from this chapter?

_____

_____

_____

_____

_____

_____

_____

With whom can you share this important principle or concept in the next week?

_____

_____

_____

Calmness Break

Go to a quiet place with the *Hymns* book or *Children's Songbook.* Read the hymns or songs quietly to yourself. Take time to ponder what you read. Be aware of the love and strength that can come to you through the Spirit as you spend this special time with yourself. Be open to feeling God's perfect love for you. Listen carefully and be aware of feelings that might answer some of the questions you may have.

Messages of Hope

Elder Richard G. Scott: "I testify that the surest, most effective, and shortest path to healing comes through application of the teachings of Jesus Christ in your life. It begins with an understanding of and appreciation for the principles of moral agency and the atonement of Jesus Christ. It leads to faith in Him and obedience to His commandments, and that brings healing" (*Ensign,* May 1994, 9).

President Spencer W. Kimball: "God is good. He is eager to forgive. He wants us to perfect ourselves and maintain control of ourselves. He does not want Satan and others to control our lives. We must learn that keeping our Heavenly Father's commandments represents the only path to total control of ourselves, the only way to find joy, truth, and fulfillment in this life and in eternity" (*Ensign,* Oct. 1982, 2).

PRINCIPLE 12

*Learning from the Past Will Help Us
to Live Well in the Present
and Give Us Hope for the Future*

CHAPTER OVERVIEW

Hope keeps us on the healing path where we connect with ourselves, with our family, with others, and with God. On the healing path we set boundaries to protect ourselves, but on this path we also can embrace God's love.

Knowing about the healing path and choosing the hope it offers is powerful, but staying on the healing path is divine. Hope says, "I can go on." Hope insists, "I will find a way." Hope echoes, "I will not quit." When the darkness of night surrounds us and we feel all alone, hope allows us to endure into the light of a new day. Hope gives us the inner courage to continue to move forward regardless of what our loved ones choose to do. With hope we can improve today and look for an even better tomorrow. Because of hope, we are able to stay connected with those who can strengthen us, support us, and give us encouragement.

With hope we educate our children directly, sensitively, and regularly about sexual matters with the goal of keeping their perspectives in line with God's will. Moving in this direction gives us hope that our posterity will learn self-mastery. "We believe all things, we hope all things, we have endured many things, and hope to be able to endure all things" (A of F 13).

Where there is hope, there is eventual healing. Where there is hope, Christ is present. Knowing that Christ is at our side gives us hope. Elder Jeffrey R. Holland reminds us:

> *Much of the comfort I am speaking of comes from the Savior's power to heal—to heal the wounds of life or of sorrow or, where necessary, of trans-*

gression. . . . Most of the healing I am speaking of is not necessarily that of administering to the physically sick. . . . No, what I refer to are those rending, wrenching illnesses of the soul that need to be healed but may be quite personal—some burden held deep inside, some weariness that is not always particularly obvious to the rest of the world (Ensign, Apr. 1998, 20–21).

CHAPTER OBJECTIVES

At the conclusion of this chapter you should—

1. Know why hope is so vital to your healing and your loved one's healing.
2. Know the importance of building hope by providing sex education to your children and being aware of appropriate times and settings where this may be done.
3. Recognize that providing appropriate sex education to your children is an ongoing stewardship from the time they are toddlers. It continues through their teenage years, through courtship, and is especially important prior to marriage. It may even continue long after they marry.
4. Realize why it is important to be hopeful and realistic about your loved one's progress and your own progress.

WHAT IS HOPE?

Hope is believing that we can be healed. Because hope is positive, it gives us the motivation and determination to continue to try. Hope allows us to approach and then become committed to the healing process.

Elder Neal A. Maxwell defined hope:

Real hope keeps us "anxiously engaged" in good causes even when they appear to be losing causes on the mortal scoreboard (see D&C 58:27). Likewise, real hope is much more than wishful musing. It stiffens, not slackens, the spiritual spine. Hope is serene, not giddy, eager without being naive, and pleasantly steady without being smug. Hope is realistic anticipation which takes the form of a determination—not only to survive adversity but, moreover, to "endure . . . well" to the end (D&C 121:8) (Ensign, Nov. 1998, 62).

Elder Maxwell detailed several important truths regarding the effects of hope. Take a moment to ponder each of them and then record how you can apply them in your own life:

"Real hope keeps us 'anxiously engaged' in good causes even when they appear to be losing causes on the mortal scoreboard" (see D&C 58:27).

_____

_____

_____

_____

"It stiffens, not slackens, the spiritual spine."

_____

_____

_____

_____

"Hope is serene, not giddy, eager without being naive, and pleasantly steady without being smug."

_____

_____

_____

_____

"Hope is realistic anticipation which takes the form of a determination—not only to survive adversity but, moreover, to 'endure . . . well to the end'" (D&C 121:8).

_____

_____

_____

_____

How do we obtain hope? Elder M. Russell Ballard explained: "As we trust in God and His plan for our happiness with all our hearts and lean not unto our own understanding (see Prov. 3:5), hope is born. Hope grows out of faith and gives meaning and purpose to all we do" (*Ensign,* May 1995, 23–24).

Where do you place your trust? How can you develop greater hope?

God wants us to have hope about our healing. Hope lifts us to greater heights. Despair is from Satan—a downward spiral that can lead to deep discouragement and even depression. Instead of looking back at what might have been, God would have us press forward in faith.

Hope: A belief that healing is possible and can happen to me.

Despair: A pessimistic, hopeless attitude that allows me to stay in the victim's role.

Words of hope:	Words of despair:
Ambition	Defeat
Aspiration	Cynicism
Belief	Disbelief
Gain	Loss
Confidence	Doubt
Desire	Hopelessness
Reachable Goals	Failure
Motivation	Pessimism

Commitment to Healing

In addition to hope, our commitment to healing is paramount. Here are some comments from others:

"I'm going to try really hard over the next few months to heal from this pain."

"I want to stay focused so I can get through this problem."

"I think I can get through this."

Even though these statements sound like these individuals want to heal from the pain, how high is their commitment?

_____

_____

_____

How high is your commitment to heal from the hurt caused by your loved one's behavior?

_____

_____

_____

Our commitment to heal is vital. Here is one woman's comment: "I'll do whatever it takes to get peace of mind and assurance from the Lord that I am doing the right thing." Notice the difference in her level of commitment compared to the ones above. She is willing to do whatever it takes to heal. President Joseph Fielding Smith taught, "I've learned from my own experience that when you want to change, really want to change, you can do it" (*New Era*, Jan. 1971, 5).

What does "whatever it takes" really mean to us? A diligent effort regarding prayer, fasting, and scripture study is always necessary for healing. We may need to consider our relationships with others and make necessary improvements. It may mean we meet with a counselor on a regular basis and apply therapeutic techniques in our lives. All these elements of healing indicate that we are giving up our will, surrendering our trials, striving to overcome our weaknesses, and learning to rely more on the Savior.

Will we get discouraged along the way? Certainly! We will not stay discouraged, however, because we will not be alone. From the *Book of Mormon,* Ammon recounts: "Now when our hearts were depressed, and we were about to turn back, behold, the Lord comforted us, and said: Go amongst thy brethren, the Lamanites, and bear with patience thine afflictions, and I will give unto you success" (Alma 26:27).

🕮 How can you apply this scripture to your healing process?

_____

_____

_____

_____

_____

The Lord will comfort us and give us success too! Often the healing comes after we have done all that we can do and are momentarily discouraged and about to give up. This is the defining moment. At this very "edge of the cliff" moment, the desire for comfort may come along with a measure of healing, if we have truly borne with patience our afflictions and are willing to continue the healing process.

🕮 How has the Lord comforted you? Think and ponder about a specific situation.

_____

_____

_____

_____

_____

As we continue our healing, we want to take positive steps to help our children who may still be living at home understand the spiritual aspects of sexuality as well as the practical aspects. In addition, we still may have influence with our children who are married and away from home and may want to share some of these proactive steps with them so they can be better prepared to teach our grandchildren.

PARENTS' RESPONSIBILITY TO TEACH CHILDREN DIRECTLY AND PLAINLY

Children are less likely to become involved with compulsive sexual behaviors if parents teach them while they are young a spiritual perspective about their bodies and how they function. Our hope grows that the next generation will develop the proper attitudes and desires as we teach them diligently and appropriately about sex. This does not mean a one-time teaching session.

As parents, we have a stewardship to teach sex education to our children during all their growing-up years. No one is better suited to teach them than we are. Teaching our children and answering their questions regarding their bodies builds a foundation for a relationship where they are more likely to come to us when they have questions later in life.

As parents, we should try to provide sex education to our children from the time they are toddlers through courtship, to engagement, and just prior to marriage. The book *Gospel Principles* shares this insight:

> *We can begin teaching our children to have proper attitudes toward their bodies when they are very young. If we will talk to our children frankly but reverently, using the correct names for the parts and functions of their bodies, they will grow up without unnecessary embarrassment concerning their bodies. Children are naturally curious. They want to know how their bodies work. They want to know where babies come from. If we answer all such questions immediately and clearly so that they can understand us, they will continue to come to us with their questions. However, if we answer them so that they feel embarrassed, rejected, or dissatisfied, they will probably go to someone else with their questions and perhaps get incorrect ideas and improper attitudes (237).*

Some of our loved ones are in the courtship stage of life and need specific guidelines. We can share the following guidelines with any of our children or grandchildren who may be courting.

GUIDELINES FOR COURTSHIP

During the college-age years and beyond, most young adults no longer engage in "friendship dating"—getting to know the opposite sex—but rather "courtship dating"—seriously considering the person for marriage. These guidelines apply to anyone who is courting.

Set a Curfew

During courtship set a reasonable time to return home and then stick with it. Plan your dates so they will end by your curfew. Unplanned dates can lead to trouble. If your physical relationship begins to get out of control, end the date immediately and return home early.

The "Four on the Floor" Principle

Avoid compromising positions. This can usually be done by keeping your feet and your date's feet on the floor. Getting in a reclining position and lying on the couch or on the floor together usually increases the temptation and the likelihood of becoming inappropriately intimate.

Stay in Public Settings

Choose places to visit where others are usually nearby, such as walking together in the park, sitting on a park bench, or talking in the living room at home. In such settings two people can share appropriate thoughts and feelings and still have the safeguard of having others nearby.

Limit Your Physical Expression

Limit your kissing and hugging. In most cases a single goodnight kiss still displays affection but greatly reduces the risk of having things get out of control. Out-of-control kissing or making out is accompanied with out-of-control emotions and desires. Elder Joseph B. Wirthlin reminds us of how Satan tries to trap us:

> *Perhaps Satan would tempt us further by suggesting that going a little too far in our physical affection with a boyfriend or girlfriend is not so serious. However, our physical affection as we date, and even when we are engaged, must be limited to that which is conservative and wholesome—behavior far different than that which is commonly portrayed in the media of our day* (*New Era,* May 1988, 7).

Children are more likely to develop a healthy attitude and be more comfortable with sexual intimacy after marriage if we give them age-appropriate guidelines and teach them in a positive way about their bodies and the procreative powers that enable us to bring new life into the world. We should warn our children early on about pornography and how it distorts reality and diminishes the wholesomeness of sexual intimacy.

Warn Children About Pornography

We need to teach our children that Satan's goal is to distort our viewpoints about our bodies and the opposite sex. Pornography is one of the most common tactics he uses to trap his victims. Elder David B. Haight encouraged parents to teach children about the harmful, addictive effects of pornography:

> *Parents, discuss with your children of appropriate age, and in sensitive ways, the harmful effects and addictive nature of such material. Rigidly monitor the selection of television programs, movies, videocassettes, music, and other forms of entertainment for your family. Let us never, by purchasing these damaging materials, contribute to the financial success of those who deal in this material.*
>
> *We would encourage you to foster in your homes a love of knowledge through uplifting literature; wholesome books; selective movies and television; classical and exemplary popular music; entertainment that uplifts and edifies the spirit and mind* (*Ensign*, Nov. 1984, 72).

Many Church leaders have emphasized parents' responsibilities to teach their children about all forms of pornography. Elder M. Russell Ballard counseled:

> *As our children grow, they need information taught by parents more directly and plainly about what is and is not appropriate. Parents need to teach children to avoid any pornographic photographs or stories. Children and youth need to know from parents that pornography of any kind is a tool of the devil; and if anyone flirts with it, it has the power to addict, dull, and even destroy the human spirit. They need to be taught not to use vulgar language and never to use the Lord's name in vain. Crude jokes overheard should never be repeated. Teach family members not to listen to music that celebrates the sensual. Talk to them plainly about sex and the teaching of the gospel regarding chastity. Let this information come from parents in the home in an appropriate way. All family members need to know the rules and be fortified spiritually so they can keep them. And when mistakes are made, the wondrous Atonement of the Lord Jesus Christ must be understood and accepted so that through the complete and sometimes difficult*

process of repentance, forgiveness and continued hope for the future can be obtained. We must never give up our individual and family quest for eternal life (Ensign, May 1999, 86).

SAFEGUARDING OUR HOMES, PROTECTING OUR CHILDREN

We can do many things to safeguard our homes and protect our loved ones—particularly our innocent children—from the harmful effects of pornography. Elder Russell M. Ballard gave us the following suggestions:

1. *We need to hold family councils and decide what our media standards are going to be.*

2. *We need to spend enough quality time with our children that we are consistently the main influence in their lives, not the media or any peer group.*

3. *We need to make good media choices ourselves and set good examples for our children.*

4. *We need to limit the amount of time our children watch TV or play video games or use the Internet each day. Virtual reality must not become their reality.*

5. *We need to use Internet filters and TV programming locks to prevent our children from "chancing upon" things they should not see.*

6. *We need to have TVs and computers in a much-used common room in the home, not in a bedroom or a private place.*

7. *We need to take time to watch appropriate media with our children and discuss with them how to make choices that will uplift and build rather than degrade and destroy (Ensign, Nov. 2003, 18-19).*

APPLICATION TO SPOUSES

With their cooperation, we can even use some of these guidelines with a spouse who struggles with compulsive sexual behaviors. One couple decided they would have a password to get on the Internet that only the wife knew until the husband could develop more self-control. He said:

My wife suggested that she set up a password that only she knew so I could not be online unless she was present. Even though I did not want to and felt a little childish for having to do so, I agreed because at the time I had almost no self-control. There was part of me that did not want to give up the access to pornography. Not being able to get on the Internet when I was alone at home was very important to my recovery from pornography.

Our loved ones definitely need to overcome their own compulsions, but during their initial healing stages they usually need firm boundaries in order to give up the "drug of lust." Often they do not have the confidence, determination, or willpower to set their own boundaries and stick to them. We can assist by setting our own boundaries and asking for their support, clearly letting our loved ones know what we expect. We expect that they will commit *not* to use the computer when no one else is at home. We expect that they *will* meet regularly with the bishop to sincerely go through the repentance process. We expect that they *will* seek professional help and follow it.

In some cases, we will need to ask our loved ones, even though they may be reluctant, to support our decisions, especially when we feel prompted by the Spirit to do so. If our loved ones choose not to meet our expectations, then appropriate consequences should be implemented. We must then follow through with the consequences that we have agreed upon. For example, we may agree not to have the Internet for a while if the boundaries are crossed regarding the Internet password and using the service only when someone else is home. We also want to be aware of when our children may be at risk of exposure to offensive material when using the Internet and take the necessary preventive measures.

DANGER SIGNS AND SAFETY TIPS

We should be very observant and watch for behavior in children that might be out of the ordinary. At the FBI's website, there is a section entitled "What Are Signs That Your Child Might Be at Risk On-line?"

- *Your child spends large amounts of time on-line, especially at night.*

- *You find pornography on your child's computer.*

- *Your child receives phone calls from men you don't know or is making calls, sometimes long distance, to numbers you don't recognize.*

- *Your child receives mail, gifts, or packages from someone you don't know.*

- *Your child turns the computer monitor off or quickly changes the screen on the monitor when you come into the room.*

- *Your child becomes withdrawn from the family.*

- *Your child is using an on-line account belonging to someone else. (U.S. Department of Justice/FBI, www.fbi.gov)*

Here are some other suggestions from the same website on what to teach our children about using the Internet:

There are some very important things that you need to keep in mind when you're on your computer at home or at school.

1. *First, remember never to give out personal information such as your name, home address, school name, or telephone number in a chat room or on bulletin boards. Also, never send a picture of yourself to someone you chat with on the computer without your parent's permission.*

2. *Never write to someone who has made you feel uncomfortable or scared.*

3. *Do not meet someone or have them visit you without the permission of your parents.*

4. *Tell your parents right away if you read anything on the Internet that makes you feel uncomfortable.*

5. *Remember that people online may not be who they say they are. Someone who says that "she" is a "twelve-year-old girl" could really be an older man.*

The above guidelines are for children, but many suggestions are important reminders for us as well. The Spirit can also tell us when our children or grandchildren are in danger.

WAYS TO HELP LOVED ONES

We want to find ways that genuinely help our loved ones. We do not want to enable them to stay in their compulsive behaviors. Here are some suggestions that have worked well for others:

- Strive to keep consistency in life. Stick to a regular routine and schedule.

- When you see progress, let him know that you appreciate the effort he is making. Compliment him for even the slightest sign of improvement.

- Avoid preaching or lecturing to your loved one about his behavior.

- Avoid giving rewards, incentives, or bribes to change his behavior.

- Allow your loved one to experience the natural consequences of his behavior. Avoid trying to protect them or minimizing the consequences in any way. If a loved one loses a job because he was looking at pornography while at work, let him find another job himself. You can still be supportive but not take over his responsibility to find work. Let him experience the full consequences of his behavior.

- Avoid inappropriate punishments for his behavior, but let the natural consequences play out.

- Let your loved one be responsible for his own duties and obligations by setting and keeping boundaries. He may inappropriately feel that you are punishing him when you hold a boundary. Only you can determine when your response to his behavior is vindictive or appropriate.

- Avoid threatening him. If an appropriate boundary is necessary, simply follow through in setting that boundary without making threats.

- Avoid making excuses for your loved one's lack of responsibility. Let him tell others why he was late or why a deadline was not met. Do not cover for him.

- Realize that your loved one's compulsive sexual behaviors have been going on for some time, and it will take him time to change. Even if he really wants to change, it will still take time.

- Accept the fact that patterns of behavior do not automatically change just because we want them to, and the likelihood that a loved one will lapse is high.

- Accept the fact that a lapse is part of the healing process; your loved one is not likely to learn how to surrender the "drug of lust" all at once.

- When your loved one "acts out," wait until emotions have calmed down before talking with him about the episode.

- Talk honestly and openly with your loved one. Tell him how his behavior makes you feel. Focus on his behavior and your feelings about the behavior. Explain in detail how his behavior affects you and the family.

- Reassure your loved one of your love for him if you still feel love. Sometimes the trauma of continual emotional abuse and the "acting out" by a spouse may destroy the love we once felt for him. Sometimes love wanes. Make it clear that you dislike and will not accept his compulsive behaviors.

- Invite your loved one to participate with the family. This may include family home evening, scripture study, household chores, and vacations. (An exception may occur when your loved one has been involved with child abuse and you will have children present.)

- Ask for the Lord's help to remain patient, encouraging, and calm—even when it is not easy.

Even though our loved ones may choose not to change right now, we can still be comforted. The Lord will not leave us alone. In the meantime, it is important for us to find some common ground with our loved ones.

COMMON GROUND

Often when our loved ones are engaged in compulsive sexual behaviors, we have much less in common with them. We may no longer have the gospel in common since our loved ones have chosen to stray. In many cases bringing up the gospel or talking about repentance may, for the time being, drive a wedge in our relationship. When our loved ones are single adults or married children who do not live at home, it may be even more difficult to find common ground.

In what ways can we reach our loved ones? Perhaps they will respond later to the Spirit and initiate a gospel conversation, but for now many of them may be apathetic or have little interest in the Church.

What can we do to stay connected with them even though we have few things in common? One mother who had three out of her four children fall away from the Church shared:

> *Without question we love each other, but sometimes finding common ground is difficult. I go back and forth with my feelings—missing them and wanting to be a part of their lives, yet being relieved at not always having to participate in their lives. It is painful to remember the dreams I used to have for them. But I don't want to torture them or me with my disappointment, so I work hard at living my life in the present instead of the past* (Ensign, Feb. 2004, 44).

Finding common ground is not easy, but we can pray for help and direction. One mother who prayed endlessly to reach her wayward daughter felt impressed to call her every week. Even though they lived in the same city, they did not regularly talk with each other. The mother recounted:

> At first I was so nervous and scared. I knew I was impressed to call her every week, but I had no idea what I was going to talk about. She was so far away from the Church it seemed that we had very little in common. The first week went fine because it did not seem out of the ordinary for me to call. The second week was okay, but on the third week my daughter rudely said, "Why are you calling so often?" This was hard to take and before I could even think of a response I blurted out, "Because I love you!" The phone went silent. This was a very awkward moment for the two of us, but we got through it. I continued my weekly calls for nearly two years before there were some very slight changes in my daughter's attitude toward me. I'm not sure why she had become so hateful towards me, but I could not dwell on that and had to focus on what I was inspired to do now. I believe the weekly calls made a difference in her life. Today, nearly five years later, she married the man she was living with, they went through the repentance process, and have been sealed in the temple.

This mother followed her inspiration to call her daughter every week, and her calls impacted her daughter and helped to bring about change. It will not be easy to find common ground with our loved ones who have strayed, but we can, through prayer, seek guidance and follow through with the inspiration we receive.

After pondering what common ground may exist with your loved one, record your impressions and consider when to begin implementing this step:

It would be wonderful if all of our loved ones responded in a similar positive way as this woman's daughter did, but many will not.

How does it make us feel when we see someone else's loved one making changes and repenting, but not ours? This is a single mother's viewpoint as she continues to show love to her three less-active children:

> *It has sometimes been difficult for me in testimony meetings to listen to faith-promoting stories about a miraculous healing, a surprising conversion, or a son or daughter who came back to church. I could become cynical if I allowed myself. What about all the righteous people who die tragically? Faith doesn't always cure. And why does Heavenly Father seem to answer other parents' prayers and not mine?*
>
> *But I choose not to be cynical. Instead I rejoice with my brothers and sisters when their prayers are answered, and I accept the fact that faith in the Lord Jesus Christ is much more than being able to pray down a miracle from heaven. In the final analysis, such faith is really faithfulness. What really matters is that I remain true to the knowledge and testimony I have and that I stay open to the growing and learning process by acknowledging my limitations and seeking divine guidance (Ensign, Feb. 2004, 48).*

Another mother shared:

> *My son has chosen to live in the gay lifestyle. He moved out and got an apartment with another man. I did not feel comfortable going to his apart-ment. After talking to my counselor, discussing some options, and following the Spirit, I felt directed to invite my son to go to lunch with me every Friday. We both enjoy eating out. This is one thing we have in common. He is far away from the teachings of the Church and appears to have given up his testimony. It does not do any good to talk about the Church or repentance. It puts a deeper wedge between us. For now, I will go to lunch with him. I will try to empathize with him, even though I do not agree with his lifestyle. I can begin to see life through his eyes even though I do not have to agree with his viewpoint or behavior. We can still have a relationship with each other and find other things we have in common.*

For now, there has been no change in this son's behavior or negative attitude toward the Church. The son is accountable and responsible for his behavior. The mother has decided to focus on staying in touch with her son and being there for him.

When a loved one no longer lives at home, what are the benefits of staying in touch with him or her? What are some ways you could you stay in touch with him or her?

_____

_____

_____

_____

_____

_____

Elder Neal A. Maxwell reminds us: "Even yesterday's righteous experience does not guarantee us against tomorrow's relapse. A few who have had supernal spiritual experiences have later fallen. Hence, enduring well to the end assumes real significance, and we are at risk till the end!" (*Ensign,* July 1982, 52).

Where are you now with your healing compared to where you want to be?

_____

_____

_____

_____

_____

What areas of your life need more focus and attention?

_____

_____

_____

_____

🌿 Are you really striving to be truthful with yourself and others? Where can you make improvements?

_____

_____

_____

_____

_____

_____

_____

_____

_____

_____

Elder Marvin J. Ashton taught:

> When one considers the bad feeling and the unpleasantness caused by contention, it is well to ask, "Why do I participate?" If we are really honest with ourselves, our answers may be something like: "When I argue and am disagreeable, I do not have to change myself. It gives me a chance to get even." "I am unhappy and I want others to be miserable too." "I can feel self-righteous. In this way I get my ego built up." "I don't want others to forget how much I know!" Whatever the real reason, it is important to recognize that we choose our behavior. At the root of this issue is the age-old problem of pride. "Only by pride cometh contention" (Prov. 13:10) (*Ensign,* May 1978, 9).

Being honest with ourselves means recognizing that other issues may be related to our unhappiness and relational issues. Improving ourselves by learning and implementing communication skills, anger management, stress management, and goal setting enhances overall healing. We deal with our own emotional issues and seek guidance and direction through the Spirit in resolving them.

When was the last time you read your patriarchal blessing? Carefully consider the problem you are currently striving to overcome, and then re-read your patriarchal blessing. Does your blessing contain possible answers and solutions that may have previously gone unnoticed?

📝 The same questions apply to your study of the scriptures. As you read the scriptures, relate them to your own personal challenges. What inspiration and revelation have you received during your scripture study time?

_____

_____

_____

_____

_____

Even though we can obtain outside help, we should keep in mind the counsel of Elder Boyd K. Packer regarding our emotional problems: "Ultimately it is the member who must solve them" (*Ensign,* May 1978, 92).

HOPE FOR PARENTS OF WAYWARD CHILDREN

The Prophet Joseph Smith declared—and he never taught a more comforting doctrine—that the eternal sealings of faithful parents and the divine promises made to them for valiant service in the Cause of Truth would save not only themselves, but likewise their posterity. Though some of the sheep may wander, the eye of the Shepherd is upon them, and sooner or later they will feel the tentacles of Divine Providence reaching out after them and drawing them back to the fold. Either in this life or the life to come, they will return. They will have to pay their debt to justice; they will suffer for their sins; and may tread a thorny path; but if it leads them at last, like the penitent Prodigal, to a loving and forgiving father's heart and home, the painful experience will not have been in vain. Pray for your careless and disobedient children; hold on to them with your faith. Hope on, trust on, till you see the salvation of God (Orson F. Whitney, *Conference Report,* Apr. 1929, 110).

President Brigham Young taught:

Let the father and mother, who are members of this Church and Kingdom, take a righteous course, and strive with all their might never to do a wrong, but to do good all their lives; if they have one child or one hundred children, if they conduct themselves towards them as they should, binding them to the Lord by their faith and prayers, I care not where those children go, they are bound up to their parents by an everlasting tie, and no power of earth or hell can separate them from their parents in eternity; they will return again to the fountain from whence they sprang (quoted in Joseph Fielding Smith, *Doctrines of Salvation*, comp. Bruce R. McConkie, 2:90-91).

President Lorenzo Snow gave us hope for ourselves and loved ones:

If you succeed in passing through these trials and afflictions and receive a resurrection, you will, by the power of the Priesthood, work and labor, as the Son of God has, until you get all your sons and daughters in the path of exaltation and glory. This is just as sure as that the sun rose this morning over yonder mountains. Therefore, mourn not because all your sons and daughters do not follow in the path that you have marked out to them, or give heed to your counsels. Inasmuch as we succeed in securing eternal glory, and stand as saviors, and as kings and priests to our God, we will save our posterity (*Collected Discourses*, comp. Brian H. Stuy, 3:364).

Elder Boyd K. Packer reminds us that:

The measure of our success as parents . . . will not rest solely on how our children turn out. That judgment would be just only if we could raise our families in a perfectly moral environment, and that now is not possible.

It is not uncommon for responsible parents to lose one of their children, for a time, to influences over which they have no control. They agonize over rebellious sons or daughters. They are puzzled over why they are so helpless when they have tried so hard to do what they should.

It is my conviction that those wicked influences one day will be overruled. . . . We cannot overemphasize the value of temple marriage, the binding ties of the sealing ordinance, and the standards of worthiness required of them. When parents keep the covenants they have made at the altar of the temple, their children will be forever bound to them (*Ensign*, May 1992, 68).

WHAT HAVE WE BECOME?

Our hope will continue as we accept the reality that change in behavior for us and for our loved ones will take some time. President Hinckley reminds us: "Those changes may not be measurable in a day or a week or a month. Resolutions are quickly made and quickly forgotten. But, in a year from now, if we are doing better than we have done in the past, then the efforts of these days will not have been in vain" (*Ensign,* Nov. 2000, 88). This is truly a message of hope and comfort.

Elder Neal A. Maxwell expressed, "We fall short. If we stumble, let us arise and continue the climb. The Lord will bless us because we are possessed of truths about 'things as they really are, and . . . things as they really will be' (Jacob 4:13). These truths beckon us, even in our imperfections, to be better" (*Ensign,* Sept. 1998, 12).

We should strive to be *patient with our healing.* Change is a process, and patience is required. Elder Henry B. Eyring explained this process: "In time we can become an example of a disciple who is born again through the Atonement. It may be gradual. It may be hard for us to discern in ourselves. But it will be real" (*Ensign,* May 2002, 28).

The Lord sets the finish line for each of us. This line is customized based on our abilities, talents, and the intent of our hearts. Because of His perfect love and mercy, He will adjust the finish line to our abilities when we have embraced the Atonement, repented of our sins, and are focused toward eternal life.

The good news is that through the Atonement of Christ we can all receive the same eternal blessing. Elder Jeffrey R. Holland stated, "I know that if we will be faithful, there is a perfectly tailored robe of righteousness ready and waiting for everyone, robes 'made white in the blood of the Lamb'" (*Ensign,* May 2002, 64).

You have spent a considerable amount of time completing this book. The key for continued healing is applying the principles that you have learned each day of your life. The daily application of principles is the key. Speaking about this vital step, President Gordon B. Hinckley remarked:

> *All of us have been edified. The test will come in the application of the teachings given. If, hereafter, we are a little more kind, if we are a little more neighborly, if we have drawn nearer to the Savior, with a more firm resolution to follow His teachings and His example, then this conference will have been a wonderful success* (*Ensign,* Nov. 2000, 88).

While on the journey to healing, what have we become? The Prophet Joseph Smith was commanded to translate the Bible. That was the beginning. One might suppose the ending would be to finish the translation, but the Lord did not require a complete translation of the Bible. In the process of translating the Bible, Joseph Smith received eight powerful revelations that are vitally important to the doctrine of the restored gospel of Jesus Christ. Eight sections of the Doctrine and Covenants are the result of revelations received during the process of Joseph's efforts to translate the Bible! The question I've pondered is this: What did we (as a Church) receive or become in the process of the Prophet Joseph Smith translating the Bible?

At times we focus too much on the end results (our loved ones' overcoming their compulsions) rather than what we should be learning and becoming in the process. We often keep track of how many chapters we have completed in our healing process and look with impatience to the last chapter. We focus more on tangible lists rather than on virtues acquired. We often become discouraged when we have to stop and rewrite a chapter. Consider this: It may be more realistic and more consistent with gospel principles to track our healing progress by the virtues we have acquired along the way. Are *we* more teachable, humble, or sincere? Do *we* pray with more intent? Have *we* decided to turn our will over to God? Can *we* extend more charity to others? If the answer is yes, then have *we* not made progress in overcoming *our own* obsessions or compulsions?

Elder Dallin H. Oaks expressed: "It is not enough for anyone just to go through the motions. The commandments, ordinances, and covenants of the gospel are not a list of deposits required to be made in some heavenly account. The gospel of Jesus Christ is a plan that shows us how to become what our Heavenly Father desires us to become" (*Ensign,* Nov. 2000, 32).

CONCLUSION

Our goals should cause us to stretch, but they must also be attainable. Mortality is for progression, not perfection. In mortality, we strive for *more* holiness, not *perfect* holiness. We work to achieve more striving within, not perfect striving. We pray for more patience, not perfect patience. And, yes, we can all benefit by having more sorrow for sin. Here are the words of the hymn "More Holiness Give Me" (*Hymns,* 131):

> *More holiness give me,*
> *More strivings within,*
> *More patience in suff'ring,*
> *More sorrow for sin,*
> *More faith in my Savior,*
> *More sense of his care,*
> *More joy in his service,*
> *More purpose in prayer.*

More gratitude give me,
More trust in the Lord,
More pride in his glory,
More hope in his word,
More tears for his sorrows,
More pain at his grief,
More meekness in trial,
More praise for relief.

More purity give me,
More strength to o'ercome,
More freedom from earthstains,
More longing for home.
More fit for the kingdom,
More used would I be,
More blessed and holy
More, Savior, like thee.

We can become more! What joy and happiness! Yes, we have a purpose here in mortality, and by surrendering our trials and staying on the healing path, we can reach what the scriptures teach: "And men are, that they might have joy" (2 Ne. 2:25).

On April 6, 2000, I was in Oklahoma City on a business trip. I had a recommend to watch the dedication of the Palmyra New York Temple by satellite. I arrived at the Oklahoma City Stake Center about forty-five minutes prior to the beginning of the service and sat on the back row.

About fifteen minutes before the dedication began, a family with five children walked in. They chose to sit in the pew just in front of me. There was not enough room for the entire family, and so two of the sons sat back with me. The one son who sat next to me had Down's Syndrome and appeared to be in his late twenties. I smiled at him and shook his hand. I told him my name and asked for his. I had some Life Savers, and so I gave him one. He was now my friend.

The service began and I shifted on the bench to get a little more comfortable. Then I leaned forward and rested my hands and arms on my legs. My friend did the same. A few minutes later I leaned back and so did he. I had been on my feet most of the day teaching a seminar and my feet were sore and tired. I removed my shoes and so did he. When I crossed my legs, he crossed his legs. When I uncrossed my legs, he did the same. When I smiled at him, he smiled back at me. He followed every move I made, but suddenly I realized that I was the one who wanted to be like him.

He did not ask me what I did for a living or what make of car I drove. He did not ask me whether I was rich or poor. He did not ask what positions I had held in the Church or whether I was married or single. He accepted me just as I was, and he was just himself—totally open and sincere. No pretense. No facade. No front of any kind.

I was in a sacred meeting witnessing the dedication of a temple and sitting next to an angel. I wanted to be innocent like him. I wanted to be clean and whole. I wanted to be less judgmental. I wanted to just be a friend to those around like he was. I wanted people to feel the Spirit just by sitting next to me as I did sitting next to him. He followed every move I made, yet, how I wanted to be like *him*. And then the thought came to me that through the Atonement of Christ I can be all of those things and have a nature as divine as my friend's.

I hope that this book has not weighed you down, but instead has given you hope. I feel much like Mormon who said, "My son, be faithful in Christ; and may not the things which I have written grieve thee, to weigh thee down unto death; but may Christ lift thee up, and may his sufferings and death, and the showing his body unto our fathers, and his mercy and long-suffering, and the hope of his glory and of eternal life, rest in your mind forever" (Moro. 9:25).

President Gordon B. Hinckley encouraged: "Let us all try to stand a little taller, rise a little higher, be a little better. Make the extra effort. You will be happier. You will know a new satisfaction, a new gladness in your heart" (*Ensign,* Sept. 1999, 5).

Elder Howard W. Hunter said, "Sooner or later, and we pray sooner than later, everyone will acknowledge that Christ's way is not only the right way, but ultimately the only way to hope and joy" (*Ensign,* May 1993, 65).

Thank you and may your joy be full!

REVIEW OF PRINCIPLES

How would you define hope?

_____

_____

_____

_____

What are some specific things you have done that have given you hope now and for the future?

_____

_____

_____

_____

_____

What steps can you take to increase your hope by providing sex education to your children?

_____

_____

_____

_____

_____

How can you help to provide a safe environment for your children so they are not exposed to inappropriate material on the Internet or other sources?

_____

_____

_____

_____

_____

What are some areas where you can establish some common ground with loved ones who have strayed?

_____

_____

_____

_____

_____

What have you become through this trial with your loved one?

_____

_____

_____

_____

_____

_____

_____

What are some skills or techniques you have learned in this chapter that you will try to implement in your relationships with yourself and others in the next thirty days?

_____

_____

_____

_____

_____

_____

_____

_____

What is the single most important principle or concept you have learned from this chapter?

_____

_____

_____

_____

_____

_____

With whom can you share this important principle or concept in the next week?

_____

_____

_____

_____

Calmness Break

Humor can diffuse anger and other negative emotions; humor can help us cope with the stress of our loved ones' choices and increase our hope. Sometimes it is healthy to stop and just laugh at ourselves and some of the choices we make. We may benefit by reading the funny papers on a regular basis or by reading one or two appropriate joke books. We can keep a file of clean humor to review when we feel stressed. There is nothing quite like a good laugh. It helps us get rid of tension, feel more relaxed, and see our situation from a new, more hopeful perspective.

How can humor help you during your healing?

_____

_____

_____

_____

_____

_____

MESSAGES OF HOPE

Elder Jeffrey R. Holland: "My declaration is that this is precisely what the gospel of Jesus Christ offers us, especially in times of need. There is help. There is happiness. There really is light at the end of the tunnel. It is the Light of the World, the Bright and Morning Star, the 'light that is endless, that can never be darkened.' It is the very Son of God Himself. In loving praise far beyond Romeo's reach, we say, 'What light through yonder window breaks?' It is the return of hope, and Jesus is the Sun. To any who may be struggling to see that light and find that hope, I say: Hold on. Keep trying. God loves you. Things will improve. Christ comes to you in His 'more excellent ministry' with a future of 'better promises.' He is your 'high priest of good things to come'" (*Ensign,* Nov. 1999, 36).

President James E. Faust: "Who are good parents? They are those who have lovingly, prayerfully, and earnestly tried to teach their children by example and precept 'to pray, and to walk uprightly before the Lord.' This is true even though some of their children are disobedient or worldly. Children come into this world with their own distinct spirits and personality traits. Some children 'would challenge any set of parents under any set of circumstances. . . . Perhaps there are others who would bless the lives of, and be a joy to, almost any father or mother.' Successful parents are those who have sacrificed and struggled to do the best they can in their own family circumstances" (*Ensign,* May 2003, 61).

Addiction Recovery Programs

LDS-Based Support Groups

LDS Family Services Addiction Recovery Program. For information on these groups, contact your local LDS Family Services agency or call LDS Family Services at (800) 453-3860, extension 2-3646.

Finding a Group in Your Area

Many groups offer separate support groups for wives to attend while their husbands attend recovery groups. For a list of support groups in your area, check www.providentliving.org, click "Social And Emotional Strength," then click "Addiction Recovery Support Groups," or call your local LDS Family Services agency. Look for support groups, as these are designed for the wife whose husband is struggling with compulsive sexual behaviors.

Evergreen International Inc.
(support group for those struggling with same-sex attraction)
307 West 200 South, Suite 4006, Salt Lake City, UT 84101
phone: (800) 391-1000
website: www.evergreeninternational.org
email: info@evergreeninternational.org

Additional LDS Resources

For more information on compulsive sexual behaviors, check www.providentliving.org, click "Social And Emotional Strength," then click "Library of Helpful Information." Another helpful resource is BYU's website, www.byu.edu. From the home page, click on the "Search" link. Many helpful articles can be found on the topic of your choice; for example, abuse, pornography, or same-sex attraction.

Non-LDS Support Groups

Sexaholics Anonymous (615) 370-6062, P.O. Box 3565, Brentwood, TN 37024
website: www.sa.org

Index

A

through, 56; natural reaction, 57; lapses bring back, 71; to get out of, 87; diffuse, 90, 100; let go, 113; surrender, 114; may drive us away from God, 153; avoid double and triple, 162; walk through using FEET, 163; self-anger, 164; thoughts that fuel, 166; told myself to stay angry at Nephi, 168; tell myself to surrender, 169; letting go of, 170; victim of, 172; writing about it diffuses, 179; Atonement healed, 215; anger and the Atonement, 216; have a right to feel, 229; what level it climbs, 234; when it takes over the strength of reason leaves, 236; stunts our spiritual growth, 239; Prodigal Son, elder son's response, 245-248; slow to anger better than the mighty, 253; melted away, 259; support system, talk about our emotions, 273; participants may recognize in others, 275; not responsible for husband's, 302; pops up from time to time, 361; forgiveness cannot stay when anger present, 374; takes neither strength nor intelligence to brood, 376; cycle of physical abuse, 401; anger management, 443; humor can diffuse, 452

anguish Nephi's anguish because of brothers, 4; Lord can relieve anguish, 113; synonymous with pain, 213; thirteen years of anguish in marriage, 259; Alma suffers anguish for his sins, 371

answer(s) come at different times, vii; to "why me," 27; come when we ask "what" not "why," 28; for "what if's," 41; to "why did this happen," 50; may never come for some questions, 74; about God's love, 96; from prayers, 135; from scriptures, 136; come a piece at a time, 149; move forward despite not having, 213; are small and simple, 220; not wise to demand, 244; from scriptures, 326, 381; listening for, 346; problem with seeking immediate, 355; in the words of the Brethren, 356; from prophets, 384; live a life worthy of, 415

anxiety due to exercises in this book, ix, 207; wrongly using anger, 23; part of depression, 25; taking action will reduce, 37; trust in God to reduce, 127; break into small pieces, 128; caused by impatience, 155; discuss feelings to reduce, 164; caused by controlling spouse, 194; from focusing on "if only," 345; before seeking counseling, 405; at thought of leaving relationship, 406; due to physical abuse, 407

apologizing part of the abuse cycle, 401

apostle(s) Article of Faith 6, xiii; trust the words of, 135; submit to the words of, 213; inspired counsel can direct our lives, 303; study and ponder words on intimacy, 307; receive spiritual help from, 340; part of Christ's committee, 353

appease Atonement appeases justice, 8; lust is hunger to appease an appetite, 64; appease husband by dressing sexy, 102; lie to appease us, 106; lack of boundaries and appeasing loved one, 289

appetites part of compulsive behaviors cycle, 54; lust is gratifying personal appetites, 310

appraisal(s) preparing for divorce with, 421

Article of Faith 1, xii

Article of Faith 2, xii

Article of Faith 3, xiii, 206, 371

Article of Faith 4, xii, xiii, 146, 206, 340

Article of Faith 5, xiii, 266

Article of Faith 6, xiii, 340

Article of Faith 7, xiii, 146, 206, 266, 340

Article of Faith 8, xiii

Article of Faith 9, xiii, 340

Article of Faith 10, xii

Article of Faith 11, xii

Article of Faith 12, xiii, xiv, 281, 282, 398

Article of Faith 13, x, xiii, xiv, 281, 322, 418, 426

Son, father, and elder son's behaviors, 246; adjust our thinking to change, 252; do not accept or condone, 255; already paid through the Atonement, 261; loved ones responsible for, 275; dislike our behaviors, still love ourselves, 366; deciding whether to divorce worksheet, 413-415

beliefs changing to create healthier feelings, 206; irrational, 245, 249; correlate with divine perspective, 252; truth frees us from false, 253; about our loved ones' behaviors, 254; Satan's worldly, 325; take time to reaffirm, 380; emotional abuse due to insulting beliefs, 402

Benson, Ezra Taft promptly terminate temptations, 68; repentance is a subtle, sometimes imperceptible process, 81-82, 372; only Christ can change human nature, 114, 189; selfishness is a common face of pride, 114; becoming Christlike is a lifetime pursuit, 199; true fitness involves mental and spiritual, 235; self-control is mastering emotions, 265; certain blessings only found in scripture study, 333-334; discover strengths through prayer, 352; necking and petting, 387-388; warns against pornography, 389

betrayal, (ed), feel betrayed after discovery, vii, 71; trusting after betrayal is difficult, 98; how we view our situation, 197; lost trust due to betrayal, 310

Bible Dictionary Conversion, 153; Prayer, 341; mind of Christ and the wishes of Christ, 345

binocular "binocular vision" separates loved ones from behaviors, 230

birthday(s) remember birthdays of support group, 274; boy baptized by brother (not father) on birthday, 418

bishop build a strong support system with him, xiii; don't worry about what bishop will think, 3; best initial source for guidance, 5; times to disclose information to, 6; discussing situation makes it better, 35; choose to initiate appointments, 37; counsel with bishop when making divorce decision, 39; has spouse ever counseled with bishop, 69; how can bishop help in a lapse, 72; serious about changing if meeting with bishop, 83; when to involve bishop when confronting spouse, 108; part of diffusing fear, 121; contacting is important and urgent, 131; choose to meet with bishop even if loved one doesn't, 182; let bishop handle slip-ups, 187; story of woman whose brother was a bishop, 189; valuable resources for wandering loved ones, 266; seek counsel from, 267; help to make sound decisions, 268; counsel may be simple, 269; part of support system, 272; part of God's committee, 353; advice proved crucial, 382; seek counsel before divorce decision, 383; husband wanted to look good for the bishop by lying, 403; let bishop know about abuse, 404; make full disclosure regarding abuse, 410; draw upon ward family, 418

bitterness unwanted feelings, ix; due to lapse, 56, 71; is an emotional infection, 86; one of Satan's traps, 105; part of natural man, 115; surrender to the Lord, 145; may drive us away from God, 153; natural response to loved one, 158; stunts our spiritual growth, 169, 239; Atonement can cleanse from, 205; exercises in books may bring, 207; leaves a little at a time, 362; Alma removed from, 372; avoid to heal more quickly, 397

blame, blamed for what happened as a child, 10; for what spouse did, 52; not serious about change if continues to blame others, 83; directed at you from spouse, 98; husband blames wife for problems, 102; fear of being, 117; cannot blame others, 184; from Satan's committee, 349; reason why women stay in abusive relationships, 406

by spiritual boundaries, 303; can do
all things through Him, 318; learn of
Him through scriptures, 326; the Great
Healer, 338; knows us personally, 339;
connected to Him through prayer, 341;
becoming one with Him, 345; choose
His committee, 351; accepts our offering
as we try, 363; gives perfect love, 364;
can save all mankind, 371; strengthen
relationship to Him through forgiveness,
376; sees beyond the sins to the sinner,
385; promises complete forgiveness,
386; perfect match with His Atonement,
392; draw nearer to Him through sacred
music, 418; He brings hope, 426; allows
us to have a divine nature, 449

church we believe in same organization
as Primitive Church, xiii, 340; happens
despite going to church, 20; husband
held leadership positions, 21; membership placed at risk due to behaviors, 61;
serious about changing if living church
standards, 84; trust church leaders,
135; anger followed me even to church,
172; we both grew up in the Church,
180; husband relapsed while wife was
at church, 185; loved one serves in
Church and has problems, 191; feeling
inferior at church, 193; wife's children
cut themselves off from Church, 196;
helps us keep balance, 208; leaders have
ordained power to help us, 266; leaders
should reach out with love, 267; man
and woman are coequals in the Church,
290; offers help to the struggling, 357;
calling does not determine value, 364;
Alma tried to destroy the church, 369;
husband held a responsible calling at
church, 380; attendance helps those
struggling, 386; teachings and immorality, 387; can't be abusive and have
good standing in Church, 401; church
discipline, 409; teachings about divorce,
416; set a foundation by staying active,
417; common ground when loved one is
uninterested in church, 439

cleansing emotional cleansing through
writing, 49, 85

Cline, Victor B. Testimonial page

closeness husband gives wife closeness
she needs, 83; danger of closeness
with support group, 276; intimacy is
emotional and physical closeness, 289;
women sometimes prefer closeness to
intimacy, 308

co-worker sends herself flowers, 178

codependent definition of, 290; boundaries help to reduce codependent relationships, 290

coequals husband and wife are coequals,
290

Collected Discourses God will never
desert us, 30; Joseph F. Smith compulsive behaviors cycle, 54; Lorenzo Snow
speaks about wayward children, 445

Colorado plane ride nearly diverted to
Colorado, 6

committee Satan's committee, 348;
Christ's committee, 351

communicate openly with loved one, 99;
letter to loved one, 120; communicate
through prayer, 341; communicate with
children about online dangers, 408

compare feelings now with feelings
then, 22; our pains nothing compared
to Christ's, 46; comparing yourself to
other women, 130, 193, 194, 195; don't
compare your situation to others, 271;
compare strength of extended family
relationships over time, 274

compliment(s) loved ones for little successes, 75, 437; compliment that loved
one trusts enough to tell, 180; withholding compliments is emotional abuse, 407

compulsive sexual behaviors cause great
trauma, i; are addictions to the drug
of lust, vi; problem for both men and
women, viii; cause many emotional
responses, 1; innocent victims, 9;

caused by emotional issues, 15; cause destructive consequences, 31; allowed by God due to agency, 32; violation of covenants, 35; cycle of compulsive addiction, 52; anyone can be healed, 54; our loved ones are responsible, 58; cycle, 61; caused by emotional and spiritual, not sexual, problems, 62; are learned behaviors, 63; driven by lust, 65; require addicts to refold their minds, 81; done to cover up emotional pain, 85; loved ones try to blame us, 102; bring darkness into life, 103; "that's just the way I am," 105; chosen by loved one, not us, 107; need accurate information to protect family, 110; becoming too tolerant, 111; turn issue over to the Lord, 145; let spouse know the pain they cause us, 173; email from woman whose husband was caught in compulsive behaviors, 180; used to cover up inadequacies, 183; healthy replacements, 224; advice to help church leaders, 270; positives and negatives of support groups, 276; difficulty for newly married man with compulsive past, 308; distort sexual intimacy, 312; cause uncertainty about future, 323; feelings from spouses, 370; avoid judging, 377; may cause criminal consequences, 398; create serious spiritual consequences, 399; can be lessened if parents teach children correct principles about sex, 432; take time to change, 438

computer argument about filtering software, 17; panic response to, 130; used at work to view pornography, 163; story of husband viewing pornography while wife out of town, 185; installing a filter, 303; kept in a common room, 408; not used when home alone, 436; what to teach children, 437

condemn Christ condemns sin not sinner, 62; condemn not, 361; President Hinckley condemns abuse, 401, 407

condones society condones drug discussion but ignores sexual addiction discus-

sion, ii; silence condones behaviors, 107

confessing not serious about change if won't confess, 83; confessing to the wife is important, 187

confidential, confidentiality names withheld for confidentiality, viii; keep information confidential, 6, 36; "please do" keep our situation confidential, 272

confront, confronted, confronting the real issues for healing, 14; trials and tribulations, 28; gather information to confront issues, 74; give careful consideration before, 87; husband about affair, 106; about lying, 107; create a good plan before, 108; important to, 185

confuse, confused, confusing feeling after discovery, vii; Satan takes advantage when we are, 51; about two sides of husband's personality, 100; trust in God, 138; about spiritual promptings, 182; column with words, 228; overcome through scriptures, 381; about son's homosexual behavior, 385; logic about whether or not to divorce, 414

connected with others keeps loved one on healing path, 75; with God through thoughts and prayers, 96; through mediation, 161; through the Atonement, 174; pain decreases as we stay connected, 213; with God to change behaviors, 224; with loved one despite behaviors, 256; to the spiritual conduit, 258; to family members, 274; through spiritual boundaries, 303; through prayer, 341; through hope, 426; despite not having things in common, 439

consequences don't suffer consequences of another's sins, iii; we suffer consequences of their choices 9, 27; we did not make the choices that led to, 32; for any temptation, 49; allow loved one to experience, 60; loved one did not consider, 65; they believe they can avoid, 106; did not see the long-term, 153; do not soften the natural, 158; openness

D

252; pleading with for comfort and direction, 259; Church leaders called of, 266; sons or daughters of, accept ourselves as total package, 282; God-given power to choose "yes" or "no," 285; boundaries allow us to be better stewards, 287; given us our bodies, 306; sexual intimacy in marriage covenant ordained of, 307; bodies temples of (chart), 309; His words have healing power, 325; be still and know that I am, 326; God heard the voice of the lad, 331; what greater witness than from, 332; a personal, living, 339; believe all that God has revealed, 340; communicate with through prayer, 341; respect God's will, 344; yielding their hearts unto, 346; letting go and letting God, 348; look to God and live, 350-351; listen only to God's committee, 352; God's timetable, 355; let God serve justice, 363; hath been my support, 366; going about to destroy the church of, 369; unforgiving, we close the door on God, 379; stay married or divorce involves at least, wife, husband, and God, 383; unthinkable that God absolves serious sins upon a few requests, 390; God be merciful to me a sinner, 397; child abuse, will be held accountable before, 407; God is good, eager to forgive, 425; stay connected with, 426; trust in, not our own understanding, 429; God loves you. Things will improve, 453

gospel compulsive behaviors despite trying to live gospel, 20; attend support groups centered on gospel, 72, 309; likened to a huge hospital, 146; trials allow us to apply the gospel, 152; happiness comes by truly living, 180; is loving one who has gone astray, 233; is the plan of happiness, 345; truths bring help to those struggling, 357; no one is living the gospel perfectly, 364; living gospel principles brings forgiveness, 374; love is the essence of, 375; is

truly learned by going through difficult times, 379; likened unto climbing a ladder, 384; setting a gospel foundation, 417; teach children gospel about chastity, 434; conversations about may make things difficult, 439; is a plan, not a list of deposits, 447; offers hope and happiness, 453

gospel-centered guidance importance of seeking, 5

grace despite the choices of others, vi; Christ is full of, 27; at work in our hearts, 196; saved by, 207, 391; reaching throne of, 341

grandson analogy of playing with marbles, 211

gratification lust done for self-gratification, v, 64; selfishness focuses on self-gratification, 114; pornography for gratification, 181; sought gratification elsewhere, 311

gratitude and love go together, 114; through the Atonement, 196; for support system, 279; express every day in prayer, 342; for help received, 354; for the gospel, 419

Gray, Dan Testimonial page

grief God comforted, ii; more than tears of, 196; life is not free of, 204; synonym for pain, 213; distortions from truth cause, 248; shrouds hope, 266

ground healing takes relationship to higher ground, x; led Israel through Red Sea on dry ground, 57; rules for open letter experience, 120; find common ground, 439

guide, guidance Savior will guide those that mourn, ii; allow Articles of Faith to guide us, xii; allow Spirit to guide, 5; guidance received in the middle of the night, 33; peace comes in pleading for guidance, 101; God and Christ our lighthouse to guide safely, 116; parents should seek guidance for each family member, 124; He will guide even though path is unknown, 148; broken heart can receive guidance, 196; purpose of bishop, 267; from the words of apostles and prophets, 303; from truth in the scriptures, 325; comes through pondering and studying, 327; received through prayer, 346; comes after expressing gratitude, 354; from Spirit may be specific and pointed, 381; regarding divorce comes through prayer, 416; from scriptures, 417; from bishop, 418

guilt avoid the guilt trip of blaming yourself, ii; gets in the way of healing, 9; diffuse by recognizing humanness, 22; from using anger in wrong way, 23; don't carry guilt for mistakes of others, 32; reduced by learning compulsive cycle, 48; causes loved ones to reach again for lust, 54; not serious about change if using guilt to manipulate, 83; loved ones try to get us to carry, 102; fosters feelings of hopelessness and depression, 216; for being angry, 238; keeps us from asking for help, 272; avoided by boundaries, 285; pray for strength to give up inappropriate guilt, 345; caused by demanding 100 percent forgiveness, 362; women feel guilt for being abused, 402

H

Haight, David B. pornographic addictions require coarser content and lead to evil actions, 67; discuss with children, 434

Hales, Robert D. act with faith, don't react with fear, 124; focus on the eternities, 151; none exempt from realities of mortality, 152; never tested beyond our ability to endure, 155; Holy Ghost withdraws from angry hearts, 168; eligibility to partake of Atonement, 205; battle pain moment by moment, 216-217; be healed with His Spirit, 338; we must

change, not the commandments, 385

half-truths used to cover tracks, 73; are not acceptable, 99

happiness not limited by choices of another, vi; even if loved ones don't repent, viii; can be restored despite sin, 47; comes in making stand with the Lord, 112; in using agency the way God wants, 136; in living the commandments each day, 180; regardless of what husband does, 182; through self-mastery, 198; the great plan of happiness, 240; is an internal event, 241; comes from eternal truths, 308; God seeks our happiness above all other concerns, 339; from recognizing and following the Spirit, 353; is not possible through revenge, 376; seek happiness and comfort of spouse, 413; through mutual respect and righteousness, 415; the objective of the gospel, 453

hard-hearted leave a place in heart to forgive, 379

harmful anger can be, 22; teach children harmful effects of promiscuity, 196; effects of pornography vs. contaminated food, 307; abuse is harmful to victim, 402; effects of pornography, 434; protecting against harmful effects, 435

heal, healing through isolation and solitude, ii; power of the Atonement, vi; delayed by avoiding feelings, ix; will be difficult, xi; twelve principles for spiritual and emotional healing, xii; by learning from others, 2; requires discovering underlying issues, 14; guided by Holy Ghost, 32; postponed by impatience, 35; one step at a time, 39; possible for everyone, 54; enhanced by examining the past, 70; complete honesty required, 72; taking responsibility for behaviors, 73; how long it takes, 82; takes time, 84; through therapeutic letter writing, 87; explicit details may be damaging, 109; based on what we are willing to sur-

I

lust, lustful the drug, iv; counterfeit love,
v; escape from real emotions, 15; kills
love and controls behaviors, 64; driving
force in all compulsive sexual behaviors, 65; is addictive, 66; has no boundaries, 67; prevents development of true
love, 68; loved one mistakenly wants
love and lust, 105; do not compete with
the drug, 159; getting married does not
solve addiction, 181; problem is addiction to lust, 184; false god that cannot
be satisfied, 191; no woman can ever
satisfy husband's lust, 192; fulfilling
lustful acts rewards husband for bad
behavior, 307; deadly to loving relationships, 308; creates a wedge in marriage,
310; already committed adultery in his
heart, 389; a poor use of agency, 399;
boundaries needed, 436; hard to give
up all at once, 438

M

manipulation, manipulative not serious
about changing if manipulative, 84;
becoming tolerant of manipulation, 111;
boundaries limit contact with manipulative, 287; through passive-aggressive
behavior, 300

married a returned missionary, 11; despite
knowing about boyfriend's addiction, 56; in the temple yet struggling,
64; behaviors began before marriage,
69; reply about staying married, 124;
husband struggled despite marriage in
the temple, 180, 380; behaviors not satisfied by marriage, 181; wouldn't matter

to whom the addict was married, 191;
issue long before marriage, 199; does
not give us right to sexual dominion,
306; couples commanded to have sex,
311; rape can occur when married, 402;
deciding to divorce worksheet, 413

marrow analogy of bone marrow transplant to Atonement, 391

masturbation discovery consumes waking
hours, vii; violation of covenants, 35;
starting point for compulsive behaviors, 69; shocked after disclosure, 180;
addicted before marriage, 181; can't
satisfy lusts associated with, 192; abstain
from, 309; hope for people struggling
with, 388; seriousness of, 389

Maxwell, Neal A. ask what rather than
why, 28; lust prevents development
of true love, 67-68; God knows us
individually, 96; we must surrender to
the Lord's terms, 115; count to ten when
angry, 163; defining moments in life,
235-236; don't demand a rose garden,
244; give genuine support, not isolation,
280; faith requires trust in God's timing,
355; individual worth does not fluctuate,
364; hope keeps us anxiously engaged,
427; enduring to the end, 442; if we
stumble, let us rise, 446

medications take prescribed medications,
132

meditate choice to take action, 38; find
quiet moments to, 161

passive-aggressive maneuvers and behaviors, 300

passwords only help in short-term, 186

patience Christ is full of, 27; bear with patience thine afflictions, 33, 431; required to obtain direction, 122; submit patiently to the Lord's will, 139; developed through trials, 154; accepting the Lord's timetable, 155; don't expect instantaneous solutions, 156; brings hope, 323; suffer afflictions with patience, 343; required for forgiveness, 360; needed to glimpse the blessings, 398; required for change, 446; pray for more, 447

patient with wayward children, iii; let loved ones share information when ready, 76; putting off the natural man, 115, 147, 212; when God lets you struggle to grow, 149; waiting for husband to come clean, 188; express love in many ways, 309; ask for Lord's help, 439; with our healing, 446

pattern becomes ingrained over time, 49; woman quitting soft drinks went back to original pattern, 80; progress followed by no progress, 81; replacing irrational thought patterns, 158; healthy replacements, 222; stop pattern of being victims, 238; using "musts or demands" with God, 243

peace taking action to bring peace, iii; daily healing brings peace, ix; peace I leave with you, x; requires faith and trust, 34; journey from despair to peace, 90; comes on my knees, 101; surrendering wills to Christ brings peace, 145; righteousness brings peace, 174, 209; comes only as we bring our perspectives in line with His, 248; learn of me and you will have peace, 303; to the degree we come to Christ, we find peace, 326; Heavenly Father sends promised peace, 332; brought by the Spirit, 338; based upon faith and testi-

mony, 359; forgiveness is about peace, 367; no peace in nursing a grudge, 376; felt in the temple, 418

Penrose, Charles W. "School Thy Feelings," 235

perfect, perfectionism God's nature of justice and mercy, 8; light groweth brighter and brighter to perfect day, 40; challenge darkness when we speak of perfect life, 62; did parents expect loved one to be perfect, 70; understanding loved one's addiction, 70, Godhead has perfect love for us, 96, 112; love casteth out fear, 119; Lord has perfect love for loved ones, 124; be as perfect as you can, 128; remind yourself daily of His perfect love, 184; endless hunt to find a perfect woman, 191; accept progress, not perfection, 199; don't expect a perfect solution, 269; scriptures are a perfect foundation, 324; God and Christ only can give perfect love, 364; Lord has perfect knowledge, 377; match of the Atonement, 391; strive for more holiness, not perfect holiness, 447

perplexed but not in despair, 234; we choose our emotions, 238; unhealthy emotion, 253; by their behaviors, 258

Perry, L. Tom agency opens possibility for sin, 241-242; husband and wife are equal partners, 290

persecuted but not forsaken, 234; we choose our emotions, 238; unhealthy emotions, 253

personal compulsive behaviors feel like personal attack, i, 69; lust driven by personal appetite, v; assurance of Holy Ghost is basis for testimony, 5; which personal weakness can I overcome, 28; God loves us personally, 112; effort is necessary to accomplish personal desires, 157; pornography makes intimacy for personal gratification, 181; Principle 7: Personal Honesty Is Essential to Set Boundaries, 281;

healing takes time, 84; wife tries to be as alluring as a porn star, 102; don't compete with women in pornography, 159; husband used work computers, 163; shocking confession from husband, 180; addicted long before he met you, 181; Satan convinces that there are no consequences, 183; husband addicted for thirteen years, 259; son loses job for viewing pornography, 291; boundary of no porn in home, 301; makes it difficult to understand love, 307; cannot vomit it back, 308; chart about lies, fantasy, and lust, 308; husband hooked at work, 310; growing up with pornography-addicted father, 347; forgiveness from, 389; addiction grows more explicit, 399; warn children about, 434

postpone impatience postpones healing, 35; spouse-bashing postpones healing, 276

pray, prayer, prayers He hears your prayers, xi; don't get so angry you can't pray, 22; God is quick to answer, 27; may contain whys, 28; put son's name on prayer rolls, 31; pray always and be believing, 47; essential to give up lust, 68; understand the surrender prayer, 97; of the psalmist, 112; surrender prayer, 113; to come off conqueror, 132; trust in, 135; for wisdom and understanding, 136; stay connected to God, 161; for six months to love husband again, 192; different than they used to be, 196; simple counsel from bishop, 269; God sometimes says no, 282; for help to keep boundaries, 317; President Hinckley praying for answers, 326; Principle 9: Personal Revelation through Prayer and Fasting, 339; a sacred privilege, 341; helps us solve problems, 342; for all people, 343; Bible Dictionary definition, 345; to avoid temptation, 351; answers are not immediate, 355; must be greater than or equal to sin, 390; for those who hate us, 397; when deciding to divorce,

415; for help to find common ground, 439; for disobedient children, 444

prefer using assertive behavior to state what you prefer, 16; to be told about lapse, 73; may not be realistic, 122; vocalize what we prefer, 253; not to engage in sexual activity, 299; other ways to express love, 309

pretend that situation doesn't exist makes it worse, 35; loved ones pretend not to be bothered, 103; that they are minor problems, 107; that situation doesn't hurt, 173; to be happy, 281; loved one may cover up hurt and pretend, 377

priesthood dad unable to ordain son, 118; blessings offered from leaders, 266; blessings lift and sustain us, 359; abandon immorality before receiving, 388; used to exercise unrighteous dominion, 403; no man with priesthood should abuse, 409; power will save wayward sons and daughters, 445

Principle 1 Agency, We Choose Our Behavior, 1

Principle 2 We Are Responsible for Our Behavior, 48

Principle 3 The Godhead Has Perfect Love for Us, 96

Principle 4 With Faith, We Can Surrender Our Trials to the Lord Jesus Christ–He Invites Us to, 145

Principle 5 Our Only Hope Is Christ's Atonement and Its Power to Heal, 205

Principle 6 Your Bishop Is Called of God, 266

Principle 7 Personal Honesty Is Essential to Set and Keep Boundaries, 281

Principle 8 God's Words Have Healing Power, 323

Principle 9 Personal Revelation through Prayer and Fasting, 339

Principle 10 Being Kind and Forgiving Is Healing, 360

U

and anguish, 259; appreciate my bishop's guidance, 268; interested in sex, but not as often, 298; times when I prefer not to engage in sexual intimacy, 299; not right to bring pornography into home, 302; decisions according to spiritual direction, 304; need money in account, 305; very uncomfortable with that, 307; never would have happened, 348; bringing child sexual abuse charges against husband, 354; don't know what word forgiveness means, 360; relief not to be everything to everyone, 365; disgusting to me, 370; blood curdles when someone says I must forgive, 373; could not change what had happened, 377; goal of forgiving husband, 380; most difficult decision of my life, 383; set up a password, 436

will "I will" thoughts and statements, 133

Wirthlin, Joseph B. draw strength and hope from the Lord, 47; developing faith, hope, and charity is a step-by-step process, 95; Heavenly Father will guide every step, 115, 280; Savior's love extends to everyone, 144; growth comes slowly, 164, 198; anger stunts spiritual growth, 169, 239; all have unique life experiences, 229; climb from where we are, 383-384; be conservative in affection when dating, 433

wisely think before sharing information, 6

wish our shattered dreams could be put back together, 174; use agency to state what we wish, 254; list the boundaries you wish to set, 313; wish to give up, 384

withdrawal symptoms when giving up lust, 67; when quitting addictions, 68; from others is unhealthy, 75; impacts us emotionally, 300; penalty for not filing QDRO, 421

wonderful spiritual help from God, ii; German pie, iv; father and husband, 21; side of personality, 50; title for Christ, 97; promise of eternal life, 152; choice

to marry in temple, 180; blessing from brother, 189; to address the real issues, 194; counsel to married couples, 311; laboratory for learning, 398

wounded heart, 4; by betrayal, 98

wrong aware of wrong choices but not consequences, v; became addicted even though he knew it was wrong, 11; suffering when you did nothing wrong, 21; wrong use of anger, 23; Jesus saw sin as wrong, 62; rationalizing wrong behavior keeps us stuck, 107; acted as if nothing had gone wrong, 187; agency to choose between right and wrong, 235; catch ourselves when listening to wrong committee, 351; forgiveness when I didn't do anything wrong, 373; any kind of abuse is wrong, 401

www.fbi.gov suggestions to minimize online exploitation, 408; danger signs and safety tips for children, 437

Y

Young, Brigham wicked anger and righteous anger, 22, 236; those doing their best are perfect, 128; superior blessings require severe trials, 154; do right as well as you know how, 334; children bound to parents, 444-445

Z

Zarephath widow and Elijah, 329

Zoramites sinful but loved by Alma, 343; were able to change, 345

Beginning Workbook

Turn Yourselves and Live: Is Any Thing Too Hard for the Lord?

This is a user-friendly workbook to help members of the Church who are struggling to overcome compulsive sexual behaviors. The book addresses all types of sexual addictions and includes scriptural references, quotes by General Authorities, and excerpts from the *Ensign* that offer real answers. Readers will be led to identify their root problems, get out of denial, distinguish the difference between irrational thoughts and rational Christ-centered thoughts, and defuse "trigger points" in a Christ-centered way. Insights and success stories from others point to the Atonement and illustrate its mighty power to enable any humble believer in Christ to escape the chains of pornography and any other compulsive sexual behavior.

Extended Workbook

"...Line Upon Line, Precept Upon Precept..."

This book provides follow-up and follow-through for anyone struggling with compulsive sexual behaviors. Rod W. Jeppsen's first book on this subject, *Turn Yourselves and Live: Is Any Thing Too Hard for the Lord?* offers an effective beginning approach. Now *Line Upon Line, Precept Upon Precept* makes available a practical, extended workbook (400 pages) that includes numerous enlightening and motivating examples, valuable exercises, and poignant observations by those who have previously engaged in such behavior. This workbook will help you uncover and heal from core issues that drive the behavior; it shows you how to surrender inappropriate thoughts and actions, stay on the healing pathway, and avoid relapse. Each chapter discusses one of the "Twelve Principles for Spiritual and Emotional Healing." These principles, based on the Articles of Faith, are reinforced with salient quotations by members of the First Presidency and the Quorum of the Twelve. The restored gospel of Jesus Christ encompasses a complete plan for healing. *Line Upon Line, Precept Upon Precept* focuses on that plan and shows you how to apply its precepts on a daily basis.

New Release:

December 2005

Agency and Boundaries

God has given you moral agency: the right to choose and make decisions. However, do you feel compelled to smooth things over when dealing with others and sometimes go against what is personally important to you? Is it difficult to tell others "no" and stick to it? Do you find yourself saying, "Why did I agree to do that? I can't do one more thing!" When dealing with your spouse, children, co-workers, or neighbors and decision times come, do you get caught in the middle of, "Should I say 'yes?'" or, "Should I say 'no?'" Do you feel guilty for saying "no" and change it to "yes." Saying "yes" too often is unhealthy for us, our loved ones, and our associates. This workbook helps readers identify what's important in their lives and explore where they want to set boundaries. The book includes numerous ideas on how we can maintain boundaries that tell us and others where our responsibilities in the relationship begin and end. When we focus on what we are responsible for and let others be responsible for their own areas of stewardship, we have more emotional energy to improve our lives and become who God wants us to be.

If you want to share your comments about this book or share ideas that have helped you in your healing process, please write or send an email to:

Rod W. Jeppsen
P.O. Box 95122
South Jordan, UT 84095-0122

Email: rwjeppsen@aol.com